Julia S. Pretl's

Big Book of

BEAD
WORK

Julia S. Pretl's
Big Book of
BEAD
WORK

32 Projects for Adventurous Beaders

Creative Publishing international
Minneapolis, MN

Creative Publishing international

First published in the United States of America by
Creative Publishing international, Inc., a member of
Quayside Publishing Group
400 First Avenue North
Suite 300
Minneapolis, MN 55401
1-800-328-3895
www.creativepub.com
Visit www.Craftside.Typepad.com for a behind-the-scenes peek at our crafty world!

ISBN-13: 978-1-58923-527-4
ISBN-10: 1-58923-527-4

10 9 8 7 6 5 4 3 2 1

Illustrations: Julia S. Pretl
Photographs: Allan Penn

Printed in China

CONTENTS

Part 1: Bags 6

Chapter 1	What Is Bead Knitting?	8
Chapter 2	Knitting Tutorial	12
Chapter 3	Making a Bending Knitted Sample	18
Chapter 4	Working with Patterns	27
	Two Easy Cuff Bracelets	30
	Pinwheel Purse	32
Chapter 5	Shaping the Knitting	38
	Dusk Necklace	44
	Olive's Star Box	48

	Dragon Bag	54
	Blue Garden Drawstring Purse	60
Chapter 6	Double Knitting	68
	Tumble Bag	74
	Luna Purse	78
	China Sea Bag	84
	Antiquity Purse	90
Chapter 7	Finishing Techniques	97
Chapter 8	Assembly and Lining	102
Chapter 9	Designing Your Own Patterns	106

Part 2: Necklaces 110

Chapter 10	Getting Started	112
Chapter 11	Making Ladders	120
Chapter 12	Assembly	126
Chapter 13	Decorative Elements	130
Chapter 14	Finishing	134
Chapter 15	The Projects	138
	Urchin	140
	New Mexico	144

	Chartreuse	152
	Drab	158
	Meadow	166
	Ember	174
	Spike	180
	Gradient	188
	Eagle Feather	196
	Trellis	204

Part 3: Boxes 212

Chapter 16	Getting Started	214
Chapter 17	Building the Base	218
Chapter 18	Building the Sides	228
Chapter 19	Lids, Finials, and Feet	237
Chapter 20	Patterns and Word Maps	242
Chapter 21	Patterns for Triangle Boxes	247
	Kaleidoscope	248
	Egypt	251
	Red Knot	255
Chapter 22	Patterns for Hexagon Boxes	261
	Tuffet	262
	Deco Pagoda	265
	New School	270

Chapter 23	Patterns for Pentagon Boxes	279
	Star	280
	Flower	283
	Dragon	288
Chapter 24	Patterns for Square Boxes	293
	Tempest	294
	Tomcat	297
	Shinjin	302

Blank Worksheets for Your Original Designs	309
Notes about the DVD	318
Index	319

PART 1: BAGS

Chapter 1

What Is Bead Knitting?

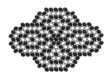

When I began my foray into bead knitting in the early 1990s, I was unaware that the craft even existed. I had been beading for several years, and I decided to take a break and learn how to knit. I picked up a copy of *Mary Thomas's Knitting Book* and opened to the first page. With visions of hand-knit socks and sweaters in my mind, I studied every paragraph. When I reached page 131 (exactly halfway through the book), everything changed. The chapter was entitled "Beaded and Bead Knitting." I glanced at my bead stash, and I knew that I would not be making socks and sweaters.

The first part of the chapter did not interest me much. In the technique that is known as beaded knitting, beads are placed between the stitches as the knitting progresses, individually or in multiples. Beaded knitting seemed more a form of embellishing hand-knitted fabric than actual beadwork. I recalled the tiny swag bags made with the technique that I'd seen at my local bead store months earlier. Most used only one bead color. As lovely as they were, I wanted to knit pictures.

Bead knitting fit the bill perfectly. In bead knitting, the beads are prestrung in a particular order and knitted into the stitch—rather than between them—creating a dense yet amazingly supple fabric. The colors come together to create an elaborate tapestry.

I searched in vain for more bead knitting instruction. The little that I found seemed geared toward knitters who were already comfortable with knitting techniques. I made numerous rectangular pieces, which was all that I could do with my limited knitting experience. Desperate to learn more, I sat down with the Mary Thomas book once again, first practicing the traditional way that the stitches were made, and then, through trial and error, adapting them to bead knitting.

Thrilled with my results, I set out to create instructions to share with other beaders. I began by teaching a bead knitting class. It was a disaster. My students could not see what I was doing with the thin needles and the tiny glass beads. I wondered if diagrams would be clear enough and, after several years of contemplation, realized that advances in technology had afforded me another option. I would make a video, with the camera close enough so that the image of my hands manipulating the tiny beads virtually could fill a television or computer screen. I purchased a digital video camera, and, after a great deal of practice, I succeeded. The result is the enclosed DVD.

How to Use the Book and DVD

All beaders—and all knitters—gradually develop their own style and find a way of working that is best for them. The instructions and diagrams in this book illustrate what works best for me, and I hope they will be valuable guidelines to help you find what will ultimately work best for you.

Consider the information in this book as a learning tool and not as fixed rules to follow. Experiment with and practice each step before moving on to the next. It is important that you become comfortable with a technique before tackling a project to avoid frustration.

Each technique that is introduced is followed by two or more projects, so you can apply what you learn as you go. At least one project for each technique is designed for larger beads (size 8) and at least one for smaller beads (size 11), but you can work with any size bead for any project.

The finished size of each project is provided with the list of materials, but you might want to try working with a different size bead, which would vary the end result. For instance, an average size bag in size 8s would be a small amulet pouch in size 11s. Feel free to change colors and to embellish to suit your own tastes. Be creative!

Throughout the book, the lessons are keyed with a DVD symbol and a number (1). The number indicates the DVD chapter that contains the corresponding information in video format.

Read through each chapter before you begin working. Watch the corresponding sections of the DVD until you understand each technique.

The DVD is a classroom in almost every sense. You will find twenty bead knitting lessons designed for right-handers and the same twenty adapted for those who are more comfortable using their left hands. Each lesson demonstrates one of the basic techniques in bead knitting and corresponds to the information about that technique presented in the book.

Read the text and study the illustrations. Then watch the DVD to learn the movement of the stitch. Whenever you need to refresh your memory, refer to the video.

The DVD is very easy to navigate. You can play it either on a television set or on a computer with a DVD drive. (For more information about how to work with the DVD, see the instructions on page 318.)

Also included on the DVD are high-resolution duplicates of each pattern in the book. The patterns are provided as PDFs so that you may view them on your computer screen or print them out so you can mark them up as you work. Each pattern is accompanied by a word map, which many people find easier to use than the graphed pattern when stringing beads. I suggest that you work with the two together.

Tools and Materials

Bead knitting needles, also used for knitting fine lace, are made of steel and are very small in diameter (see facing page, top). They are sold in sizes that range from 00000000 (8/0), which are unbelievably thin, to a comparably larger size 0. They are usually packaged in sets of five. The projects in this book require size 0000 (1.25 mm) and size 00 (1.75 mm).

Seed beads come in a variety of sizes. The most common, from smallest to largest, are size 15, size 11, and size 8.

The three swatches on the facing page show 1" (2.5 cm) squares that have been bead knitted in each size of bead. Notice that the red swatch, made with size 15s, uses significantly more beads than the blue swatch, made with size 8s, allowing for a more detailed texture pattern.

The most commonly available seed beads are from the Czech Republic and from Japan (sold primarily under the names Miyuki, TOHO, and Matsuno). The overall size and shape of the beads often differ from one manufacturer to another, but, as long as you use only one size of seed bead within a project, you can combine brands.

Silk thread is the best choice for bead knitted projects. Silk is relatively expensive, but the beautiful drape that it provides in the finished fabric is worth the cost. Look for a firm, smooth fiber with a gentle twist. My favorite brand is Gudebrod Brothers Champion Silk.

Cotton thread is less expensive and can be found at most craft and yarn stores, but it is not especially durable. Although I do not recommend cotton for keepsake projects, it is a good choice when you are practicing bead knitting. The most common types of cotton thread are crochet cotton and perle cotton.

You will also need these other miscellaneous tools and findings. You can find them in any craft or beading shop. The specific materials, tools, and techniques you will need for each of the ten projects are listed with the pattern and instructions on pages 30–90.

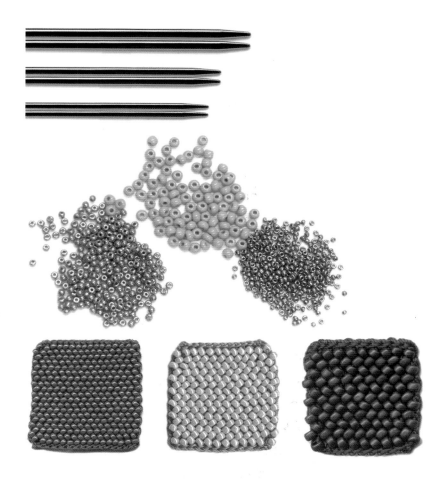

- Steel crochet hooks, sizes 9 to 12 (for picking up dropped stitches and adding decorative edge)
- Lining fabric
- Large beads (for embellishment)
- Jump rings, cord/chain, and clasps (for finishing the bag)

Chapter 2

Knitting Tutorial

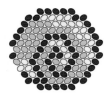

This chapter will help those of you who have never knit before learn the basic stitches required for bead knitting. Those with knitting experience should review this tutorial, too, because some bead knitting stitches are variations of those used in traditional knitting.

First practice the basic knitting stitches with needles and yarn in the size you find most comfortable. If you are new to knitting, I suggest size 4 or size 5 needles and a sport-weight yarn. Then as you begin to get the feel of it, work your way down to smaller, size 00 needles, and size 10 crochet cotton.

The instructions and diagrams in this book are written for right-handed knitting, but both right-handed and left-handed demonstrations are included on the DVD.

Estimating the Length of the Tail

1. Cast on 10 stitches.

2. Pull the stitches off the needle, and measure the length of the thread you used to cast on the 10 stitches.

3. To determine the total length of the tail you will need for your project, multiply this measurement by one-tenth of the total cast-on stitches for your project.

---

1 Casting On

Step 1: Make a slipknot approximately 18" (45.7 cm) from the end of your thread. You will need this "tail" to create your cast-on row. Leave a longer tail for wider projects, or estimate the amount of thread with the method described in the box at left.

Step 2: Insert the tip of the needle, and tighten the slipknot around it. Grasp the needle just below the knot with the thumb and index finger of your left hand. Drape the tail of the thread over your thumb, and drape the spool end over your index finger. Gather both ends with your right hand, and

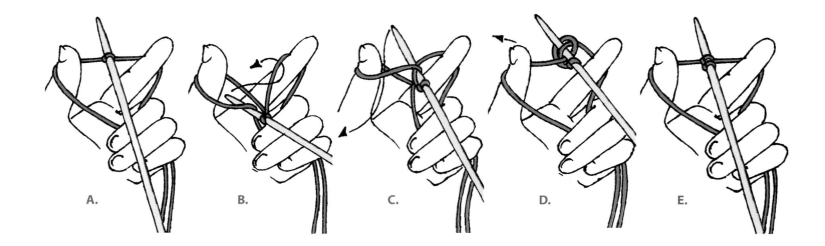

A. **B.** **C.** **D.** **E.**

wrap them twice around the pinky finger of your left hand. Close the last three fingers of your left hand around the thread to control tension.

Step 3: Grasp the bottom portion of the needle with your right hand, and rest your index finger on the slipknot. Allow a little bit of the spool thread to slide from your pinky finger as you separate the thumb and index finger of your left hand, leaving a space of about 3" (7.6 cm) between them. The needle should be in the center (A).

Step 4: With your right hand, move the tip of the needle downward to catch the lower strand of the thread that is looped around your thumb. Then move the needle up and over the lower portion of the strand that is looped around your index finger (B).

Step 5: Swing the tip of the needle back through the thumb loop, bringing with it the thread from the index-finger loop (C).

Step 6: Let the loop drop from your thumb, and, in a single motion, catch the spool end of the thread again. (It should already be positioned against the outer edge of your thumb.) Pull your thumb back to tighten the stitch around the needle (D).

You now have cast on two stitches (E). Let out a bit more spool thread, if necessary, and repeat this process to make a third stitch. Repeat until you have the desired number of stitches on your needle.

After the motion of casting on becomes more fluid, you may find it easier to hold the needle stationary and maneuver the thread around it with your left hand.

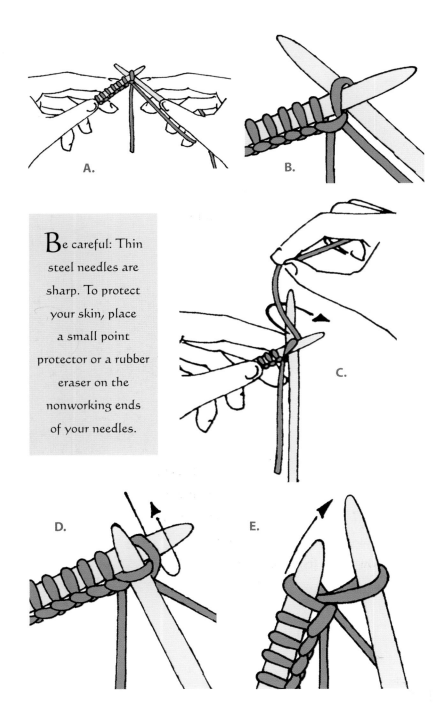

A.

B.

C.

D.

E.

Be careful: Thin steel needles are sharp. To protect your skin, place a small point protector or a rubber eraser on the nonworking ends of your needles.

◗ 2 The Knit Stitch

Step 1: Hold the needle with the cast-on stitches in your left hand, between your thumb and third finger, about 1" (2.5 cm) below the tip. Press the lower portion of the needle to the back edge of your hand by curling the last two fingers loosely around it. Rest your left index finger on the first stitch, where the thread wraps around the back of the needle. This finger will alternately control the needle and manipulate the stitches. Hold the empty needle in your right hand in the same way (A).

Step 2: Push the first cast-on stitch forward with your left index finger, and insert the second, empty needle into the back leg of the stitch so that it is behind the first needle (B). Press your right index finger against the back of the second needle, keeping it in the stitch. Remove your right hand from the second needle, and, holding the thread behind the needles, wrap the spool end of the thread twice around your right pinky finger. Curl the last two fingers of your right hand around the thread to hold the tension.

Step 3: With your right thumb and index finger, grasp the thread close to the needles, and wrap the thread in front of and around the top portion of the empty needle (C). Resume your grasp on the second needle. To keep your fingers curled around the thread, rest the knuckles of your last two fingers on top of the second needle, still holding it to the back edge of your hand. There should be very little slack in the thread between your pinky finger and the needles.

Step 4: Keep the thread tension tight by increasing your grip on the pinky thread. Maintaining constant contact between the two needles, slide the right-hand needle downward until the tip clears the left-hand needle. Then slide it back up again, bringing with it a new stitch. The two needles have now reversed positions, with the right-hand needle in front (D).

Step 5: With the last two fingers of your left hand, pull down on the lower portion of the needle while sliding the stitches

After several rows—knitting one row and purling the next—the fabric will begin to curl. This is normal in a pattern of alternating knit and purl rows, which is called stockinette stitch.

toward the tip with your thumb and index finger so that the first stitch drops off the needle (E). (You may need to give the starting tail of the thread a tug to keep the first stitch from stretching out.)

Step 6: Insert the tip of the right-hand needle into the next stitch, and repeat. Continue until you have knitted every stitch on the needle.

▷ 3 The Purl Stitch

Step 1: Hold the needle with the stitches in your left hand and the empty needle in your right hand. Insert the empty needle into the front leg of the first stitch. The thread should now be in front of the needles. If it is not, bring the thread under the needles to move it to the proper position.

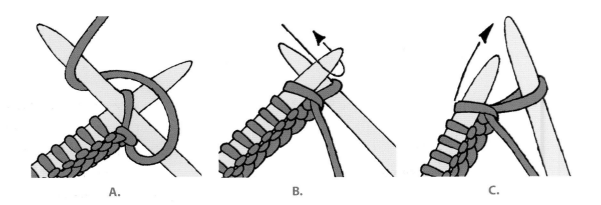

A.   B.   C.

Step 2: Hold the empty needle in the stitch between your left thumb and index finger. With your right hand, wrap the thread behind and then over and around the top of the empty needle (A).

Step 3: Return your right hand to the needle, and, maintaining contact between the two needles at all times, slide the right-hand needle downward until the tip clears the left-hand needle. Then slide it back up again, taking with it a new stitch. The two needles have now reversed positions, with the right-hand needle behind the left-hand needle (B).

Step 4: With your left hand, slide the stitches to the tip of the needle until the first stitch drops off (C).

A mistake beginners sometimes make is to accidentally hold the thread behind the needles while purling. The end result of this is a "yarn over" on the right-hand needle, which creates an additional stitch. Make sure that you have created only one new stitch each time you purl. Continue until you have purled each of the remaining stitches.

Practice alternating the knit stitch (this stitch will create the "right" side of your knitting) and the purl stitch (this stitch will create the "wrong" side) until you are comfortable with both techniques. Notice the difference in the surface texture of each side of the knitting.

The Combination Method

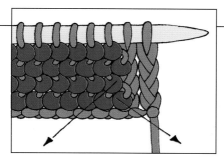

When constructing a "yarn only" knitted fabric, a knitter can use a variety of flat and twisted stitches—but when bead knitting, the options are much more limited. Bead knitters must always use a twisted stitch to position the bead on the correct side of the fabric.

There are two common flat stitches in traditional knitting. The first is the Western knit stitch, in which the needle is inserted into the front leg of the stitch and the yarn is thrown (wrapped) under and around that needle. To purl, the needle is inserted into the front leg of the stitch, and the yarn is thrown over the needle.

The second method, the Eastern knit stitch (traditionally used in eastern Europe), is the reverse. The needle is inserted into the back of the stitch, and the yarn is thrown over the needle to knit. To purl, the needle is inserted into the back of the stitch, and the yarn is thrown under the needle. Western and Eastern flat stitches appear similar in a completed fabric.

Both Eastern and Western knitting have a twisted variation in which the yarn is thrown in the same direction as the flat version, but the leg of the stitch into which the needle is inserted is reversed. For example, to make a twisted Western knit stitch, you would insert the needle into the back leg of the stitch and then wrap the thread under and around the needle.

Traditionally, bead knitting was created with the knit and purl versions of either of these twisted stitch methods, depending on the region. The difference in the fabric is in which leg crosses in front of the other in the respective knit/purl rows. Although these methods both hold the bead within the stitch, the fabric tends either to bias (slant) or, in a tubular fabric, to twist.

My solution is to use the "combination method," which—as the name indicates—combines the Western and Eastern methods. I work with the flat-stitch versions of each method. The stitches naturally twist each other, without creating a bias fabric.

When you work an Eastern knit stitch with a Western purl stitch, the thread takes a longer route. The result is a slightly looser stitch, which creates a space in which to easily insert a bead. Also, the first bead in each row protrudes, or "kicks out," creating a staggered effect along the edge of the knitting and eliminating the problem of a biased fabric, as shown in the illustration above.

Chapter 3

Making a Bead Knitted Sample

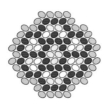

Before you tackle a project, I suggest you create a practice swatch that is approximately 2" × 2" (5.1 × 5.1 cm). Begin with two size 00 knitting needles and at least 10 yards (9.1 m) of size 5 perle cotton (or size 10 crochet cotton or size FF silk thread). You'll need at least 10 grams of size 8 seed beads and a twisted wire needle.

To string your beads, first insert the end of the thread into the eye of a twisted wire needle. If you don't have a twisted wire needle, cut a short length of a very thin piece of thread (6" to 8" [15.2–20.32 cm]), and insert both ends into the same side of the eye of a beading needle. You can then insert the bead knitting thread into the thread loop. Pull tightly on both ends of the thin thread.

When you string beads for a pattern, you will pick up the beads one at a time. But for this practice piece, which may be a solid color or a mix of colors with no particular pattern (what I call "bead soup"), you can simply use the scoop method.

Pour about 10 grams of beads into a shallow bowl and slide the threaded needle horizontally through them. After a few passes, you will have a number of beads on the needle. Slide these beads down onto the thread and begin scooping again. When you have strung most of the beads in the bowl, you are ready to start knitting.

If your beads are on a hank—a strand of beads that are all the same color—you can transfer them from the hank thread directly to the bead knitting thread simply by sliding the twisted wire needle through the beads on the hank and sliding them onto the bead knitting thread.

4 Knit Stitch with Beads

Cast on 22 stitches for your practice piece. Beginners should knit at least one empty (yarn only) row of knit stitches and one empty row of purl stitches before starting to add beads to the knitting.

Step 1: Slide 1" to 2" (2.5–5.1 cm) of beads to the top of the thread so that the beads touch the needles. Wrap the end of the thread several times around your right pinky finger to create tension, with the beads spanning your palm.

Step 2: When your hand is in its natural knitting position, the beads should fill approximately one-half of the thread in the palm of your hand. Push all the beads toward your pinky finger, leaving the top half of the thread free for knitting.

Step 3: Start the first beaded row by knitting 2 stitches without beads. These stitches will form the outer edge, or selvage, of your knitting.

Step 4: Knit into the back leg of the third stitch, and wrap the thread over the right-hand needle. With your right thumb, push the first bead to the top of the thread and around the back of the right-hand needle until the bead is resting against both needles (A).

Step 5: Hold the bead in place with your left index finger, and open the stitch by pulling the two needles apart. Push the

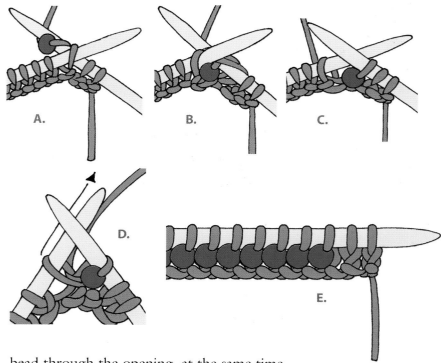

bead through the opening, at the same time pulling the needle in your left hand toward you, over the bead (B).

Step 6: Slide the right-hand needle downward and then up again so that it is in front of the left-hand needle (C). Slide the original stitch off of the needle to complete the stitch (D).

Step 7: Slide the next bead to the top of the thread, and continue knitting with beads until you have reached the last 2 stitches. Knit these 2 selvage stitches without beads (E).

5 Purl Stitch with Beads

As you continue knitting in stockinette stitch, your next row of knitting will be a purl row.

Step 1: Slide 1" to 2" (2.5–5.1 cm) of beads into your right hand. Purl the first two stitches of the row without beads to form the selvage end of the fabric.

Step 2: Purl into the front leg of the next stitch, and wrap the thread behind, over, and around the right-hand needle.

Step 3: Slide the first bead to the top of the thread until it touches both needles. Hold the bead in place with your left thumb, and open the stitch by pulling the two needles apart (A). Push the bead through the opening, and pull the right needle toward you and over the bead (B).

Step 4: Slide the right-hand needle downward and then up again so that it is in front of the left-hand needle. Slide the original stitch off the left-hand needle to complete the stitch (C).

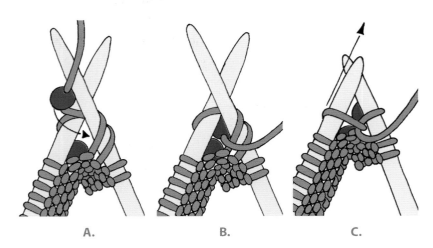

A.   B.   C.

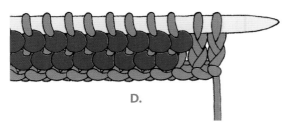

D.

Step 5: Slide the next bead to the top of the thread, and continue purling with beads until you have reached the last 2 stitches. Purl these 2 selvage stitches without beads (D).

As you purl, keep your left thumb pressed against the needles to prevent the bead from moving to the back of the fabric. If a bead occasionally flips to the back, simply push it over the needle to the front.

Continental Bead Knitting

My preferred method of bead knitting is the English method (holding the working yarn in the right hand). Knitters who prefer the Continental method (holding the working yarn in the left hand) can follow the same general steps for bead knitting by making these few adjustments.

Knit Stitch

1. Keep 1" (2.5 cm) of beads behind the left index finger. Knit into the back of the stitch.
2. Pick the thread from underneath.
3. With your right index finger, slide a bead down the thread until it touches both needles.
4. Push the bead through the stitch with your right index finger, and then pull the loop through the stitch.

Purl Stitch

1. Keep 1" (2.5 cm) of beads behind the left index finger. Knit into the front of the stitch.
2. Wrap the thread under and around the right-hand needle.
3. With your right index finger, slide a bead down the thread until it touches both needles.
4. Push the bead through the stitch with your right or left thumb (whichever works better for you), and then pull the loop through the stitch.

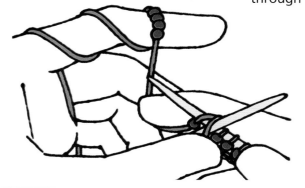

Because of the nature of the stitch, as you purl with beads, the bead directly below the one that you just worked will inevitably move between the stitches to the back of the fabric. With your left thumb, simply push it back into place, and hold it there until you insert the needle into the next stitch.

Continue knitting and purling with your beads until your practice piece is about 2" (5.1 cm) long (approximately 22 rows). Now you will bind off the stitches to create a finished edge.

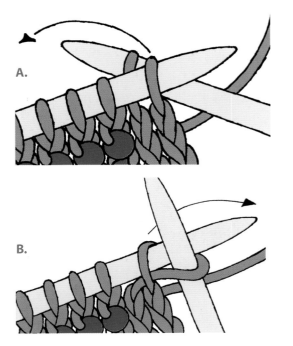

A.

B.

Binding Off

To finish your bead knitted fabric, you must bind off. I suggest that beginning bead knitters complete at least one empty (yarn only) row before binding off. It is easier to bind off on a knit row.

9 Simple Bind-Off

A simple bind-off results in a firm, relatively inflexible edge with very little elasticity. Keep your tension loose to prevent the fabric edge from contracting.

Step 1: Knit the first 2 stitches. Insert the needle in your left hand into the first of the 2 stitches, and lift it over the second stitch and off the needle (A). Keep a firm tension on the spool thread so that you don't pull off the second stitch as well.

Step 2: Slide the lifted stitch off the needle in your left hand (B).

Step 3: Knit the next stitch, and repeat the process. (You should never have more than 2 stitches on the needle in your right hand.) Pull the last stitch until it is 3" to 4" (7.6–10.7 cm) long.

Step 4: Cut the thread from the spool, and pull so that the free end slides through the stitch. Tighten the corner knot to secure.

10 Suspended Bind-Off

A suspended bind-off results in a firm yet elastic edge.

Step 1: Follow Step 1 for the simple bind-off, but do not slide the lifted stitch off the left needle.

Step 2: Insert the right-hand needle into the back leg of the next stitch (not the lifted stitch), and wrap the thread over the needle (A).

Step 3: Complete the stitch, bringing the new loop out between the working stitch and the lifted one, and slide both stitches off the needle (B). You will have 2 stitches on the needle in your right hand.

Step 4: Lift the first stitch over the second, and repeat the process. When only 2 stitches remain, lift the first stitch over the second, and follow Step 4 for the simple bind-off to finish.

Some patterns may end on a knit row, requiring you to bind off on a purl row. Although it is possible, binding off on a purl row tends to make the stitches tight. A better solution is to knit an extra row without beads so that you can bind off on a knit row.

Fixing Mistakes

6 Picking Up Dropped Stitches

Bead knitting requires thin thread, which is often slippery, so it is easy to drop a stitch. Fortunately, stitches with beads will not unravel because the thread contracts around the loop below the bead and holds it in place. However, dropped stitches can unravel in unbeaded areas of the knitting.

When you drop a stitch, the stitch unravels, and a gap will appear in the knitting, leaving a "ladder" of straight thread strands. When this happens, stay calm! Get a small crochet hook. From the right side of the fabric (regardless of whether you are working a knit or purl row), insert the crochet hook into the dropped stitch and then into the space above the lowest ladder

You can also bind off on a purl row—and create a satisfactory fabric edge—by knitting into the front leg of each stitch.

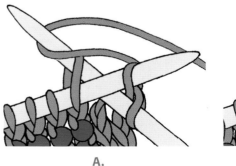

A.

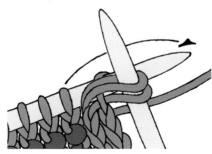

B.

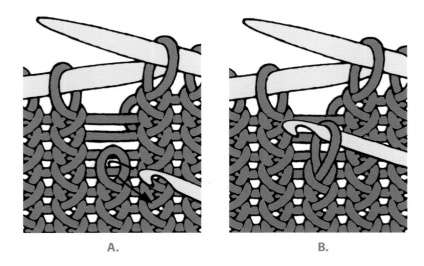

A.   **B.**

strand (A). With the hook, catch the strand, and pull it through the stitch (B). Repeat this process for each strand of the ladder until you reach the working row of your bead knitting. Transfer the stitch back to the knitting needle and continue working.

Cutting and Joining Thread

Sometimes you will need to cut your thread, either to add more beads or to correct a stringing error. Always rejoin the thread at the beginning of a row.

Leave a tail of at least 6" to 8" (15.2–20.3 cm), and cut the working thread. Make a slipknot at the end of a new spool of thread, once again leaving a

6" to 8" (15.2–20.32 cm) tail. Slide the slipknot to the top of the tail of the bead knitting so that it sits as close to the fabric as possible, as shown in the drawing below. Pull tightly on both ends of the new thread to close the loop around the working thread. You will feel a small "pop" when the new thread is attached securely.

7 Removing Stitches

At times, you may make a mistake that requires you to remove some of your stitches. You may discover a mistake in the sequence of bead colors (when knitting a pattern) or simply in the knitted fabric itself.

If the error is no more than one row prior to your working row, it is easier to take out the stitches one at a time than it is to remove the work from the needle to remove

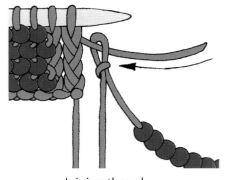

Joining thread

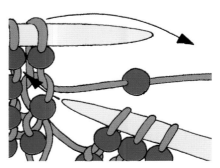

Removing a single stitch

the entire row. When removing stitches in knit rows, keep the thread in the back of the work; when removing stitches in purl rows, keep the thread in front of the work.

Pick out the incorrect stitches with the right-hand needle. Insert the needle into the stitch below the stitch you want to remove, as shown in the drawing above. Drop the last stitch, and pull the thread to undo the stitch. (You may have to ease the bead out of the stitch before you can pull out the thread.) Continue removing stitches one by one until you reach the error in the knitting, and resume knitting to fix it.

If you have to cut the thread to correct a stringing error, remove all the stitches to the beginning of the row. Correct the error, and rejoin the thread to the knitting, as described on page 24.

8 Removing Multiple Rows

If the error is two or more rows prior to your working row, it's best to remove entire rows of knitting to correct the mistake.

With the right side of the work facing you, locate the row below the error. Remember, because bead-knit stitches are twisted, one leg of the loop always sits in front of the other. (This positioning is more noticeable in stitches with beads because the front leg holds the bead.)

Starting at one edge of the beaded fabric, insert an empty needle into the front leg of each stitch, including the selvage (end) stitches. Move the stitches to the center of this needle to hold them, as shown below.

Remove the stitches at the top of your bead knitting from the working needle. Undo each row, easing the beads

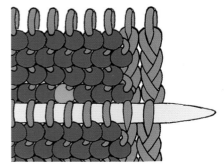

Holding stitches to remove multiple rows

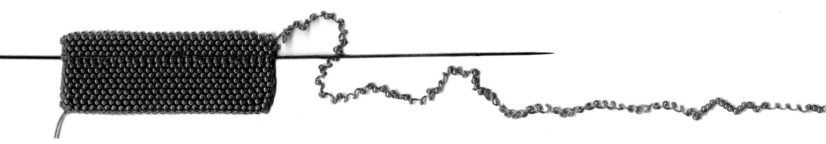

out one at a time. Fix the error and then resume knitting.

If the unraveled thread is curly (from having been knit), wind it tightly back around the spool. It will smooth out after several hours.

Blocking

After you bind off the knitting, you may find that the fabric is misshapen along its width or length or has curled at the edges. To correct this problem, dampen the fabric by lightly spraying the wrong side of the fabric with water. Then lay the fabric on a smooth, flat surface. Press the surface of the fabric with your fingers while gently reshaping the length and width. Then allow the knitting to dry thoroughly. This method for reshaping a knit fabric is called blocking.

After the fabric has dried, if the problem persists, lay the knitting on a folded towel or a cardboard box, and pin the edges securely, making sure not to damage the threads or beads. Spray the fabric again. When it has dried thoroughly, the fabric will be flat and very supple.

Chapter 4
Working with Patterns

There are ten projects in this book. To help you gradually develop and expand your bead knitting skills, each project incorporates the techniques introduced in the preceding chapters. At least one project for each technique is designed for large beads (size 8) and at least one for smaller beads (size 11). Before working an entire bead knitted bag, you might want to practice your bead-knitting and graph-reading skills by making the Two Easy Cuff Bracelets (page 30).

The instructions for every project have six components: a materials list, a color list, a graphed pattern, a word map, knitting instructions, and finishing suggestions.

The materials list provides an estimate of the quantity of thread and beads you'll need to complete the project. Bead amounts are rounded up to the nearest gram, and weights may vary slightly, depending on the exact bead size and finish (matte, glossy, etc.). The estimate is only for the bead knitted portion of the project and does not include the fringe, strap, or any additional finishing details.

The actual amount of thread you'll need may vary, depending on the amount of tension in your own knitting. It's always a good idea to purchase extra, just in case. (The thread estimates are also only for the bead knitted portion of the project.) The materials list also includes a list of the optional beads and findings I used to create the project sample shown in the photograph.

The color list references both the graphed pattern and the word map. The suggested colors correspond with the colors on the pattern. Each color also has a corresponding letter, which indicates that color on the word map. The color choices are only suggestions. You will be working with a maximum of eight colors per project, so it is easy to experiment with your own colors to make the project suit your taste.

The graphed pattern for the project may show the entire design or, in the case of a repeating pattern, one unit of the design. The numbers on either the right or left side of the graph help while stringing beads and while knitting. The arrow beside each number indicates the direction in which that row, and all other even rows, will be strung. (If you want to make notes while you work or enlarge the pattern, you'll find a printable graphed pattern for each project in electronic format on the DVD.)

The word map lists the color letter of each bead, followed by the number of beads of that color to string. Word maps are read from top to bottom (divide them into sections if necessary). Each row is read from left to right. For flat bead knitting (for example, for the Two Easy Cuff Bracelets), the codes L-R (left to right) or R-L (right to left) indicate the stringing direction of that row of the pattern. For projects with shaping (increases or decreases), the total number of beads in the affected row or rows is also provided.

Depending on your preference, you can work following the graphed pattern only or refer to the pattern and word map together.

The knitting instructions provide guidelines. Depending on the project, these instructions may be basic (how many stitches to cast on, whether to start with a knit or a purl row) or more complex (how many stitches to increase or decrease in each row).

The finishing suggestions simply indicate how I finished the project shown in the photograph, but you may want to add your own finishing touches. Chapters Seven and Eight provide more detailed instruction for making eyelets, fringe, and linings.

Reading Graphed Patterns and Word Maps

The graphed pattern indicates the correct order in which to string the beads for knitting. When knitting, you read the graph from bottom to top. When stringing, you read the graph from top to bottom.

For example, if you were to knit the pattern shown on the facing page, the red bead in the lower right-hand corner is the first one you would knit. You would begin the stringing sequence at the upper right-hand corner of the graph and wind back and forth down the pattern (left to right

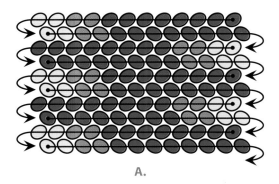

A.

and right to left across the rows) until you reach this bead. The word map shows how to read this pattern for stringing:

Row 10: Red (7); Dk. Gray (2); Lt. Gray (2)
Row 9: Lt. Gray (2); Dk. Gray (2); Red (7)
Row 8: Lt. Gray (2); Dk. Gray (2); Red (7)
Row 7: Red (7); Dk. Gray (2); Lt. Gray (2)
Row 6: Red (7); Dk. Gray (2); Lt. Gray (2)
Row 5: Lt. Gray (2); Dk. Gray (2); Red (7)
Row 4: Lt. Gray (2); Dk. Gray (2); Red (7)
Row 3: Red (7); Dk. Gray (2); Lt. Gray (2)
Row 2: Red (7); Dk. Gray (2); Lt. Gray (2)
Row 1: Lt. Gray (2); Dk. Gray (2); Red (7)

The key to reading a graphed pattern is in the staggered rows. Remember that the bead that protrudes, or kicks out, is always at the beginning of the row and is the last bead you will string in that row. Always begin reading at the opposite, or recessed, end of the row.

Because you knit up from the bottom row of the graph, you begin stringing at the top. (Left-handed knitters read patterns the same way, but their beadwork will be a mirror image of the pattern in the graph.)

Count twice, knit once! Perhaps the most frustrating error you can make is to string your beads incorrectly—especially because it is difficult to know whether the sequence of beads is correct until you have completed at least 2 rows. So, organize your beads carefully.

Double-check the bead order after stringing each row, or, at the very least, count the beads to be sure you have strung the correct number for the row. (I've trained my eye to group the beads in fives, which makes for faster counting.) Checking each row is time-consuming, but it's less time-consuming than removing rows and restringing beads!

I also like to keep a pile of small paper squares on hand, no larger than 1/4" (6 mm) or so, to string after I've strung each row of beads. I tear each square from the thread as I complete the previous row. (If you are using a twisted wire needle, you will need to poke a hole in each square before you can string them.)

When you are knitting, you read the graph from bottom to top. When you are stringing, you read the graph from top to bottom.

TWO EASY CUFF BRACELETS

Materials

Size 8 Beads:

- color A: white;
  80 beads (2 grams)
- color B: cream;
  80 beads (2 grams)
- color C: jade;
  80 beads (2 grams)
- color D: copper;
  60 beads (2 grams)
- color E: plum; 360 beads
  (9 grams)

size F silk thread; 11 yards

2 needles, size 00

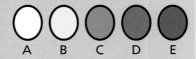

Optional
(for finishing)

- lining material
- backbars
- jump rings
- clasp

Finished Size

1" wide x 4" long
(2.5 x 10.7 cm), exclusive of
strap and embellishments

Knitting Instructions

- Cast on 15 stitches (2 empty stitches
  on each edge).
- Knit and purl 1 row each without
  beads.
- Begin adding beads on a knit row.
- Repeat the pattern segment 5 times
  (more if necessary).
- Work at least 1 row without
  beads, and then end with a simple
  bind-off.

Finishing Suggestions

Line the back with fabric. Sandwich
a backbar or jump rings between
layers, and attach a clasp.

Design Variation

Both bracelets are made with the
same pattern but with different size
beads and slight variations. The
bracelet on the left is made using size
11 beads instead of size 8 and with a
different color scheme. I also doubled
each row and worked additional
repeats. You can create many variations simply by changing colors, bead
size, or the style of the findings.

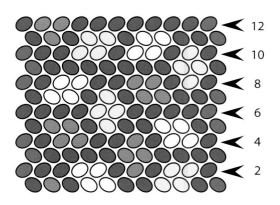

Word Map

Each row = 11 beads
Repeat pattern segment 5 times (more
if necessary).

Row 12 (R-L): D(1); E(7); C(2); E(1)
Row 11 (L-R): E(1); C(1); E(1); B(2); E(1);
  A(2); E(2); D(1)
Row 10 (R-L): E(1); B(1); E(1); A(2); E(1);
  B(2); E(2); D(1)
Row 9 (L-R): D(1); E(7); B(2); E(1)
Row 8 (R-L): E(1); B(1); E(1); C(2); E(2);
  A(2); E(1); D(1)
Row 7 (L-R): E(1); A(2); E(1); B(1); E(1);
  C(2); E(2); D(1)
Row 6 (R-L): D(1); E(4); B(2); E(4)
Row 5 (L-R): E(1); C(2); E(1); B(1); E(2);
  A(2); E(1); D(1)
Row 4 (R-L): E(1); A(2); E(1); C(1); E(2);
  C(2); E(1); D(1)
Row 3 (L-R): D(1); E(4); C(2); E(4)
Row 2 (R-L): E(1); B(2); E(1); C(1); E(1);
  A(2); E(2); D(1)
Row 1 (L-R): E(1); C(1); E(1); A(2); E(2);
  B(2); E(1); D(1)

PINWHEEL PURSE

Materials

Size 11 Beads:

- color A: aquamarine; 3,246 beads (30 grams)
- color B: teal; 3,245 beads (30 grams)
- color C: purple; 3,244 beads (30 grams)

size E silk thread; 106 yards

2 needles, size 0000

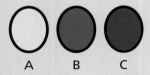

A   B   C

Optional (for finishing)

- lining material
- twisted cord
- jump rings
- accent beads

Finished Size

5" wide x 4½" long (12.7 x 11.4 cm), exclusive of strap and embellishments

Knitting Instructions

- Cast on 63 stitches (2 empty stitches on each edge).
- Knit and purl 1 row each without beads.
- Begin adding beads on a knit row.
- Repeat the pattern segment 2 times, and then complete only the first 33 rows of the pattern for the flap.
- Complete at least 1 row without beads, and end with a simple bind-off.

Finishing Suggestions

Line the entire fabric, and then fold it so that the pattern lines up correctly. Sew the sides to close. Add a strap and fringe if desired.

Word Map

*Each row = 59 beads
*Repeat the pattern segment 2 times, and then complete only the first 33 rows for the flap.

Row 66 (R-L): A(9); B(9); C(9); A(9); B(9); C(9); A(5)

Row 65 (L-R): A(4); C(1); A(3); C(5); B(1); C(3); B(5); A(1); B(3); A(5); C(1); A(3); C(5); B(1); C(3); B(5); A(1); B(3); A(5); C(1)

Row 64 (R-L): C(1); A(3); B(2); C(2); B(5); C(2); A(2); C(5); A(2); B(2); A(5); B(2); C(2); B(5); C(2); A(2); C(5); A(2); B(2); A(6)

Row 63 (L-R): A(4); B(5); A(1); C(3); A(5); C(1); B(3); C(5); B(1); A(3); B(5); A(1); C(3); A(5); C(1); B(3); C(5); B(1); A(2); C(2)

Row 62 (R-L): C(2); A(1); B(1); C(6); B(2); C(1); A(6); C(2); A(1); B(6); A(2); B(1); C(6); B(2); C(1); A(6); C(2); A(1); B(6); A(4)

Row 61 (L-R): A(2); C(1); A(1); B(5); A(1); C(1); B(1); C(1); A(5); C(1); B(1); A(1); B(1); C(5); B(1); A(1); C(1); A(1); B(5); A(1); C(1); B(1); C(1); A(5); C(1); B(1); A(1); B(1); C(5); B(1); A(1); C(3)

Row 60 (R-L): C(3); B(1); C(6); B(1); A(1); C(1); A(6); C(1); B(1); A(1); B(6); A(1); C(1); B(1); C(6); B(1); A(1); C(1); A(6); C(1); B(1); A(1); B(6); A(1); C(1); A(2)

Row 59 (L-R): A(1); C(2); A(1); B(5); A(1); B(2); C(1); A(5); C(1); A(2); B(1); C(5); B(1); C(2); A(1); B(5); A(1); B(2); C(1); A(5); C(1); A(2); B(1); C(5); B(1); C(4)

Row 58 (R-L): C(4); B(2); C(2); B(2); A(3); C(2); A(2); C(2); B(3); A(2); B(2); A(2); C(3); B(2); C(2); B(2); A(3); C(2); A(2); C(2); B(3); A(2); B(2); A(2); C(3); A(1)

Row 57 (L-R): C(5); A(3); C(1); B(5); C(3); B(1); A(5); B(3); A(1); C(5); A(3); C(1); B(5); C(3); B(1); A(5); B(3); A(1); C(5)

Row 56 (R-L): C(5); A(9); B(9); C(9); A(9); B(9); C(9)

Row 55 (L-R): A(9); C(9); B(9); A(9); C(9); B(9); A(5)

Row 54 (R-L): A(4); B(1); C(3); B(5); C(1); A(3); C(5); A(1); B(3); A(5); B(1); C(3); B(5); C(1); A(3); C(5); A(1); B(3); A(5); B(1)

Row 53 (L-R): B(1); A(3); B(2); C(2); B(2); C(3); A(2); B(2); A(2); B(3); C(2); A(2); C(2); A(3); B(2); C(2); B(2); C(3); A(2); B(2); A(2); B(3); C(2); A(2); C(2); A(4)

Row 52 (R-L): A(3); C(1); A(5); C(1); B(2); A(1); B(5); A(1); C(2); B(1); C(5); B(1); A(2); C(1); A(5); C(1); B(2); A(1); B(5); A(1); C(2); B(1); C(5); B(1); A(2); B(2)

Row 51 (L-R): B(2); A(1); B(1); C(6); B(1); C(1); A(1); B(6); A(1); B(1); C(1); A(6); C(1); A(1); B(1); C(6); B(1); C(1); A(1); B(6); A(1); B(1); C(1); A(6); C(1); A(3)

Row 50 (R-L): A(2); B(1); C(1); A(5); C(1); B(1); C(1); A(1); B(5); A(1); C(1); A(1); B(1); C(5); B(1); A(1); B(1); C(1); A(5); C(1); B(1); C(1); A(1); B(5); A(1); C(1); A(1); B(1); C(5); B(1); A(1); B(3)

Row 49 (L-R): B(4); C(6); B(1); A(2); B(6); A(1); C(2); A(6); C(1); B(2); C(6); B(1); A(2); B(6); A(1); C(2); A(6); C(1); B(1); A(2)

Row 48 (R-L): A(1); B(2); C(1); A(5); C(3); A(1); B(5); A(3); B(1); C(5); B(3); C(1); A(6); C(2); A(1); B(6); A(2); B(1); C(5); B(5)

Row 47 (L-R): B(6); C(2); B(2); A(5); B(2); A(2); C(5); A(2); C(2); B(5); C(2); B(2); A(5); B(2); A(2); C(5); A(2); C(2); B(3); A(1)

Row 46 (R-L): B(5); C(3); B(1); C(5); A(3); C(1); A(5); B(3); A(1); B(5); C(3); B(1); C(5); A(3); C(1); A(5); B(3); A(1); B(5)

Row 45 (L-R): B(5); A(9); C(9); B(9); A(9); C(9); B(9)

Row 44 (R-L): C(9); A(9); B(9); C(9); A(9); B(9); C(5)

Row 43 (L-R): C(4); B(1); C(3); B(5); A(1); B(3); A(5); C(1); A(3); C(5); B(1); C(3); B(5); A(1); B(3); A(5); C(1); A(3); C(5); B(1)

34

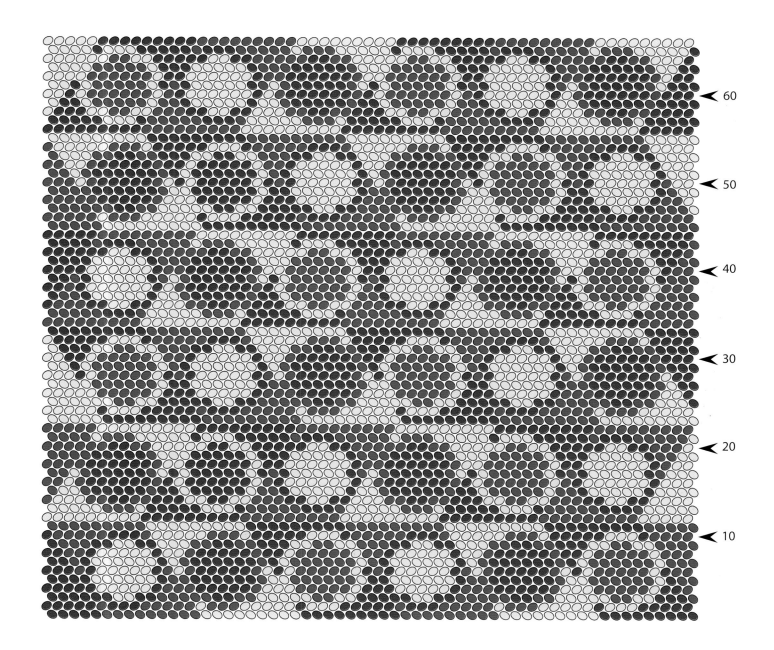

60

50

40

30

20

10

Row 42 (R-L): B(1); C(3); A(2); B(2); A(5); B(2); C(2); B(5); C(2); A(2); C(5); A(2); B(2); A(5); B(2); C(2); B(5); C(2); A(2); C(6)

Row 41 (L-R): C(4); A(5); C(1); B(3); C(5); B(1); A(3); B(5); A(1); C(3); A(5); C(1); B(3); C(5); B(1); A(3); B(5); A(1); C(2); B(2)

Row 40 (R-L): B(2); C(1); A(1); B(6); A(2); B(1); C(6); B(2); C(1); A(6); C(2); A(1); B(6); A(2); B(1); C(6); B(2); C(1); A(6); C(4)

Row 39 (L-R): C(2); B(1); C(1); A(5); C(1); B(1); A(1); B(1); C(5); B(1); A(1); C(1); A(1); B(5); A(1); C(1); B(1); C(1); A(5); C(1); B(1); A(1); B(1); C(5); B(1); A(1); C(1); A(1); B(5); A(1); C(1); B(3)

Row 38 (R-L): B(3); A(1); B(6); A(1); C(1); B(1); C(6); B(1); A(1); C(1); A(6); C(1); B(1); A(1); B(6); A(1); C(1); B(1); C(6); B(1); A(1); C(1); A(6); C(1); B(1); C(2)

Row 37 (L-R): C(1); B(2); C(1); A(5); C(1); A(2); B(1); C(5); B(1); C(2); A(1); B(5); A(1); B(2); C(1); A(5); C(1); A(2); B(1); C(5); B(1); C(2); A(1); B(5); A(1); B(4)

Row 36 (R-L): B(4); A(2); B(2); A(2); C(3); B(2); C(2); B(2); A(3); C(2); A(2); C(2); B(3); A(2); B(2); A(2); C(3); B(2); C(2); B(2); A(3); C(2); A(2); C(2); B(3); C(1)

Row 35 (L-R): B(5); C(3); B(1); A(5); B(3); A(1); C(5); A(3); C(1); B(5); C(3); B(1); A(5); B(3); A(1); C(5); A(3); C(1); B(5)

Row 34 (R-L): B(5); C(9); A(9); B(9); C(9); A(9); B(9)

Row 33 (L-R): C(9); B(9); A(9); C(9); B(9); A(9); C(5)

Row 32 (R-L): C(4); A(1); B(3); A(5); B(1); C(3); B(5); C(1); A(3); C(5); A(1); B(3); A(5); B(1); C(3); B(5); C(1); A(3); C(5); A(1)

Row 31 (L-R): A(1); C(3); A(2); B(2); A(2); B(3); C(2); A(2); C(2); A(3); B(2); C(2); B(2); C(3); A(2); B(2); A(2); B(3); C(2); A(2); C(2); A(3); B(2); C(2); B(2); C(4)

Row 30 (R-L): C(3); B(1); C(5); B(1); A(2); C(1); A(5); C(1); B(2); A(1); B(5); A(1); C(2); B(1); C(5); B(1); A(2); C(1); A(5); C(1); B(2); A(1); B(5); A(1); C(2); A(2)

Row 29 (L-R): A(2); C(1); A(1); B(6); A(1); B(1); C(1); A(6); C(1); A(1); B(1); C(6); B(1); C(1); A(1); B(6); A(1); B(1); C(1); A(6); C(1); A(1); B(1); C(6); B(1); C(3)

Row 28 (R-L): C(2); A(1); B(1); C(5); B(1); A(1); B(1); C(1); A(5); C(1); B(1); C(1); A(1); B(5); A(1); C(1); A(1); B(1); C(5); B(1); A(1); B(1); C(1); A(5); C(1); B(1); C(1); A(1); B(5); A(1); C(1); A(3)

Row 27 (L-R): A(4); B(6); A(1); C(2); A(6); C(1); B(2); C(6); B(1); A(2); B(6); A(1); C(2); A(6); C(1); B(2); C(6); B(1); A(1); C(2)

Row 26 (R-L): C(1); A(2); B(1); C(5); B(3); C(1); A(5); C(3); A(1); B(5); A(3); B(1); C(5); B(3); C(1); A(5); C(3); A(1); B(5); A(5)

Row 25 (L-R): A(6); B(2); A(2); C(5); A(2); C(2); B(5); C(2); B(2); A(5); B(2); A(2); C(5); A(2); C(2); B(5); C(2); B(2); A(3); C(1)

Row 24 (R-L): A(5); B(3); A(1); B(5); C(3); B(1); C(5); A(3); C(1); A(5); B(3); A(1); B(5); C(3); B(1); C(5); A(3); C(1); A(5)

Row 23 (L-R): A(5); C(9); B(9); A(9); C(9); B(9); A(9)

Row 22 (R-L): B(9); C(9); A(9); B(9); C(9); A(9); B(5)

Row 21 (L-R): B(4); A(1); B(3); A(5); C(1); A(3); C(5); B(1); C(3); B(5); A(1); B(3); A(5); C(1); A(3); C(5); B(1); C(3); B(5); A(1)

Row 20 (R-L): A(1); B(3); C(2); A(2); C(5); A(2); B(2); A(5); B(2); C(2); B(5); C(2); A(2); C(5); A(2); B(2); A(5); B(2); C(2); B(6)

Row 19 (L-R): B(4); C(5); B(1); A(3); B(5); A(1); C(3); A(5); C(1); B(3); C(5); B(1); A(3); B(5); A(1); C(3); A(5); C(1); B(2); A(2)

Row 18 (R-L): A(2); B(1); C(1); A(6); C(2); A(1); B(6); A(2); B(1); C(6); B(2); C(1); A(6); C(2); A(1); B(6); A(2); B(1); C(6); B(4)

Row 17 (L-R): B(2); A(1); B(1); C(5); B(1); A(1); C(1); A(1); B(5); A(1); C(1); B(1); C(1); A(5); C(1); B(1); A(1); B(1); C(5); B(1); A(1); C(1); A(1); B(5); A(1); C(1); B(1); C(1); A(5); C(1); B(1); A(3)

Row 16 (R-L): A(3); C(1); A(6); C(1); B(1); A(1); B(6); A(1); C(1); B(1); C(6); B(1); A(1); C(1); A(6); C(1); B(1); A(1); B(6); A(1); C(1); B(1); C(6); B(1); A(1); B(2)

Row 15 (L-R): B(1); A(2); B(1); C(5); B(1); C(2); A(1); B(5); A(1); B(2); C(1); A(5); C(1); A(2); B(1); C(5); B(1); C(2); A(1); B(5); A(1); B(2); C(1); A(5); C(1); A(4)

Row 14 (R-L): A(4); C(2); A(2); C(2); B(3); A(2); B(2); A(2); C(3); B(2); C(2); B(2); A(3); C(2); A(2); C(2); B(3); A(2); B(2); A(2); C(3); B(2); C(2); B(2); A(3); B(1)

Row 13 (L-R): A(5); B(3); A(1); C(5); A(3); C(1); B(5); C(3); B(1); A(5); B(3); A(1); C(5); A(3); C(1); B(5); C(3); B(1); A(5)

Row 12 (R-L): A(5); B(9); C(9); A(9); B(9); C(9); A(9)

Row 11 (L-R): B(9); A(9); C(9); B(9); A(9); C(9); B(5)

Row 10 (R-L): B(4); C(1); A(3); C(5); A(1); B(3); A(5); B(1); C(3); B(5); C(1); A(3); C(5); A(1); B(3); A(5); B(1); C(3); B(5); C(1)

Row 9 (L-R): C(1); B(3); C(2); A(2); C(2); A(3); B(2); C(2); B(2); C(3); A(2); B(2); A(2); B(3); C(2); A(2); C(2); A(3); B(2); C(2); B(2); C(3); A(2); B(2); A(2); B(4)

Row 8 (R-L): B(3); A(1); B(5); A(1); C(2); B(1); C(5); B(1); A(2); C(1); A(5); C(1); B(2); A(1); B(5); A(1); C(2); B(1); C(5); B(1); A(2); C(1); A(5); C(1); B(2); C(2)

Row 7 (L-R): C(2); B(1); C(1); A(6); C(1); A(1); B(1); C(6); B(1); C(1); A(1); B(6); A(1); B(1); C(1); A(6); C(1); A(1); B(1); C(6); B(1); C(1); A(1); B(6); A(1); B3

Row 6 (R-L): B(2); C(1); A(1); B(5); A(1); C(1); A(1); B(1); C(5); B(1); A(1); B(1); C(1); A(5); C(1); B(1); C(1); A(1); B(5); A(1); C(1); A(1); B(1); C(5); B(1); A(1); B(1); C(1); A(5); C(1); B(1); C(3)

Row 5 (L-R): C(4); A(6); C(1); B(2); C(6); B(1); A(2); B(6); A(1); C(2); A(6); C(1); B(2); C(6); B(1); A(2); B(6); A(1); C(1); B(2)

Row 4 (R-L): B(1); C(2); A(1); B(5); A(3); B(1); C(5); B(3); C(1); A(5); C(3); A(1); B(6); A(2); B(1); C(6); B(2); C(1); A(5); C(5)

Row 3 (L-R): C(6); A(2); C(2); B(5); C(2); B(2); A(5); B(2); A(2); C(5); A(2); C(2); B(5); C(2); B(2); A(5); B(2); A(2); C(3); B(1)

Row 2 (R-L): C(5); A(3); C(1); A(5); B(3); A(1); B(5); C(3); B(1); C(5); A(3); C(1); A(5); B(3); A(1); B(5); C(3); B(1); C(5)

Row 1 (L-R): C(5); B(9); A(9); C(9); B(9); A(9); C(9)

Chapter 5

Shaping the Knitting

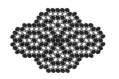

A bead knitter works with increases and decreases to shape the body of a bead knitted fabric. Edge increases make the piece gradually widen at the selvages while keeping the fabric flat. Similarly, edge decreases narrow the width of the fabric at the selvages. By increasing and decreasing within the rows of knitting, the fabric becomes wider overall, which gives it extra volume and dimension.

11 Edge Increases

An edge increase is made over 2 rows. In the first row, you make an extra stitch by knitting or purling into the same stitch twice. In the second row, you add a bead to the edge of the beaded row, leaving only 2 unbeaded edge stitches.

Increasing in a Knit Row

Step 1: Insert the right-hand needle into the front leg of the first stitch.

Step 2: Wrap the thread over and around the needle, and pull a loop through, but do not drop the stitch from the left-hand needle (A).

Step 3: Position the right-hand needle so that you can knit into the back leg of the same stitch (B).

Step 4: Allow the stitch to drop from the left-hand needle, and knit the next stitch without a bead. You now have 3 stitches without beads at the beginning of the row. Complete the increase in the next purl row by leaving only 2 empty stitches at the end of the row.

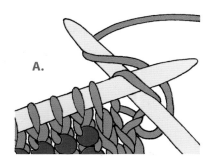

A.

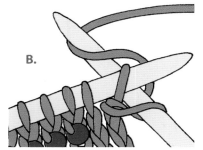

B.

Increasing in a Purl Row

Step 1: Purl the back leg of the first stitch (A). Leave the stitch on the left-hand needle.

Step 2: Bring the right-hand needle to the front, and purl the front leg of the same stitch (B). Allow the stitch to drop from the left-hand needle.

Step 3: Purl the remainder of the row with a bead in each stitch and 2 stitches without beads at the end.

Step 4: Complete this increase in the next knit row by leaving only 2 stitches at the end of the row.

Increases can be made at the start of every row, or they can be staggered, which will create a more gradual slope. Also, you don't have to increase both edges—you can increase on only one side to create an asymmetrical effect in the design.

12 Edge Decreases

An edge decrease is made over 2 rows. In the first row a bead is omitted. In the next row, the unbeaded stitch is bound off.

Decreasing in a Knit Row

Step 1: Knit the first 3 stitches without beads. Bead knit to the end of the row, leaving the last 2 stitches unbeaded.

Step 2: Purl to the end of the row until you reach the 3 unbeaded stitches. Purl the first of these stitches without a bead.

Step 3: Insert the right-hand needle into the next stitch as if to purl. Transfer the stitch from the left-hand needle to the right-hand needle without purling. This is called a slipped stitch.

Step 4: Purl the third stitch without a bead. The left-hand needle is now empty. Insert the left-hand needle into the slipped

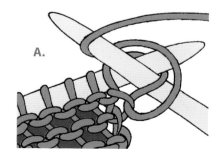

A.

B.

Example of Edge Shaping

Cast on 11 stitches. Complete 2 rows without beads.
Row 1 is the bottom row.

Row 1: Increase by 1 stitch; knit 7 beads.

Row 2: Increase by 1 stitch; purl 8 beads.

Row 3: Increase by 1 stitch; knit 9 beads.

Row 4: Increase by 1 stitch; purl 10 beads.

Row 5: Increase by 1 stitch; knit 11 beads.

Row 6: Purl 12 beads.

Row 7: Omit 1 bead; knit 11 beads.

Row 8: Omit 1 bead; purl 10 beads; eliminate 1 stitch.

Row 9: Omit 1 bead; knit 9 beads; eliminate 1 stitch.

Row 10: Omit 1 bead; purl 8 beads; eliminate 1 stitch.

Row 11: Omit 1 bead; knit 7 beads; eliminate 1 stitch.

Purl the next row without beads, eliminating the
extra stitch at the end of the row.

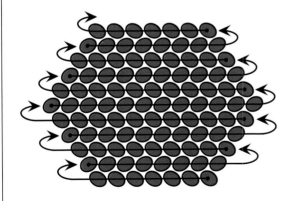

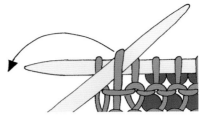

Bind off a knit
decrease in a
purl row.

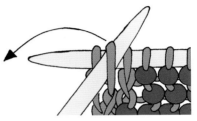

Bind off a purl
decrease in a
knit row.

stitch, and lift it over the last purled stitch.
Allow it to drop from the needle. You have
made a decrease.

Decreasing in a Purl Row

Purl the first 3 stitches without beads.
Complete the decrease by binding off the
stitch at the end of the subsequent knit row,
as shown above.

Shaping within a Row

An increase within a row is made over two
rows. It may occur anywhere within the
row, and any number of increases may be
made. This adds body to your bead knitting
and is useful when creating a round bag.

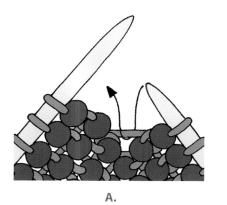

A.

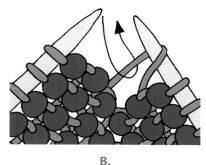

B.

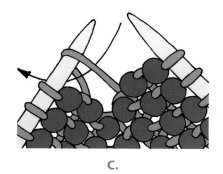

C.

▶ 13 Increasing within a Row

Step 1: Knit to the point where you want to add a new stitch. Working from back to front, insert the tip of the needle in your right hand beneath the "running thread" between the stitch below the one that was just knitted and the one that you will knit next (A).

Step 2: Transfer the running thread to the needle in your left hand by inserting the needle into the loop from front to back (B).

Step 3: Remove the needle in your right hand from the front of the loop, and reinsert it into the back leg, as if you were knitting a regular stitch (C). It may be necessary to push the thread forward a bit to make a space in which to insert the needle.

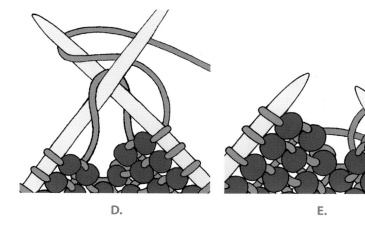

D.

E.

Step 4: Wrap the thread over and around the right-hand needle, and complete the new stitch without adding a bead (D, E). Allow the running thread to drop from the needle in your left hand. Knit until you want to make the next increase.

Step 5: Complete the increase in the subsequent purl row by purling each stitch, adding beads to the new stitches that were created in the previous row.

Because increases made within the row are visible in the beadwork (although less so with smaller beads), they are much more attractive when carefully organized. This can be done in two ways:

1. Add a new stitch after the first or second bead of every increase row and another before the last or next-to-last bead. This method of increasing creates an effect similar to that of an edge increase in that the body of the beadwork fabric remains flat. This method is also used to increase when double knitting (page 68).

2. Add new stitches incrementally, giving the appearance of triangular wedges. For example, there may be 1 bead between each increase in the first row, 2 beads between increases in the third row, and 3 beads between increases in the fifth row (see the graphed pattern for the Blue Garden Draw-string Purse, page 60).

14 Decreasing within a Row

A decrease within a row is made over 2 rows and acts as a complement to an increase within a row.

Step 1: Begin a decrease on a purl row by omitting the desired beads from the row, leaving an empty stitch where each decrease is to be made.

Step 2: Complete each decrease in the subsequent knit row by eliminating each empty stitch. Knit the row until you reach the first empty stitch.

Step 3: Slip the empty stitch from the left-hand needle to the right-hand needle. Knit a bead into the next stitch.

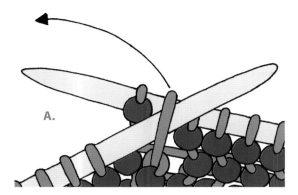

Step 4: Insert the needle in your left hand into the slipped stitch, and lift it over the beaded stitch and off the needle (A). Pull the stitch over the bead so that it is concealed between that bead and the bead below it (B). Continue knitting until the next empty stitch.

Organize decreases as you would organize increases. When eliminating empty stitches with an incremental (wedge) decrease, take special care when counting the number of beads between each decrease. It is easy to forget to count the bead above the decrease stitch, which can throw off your count.

Increases and decreases can be made within the same row, or you can stagger rows for more gradual shaping.

If you make a large number of increases within a single row—particularly if they are made on consecutive rows—your bead knitting will likely appear bunched until you knit several rows without increases or remove the knitting from the needles. In some cases, this bunching may make it difficult for you to continue knitting because the stitches are so close together. If this happens, simply transfer half of the stitches to a third needle, and knit from needle to needle without increasing until the knit fabric is smooth.

Be creative. You can adapt many other traditional knitting techniques to bead knitting!

DUSK NECKLACE

Materials

Size 8 Beads:

- color A: lavender;
  734 beads (19 grams)
- color B: light green;
  69 beads (2 grams)
- color C: purple; 66 beads
  (2 grams)
- color D: black; 671 beads
  (17 grams)

size FF silk thread; 24 yards

2 needles, size 00

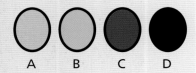

A   B   C   D

Optional (for finishing)

- lining material
- bead stringing wire
- jump rings
- clasp
- sterling crimps
- 10mm accent beads
- pressed glass leaves

Finished Size

5" wide x 4½" long
(12.7 x 11.4 cm),
exclusive of strap
and embellishments

Knitting Instructions

- Cast on 32 stitches (2 empty stitches on each edge).
- Knit 1 row without beads.
- Begin adding beads on a purl row.

Row 1:

Purl a bead into each of 28 stitches (leave the first and last 2 stitches unbeaded).

Row 2:

Increase by 1 stitch to begin the (knit) row.

Row 3–27:

- All odd (purl) rows: Decrease by 1 bead to begin each row. Complete the increase from the previous row by knitting a bead into the first of the last 3 empty stitches.
- All even (knit) rows: Increase by 1 stitch to begin each row. Complete the decrease from the previous row by eliminating the last stitch.

Row 28:

Do not increase. Complete the decrease from the previous row by eliminating the last stitch.

Row 29:

Increase by 1 stitch to begin the row.

Row 30–54:

- All even (knit) rows: Decrease by 1 bead at the beginning of each row. Complete the increase from the previous row by knitting a bead onto the first of the last 3 empty stitches.
- All odd (purl) rows: Increase by 1 stitch at the beginning of each row. Complete the decrease from the previous row by eliminating the last stitch.

Row 55:

Do not increase. Complete the decrease from the previous row by eliminating the last stitch.

Work at least 1 row without beads, and end with a simple bind-off.

Finishing Suggestions

Line with fabric. Add a strap. Add fringe if you'd like.

Word Map

* Each row = 28 beads

Row 55 (R-L): A(4); C(1); D(1); A(1); D(1); B(1); A(2); D(2); B(1); A(2); B(1); A(3); D(1); C(1); A(1); D(1); A(4)

Row 54 (L-R): D(2); A(1); D(2); C(2); D(2); A(1); B(2); A(1); B(2); A(1); D(2); B(2); D(2); C(2); A(4)

Row 53 (R-L): A(6); D(1); A(3); D(1); A(1); D(1); A(2); D(5); A(2); D(1); A(2); D(2); A(1)

Row 52 (L-R): D(1); B(2); A(2); D(1); A(3); D(1); A(2); D(3); A(2); D(3); A(1); D(1); A(6)

Row 51 (R-L): A(7); D(2); A(4); D(1); A(2); D(1); A(2); D(2); A(1); D(4); B(1); A(1)

Row 50 (L-R): D(2); A(3); D(2); A(2); D(2); A(1); D(1); A(1); D(4); A(1); D(1); A(1); B(2); A(5)

Row 49 (R-L): A(5); D(1); B(1); A(1); D(1); A(1); D(1); A(3); D(4); A(2); C(2); A(3); D(2); A(1)

Row 48 (L-R): A(2); D(2); A(2); C(1); D(2); A(3); D(3); A(2); D(3); A(2); D(2); A(4)

Row 47 (R-L): A(3); C(1); D(1); A(2); D(2); A(3); D(2); C(2); A(1); D(3); A(1); D(2); A(1); D(1); A(1); D(2)

Row 46 (L-R): B(2); A(1); D(2); A(2); D(2); A(1); D(2); C(1); D(1); A(1); D(2); A(3); D(1); A(1); D(1); C(2); A(3)

Row 45 (R-L): A(6); D(2); A(3); D(1); A(2); D(1); A(1); D(1); A(4); D(2); B(1); A(3); B(1)

Row 44 (L-R): A(2); D(1); B(2); A(3); D(2); A(1); D(2); A(1); C(1); D(4); A(2); D(1); A(6)

Row 43 (R-L): A(4); B(1); D(1); A(1); D(1); A(1); D(1); A(3); C(2); D(1); A(2); D(1); A(1); D(3); A(2); D(1); C(1); A(1)

Row 42 (L-R): C(2); D(2); A(3); D(1); A(1); D(1); A(2); D(2); B(2); A(2); D(1); A(1); D(2); B(2); A(4)

Row 41 (R-L): A(7); D(1); A(1); D(4); B(1); D(1); A(1); D(2); B(1); D(3); C(1); A(1); D(1); A(3)

Row 40 (L-R): D(1); A(2); D(1); C(2); A(2); B(2); A(1); D(3); A(2); D(1); A(1); D(2); A(8)

Row 39 (R-L): A(9); D(1); A(2); D(1); A(1); D(1); A(4); D(9)

Row 38 (L-R): A(2); B(1); A(2); D(6); A(2); D(1); C(2); D(1); A(1); D(1); A(9)

Row 37 (R-L): A(10); D(2); A(1); C(1); D(1); A(1); D(5); A(2); D(2); B(2); D(1)

Row 36 (L-R): D(2); A(1); C(2); A(3); D(6); A(2); D(1); A(10); D(1)

Row 35 (R-L): D(2); A(9); D(2); A(1); D(5); A(3); D(2); C(1); A(1); D(1); A(1)

Row 34 (L-R): A(1); D(2); A(2); D(9); A(1); D(1); A(9); D(3)

Row 33 (R-L): D(4); A(7); D(2); A(1); D(8); A(1); D(1); A(1); D(1); A(2)

Row 32 (L-R): D(4); A(2); D(1); A(2); D(5); A(1); D(2); A(1); D(1); A(3); D(6)

Row 31 (R-L): D(10); A(1); D(7); A(3); D(3); A(2); C(1); D(1)

Row 30 (L-R): C(2); A(1); D(1); A(2); D(2); A(2); D(18)

Row 29 (R-L): D(18); A(2); D(1); A(2); D(3); A(2)

Row 28 (L-R): D(2); A(1); B(1); D(3); A(1); D(20)

Row 27 (R-L): D(22); A(1); B(2); A(2); D(1)

Row 26 (L-R): D(2); A(1); D(2); A(3); D(2); A(1); D(17)

Row 25 (R-L): D(17); A(2); D(2); A(1); D(1); A(1); D(2); A(2)

Row 24 (L-R): A(1); D(1); A(4); D(2); A(1); D(1); A(1); D(9); A(2); D(6)

Row 23 (R-L): D(4); A(6); D(2); A(1); D(4); A(1); D(1); A(2); D(2); A(1); D(2); C(2)

Row 22 (L-R): D(1); C(1); A(2); D(2); A(2); D(2); A(2); D(2); A(2); D(1); A(9); D(2)

Row 21 (R-L): D(1); A(10); D(1); A(2); D(2); A(3); D(2); A(1); D(1); A(1); D(1); A(1); D(1); A(1)

Row 20 (L-R): A(2); D(4); A(2); C(2); A(1); D(3); A(1); D(2); A(11)

Row 19 (R-L): A(10); D(1); A(3); D(4); C(1); D(2); B(1); A(2); C(1); D(2); A(1)

Row 18 (L-R): D(2); A(1); C(2); D(1); B(2); A(1); D(4); A(1); D(1); A(1); D(2); A(10)

Row 17 (R-L): A(9); D(1); A(1); D(1); C(1); D(1); A(1); D(3); A(2); D(2); A(1); D(2); A(2); D(1)

Row 16 (L-R): A(1); D(3); A(1); D(1); A(2); D(4); A(2); D(1); C(2); A(1); D(2); C(1); A(7)

Row 15 (R-L): A(6); C(2); A(1); D(1); A(2); D(3); B(1); A(1); D(1); A(1); D(4); A(4); D(1)

Row 14 (L-R): B(1); D(2); C(2); A(2); D(1); A(2); D(1); A(1); B(2); A(1); D(1); A(2); D(1); A(9)

Row 13 (R-L): A(7); B(1); D(1); A(3); D(2); A(3); D(2); A(1); D(3); C(1); D(1); A(1); B(2)

Row 12 (L-R): A(3); D(3); A(1); B(2); A(4); D(2); A(1); D(2); A(2); B(2); A(6)

Row 11 (R-L): A(9); D(2); A(3);
 D(4); A(1); B(1); D(1); A(3);
 D(2); A(1); D(1)

Row 10 (L-R): A(1); D(2); A(2);
 D(2); A(1); D(2); A(2); D(2);
 A(2); D(5); A(7)

Row 9 (R-L): A(4); D(3); A(1);
 D(1); A(2); D(1); A(1); B(2);
 D(1); A(1); D(1); A(2); D(1);
 A(1); D(1); B(1); A(4)

Row 8 (L-R): D(1); A(1); D(2);
 B(2); A(1); C(1); D(5); A(1); B(1);
 D(2); A(2); D(1); A(2); D(1); A(1);
 D(1); A(3)

Row 7 (R-L): A(3); D(1); A(1); D(1);
 C(2); D(1); A(2); D(1); A(5); D(1);
 A(1); C(2); D(3); A(1); D(2); B(1)

Row 6 (L-R): B(2); A(1); D(1); A(3);
 D(1); A(7); D(2); A(3); D(1); C(1);
 A(1); D(1); A(1); D(1); A(2)

Row 5 (R-L): A(1); B(2); A(1); D(1);
 A(1); D(4); A(2); D(5); A(1); D(2);
 A(1); D(4); A(3)

Row 4 (L-R): A(1); D(3); A(3); D(2);
 A(1); D(2); A(2); D(1); A(3); D(1);
 A(1); D(1); A(2); D(1); A(2);
 B(1); A(1)

Row 3 (R-L): A(4); D(2); A(1);
 D(1); A(1); D(2); C(1); D(3);
 A(5); D(1); A(1); B(2); D(1);
 A(1); D(2)

Row 2 (L-R): A(1); C(2); D(1);
 A(1); B(1); D(2); B(2); A(2);
 D(2); A(1); D(1); C(2); A(1);
 D(2); A(2); C(2); A(3)

Row 1 (R-L): A(3); C(1); A(4);
 D(1); A(3); D(1); A(2); D(3);
 B(1); A(1); D(1); A(3); D(1);
 C(1); A(2)

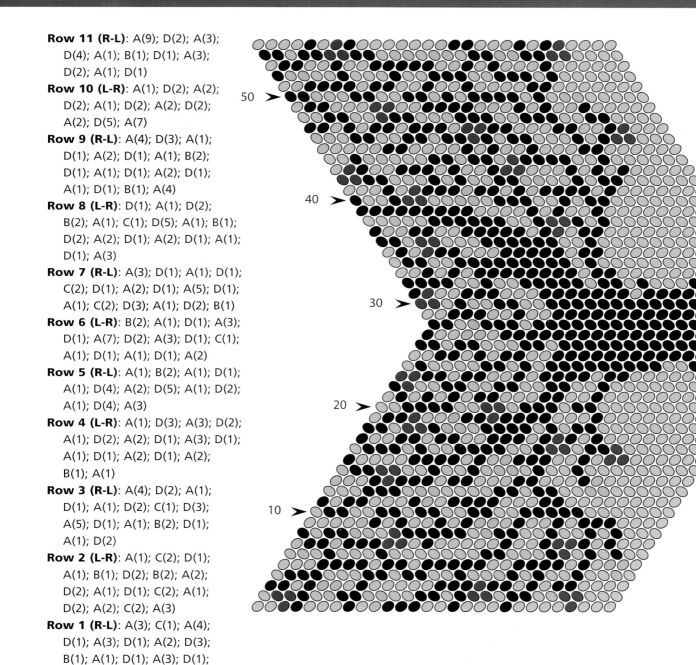

OLIVE'S STAR BOX

Materials
Size 11 Beads:
- color A: pale pink; 1,277 beads (12 grams)
- color B: dusty rose; 2,218 beads (21 grams)
- color C: navy blue; 1,569 beads (15 grams)

size E silk thread; 57 yards

2 needles, size 0000

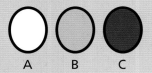

A   B   C

Optional (for finishing)
- lining material
- twisted cord
- jump rings
- accent beads

Finished Size
7" wide x 3½" long (17.8 x 8.9 cm), exclusive of strap and embellishments

Knitting Instructions
- Cast on 5 stitches (2 empty stitches on each edge).
- Purl 1 row without beads.
- Begin adding beads on a knit row.

Row 1:
Increase by 1 stitch to begin the row.

Rows 2–74:
Increase by 1 stitch to begin each row. Complete the increase from the previous row by knitting/purling a bead onto the first of the last 3 empty stitches.

Row 75:
Do not increase. Complete the increase from the previous row by knitting a bead into the first of the last 3 empty stitches.

Rows 76–116:
Decrease by 1 bead to begin each row. Complete the decrease from the previous row by eliminating the last stitch.

Knit the subsequent row without beads, eliminating the last stitch. Work at least 1 more row without beads, and end with a simple bind-off.

Finishing Suggestions
Line the entire fabric. Fold at the widest point, matching the pattern on each edge, and sew the edges. Embellish and add straps if you'd like.

Word Map

Row 116 (R-L): B(34), *34 beads*
Row 115 (L-R): B(35), *35 beads*
Row 114 (R-L): B(36), *36 beads*
Row 113 (L-R): B(37), *37 beads*
Row 112 (R-L): B(38), *38 beads*
Row 111 (L-R): B(39), *39 beads*
Row 110 (R-L): B(40), *40 beads*
Row 109 (L-R): B(41), *41 beads*
Row 108 (R-L): B(42), *42 beads*
Row 107 (L-R): B(43), *43 beads*
Row 106 (R-L): B(44), *44 beads*
Row 105 (L-R): B(45), *45 beads*
Row 104 (R-L): B(46), *46 beads*
Row 103 (L-R): B(47), *47 beads*
Row 102 (R-L): B(48), *48 beads*
Row 101 (L-R): B(49), *49 beads*
Row 100 (R-L): B(50), *50 beads*
Row 99 (L-R): C(3); B(45); C(3), *51 beads*
Row 98 (R-L): A(3); C(2); B(42); C(2); A(3), *52 beads*
Row 97 (L-R): C(3); A(2); C(1); B(41); C(1); A(2); C(3), *53 beads*
Row 96 (R-L): C(1); A(2); C(2); A(1); C(1); B(40); C(1); A(1); C(2); A(2); C(1), *54 beads*
Row 95 (L-R): A(2); C(1); A(2); C(5); B(35); C(5); A(2); C(1); A(2), *55 beads*
Row 94 (R-L): C(2); A(2); C(2); A(4); C(2); B(32); C(2); A(4); C(2); A(2); C(2), *56 beads*
Row 93 (L-R): A(2); C(1); A(1); C(1); A(2); C(3); A(2); C(1); B(31); C(1); A(2); C(3); A(2); C(1); A(1); C(1); A(2), *57 beads*
Row 92 (R-L): C(2); A(1); C(2); A(1); C(2); A(2); C(2); A(1); C(1); B(30); C(1); A(1); C(2); A(2); C(2); A(1); C(2); A(1); C(2), *58 beads*

Row 91 (L-R): A(2); C(5); A(2); C(1); A(2); C(5); B(25); C(5); A(2); C(1); A(2); C(5); A(2), *59 beads*
Row 90 (R-L): A(1); C(2); A(4); C(2); A(2); C(2); A(4); C(2); B(22); C(2); A(4); C(2); A(2); C(2); A(4); C(2); A(1), *60 beads*
Row 89 (L-R): A(1); C(1); A(2); C(3); A(2); C(1); A(1); C(1); A(2); C(3); A(2); C(1); B(21); C(1); A(2); C(3); A(2); C(1); A(1); C(1); A(2); C(3); A(2); C(1); A(1), *61 beads*
Row 88 (R-L): C(2); A(1); C(2); A(2); C(2); A(1); C(2); A(1); C(2); A(2); C(2); A(1); C(1); B(20); C(1); A(1); C(2); A(2); C(2); A(1); C(2); A(1); C(2); A(2); C(2); A(1); C(2), *62 beads*
Row 87 (L-R): C(4); A(2); C(1); A(2); C(5); A(2); C(1); A(2); C(5); B(15); C(5); A(2); C(1); A(2); C(5); A(2); C(1); A(2); C(4), *63 beads*
Row 86 (R-L): A(4); C(2); A(2); C(2); A(4); C(2); A(2); C(2); A(4); C(2); B(12); C(2); A(4); C(2); A(2); C(2); A(4); C(2); A(2); C(2); A(4), *64 beads*
Row 85 (L-R): A(1); C(3); A(2); C(1); A(1); C(1); A(2); C(3); A(2); C(1); A(1); C(1); A(2); C(3); A(2); C(1); B(11); C(1); A(2); C(3); A(2); C(1); A(1); C(1); A(2); C(3); A(2); C(1); A(1); C(1); A(2); C(3); A(1), *65 beads*
Row 84 (R-L): C(2); A(2); C(2); A(1); C(2); A(1); C(2); A(2); C(2); A(1); C(2); A(1); C(2); A(2); C(2); A(1); C(1); B(10); C(1); A(1); C(2); A(2); C(2); A(1); C(2); A(1); C(2); A(2); C(2); A(1); C(2); A(2); C(2), *66 beads*
Row 83 (L-R): C(1); A(2); C(1); A(2); C(5); A(2); C(1); A(2); C(5); A(2); C(1); A(2); C(5); B(5); C(5); A(2); C(1); A(2);

C(5); A(2); C(1); A(2); C(5); A(2); C(1); A(2); C(1), *67 beads*
Row 82 (R-L): A(1); C(2); A(2); C(2); A(4); C(2); A(2); C(2); A(4); C(2); A(2); C(2); A(4); C(2); B(2); C(2); A(4); C(2); A(2); C(2); A(4); C(2); A(2); C(2); A(4); C(2); A(2); C(2); A(1), *68 beads*
Row 81 (L-R): C(1); A(2); C(1); A(1); C(1); A(2); C(3); A(2); C(1); A(1); C(1); A(2); C(3); A(2); C(1); A(1); C(1); A(2); C(3); A(2); C(1); B(1); C(1); A(2); C(3); A(2); C(1); A(1); C(1); A(2); C(3); A(2); C(1); A(1); C(1); A(2); C(3); A(2); C(1); A(1); C(1); A(2); C(1), *69 beads*
Row 80 (R-L): A(1); C(2); A(1); C(2); A(1); C(2); A(2); C(2); A(1); C(2); A(1); C(2); A(2); C(2); A(1); C(2); A(1); C(2); A(2); C(2); A(1); C(2); A(1); C(2); A(2); C(2); A(1); C(2); A(1); C(2); A(2); C(2); A(1); C(2); A(1); C(2); A(1), *70 beads*
Row 79 (L-R): C(1); A(2); C(5); A(2); C(1); A(2); C(5); A(2); C(1); A(2); C(5); A(2); C(1); A(2); C(5); A(2); C(1); A(2); C(5); A(2); C(1); A(2); C(5); A(2); C(1); A(2); C(5); A(2); C(1), *71 beads*
Row 78 (R-L): A(2); C(2); A(4); C(2); A(2); C(2); A(4); C(2); A(2); C(2); A(4); C(2); A(2); C(2); A(4); C(2); A(2); C(2); A(4); C(2); A(2); C(2); A(4); C(2); A(2), *72 beads*
Row 77 (L-R): C(1); A(1); C(1); A(2); C(3); A(2); C(1); A(1); C(1); A(2); C(3); A(2); C(1); A(1); C(1); A(2); C(3); A(2); C(1); A(1); C(1); A(2); C(3); A(2); C(1); A(1); C(1); A(2); C(3); A(2); C(1); A(1); C(1); A(2); C(3); A(2); C(1); A(1); C(1); A(2); C(3); A(2); C(1); A(1); C(1), *73 beads*

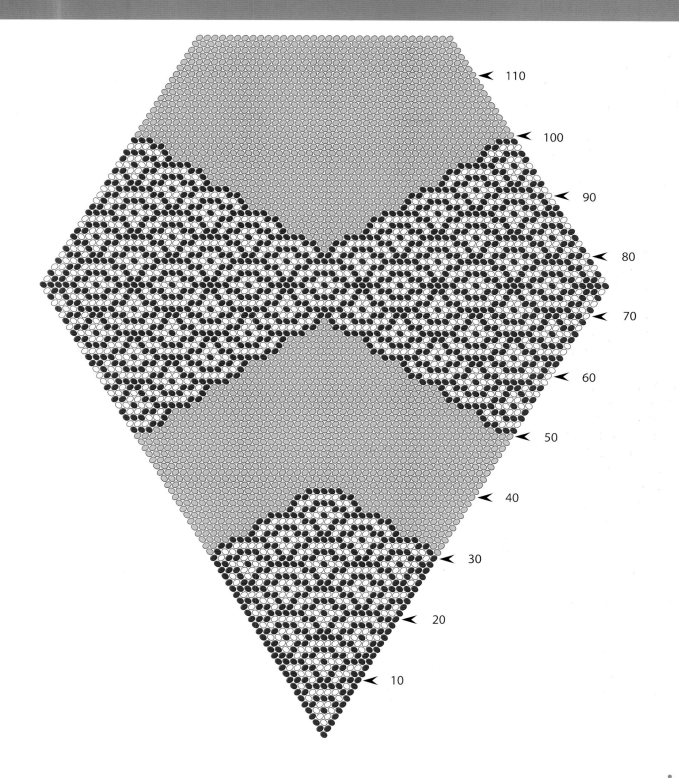

110

100

90

80

70

60

50

40

30

20

10

Row 76 (R-L): A(1); C(2); A(1); C(2);
A(2); C(2); A(1); C(2); A(1); C(2); A(2);
C(2); A(1); C(2); A(1); C(2); A(2); C(2);
A(1); C(2); A(1); C(2); A(2); C(2); A(1);
C(2); A(1); C(2); A(2); C(2); A(1); C(2);
A(1); C(2); A(2); C(2); A(1); C(2); A(1);
C(2); A(2); C(2); A(1); C(2); A(1),
74 beads

Row 75 (L-R): C(5); A(2); C(1); A(2);
C(5); A(2); C(1); A(2); C(5); A(2); C(1);
A(2); C(5); A(2); C(1); A(2); C(5); A(2);
C(1); A(2); C(5); A(2); C(1); A(2); C(5);
A(2); C(1); A(2); C(5), *75 beads*

Row 74 (R-L): A(1); C(2); A(1); C(2);
A(2); C(2); A(1); C(2); A(1); C(2); A(2);
C(2); A(1); C(2); A(1); C(2); A(2); C(2);
A(1); C(2); A(1); C(2); A(2); C(2); A(1);
C(2); A(1); C(2); A(2); C(2); A(1); C(2);
A(1); C(2); A(2); C(2); A(1); C(2); A(1);
C(2); A(2); C(2); A(1); C(2); A(1),
74 beads

Row 73 (L-R): C(1); A(1); C(1); A(2);
C(3); A(2); C(1); A(1); C(1); A(2); C(3);
A(2); C(1); A(1); C(1); A(2); C(3); A(2);
C(1); A(1); C(1); A(2); C(3); A(2); C(1);
A(1); C(1); A(2); C(3); A(2); C(1); A(1);
C(1); A(2); C(3); A(2); C(1); A(1); C(1);
A(2); C(3); A(2); C(1); A(1); C(1),
73 beads

Row 72 (R-L): A(2); C(2); A(4); C(2);
A(2); C(2); A(4); C(2); A(2); C(2); A(4);
C(2); A(2); C(2); A(4); C(2); A(2); C(2);
A(4); C(2); A(2); C(2); A(4); C(2); A(2);
C(2); A(4); C(2); A(2), *72 beads*

Row 71 (L-R): C(1); A(2); C(5); A(2);
C(1); A(2); C(5); A(2); C(1); A(2); C(5);
A(2); C(1); A(2); C(5); A(2); C(1); A(2);

C(5); A(2); C(1); A(2); C(5); A(2); C(1);
A(2); C(5); A(2); C(1), *71 beads*

Row 70 (R-L): A(1); C(2); A(1); C(2);
A(1); C(2); A(2); C(2); A(1); C(2); A(1);
C(2); A(2); C(2); A(1); C(2); A(1); C(2);
A(2); C(2); A(1); C(2); A(1); C(2); A(2);
C(2); A(1); C(2); A(1); C(2); A(2); C(2);
A(1); C(2); A(1); C(2); A(2); C(2); A(1);
C(2); A(1); C(2); A(1), *70 beads*

Row 69 (L-R): C(1); A(2); C(1); A(1);
C(1); A(2); C(3); A(2); C(1); A(1); C(1);
A(2); C(3); A(2); C(1); A(1); C(1); A(2);
C(3); A(2); C(1); B(1); C(1); A(2); C(3);
A(2); C(1); A(1); C(1); A(2); C(3); A(2);
C(1); A(1); C(1); A(2); C(3); A(2); C(1);
A(1); C(1); A(2); C(1), *69 beads*

Row 68 (R-L): A(1); C(2); A(2); C(2);
A(4); C(2); A(2); C(2); A(4); C(2); A(2);
C(2); A(4); C(2); B(2); C(2); A(4); C(2);
A(2); C(2); A(4); C(2); A(2); C(2); A(4);
C(2); A(2); C(2); A(1), *68 beads*

Row 67 (L-R): C(1); A(2); C(1); A(2);
C(5); A(2); C(1); A(2); C(5); A(2); C(1);
A(2); C(5); B(5); C(5); A(2); C(1); A(2);
C(5); A(2); C(1); A(2); C(5); A(2); C(1);
A(2); C(1), *67 beads*

Row 66 (R-L): C(2); A(2); C(2); A(1);
C(2); A(1); C(2); A(2); C(2); A(1); C(2);
A(1); C(2); A(2); C(2); A(1); C(1);
B(10); C(1); A(1); C(2); A(2); C(2);
A(1); C(2); A(1); C(2); A(2); C(2); A(1);
C(2); A(1); C(2); A(2); C(2), *66 beads*

Row 65 (L-R): A(1); C(3); A(2); C(1);
A(1); C(1); A(2); C(3); A(2); C(1); A(1);
C(1); A(2); C(3); A(2); C(1); B(11);
C(1); A(2); C(3); A(2); C(1); A(1); C(1);
A(2); C(3); A(2); C(1); A(1); C(1); A(2);
C(3); A(1), *65 beads*

Row 64 (R-L): A(4); C(2); A(2); C(2);
A(4); C(2); A(2); C(2); A(4); C(2);
B(12); C(2); A(4); C(2); A(2); C(2);
A(4); C(2); A(2); C(2); A(4), *64 beads*

Row 63 (L-R): C(4); A(2); C(1); A(2);
C(5); A(2); C(1); A(2); C(5); B(15);
C(5); A(2); C(1); A(2); C(5); A(2); C(1);
A(2); C(4), *63 beads*

Row 62 (R-L): C(2); A(1); C(2); A(2);
C(2); A(1); C(2); A(1); C(2); A(2); C(2);
A(1); C(1); B(20); C(1); A(1); C(2);
A(2); C(2); A(1); C(2); A(1); C(2); A(2);
C(2); A(1); C(1); A(1), *62 beads*

Row 61 (L-R): A(1); C(1); A(2); C(3);
A(2); C(1); A(1); C(1); A(2); C(3); A(2);
C(1); B(21); C(1); A(2); C(3); A(2);
C(1); A(1); C(1); A(2); C(3); A(2); C(2),
61 beads

Row 60 (R-L): A(1); C(2); A(4); C(2);
A(2); C(2); A(4); C(2); B(22); C(2);
A(4); C(2); A(2); C(2); A(4); C(2); A(1),
60 beads

Row 59 (L-R): A(2); C(5); A(2); C(1);
A(2); C(5); B(25); C(5); A(2); C(1);
A(2); C(5); A(2), *59 beads*

Row 58 (R-L): C(2); A(1); C(2); A(1);
C(2); A(2); C(2); A(1); C(1); B(30);
C(1); A(1); C(2); A(2); C(2); A(1); C(2);
A(1); C(2), *58 beads*

Row 57 (L-R): A(2); C(1); A(1); C(1);
A(2); C(3); A(2); C(1); B(31); C(1);
A(2); C(3); A(2); C(1); A(1); C(1); A(2),
57 beads

Row 56 (R-L): C(2); A(2); C(2); A(4);
C(2); B(32); C(2); A(4); C(2); A(2);
C(2), *56 beads*

Row 55 (L-R): A(2); C(1); A(2); C(5);
B(35); C(5); A(2); C(1); A(2), *55 beads*

Row 54 (R-L): C(1); A(2); C(2); A(1); C(1); B(40); C(1); A(1); C(2); A(2); C(1), *54 beads*

Row 53 (L-R): C(3); A(2); C(1); B(41); C(1); A(2); C(3), *53 beads*

Row 52 (R-L): A(3); C(2); B(42); C(2); A(3), *52 beads*

Row 51 (L-R): C(3); B(45); C(3), *51 beads*

Row 50 (R-L): B(50), *50 beads*

Row 49 (L-R): B(49), *49 beads*

Row 48 (R-L): B(48), *48 beads*

Row 47 (L-R): B(47), *47 beads*

Row 46 (R-L): B(46), *46 beads*

Row 45 (L-R): B(45), *45 beads*

Row 44 (R-L): B(44), *44 beads*

Row 43 (L-R): B(43), *43 beads*

Row 42 (R-L): B(42), *42 beads*

Row 41 (L-R): B(18); C(5); B(18), *41 beads*

Row 40 (R-L): B(16); C(2); A(4); C(2); B(16), *40 beads*

Row 39 (L-R): B(15); C(1); A(2); C(3); A(2); C(1); B(15), *39 beads*

Row 38 (R-L): B(14); C(1); A(1); C(2); A(2); C(2); A(1); C(1); B(14), *38 beads*

Row 37 (L-R): B(11); C(5); A(2); C(1); A(2); C(5); B(11), *37 beads*

Row 36 (R-L): B(9); C(2); A(4); C(2); A(2); C(2); A(4); C(2); B(9), *36 beads*

Row 35 (L-R): B(8); C(1); A(2); C(3); A(2); C(1); A(1); C(1); A(2); C(3); A(2); C(1); B(8), *35 beads*

Row 34 (R-L): B(7); C(1); A(1); C(2); A(2); C(2); A(1); C(2); A(1); C(2); A(2); C(2); A(1); C(1); B(7), *34 beads*

Row 33 (L-R): B(4); C(5); A(2); C(1); A(2); C(5); A(2); C(1); A(2); C(5); B(4), *33 beads*

Row 32 (R-L): B(2); C(2); A(4); C(2); A(2); C(2); A(4); C(2); A(2); C(2); A(4); C(2); B(2), *32 beads*

Row 31 (L-R): B(1); C(1); A(2); C(3); A(2); C(1); A(1); C(1); A(2); C(3); A(2); C(1); A(1); C(1); A(2); C(3); A(2); C(1); B(1), *31 beads*

Row 30 (R-L): C(1); A(1); C(2); A(2); C(2); A(1); C(2); A(1); C(2); A(2); C(2); A(1); C(2); A(1); C(2); A(2); C(2); A(1); C(1), *30 beads*

Row 29 (L-R): C(2); A(2); C(1); A(2); C(5); A(2); C(1); A(2); C(5); A(2); C(1); A(2); C(2), *29 beads*

Row 28 (R-L): C(3); A(2); C(2); A(4); C(2); A(2); C(2); A(4); C(2); A(2); C(3), *28 beads*

Row 27 (L-R): C(1); A(1); C(1); A(1); C(1); A(2); C(3); A(2); C(1); A(1); C(1); A(2); C(3); A(2); C(1); A(1); C(1); A(1); C(1), *27 beads*

Row 26 (R-L): C(1); A(1); C(2); A(1); C(2); A(2); C(2); A(1); C(2); A(1); C(2); A(2); C(2); A(1); C(2); A(1); C(1), *26 beads*

Row 25 (L-R): C(5); A(2); C(1); A(2); C(5); A(2); C(1); A(2); C(5), *25 beads*

Row 24 (R-L): C(1); A(3); C(2); A(2); C(2); A(4); C(2); A(2); C(2); A(3); C(1), *24 beads*

Row 23 (L-R): C(3); A(2); C(1); A(1); C(1); A(2); C(3); A(2); C(1); A(1); C(1); A(2); C(3), *23 beads*

Row 22 (R-L): C(1); A(1); C(2); A(1); C(2); A(1); C(2); A(2); C(2); A(1); C(2); A(1); C(2); A(1); C(1), *22 beads*

Row 21 (L-R): C(1); A(2); C(5); A(2); C(1); A(2); C(5); A(2); C(1), *21 beads*

Row 20 (R-L): C(3); A(4); C(2); A(2); C(2); A(4); C(3), *20 beads*

Row 19 (L-R): C(1); A(2); C(3); A(2); C(1); A(1); C(1); A(2); C(3); A(2); C(1), *19 beads*

Row 18 (R-L): C(3); A(2); C(2); A(1); C(2); A(1); C(2); A(2); C(3), *18 beads*

Row 17 (L-R): C(1); A(2); C(1); A(2); C(5); A(2); C(1); A(2); C(1), *17 beads*

Row 16 (R-L): C(2); A(2); C(2); A(4); C(2); A(2); C(2), *16 beads*

Row 15 (L-R): C(2); A(1); C(1); A(2); C(3); A(2); C(1); A(1); C(2), *15 beads*

Row 14 (R-L): C(3); A(1); C(2); A(2); C(2); A(1); C(3), *14 beads*

Row 13 (L-R): C(4); A(2); C(1); A(2); C(4), *13 beads*

Row 12 (R-L): C(1); A(2); C(2); A(2); C(2); A(2); C(1), *12 beads*

Row 11 (L-R): C(2); A(2); C(1); A(1); C(1); A(2); C(2), *11 beads*

Row 10 (R-L): C(3); A(1); C(2); A(1); C(3), *10 beads*

Row 9 (L-R): C(1); A(1); C(5); A(1); C(1), *9 beads*

Row 8 (R-L): C(2); A(4); C(2), *8 beads*

Row 7 (L-R): C(1); A(1); C(3); A(1); C(1), *7 beads*

Row 6 (R-L): C(2); A(2); C(2), *6 beads*

Row 5 (L-R): C(1); A(1); C(1); A(1); C(1), *5 beads*

Row 4 (R-L): C(1); A(2); C(1), *4 beads*

Row 3 (L-R): C(1); A(1); C(1), *3 beads*

Row 2 (R-L): C(2), *2 beads*

Row 1 (L-R): C(1), *1 bead*

DRAGON BAG

Materials

Size 8 Beads:

- color A: lime green; 36 beads (1 gram)
- color B: cream; 442 beads (12 grams)
- color C: yellow; 168 beads (5 grams)
- color D: gold; 126 beads (4 grams)
- color E: lavender; 118 beads (3 grams)
- color F: purple; 246 beads (7 grams)
- color G: red; 1,430 beads (36 grams)
- color H: brown iris; 698 beads (18 grams)

size FF silk thread; 52 yards

2 needles, size 00

A   B   C   D   E   F   G   H

Optional (for finishing)

- lining material
- jump rings
- 10mm accent beads
- pressed glass disks

Finished Size

4½" wide x 4½" long (11.4 x 11.4 cm), exclusive of strap and embellishments

Knitting Instructions

- Cast on 29 stitches (2 empty stitches on each edge).
- Knit 1 row without beads.
- Begin adding beads on a purl row.

Row 1:

Purl each stitch, adding beads to all but the edge stitches.

Rows 2–17:

- All even (knit) rows: Make a new stitch after the first bead and another before the last bead of each row.
- All odd (purl) rows: Complete the increases from the previous row by knitting a bead into each new stitch.

Rows 18–32:

Knit/purl each row without increases.

Rows 33–42:

- All odd (purl) rows: Omit the 2nd bead and the next-to-last bead of each row.
- All even (knit) rows: Complete the decreases made in the previous row by eliminating all empty stitches.

Row 43:

Omit the 2nd, 4th, 6th, 26th, 28th, and 30th beads

Rows 44, 46, 48 (even rows only):

Complete the decreases made in the previous row by eliminating all empty stitches.

Row 45:

Omit the 2nd, 4th, 6th, 20th, 22nd, and 24th beads.

Row 47:

Omit the 2nd, 4th, 6th, 14th, 16th, and 18th beads.

Work at least 1 row without beads, and then end with a simple bind-off.

Repeat this entire process to make the second side of the bag.

Finishing Suggestions

- Sew the 2 sides of the bag together at the edges, and then line the bag with fabric.
- Add fringe, a strap, and a bead-and-loop closure if you'd like.

Word Map

Row 48 (L-R): G(13), *13 beads*
Row 47 (R-L): G(13), *13 beads*
Row 46 (L-R): G(19), *19 beads*
Row 45 (R-L): G(19), *19 beads*
Row 44 (L-R): G(25), *25 beads*
Row 43 (R-L): G(25), *25 beads*
Row 42 (L-R): G(9); H(2); G(8); H(2); G(10), *31 beads*
Row 41 (R-L): G(7); H(3); G(11); H(3); G(7), *31 beads*
Row 40 (L-R): G(6); H(3); G(14); H(3); G(7), *33 beads*
Row 39 (R-L): G(6); H(1); F(1); H(1); G(5); H(5); G(5); H(1); F(1); H(1); G(6), *33 beads*
Row 38 (L-R): G(5); H(2); F(1); H(1); G(4); H(2); B(4); H(2); G(4); H(1); F(1); H(2); G(6), *35 beads*
Row 37 (R-L): G(5); H(1); F(2); H(1); G(4); H(1); B(2); C(3); B(2); H(1); G(4); H(1); F(2); H(1); G(5), *35 beads*
Row 36 (L-R): G(5); H(1); F(2); H(1); G(4); H(1); B(1); H(1); B(1); C(2); B(1); H(1); B(1); H(1); G(4); H(1); F(2); H(1); G(6), *37 beads*
Row 35 (R-L): G(4); H(2); F(1); E(1); F(1); H(1); G(4); H(1); B(1); H(1); B(1); C(1); B(1); H(1); B(1); H(1); G(4); H(1); F(1); E(1); F(1); H(2); G(4), *37 beads*

Row 34 (L-R): G(4); H(1); B(1); H(1); F(2); H(1); G(5); H(2); B(1); C(2); B(1); H(2); G(5); H(1); F(2); H(1); B(1); H(1); G(5), *39 beads*
Row 33 (R-L): G(4); H(1); B(2); H(1); F(2); H(1); G(5); H(1); B(1); C(1); D(1); C(1); B(1); H(1); G(5); H(1); F(2); H(1); B(2); H(1); G(4), *39 beads*
Row 32 (L-R): G(4); H(1); B(2); H(1); F(1); E(1); F(1); H(1); G(4); H(1); B(1); C(1); D(2); C(1); B(1); H(1); G(4); H(1); F(1); E(1); F(1); H(1); B(2); H(1); G(5), *41 beads*
Row 31 (R-L): G(4); H(1); B(2); H(1); F(1); E(2); F(1); H(1); G(4); H(1); B(1); C(1); D(1); C(1); B(1); H(1); G(4); H(1); F(1); E(2); F(1); H(1); B(2); H(1); G(4), *41 beads*
Row 30 (L-R): G(3); H(1); B(2); H(1); F(1); E(2); F(1); H(1); G(4); H(1); B(1); C(1); D(2); C(1); B(1); H(1); G(4); H(1); F(1); E(2); F(1); H(1); B(2); H(1); G(4), *41 beads*
Row 29 (R-L): G(3); H(1); B(2); H(1); F(1); E(3); F(1); H(1); G(2); H(1); G(1); H(1); B(1); C(1); D(1); C(1); B(1); H(1); G(1); H(1); G(2); H(1); F(1); E(3); F(1); H(1); B(2); H(1); G(3), *41 beads*
Row 28 (L-R): G(3); H(1); B(1); H(1); F(1); E(4); F(1); H(1); G(2); H(3); B(1); C(2); B(1); H(3); G(2); H(1); F(1); E(4); F(1); H(1); B(1); H(1); G(4), *41 beads*

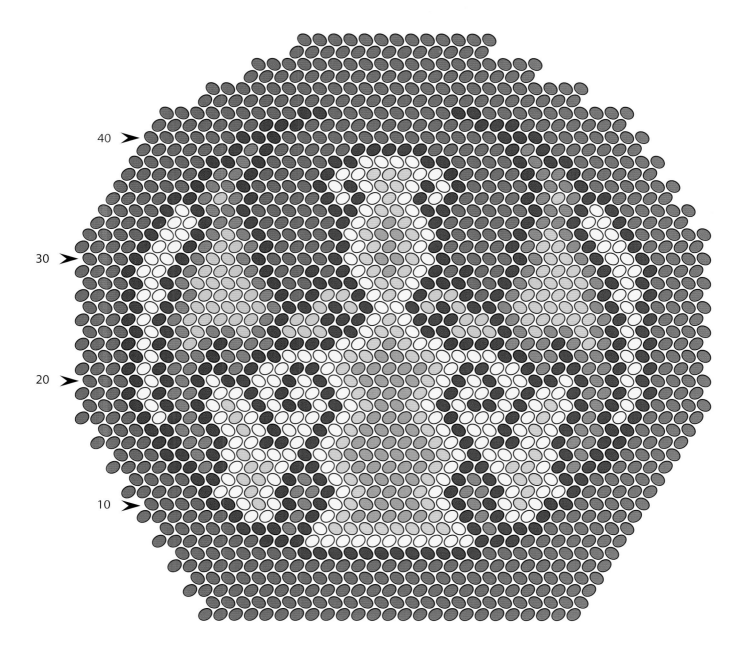

Row 27 (R-L): G(3); H(1); B(2); H(1);
F(1); E(4); F(1); H(1); G(1); H(1); A(2);
H(1); B(1); C(1); B(1); H(1); A(2); H(1);
G(1); H(1); F(1); E(4); F(1); H(1); B(2);
H(1); G(3), *41 beads*

Row 26 (L-R): G(3); H(1); B(1); H(1);
F(1); E(5); F(1); H(2); A(1); H(1); A(1);
H(1); B(2); H(1); A(1); H(1); A(1); H(2);
F(1); E(5); F(1); H(1); B(1); H(1); G(4),
41 beads

Row 25 (R-L): G(3); H(1); B(1); H(1);
F(2); E(4); F(1); H(1); A(2); H(3); B(1);
C(1); B(1); H(3); A(2); H(1); F(1); E(5);
F(1); H(1); B(1); H(1); G(3), *41 beads*

Row 24 (L-R): G(3); H(1); B(1); H(1);
F(1); E(1); F(2); E(1); F(1); H(1); A(3);
H(2); B(1); C(2); B(1); H(2); A(3); H(1);
F(1); E(1); F(2); E(1); F(1); H(1); B(1);
H(1); G(4), *41 beads*

Row 23 (R-L): G(3); H(1); B(1); H(1);
F(1); E(1); F(1); H(1); F(3); H(4); B(2);
C(1); D(1); C(1); B(2); H(4); F(3); H(1);
F(1); E(1); F(1); H(1); B(1); H(1); G(3),
41 beads

Row 22 (L-R): G(3); H(1); B(1); H(1);
F(2); H(1); F(2); H(2); B(4); C(2); D(2);
C(2); B(4); H(2); F(2); H(1); F(2); H(1);
B(1); H(1); G(4), *41 beads*

Row 21 (R-L): G(3); H(1); B(1); H(1);
F(2); H(2); F(1); H(1); B(2); H(2); B(1);
C(1); D(5); C(1); B(1); H(2); B(2); H(1);
F(1); H(2); F(2); H(1); B(1); H(1); G(3),
41 beads

Row 20 (L-R): G(3); H(1); B(1); H(1);
F(1); H(1); B(1); H(2); B(2); H(1); B(1);
H(1); B(1); C(1); D(4); C(1); B(1); H(1);
B(1); H(1); B(2); H(2); B(1); H(1); F(1);
H(1); B(1); H(1); G(4), *41 beads*

Row 19 (R-L): G(3); H(1); B(1); H(1);
F(2); H(1); B(2); H(1); B(1); H(1); B(2);
H(1); B(1); C(1); D(3); C(1); B(1); H(1);
B(2); H(1); B(1); H(1); B(2); H(1); F(2);
H(1); B(1); H(1); G(3), *41 beads*

Row 18 (L-R): G(3); H(1); B(1); H(1);
F(1); H(1); B(1); C(1); B(1); H(1); B(1);
H(2); B(1); H(1); B(1); C(1); D(2); C(1);
B(1); H(1); B(1); H(2); B(1); H(1); B(1);
C(1); B(1); H(1); F(1); H(1); B(1); H(1);
G(4), *41 beads*

Row 17 (R-L): G(4); H(1); B(1); H(1);
F(1); H(1); B(1); C(1); B(1); H(1); B(3);
H(1); B(1); C(1); D(3); C(1); B(1); H(1);
B(3); H(1); B(1); C(1); B(1); H(1); F(1);
H(1); B(1); H(1); G(4), *41 beads*

Row 16 (L-R): G(3); H(2); F(2); H(1);
B(1); C(1); B(1); H(1); B(2); H(1); B(1);
C(1); D(4); C(1); B(1); H(1); B(2); H(1);
B(1); C(1); B(1); H(1); F(2); H(2); G(4),
39 beads

Row 15 (R-L): G(4); H(2); F(2);
H(1); B(2); H(2); B(1); H(1); B(1); C(1);
D(5); C(1); B(1); H(1); B(1); H(2); B(2);
H(1); F(2); H(2); G(4), *39 beads*

Row 14 (L-R): G(3); H(2); F(1);
H(1); B(1); C(1); B(3); H(1); B(1); C(1);
D(6); C(1); B(1); H(1); B(3); C(1); B(1);
H(1); F(1); H(2); G(4), *37 beads*

Row 13 (R-L): G(4); H(2); F(1); H(1);
B(1); C(2); B(1); H(2); B(1); C(1); D(5);
C(1); B(1); H(2); B(1); C(2); B(1); H(1);
F(1); H(2); G(4), *37 beads*

Row 12 (L-R): G(4); H(2); B(1); C(2);
B(1); H(1); F(1); H(1); B(1); C(1); D(4);
C(1); B(1); H(1); F(1); H(1); B(1); C(2);
B(1); H(2); G(5), *35 beads*

Row 11 (R-L): G(5); H(1); B(2);
C(1); B(1); H(1); F(2); H(1); B(1); C(1);
D(3); C(1); B(1); H(1); F(2); H(1); B(1);
C(1); B(2); H(1); G(5), *35 beads*

Row 10 (L-R): G(4); H(2); B(1);
C(1); B(1); H(1); F(1); H(1); B(1);
C(1); D(4); C(1); B(1); H(1);
F(1); H(1); B(1); C(1); B(1);
H(2); G(5), *33 beads*

Row 9 (R-L): G(6); H(1); B(2);
H(1); F(1); H(1); B(1); C(1);
D(5); C(1); B(1); H(1); F(1); H(1);
B(2); H(1); G(6), *33 beads*

Row 8 (L-R): G(5); H(3); F(1); H(1);
B(1); C(8); B(1); H(1); F(1); H(3);
G(6), *31 beads*

Row 7 (R-L): G(7); H(3); B(11);
H(3); G(7), *31 beads*

Row 6 (L-R): G(8); H(12); G(9),
29 beads

Row 5 (R-L): G(29), *29 beads*
Row 4 (L-R): G(27), *27 beads*
Row 3 (R-L): G(27), *27 beads*
Row 2 (L-R): G(25), *25 beads*
Row 1 (R-L): G(25), *25 beads*

BLUE GARDEN DRAWSTRING PURSE

Materials

Size 11 Beads
- color A: white; 222 beads (3 grams)
- color B: pink; 138 beads (2 grams)
- color C: yellow/green; 72 beads (1 gram)
- color D: light blue; 1,446 beads (14 grams)
- color E: royal blue; 240 beads (3 grams)
- color F: navy blue; 1,422 beads (13 grams)

size E silk thread; 43 yards

2 needles, size 0000

A   B   C   D   E   F

Optional (for finishing)

lining material

twisted cord

accent beads

Finished Size

3" wide x 4" long (7.6 x 10.7 cm), exclusive of strap and embellishments

Knitting Instructions

- Cast on 16 stitches (2 empty stitches on each edge).
- Knit 1 row each without beads.
- Begin adding beads on a purl row.

Row 1:

Purl each stitch, adding beads to all but the edge stitches.

Row 2:

Increase by 1 stitch after the first bead and then after every 2 beads. The row will end with 1 bead after the last increase.

Row 3–21 (odd rows only):

Complete the increases from the previous row by purling a bead into each new stitch.

Row 4:

Make 1 new stitch after the first bead and then after every 3 beads. The row will end with 2 beads after the last increase.

Row 6:

Make 1 new stitch after the first 2 beads and then after every 4 beads. The row will end with 2 beads after the last increase.

Row 8:

Make 1 new stitch after the first 2 beads and then after every 5 beads. The row will end with 3 beads after the last increase.

Row 10:

Make 1 new stitch after the first 3 beads and then after every 6 beads. The row will end with 3 beads after the last increase.

Row 12:

Make 1 new stitch after the first 3 beads and then after every 7 beads. The row will end with 4 beads after the last increase.

Row 14:

Make 1 new stitch after the first 4 beads and then after every 8 beads. The row will end with 4 beads after the last increase.

Row 16:

Make 1 new stitch after the first 4 beads and then after every 9 beads. The row will end with 5 beads after the last increase.

Row 18:

Make 1 new stitch after the first 5 beads and then after every 10 beads. The row will end with 5 beads after the last increase.

Row 20:

Make 1 new stitch after the first 5 beads and then after every 11 beads. The row will end with 6 beads after the last increase.

Rows 22–52:

Knit/Purl each row without increases.

Row 53:

Omit the 7th bead and then every 12th bead. The row will end with 5 beads after the last omission.

Rows 54–60 (even rows only):

Complete the decreases from the previous row by eliminating all empty stitches (not including the edge stitches).

Row 55:

Omit the 6th bead and then every 11th bead. The row will end with 5 beads after the last omission.

Row 57:

Omit the 6th bead and then every 10th bead. The row will end with 4 beads after the last omission.

Row 59:

Omit the 5th bead and then every 9th bead. The row will end with 4 beads after the last omission.

Work at least 1 row without beads. Add knitted eyelets, if you want, and then end with a simple bind-off.

Finishing Suggestions

Match the pattern along the side edges, and sew the seam up the back of the pouch.

Add a strap, fabric lining, and embellishments if you want.

Word Map

Row 60 (L-R): D(48), *48 beads*

Row 59 (R-L): F(1); D(5); F(3); D(5); F(3); D(5); F(3); D(5); F(3); D(5); F(2), *48 beads*

Row 58 (L-R): B(1); F(1); D(5); F(1); B(2); F(1); D(5); F(1); B(2); F(1); D(5); F(1); B(2); F(1); D(5); F(1); B(2); F(1); D(5); F(1); B(1), *54 beads*

Row 57 (R-L): A(1); F(2); D(2); F(2); A(1); F(1); A(1); F(2); D(2); F(2); A(1); F(1); A(1); F(2); D(2); F(2); A(1); F(1); A(1); F(2); D(2); F(2); A(1); F(1); A(1); F(2); D(2); F(2); A(1); F(1), *54 beads*

Row 56 (L-R): F(2); A(1); F(1); D(2); F(1); A(1); F(4); A(1); F(1); D(2); F(1); A(1); F(4); A(1); F(1); D(2); F(1); A(1); F(4); A(1); F(1); D(2); F(1); A(1); F(4); A(1); F(1); D(2); F(1); A(1); F(2), *60 beads*

Row 55 (R-L): F(1); A(1); B(1); F(1); D(1); F(1); B(1); A(1); F(1); C(1); F(1); A(1); B(1); F(1); D(1); F(1); B(1); A(1); F(1); C(1); F(1); A(1); B(1); F(1); D(1); F(1); B(1); A(1); F(1); C(1); F(1); A(1); B(1); F(1); D(1); F(1); B(1); A(1); F(1); C(1); F(1); A(1); B(1); F(1); D(1); F(1); B(1); A(1); F(1); C(1), *60 beads*

60

50

40

30

20

10

Row 54 (L-R): C(1); F(3); D(3); F(3); C(2); F(3); D(3); F(3); C(2); F(3); D(3); F(3); C(2); F(3); D(3); F(3); C(2); F(3); D(3); F(3); C(2); F(3); D(3); F(3); C(1), *66 beads*

Row 53 (R-L): F(1); A(1); B(1); F(1); D(2); F(1); B(1); A(1); F(1); C(1); F(1); A(1); B(1); F(1); D(2); F(1); B(1); A(1); F(1); C(1); F(1); A(1); B(1); F(1); D(2); F(1); B(1); A(1); F(1); C(1); F(1); A(1); B(1); F(1); D(2); F(1); B(1); A(1); F(1); C(1); F(1); A(1); B(1); F(1); D(2); F(1); B(1); A(1); F(1); C(1), *66 beads*

Row 52 (L-R): F(2); A(1); F(1); D(4); F(1); A(1); F(4); A(1); F(1); D(4); F(1); A(1); F(4); A(1); F(1); D(4); F(1); A(1); F(4); A(1); F(1); D(4); F(1); A(1); F(4); A(1); F(1); D(4); F(1); A(1); F(4); A(1); F(1); D(4); F(1); A(1); F(2), *72 beads*

Row 51 (R-L): A(1); F(2); D(1); F(3); D(1); F(2); A(1); F(1); A(1); F(2); D(1); F(3); D(1); F(2); A(1); F(1); A(1); F(2); D(1); F(3); D(1); F(2); A(1); F(1); A(1); F(2); D(1); F(3); D(1); F(2); A(1); F(1); A(1); F(2); D(1); F(3); D(1); F(2); A(1); F(1), *72 beads*

Row 50 (L-R): B(1); F(1); D(2); F(1); B(2); F(1); D(2); F(1); B(2); F(1); D(2); F(1); B(2); F(1); D(2); F(1); B(2); F(1); D(2); F(1); B(2); F(1); D(2); F(1); B(2); F(1); D(2); F(1); B(2); F(1); D(2); F(1); B(2); F(1); D(2); F(1); B(2); F(1); D(2); F(1); B(1), *72 beads*

Row 49 (R-L): F(1); D(1); F(2); A(1); F(1); A(1); F(2); D(1); F(3); D(1); F(2); A(1); F(1); A(1); F(2); D(1); F(3); D(1); F(2); A(1); F(1); A(1); F(2); D(1); F(3); D(1); F(2); A(1); F(1); A(1); F(2); D(1); F(3); D(1); F(2); A(1); F(1); A(1); F(2); D(1); F(2), *72 beads*

Row 48 (L-R): D(2); F(1); A(1); F(4); A(1); F(1); D(4); F(1); A(1); F(4); A(1); F(1); D(4); F(1); A(1); F(4); A(1); F(1); D(4); F(1); A(1); F(4); A(1); F(1); D(4); F(1); A(1); F(4); A(1); F(1); D(2), *72 beads*

Row 47 (R-L): D(1); F(1); B(1); A(1); F(1); C(1); F(1); A(1); B(1); F(1); D(3); F(1); B(1); A(1); F(1); C(1); F(1); A(1); B(1); F(1); D(3); F(1); B(1); A(1); F(1); C(1); F(1); A(1); B(1); F(1); D(3); F(1); B(1); A(1); F(1); C(1); F(1); A(1); B(1); F(1); D(3); F(1); B(1); A(1); F(1); C(1); F(1); A(1); B(1); F(1); D(2), *72 beads*

Row 46 (L-R): D(2); F(3); C(2); F(3); D(4); F(3); C(2); F(3); D(4); F(3); C(2); F(3); D(4); F(3); C(2); F(3); D(4); F(3); C(2); F(3); D(4); F(3); C(2); F(3); D(2), *72 beads*

Row 45 (R-L): D(1); F(1); B(1); A(1); F(1); C(1); F(1); A(1); B(1); F(1); D(3); D(1); F(1); B(1); A(1); F(1); C(1); F(1); A(1); B(1); F(1); D(3); D(1); F(1); B(1); A(1); F(1); C(1); F(1); A(1); B(1); F(1); D(3); D(1); F(1); B(1); A(1); F(1); C(1); F(1); A(1); B(1); F(1); D(2); *72 beads*

Row 44 (L-R): D(2); F(1); A(1); F(4); A(1); F(1); D(4); F(1); A(1); F(4); A(1); F(1); D(4); F(1); A(1); F(4); A(1); F(1); D(4); F(1); A(1); F(4); A(1); F(1); D(4); F(1); A(1); F(4); A(1); F(1); D(2), *72 beads*

Row 43 (R-L): F(1); D(1); F(2); A(1); F(1); A(1); F(2); D(1); F(3); D(1); F(2); A(1); F(1); A(1); F(2); D(1); F(3); D(1); F(2); A(1); F(1); A(1); F(2); D(1); F(3); D(1); F(2); A(1); F(1); A(1); F(2); D(1); F(3); D(1); F(2); A(1); F(1); A(1); F(2); D(1); F(2), *72 beads*

Row 42 (L-R): B(1); F(1); D(2); F(1); B(2); F(1); D(2); F(1); B(2); F(1); D(2); F(1); B(2); F(1); D(2); F(1); B(2); F(1); D(2); F(1); B(2); F(1); D(2); F(1); B(2); F(1); D(2); F(1); B(2); F(1); D(2); F(1); B(2); F(1); D(2); F(1); B(2); F(1); D(2); F(1); B(1), *72 beads*

Row 41 (R-L): A(1); F(2); D(1); F(3); D(1); F(2); A(1); F(1); A(1); F(2); D(1); F(3); D(1); F(2); A(1); F(1); A(1); F(2); D(1); F(3); D(1); F(2); A(1); F(1); A(1); F(2); D(1); F(3); D(1); F(2); A(1); F(1); A(1); F(2); D(1); F(3); D(1); F(2); A(1); F(1); A(1); F(2); D(1); F(3); D(1); F(2); A(1); F(1), *72 beads*

Row 40 (L-R): F(2); A(1); F(1); D(4); F(1); A(1); F(4); A(1); F(1); D(4); F(1); A(1); F(4); A(1); F(1); D(4); F(1); A(1); F(4); A(1); F(1); D(4); F(1); A(1); F(4); A(1); F(1); D(4); F(1); A(1); F(4); A(1); F(1); D(4); F(1); A(1); F(2), *72 beads*

Row 39 (R-L): F(1); A(1); B(1); F(1); D(3); F(1); B(1); A(1); F(1); C(1); F(1); A(1); B(1); F(1); D(3); F(1); B(1); A(1); F(1); C(1); F(1); A(1); B(1); F(1); D(3); F(1); B(1); A(1); F(1); C(1); F(1); A(1); B(1); F(1); D(3); F(1); B(1); A(1); F(1); C(1); F(1); A(1); B(1); F(1); D(3); F(1); B(1); A(1); F(1); C(1), *72 beads*

Row 38 (L-R): C(1); F(3); D(4); F(3); C(2); F(3); D(4); F(3); C(2); F(3); D(4); F(3); C(2); F(3); D(4); F(3); C(2); F(3); D(4); F(3); C(2); F(3); D(4); F(3); C(1), *72 beads*

Row 37 (R-L): F(1); A(1); B(1); F(1); D(1); F(1); D(1); F(1); B(1); A(1); F(1); C(1); F(1); A(1); B(1); F(1); D(1); F(1); D(1); F(1); B(1); A(1); F(1); C(1); F(1); A(1); B(1); F(1); D(1); F(1); D(1); F(1); B(1); A(1); F(1); C(1); F(1); A(1); B(1); F(1); D(1); F(1); D(1); F(1); B(1); A(1); F(1); C(1); F(1); A(1); B(1); F(1); D(1); F(1); D(1); F(1); B(1); A(1); F(1); C(1), *72 beads*

Row 36 (L-R): F(2); A(1); F(1); D(1); F(2); D(1); F(1); A(1); F(4); A(1); F(1); D(1); F(2); D(1); F(1); A(1); F(4); A(1); F(1); D(1); F(2); D(1); F(1); A(1); F(4); A(1); F(1); D(1); F(2); D(1); F(1); A(1); F(4); A(1); F(1); D(1); F(2); D(1); F(1); A(1); F(2), *72 beads*

Row 35 (R-L): A(1); F(2); D(1); F(1); E(1); F(1); D(1); F(2); A(1); F(1); A(1); F(2); D(1); F(1); E(1); F(1); D(1); F(2); A(1); F(1); A(1); F(2); D(1); F(1); E(1); F(1); D(1); F(2); A(1); F(1); A(1); F(2); D(1); F(1); E(1); F(1); D(1); F(2); A(1); F(1); A(1); F(2); D(1); F(1); E(1); F(1); D(1); F(2); A(1); F(1), *72 beads*

Row 34 (L-R): B(1); F(1); D(2); F(1); E(2); F(1); D(2); F(1); B(2); F(1); D(2); F(1); E(2); F(1); D(2); F(1); B(2); F(1); D(2); F(1); E(2); F(1); D(2); F(1); B(2); F(1); D(2); F(1); E(2); F(1); D(2); F(1); B(2); F(1); D(2); F(1); E(2); F(1); D(2); F(1); B(1), *72 beads*

Row 33 (R-L): F(1); D(2); F(1); E(1); F(1); E(1); F(1); D(2); F(3); D(2); F(1); E(1); F(1); E(1); F(1); D(2); F(3); D(2); F(1); E(1); F(1); E(1); F(1); D(2); F(3); D(2); F(1); E(1); F(1); E(1); F(1); D(2); F(3); D(2); F(1); E(1); F(1); E(1); F(1); D(2); F(2), *72 beads*

Row 32 (L-R): D(4); F(1); E(2); F(1); D(8); F(1); E(2); F(1); D(8); F(1); E(2); F(1); D(8); F(1); E(2); F(1); D(8); F(1); E(2); F(1); D(4), *72 beads*

Row 31 (R-L): D(2); F(1); D(1); F(1); E(1); F(1); D(1); F(1); D(5); F(1); D(1); F(1); E(1); F(1); D(1); F(1); D(5); F(1); D(1); F(1); E(1); F(1); D(1); F(1); D(5); F(1); D(1); F(1); E(1); F(1); D(1); F(1); D(5); F(1); D(1); F(1); E(1); F(1); D(1); F(1); D(3), *72 beads*

Row 30 (L-R): D(2); F(2); D(1); F(2); D(1); F(2); D(4); F(2); D(1); F(2); D(1); F(2); D(4); F(2); D(1); F(2); D(1); F(2); D(4); F(2); D(1); F(2); D(1); F(2); D(4); F(2); D(1); F(2); D(1); F(2); D(4); F(2); D(1); F(2); D(1); F(2); D(2), *72 beads*

Row 29 (R-L): D(1); F(1); E(1); F(1); D(1); F(1); D(1); F(1); E(1); F(1); D(3); F(1); E(1); F(1); D(1); F(1); D(1); F(1); E(1); F(1); D(3); F(1); E(1); F(1); D(1); F(1); D(1); F(1); E(1); F(1); D(3); F(1); E(1); F(1); D(1); F(1); D(1); F(1); E(1); F(1); D(3); F(1); E(1); F(1); D(1); F(1); E(1); F(1); D(3); F(1); E(1); F(1); D(1); F(1); F(1); D(1); F(1); E(1); F(1); D(2), *72 beads*

Row 28 (L-R): D(1); F(1); E(2); F(1); D(2); F(1); E(2); F(1); D(2); F(1); E(2); F(1); D(2); F(1); E(2); F(1); D(2); F(1); E(2); F(1); D(2); F(1); E(2); F(1); D(2); F(1); E(2); F(1); D(2); F(1); E(2); F(1); D(2); F(1); E(2); F(1); D(1), *72 beads*

Row 27 (R-L): F(1); E(1); F(1); E(1); F(1); D(1); F(1); E(1); F(1); E(1); F(1); D(1); F(1); E(1); F(1); E(1); F(1); D(1); F(1); E(1); F(1); E(1); F(1); D(1); F(1); E(1); F(1); E(1); F(1); D(1); F(1); E(1); F(1); D(1); F(1); E(1); F(1); E(1); F(1); D(1); F(1); E(1); F(1); E(1); F(1); D(1); F(1); E(1); F(1); E(1); F(1); D(1); F(1); E(1); F(1); E(1); F(1); D(1); F(1); E(1); F(1); E(1); F(1); D(1); F(1); E(1); F(1); E(1); F(1); D(1); *72 beads*

Row 26 (L-R): D(1); F(1); E(2); F(1); D(2); F(1); E(2); F(1); D(2); F(1); E(2); F(1); D(2); F(1); E(2); F(1); D(2); F(1); E(2); F(1); E(2); F(1); D(2); F(1); E(2); F(1); D(2); F(1); E(2); F(1); D(2); F(1); E(2); F(1); D(2); F(1); E(2); F(1); D(2); F(1); E(2); F(1); D(2); F(1); E(2); F(1); D(1), *72 beads*

Row 25 (R-L): D(1); F(1); E(1); F(1); D(1); F(1); D(1); F(1); E(1); F(1); D(1); F(1); D(1); F(1); E(1); F(1); D(1); F(1); D(1); F(1); E(1); F(1); D(1); F(1); E(1); F(1); D(1); F(1); D(1); F(1); E(1); F(1); D(1); F(1); D(1); F(1); E(1); F(1); D(1); F(1); D(1); F(1); E(1); F(1); D(1); F(1); E(1); F(1); D(1); F(1); D(1); F(1); D(1); F(1); E(1); F(1); D(1); F(1); D(1); F(1); E(1); F(1); D(1); F(1), *72 beads*

Row 24 (L-R): F(1); D(1); F(2); D(1); F(2); D(1); F(2); D(1); F(2); D(1); F(2); D(1); F(2); D(1); F(2); D(1); F(2); D(1); F(2); D(1); F(2); D(1); F(2); D(1); F(2); D(1); F(2); D(1); F(2); D(1); F(2); D(1); F(2); D(1); F(2); D(1); F(2); D(1); F(1), *72 beads*

Row 23 (R-L): F(1); D(1); F(1); D(2); F(1); D(2); F(1); D(1); F(1); E(1); F(1); D(1); F(1); D(2); F(1); D(2); F(1); D(1); F(1); E(1); F(1); D(1); F(1); D(2); F(1); D(1); F(1); E(1); F(1); D(1); F(1); D(2); F(1); D(2); F(1); D(1); F(1); E(1); F(1); D(1); F(1); D(2); F(1); D(2); F(1); D(1); F(1); E(1); F(1); D(1); F(1); E(1); F(1); D(1); F(1); D(2); F(1); D(2); F(1); D(1); F(1); E(1), *72 beads*

Row 22 (L-R): E(1); F(1); D(8); F(1); E(2); F(1); D(8); F(1); E(2); F(1); D(8); F(1); E(2); F(1); D(8); F(1); E(2); F(1); D(8); F(1); E(2); F(1); D(8); F(1); E(1), *72 beads*

Row 21 (R-L): E(1); F(1); D(7); F(1); E(1); F(1); E(1); F(1); D(7); F(1); E(1); F(1); E(1); F(1); D(7); F(1); E(1); F(1); E(1); F(1); D(7); F(1); E(1); F(1); E(1); F(1); D(7); F(1); E(1); F(1); E(1); F(1); D(7); F(1); E(1); F(1), *72 beads*

Row 20 (L-R): E(1); F(1); D(4); D(3); F(1); E(2); F(1); D(4); D(3); F(1); E(2); F(1); D(4); D(3); F(1); E(2); F(1); D(4); D(3); F(1); E(2); F(1); D(4); D(3); F(1); E(2); F(1); D(4); D(3); F(1); E(1), *66 beads*

Row 19 (R-L): F(1); D(4); D(4); F(1); E(1); F(1); D(4); D(4); F(1); E(1); F(1); D(4); D(4); F(1); E(1); F(1); D(4); D(4); F(1); E(1); F(1); D(4); D(4); F(1); E(1); F(1); D(4); D(4); F(1); E(1), *66 beads*

Row 18 (L-R): F(1); D(1); F(1); D(4); F(1); D(1); F(2); D(1); F(1); D(4); F(1); D(1); F(2); D(1); F(1); D(4); F(1); D(1); F(2); D(1); F(1); D(4); F(1); D(1); F(2); D(1); F(1); D(4); F(1); D(1); F(2); D(1); F(1); D(4); F(1); D(1); F(1), *60 beads*

Row 17 (R-L): D(1); F(2); D(3); F(2); D(1); F(1); D(1); F(2); D(3); F(2); D(1); F(1); D(1); F(2); D(3); F(2); D(1); F(1); D(1); F(2); D(3); F(2); D(1); F(1); D(1); F(2); D(3); F(2); D(1); F(1), *60 beads*

Row 16 (L-R): F(1); D(1); F(1); D(3); F(1); D(1); F(2); D(1); F(1); D(3); F(1); D(1); F(2); D(1); F(1); D(3); F(1); D(1); F(2); D(1); F(1); D(3); F(1); D(1); F(2); D(1); F(1); D(3); F(1); D(1); F(1), *54 beads*

Row 15 (R-L): F(1); D(3); D(3); F(1); E(1); F(1); D(3); D(3); F(1); E(1); F(1); D(3); D(3); F(1); E(1); F(1); D(3); D(3); F(1); E(1); F(1); D(3); D(3); F(1); E(1); F(1); D(3); D(3); F(1); E(1), *54 beads*

Row 14 (L-R): E(1); F(1); D(4); F(1); E(2); F(1); D(4); F(1); E(2); F(1); D(4); F(1); E(2); F(1); D(4); F(1); E(2); F(1); D(4); F(1); E(2); F(1); D(4); F(1); E(1), *48 beads*

Row 13 (R-L): E(1); F(1); D(3); F(1); E(1); F(1); E(1); F(1); D(3); F(1); E(1); F(1); E(1); F(1); D(3); F(1); E(1); F(1); E(1); F(1); D(3); F(1); E(1); F(1); E(1); F(1); D(3); F(1); E(1); F(1); E(1); F(1); D(3); F(1); E(1); F(1), *48 beads*

Row 12 (L-R): E(1); F(1); D(3); F(1); E(2); F(1); D(3); F(1); E(2); F(1); D(3); F(1); E(2); F(1); D(3); F(1); E(2); F(1); D(3); F(1); E(2); F(1); D(3); F(1); E(1), *42 beads*

Row 11 (R-L): F(1); D(4); F(1); E(1); F(1); D(4); F(1); E(1); F(1); D(4); F(1); E(1); F(1); D(4); F(1); E(1); F(1); D(4); F(1); E(1); F(1); D(4); F(1); E(1), *42 beads*

Row 10 (L-R): F(1); D(4); F(2); D(4); F(2); D(4); F(2); D(4); F(2); D(4); F(2); D(4); F(1), *36 beads*

Row 9 (R-L): D(5); F(1); D(5); F(1); D(5); F(1); D(5); F(1); D(5); F(1); D(5); F(1), *36 beads*

Row 8 (L-R): D(30), *30 beads*

Row 7 (R-L): D(4); F(1); D(4); F(1); D(4); F(1); D(4); F(1); D(4); F(1); D(4); F(1), *30 beads*

Row 6 (L-R): F(1); D(2); F(2); D(2); F(2); D(2); F(2); D(2); F(2); D(2); F(2); D(2); F(1), *24 beads*

Row 5 (R-L): D(3); F(1); D(3); F(1); D(3); F(1); D(3); F(1); D(3); F(1); D(3); F(1), *24 beads*

Row 4 (L-R): D(18), *18 beads*

Row 3 (R-L): D(18), *18 beads*

Row 2 (L-R): D(12), *12 beads*

Row 1 (R-L): D(12), *12 beads*

Chapter 6
Double Knitting

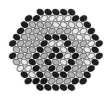

In traditional knitting, knitting in the round is done with multiple double-pointed needles or with circular needles. Unfortunately, knitting with these types of needles, fine thread, and tiny beads is not quite so easy. So I prefer to knit in the round with a technique called double knitting. Double knitting allows the knitter to work on two needles to create a tubular beadwork with a bottom seam.

Because double knitting is worked in the round, every row is a knit row. To create a twisted stitch to hold the beads, you must alternate a row of Eastern knit stitch with a row of Western knit stitch (page 17).

15 Knitting Rows without Beads

Step 1: Cast on twice the number of stitches needed for one side of the bead knitted fabric.

Step 2: The first row is knitted without beads. Knit the first stitch with Eastern knit stitch (knitting into the back leg of the stitch and wrapping the thread over and around the right-hand needle). Bring the thread forward between the needles as if to purl. Slip the second stitch to the needle in your right hand without knitting it (A). (This stitch belongs to the other half of the double fabric and will be knitted on the return row.)

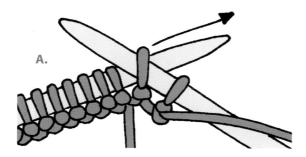

A.

B.

Step 3: Pass the thread between the needles to the back of the work, and knit the next stitch.

Step 4: Continue alternately knitting a stitch and slipping a stitch, until you reach the end of the first side of the row. Because you began with an even amount of stitches, the last stitch will be slipped.

Step 5: Turn the work over, and knit the second side the same way—knitting the stitches you previously slipped and slipping those you knitted.

In Steps 6 to 8, you will knit with Western knit stitch to twist the stitches as you complete the next row.

Step 6: Knit the first stitch with Western knit stitch (knit into the front leg of the stitch, and wrap the thread under and around the right-hand needle) (B).

Step 7: Bring the thread forward as if to purl, and slip the next stitch.

Step 8: Continue alternately knitting a stitch and slipping a stitch, until you reach the end of the first side of the row. Because you began with an even amount of stitches, the last stitch will be slipped.

Step 9: Turn the work over, and knit the second side the same way.

15 Knitting Rows with Beads

After you have knit one Eastern and one Western row without beads, begin the first beaded row. Double knitting results in a continuous tube of beads, so there are no unbeaded edge stitches.

Step 1: Knit a bead into the first stitch with Eastern stitch. Bring the thread forward, and slip the next stitch. Pass the thread back, and knit a bead into the next stitch. Complete both halves of the first beaded row (A).

Step 2: Knit the next row with Western stitch. Insert the empty needle into the front leg of the first stitch above the bead that is already on the stitch.

Step 3: Slide the first bead up to the needles. Open the stitch, and wrap the thread under and around the right-hand needle while pushing the bead through to the front (B).

When you are double knitting or knitting in the round, each row of the graphed pattern is read from left to right, regardless of the row, and every row of beads is strung twice.

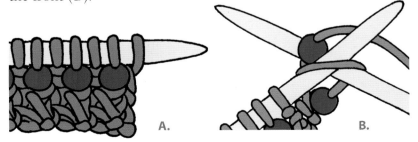

A.   B.

Step 4: Bring the thread forward, and slip the next stitch. Work both halves of the row with Western stitch.

Step 5: Continue knitting the double-knit fabric, alternating Eastern and Western beaded rows. Make sure the beads are on their respective sides of the fabric. Continue knitting to the top edge of the piece, ending with at least one unbeaded row. Now you'll need to transfer stitches to two needles to bind off to maintain the two separate sides of the bag.

16 Separating the Sides

The first step is to transfer each half of the bead knitting to a separate double-pointed needle.

Step 1: Hold the needle with the stitches in your left hand, as if to knit the

next row. In your right hand, hold two needles together, side by side, behind the beadwork.

Step 2: Insert the end of the needle that is closest to your body into the back leg of the first stitch. Slide the stitch off the original needle, pushing the rest of the stitches forward with your left index finger (A).

Step 3: Bring the two needles to the front of the beadwork. Insert the needle that is farthest from your body into the next stitch, and slide the stitch off the original needle (B).

Step 4: Continue until all stitches have been removed from the original needle. To prevent the end stitches from sliding off their needles, it is a good idea to hold the index finger of your right hand over the stitches as you proceed.

Binding Off

It can be difficult to bind off double knitting because the needles are rigid, so you'll need to transfer stitches to a flexible stitch holder.

Thread a large, blunt tapestry needle with yarn or cord that is the approximate

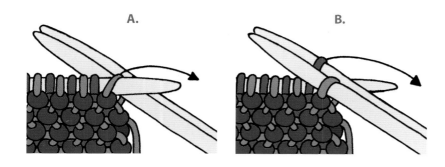

A.

B.

diameter of your knitting needles (a smooth yarn works best). Transfer all the stitches, one at a time, from the nonworking needle.

Secure both ends of the yarn by attaching a large bead or a safety pin to the end so that the stitches do not slip off.

Bind off all but the last 3 stitches from the working needle. Slide these stitches to the opposite end of the working needles and then transfer the stitches from the stitch holder to the same needle. Bind off the remaining stitches.

Double Knit Increases

Increases in double knitting must be made within the row (page 40). You cannot decrease while double knitting because the process of binding off a stitch would bind the two sides of the beadwork together. You would then decrease after the stitches have been transferred to multiple needles.

Side One

Always begin an increase on an Eastern row. Double-knit each bead of the first side until you reach the point where you would like to make your first increase.

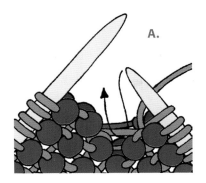
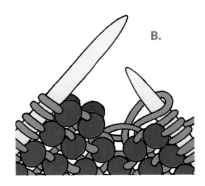

Slip the last bead before the intended increase point, and return the thread to the back of your work.

Insert the right-hand needle under the running thread and create a new knit stitch (A, B). (Do not accidentally catch the running thread from the back half of your work.)

Knit the next stitch (note that you now have an additional knit stitch). Continue knitting until you want to make your next increase. Work in this way to the end of the first side of the row.

Side Two

Begin the second side of the row as you did the first. When you reach the last increase that you made on side one, you will notice two consecutive stitches, the first stitch with a bead in it and the increased stitch without a bead. In double knitting, you

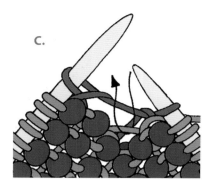

C.

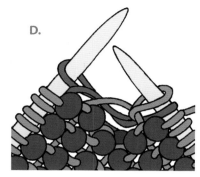

D.

must increase symmetrically on each side, so at this point, you will make the first increase for side two.

Bring the thread forward, slip the first stitch, and return the thread to the back. Lift the running thread to make a new stitch between the two consecutive stitches (C, D).

Bring the thread forward, slip the next stitch, and continue until you reach another increase point. Complete all the increases on subsequent Western (front leg) rows by knitting a bead into each new stitch.

You can make as few or as many increases as you would like within a row. Keep in mind, however, that a large number of increases in a single row may crowd your stitches on the needle. If this occurs, transfer one-half of the stitches to an extra double-pointed needle. If you are bead knitting a large piece—more than 4"

(10.7 cm) wide—you may find it easier to knit if you divide the stitches from both needles onto a third and fourth needle.

18 Working with Multiple Needles

When you have completed at least 10 rows of double knitting, you may want to transfer the stitches to three or four double-pointed needles.

Knitting with multiple needles is optional but it serves several purposes. You reduce the chance that you will knit two subsequent stitches, which would connect the two sides of the fabric. You also eliminate the additional step of slipping every other stitch, so you can knit faster. Dividing the stitches onto multiple needles also makes it possible to bind off without a stitch holder.

Bead knitting on multiple double-pointed needles can be tricky. Before you attempt it, become confident in your bead knitting skills. Before you begin a large project, practice the technique on a learning swatch.

Step 1: Transfer the stitches from the double knitting onto two needles as you did on page 70. You will see that the two sides of the fabric are separate. The needles will be too close together to continue knitting properly, however, so you will need to move some of the stitches to at least one additional needle.

Step 2: Slide all the stitches to the opposite end of the needles so that the thread exits the last stitch on the back needle in a ready-to-knit position.

Step 3: Transfer half the stitches from the front needle, one at a time, onto a third needle, as shown in the illustration.

Knitting on Multiple Needles

You need a fourth needle to begin knitting. I suggest the following method, but the correct method is whatever works best for you.

Step 1: Center the stitches on the needle that is farthest from you. You will not be working with this needle right away, so it's wise to keep the stitches as far from the ends as possible. For the same reason, center the stitches on the needle holding the other half of the stitches.

Step 2: Hold the thread above the back needle and behind the beadwork.

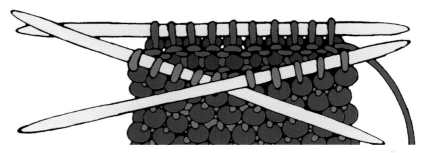

Knitting on multiple needles

Insert the index finger of your right hand between the two sides of the fabric, close to the tip of the needle. Keep the rest of your fingers wrapped around the bottom of the needle.

Step 3: Hold the empty needle above the back one as you knit into the first stitch of the front needle. Wrap the thread, and knit a bead into the first stitch. Keep the thread taut as you work to reduce the risk of creating a gap between the front and back halves of your knitting.

Step 4: Continue knitting until the left-hand needle is empty. Center the stitches that you just knit on their needle.

Step 5: Slide the stitches on the next needle toward the tip. With the empty needle, knit a bead into each stitch.

Step 6: Knit the stitches on the remaining needle in the same way.

Knitting with multiple needles can be unwieldy when you are working with a small piece because there are so few stitches and so many needles! When working with a large piece, you have more stitches, which can be distributed evenly onto the needles without interfering with your work.

TUMBLE BAG

Materials

Size 8 Beads:

- color A: lavender;
  1,792 beads (45 grams)
- color B: lime green;
  1,792 beads (45 grams)
- color C: dark pink;
  1,792 beads (45 grams)

*Note: These quantities allow
you to string each row twice
for double knitting.*

size FF silk thread; 81 yards

5 double-pointed needles,
  size 00

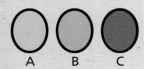

A   B   C

Optional (for finishing)

- lining material
- twisted cord

Finished Size

5" wide x 4½" long
(12.7 x 11.4 cm),
exclusive of strap and
embellishments

Knitting Instructions

- Cast on 96 stitches.
- Double-knit both sides without
  beads, using Eastern and Western
  knit stitch alternately (page 68).
- Repeat the pattern segment
  4 times.
- Separate the stitches to multiple
  needles, if you want, after the 10th
  row. If you choose to continue in
  double-knit stitch,
  pull the sides apart after each
  row to ensure that the rows are still
  separate.

- Row 1 begins with Eastern knit
  stitch.
- Knit each row with beads,
  alternating Eastern and Western
  knitting.
- Divide the stitches and complete at
  least 2 rows without beads. Add
  knitted eyelets, if desired, and end
  with a suspended bind-off.

Finishing Suggestions

Line the bag, leaving extra fabric
at the top to fold for a drawstring
casing.

Word Map
*String each row twice.
* Repeat the pattern segment 4 times.
*Each row = 48 beads
*All rows read left to right.

Row 14: A(4); B(4); C(4); A(4); B(4);
C(4); A(4); B(4); C(4); A(4); B(4); C(4)

Row 13: A(1); C(2); B(1); C(3); B(1);
C(1); B(2); A(1); B(3); A(1); B(1); A(2);
C(1); A(3); C(1); A(1); C(2); B(1); C(3);
B(1); C(1); B(2); A(1); B(3); A(1); B(1);
A(2); C(1); A(3); C(1)

Row 12: C(1); A(1); C(1); B(1); C(1);
B(2); C(1); B(1); C(1); B(1); A(1); B(1);
A(2); B(1); A(1); B(1); A(1); C(1);
A(1); C(2); A(1); C(1); A(1); C(1); B(1);
C(1); B(2); C(1); B(1); C(1); B(1); A(1);
B(1); A(2); B(1); A(1); B(1); A(1); C(1);
A(1); C(2); A(1)

Row 11: C(1); A(1); B(1); C(1); B(1);
C(1); B(1); C(1); B(1); C(1); A(1); B(1);
A(1); B(1); A(1); B(1); A(1); B(1); C(1);
A(1); C(1); A(1); C(1); A(1); C(1);
A(1); B(1); C(1); B(1); C(1); B(1); C(1);
B(1); C(1); A(1); B(1); A(1); B(1); A(1);
B(1); A(1); B(1); C(1); A(1); C(1); A(1);
C(1); A(1)

Row 10: C(1); A(1); B(1); C(1); B(1);
C(1); B(1); C(1); B(1); C(1); A(1); B(1);
A(1); B(1); A(1); B(1); A(1); B(1); C(1);
A(1); C(1); A(1); C(1); A(1); C(1);
A(1); B(1); C(1); B(1); C(1); B(1); C(1);
B(1); C(1); A(1); B(1); A(1); B(1); A(1);
B(1); A(1); B(1); C(1); A(1); C(1); A(1);
C(1); A(1)

Row 9: A(1); C(1); B(1); C(1); B(1); C(2);
B(1); C(1); B(1); A(1); B(1); A(1); B(2);
A(1); B(1); A(1); C(1); A(1); C(1);
A(2); C(1); A(1); C(1); B(1); C(1); B(1);
C(2); B(1); C(1); B(1); A(1); B(1); A(1);
B(2); A(1); B(1); A(1); C(1); A(1); C(1);
A(2); C(1)

Row 8: A(1); C(2); B(1); C(1); B(3); C(1);
B(2); A(1); B(1); A(3); B(1); A(2); C(1);
A(1); C(3); A(1); C(2); B(1); C(1); B(3);
C(1); B(2); A(1); B(1); A(3); B(1); A(2);
C(1); A(1); C(3)

Row 7: B(4); C(4); A(4); B(4); C(4); A(4);
B(4); C(4); A(4); B(4); C(4); A(4)

Row 6: B(1); A(3); B(1); A(2); C(1); A(1);
C(3); A(1); C(2); B(1); C(1); B(3); C(1);
B(2); A(1); B(1); A(3); B(1); A(2); C(1);
A(1); C(3); A(1); C(2); B(1); C(1); B(3);
C(1); B(2); A(1)

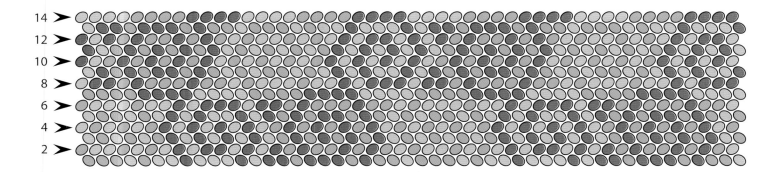

Row 5: A(1); B(2); A(1); B(1); A(1); C(1); A(1); C(1); A(2); C(1); A(1); C(1); B(1); C(1); B(1); C(2); B(1); C(1); B(1); A(1); B(1); A(1); B(2); A(1); B(1); A(1); C(1); A(1); C(1); A(2); C(1); A(1); C(1); B(1); C(1); B(1); C(2); B(1); C(1); B(1); A(1); B(1)

Row 4: A(1); B(1); A(1); B(1); A(1); B(1); C(1); A(1); C(1); A(1); C(1); A(1); C(1); A(1); B(1); C(1); B(1); C(1); B(1); C(1); B(1); C(1); A(1); B(1); A(1); B(1); A(1); B(1); A(1); B(1); C(1); A(1); C(1); A(1); C(1); A(1); C(1); A(1); B(1); C(1); B(1); C(1); B(1); C(1); B(1); C(1); A(1); B(1)

Row 3: A(1); B(1); A(1); B(1); A(1); B(1); C(1); A(1); C(1); A(1); C(1); A(1); C(1); A(1); B(1); C(1); B(1); C(1); B(1); C(1); C(1); B(1); C(1); A(1); B(1); A(1); B(1); A(1); B(1); A(1); B(1); C(1); A(1); C(1); A(1); C(1); A(1); C(1); A(1); B(1); C(1); B(1); C(1); B(1); C(1); A(1); B(1)

Row 2: B(1); A(2); B(1); A(1); B(1); A(1); C(1); A(1); C(2); A(1); C(1); A(1); C(1); B(1); C(1); B(2); C(1); B(1); C(1); B(1); A(1); B(1); A(2); B(1); A(1); B(1); A(1); C(1); A(1); C(2); A(1); C(1); A(1); C(1); B(1); C(1); B(2); C(1); B(1); C(1); B(1); A(1)

Row 1: B(3); A(1); B(1); A(2); C(1); A(3); C(1); A(1); C(2); B(1); C(3); B(1); C(1); B(2); A(1); B(3); A(1); B(1); A(2); C(1); A(3); C(1); A(1); C(2); B(1); C(3); B(1); C(1); B(2); A(1)

Luna Purse

Materials

Size 11 Beads:
- color A: white; 152 beads (2 grams)
- color B: yellow; 44 beads (1 gram)
- color C: chartreuse; 684 beads (7 grams)
- color D: mint; 460 beads (5 grams)
- color E: lime green; 624 beads (6 grams)
- color F: red; 366 beads (4 grams)
- color G: dark green; 1,156 beads (11 grams)
- color H: lavender; 4,434 beads (41 grams)

Note: These quantities allow you to string each row twice for double knitting.

size E silk thread; 91 yards

5 double-pointed needles, size 0000

A   B   C   D   E   F   G   H

Optional (for finishing)
- lining material
- twisted cord

Finished Size
4½" wide x 4½" long (11.4 x 11.4 cm), exclusive of strap and embellishments

Knitting Instructions
- Cast on 120 stitches.
- Double-knit both sides without beads, using Eastern and Western knit stitch alternately (page 68).
- Separate the stitches to multiple needles, if you want, after the 10th row. If you choose to continue in double-knit stitch, pull the sides apart after each row to ensure that the rows are still separate.
- Row 1 begins with Eastern knit stitch.
- Knit each row with beads, alternating Eastern and Western knitting.
- Divide the stitches and complete at least 2 rows without beads. Add knitted eyelets, if desired, and end with a suspended bind-off.

Finishing Suggestions
Add crocheted eyelets, if you'd like. Line the bag. Add a strap.

Word Map

*String each row twice.
*Each row = 60 beads
*All rows read left to right.

Row 66: H(60)

Row 65: H(60)

Row 64: H(60)

Row 63: H(4); G(2); F(5); H(38); F(5); G(2); H(4)

Row 62: H(4); G(1); D(1); G(2); F(5); H(35); F(5); G(2); D(1); G(1); H(3)

Row 61: H(3); G(1); D(3); G(1); E(3); F(4); H(30); F(4); E(3); G(1); D(3); G(1); H(3)

Row 60: H(3); G(3); D(2); G(3); E(3); F(3); H(27); F(3); E(3); G(3); D(2); G(3); H(2)

Row 59: H(3); G(1); E(1); G(2); D(3); G(3); E(2); F(3); H(24); F(3); E(2); G(3); D(3); G(2); E(1); G(1); H(3)

Row 58: H(4); G(1); E(2); G(2); D(4); G(2); E(2); F(3); H(5); F(1); H(9); F(1); H(5); F(3); E(2); G(2); D(4); G(2); E(2); G(1); H(3)

Row 57: H(4); G(1); E(3); G(5); B(1); F(7); H(4); F(1); H(8); F(1); H(4); F(7); B(1); G(5); E(3); G(1); H(4)

Row 56: H(5); G(1); E(7); B(1); A(2); F(1); C(3); F(2); H(4); F(1); H(7); F(1); H(4); F(2); C(3); F(1); A(2); B(1); E(7); G(1); H(4)

Row 55: H(4); G(1); E(6); G(1); B(1); A(3); F(1); C(4); F(2); H(2); F(1); H(8); F(1); H(2); F(2); C(4); F(1); A(3); B(1); G(1); E(6); G(1); H(4)

Row 54: H(5); G(1); E(4); G(2); C(1); B(1); A(2); F(1); C(5); F(2); H(2); F(1); H(7); F(1); H(2); F(2); C(5); F(1); A(2); B(1); C(1); G(2); E(4); G(1); H(4)

Row 53: H(5); G(1); E(2); G(2); C(3); B(2); F(1); G(1); C(6); F(2); H(1); F(1); H(6); F(1); H(1); F(2); C(6); G(1); F(1); B(2); C(3); G(2); E(2); G(1); H(5)

Row 52: H(6); G(3); C(2); G(3); D(3); G(4); C(3); F(2); H(1); F(1); H(5); F(1); H(1); F(2); C(3); G(4); D(3); G(3); C(2); G(3); H(5)

Row 51: H(5); G(1); C(3); G(2); D(9); G(3); C(1); F(2); H(1); F(2); H(2); F(2); H(1); F(2); C(1); G(3); D(9); G(2); C(3); G(1); H(5)

Row 50: H(6); G(4); D(3); G(7); D(3); G(2); C(1); F(1); H(2); F(1); H(1); F(1); H(2); F(1); C(1); G(2); D(3); G(7); D(3); G(4); H(5)

Row 49: H(5); G(1); E(3); G(4); E(6); G(3); D(2); G(2); F(1); H(1); F(1); A(2); F(1); H(1); F(1); G(2); D(2); G(3); E(6); G(4); E(3); G(1); H(5)

Row 48: H(6); G(1); E(8); G(5); C(2); G(2); D(2); G(1); F(7); G(1); D(2); G(2); C(2); G(5); E(8); G(1); H(5)

Row 47: H(5); G(1); E(6); G(3); C(8); G(4); F(2); A(2); F(2); G(4); C(8); G(3); E(6); G(1); H(5)

Row 46: H(6); G(7); C(14); G(1); A(5); G(1); C(14); G(7); H(5)

Row 45: H(7); G(1); C(10); G(9); A(6); G(9); C(10); G(1); H(7)

Row 44: H(8); G(1); C(5); G(5); E(7); G(2); A(5); G(2); E(7); G(5); C(5); G(1); H(7)

Row 43: H(8); G(6); E(8); G(2); E(1); G(1); D(1); G(1); A(4); G(1); D(1); G(1); E(1); G(2); E(8); G(6); H(8)

Row 42: H(9); G(1); E(10); G(3); C(1); G(2); D(1); G(1); A(5); G(1); D(1); G(2); C(1); G(3); E(10); G(1); H(8)

Row 41: H(9); G(3); E(5); G(3); C(3); G(1); D(2); G(2); A(4); G(2); D(2); G(1); C(3); G(3); E(5); G(3); H(9)

Row 40: H(12); G(6); D(1); G(1); C(2); G(2); D(2); G(2); A(5); G(2); D(2); G(2); C(2); G(1); D(1); G(6); H(11)

Row 39: H(11); G(1); D(6); G(1); C(1); G(2); D(3); G(1); E(1); G(1); A(4); G(1); E(1); G(1); D(3); G(2); C(1); G(1); D(6); G(1); H(11)

Row 38: H(10); G(2); D(6); G(1); C(1); G(1); D(4); G(1); E(2); G(1); A(3); G(1); E(2); G(1); D(4); G(1); C(1); G(1); D(6); G(2); H(9)

Row 37: H(8); G(2); D(6); G(2); C(1); G(1); D(4); G(1); E(3); G(1); A(2); G(1); E(3); G(1); D(4); G(1); C(1); G(2); D(6); G(2); H(8)

Row 36: H(8); G(1); D(7); G(1); C(2); G(1); D(4); G(1); E(4); G(1); A(1); G(1); E(4); G(1); D(4); G(1); C(2); G(1); D(7); G(1); H(7)

Row 35: H(7); G(1); D(7); G(1); C(3); G(1); D(3); F(1); E(4); G(4); E(4); F(1); D(3); G(1); C(3); G(1); D(7); G(1); H(7)

Row 34: H(7); G(1); D(7); G(1); C(3); G(1); F(4); E(4); G(1); H(3); G(1); E(4); F(4); G(1); C(3); G(1); D(7); G(1); H(6)

Row 33: H(7); G(1); D(6); G(1); C(3); G(1); F(1); A(2); F(1); E(4); G(1); H(4); G(1); E(4); F(1); A(2); F(1); G(1); C(3); G(1); D(6); G(1); H(7)

Row 32: H(8); G(1); D(4); G(2); C(3); G(1); B(1); A(3); F(1); E(3); G(1); H(5); G(1); E(3); F(1); A(3); B(1); G(1); C(3); G(2); D(4); G(1); H(7)

Row 31: H(8); G(1); D(3); G(1); C(4); G(2); B(1); A(2); F(1); G(1); E(2); G(1); H(6); G(1); E(2); G(1); F(1); A(2); B(1); G(2); C(4); G(1); D(3); G(1); H(8)

Row 30: H(9); F(1); D(2); G(1); C(4); G(1); E(1); G(1); B(3); G(1); E(3); G(1); H(5); G(1); E(3); G(1); B(3); G(1); E(1); G(1); C(4); G(1); D(2); F(1); H(8)

Row 29: H(9); F(1); D(1); G(1); C(5); G(1); E(1); G(4); E(3); G(1); H(6); G(1); E(3); G(4); E(1); G(1); C(5); G(1); D(1); F(1); H(9)

Row 28: H(10); F(1); G(1); C(5); G(1); E(2); G(1); C(2); G(1); E(2); G(1); H(7); G(1); E(2); G(1); C(2); G(1); E(2); G(1); C(5); G(1); F(1); H(9)

Row 27: H(9); F(1); G(1); C(5); G(1); E(2); G(1); C(2); G(1); E(2); G(1); H(8); G(1); E(2); G(1); C(2); G(1); E(2); G(1); C(5); G(1); F(1); H(9)

Row 26: H(10); F(2); C(5); G(1); E(1); G(1); C(3); G(1); E(1); G(1); H(9); G(1); E(1); G(1); C(3); G(1); E(1); G(1); C(5); F(2); H(9)

Row 25: H(11); F(2); C(3); G(1); E(2); G(1); C(2); G(1); E(2); G(1); H(8); G(1); E(2); G(1); C(2); G(1); E(2); G(1); C(3); F(2); H(11)

Row 24: H(13); F(1); C(2); G(1); E(2); G(1); C(3); G(1); E(1); G(1); H(9); G(1); E(1); G(1); C(3); G(1); E(2); G(1); C(2); F(1); H(12)

Row 23: H(13); F(1); C(1); G(1); E(2); G(1); C(3); G(1); E(1); G(1); H(10); G(1); E(1); G(1); C(3); G(1); E(2); G(1); C(1); F(1); H(13)

Row 22: H(14); F(1); C(1); G(1); E(2); G(1); C(2); G(1); E(1); G(1); H(11); G(1); E(1); G(1); C(2); G(1); E(2); G(1); C(1); F(1); H(13)

Row 21: H(13); F(1); C(1); G(1); E(2); G(1); C(2); G(1); E(1); G(1); H(12); G(1); E(1); G(1); C(2); G(1); E(2); G(1); C(1); F(1); H(13)

Row 20: H(14); F(1); G(1); E(2); G(1); C(2); G(1); E(1); G(1); H(13); G(1); E(1); G(1); C(2); G(1); E(2); G(1); F(1); H(13)

Row 19: H(14); F(2); E(1); G(1); C(3); G(2); H(14); G(2); C(3); G(1); E(1); F(2); H(14)

Row 18: H(16); F(1); E(1); G(1); C(2); G(1); H(17); G(1); C(2); G(1); E(1); F(1); H(15)

Row 17: H(16); F(1); E(1); G(1); C(1); G(1); H(18); G(1); C(1); G(1); E(1); F(1); H(16)

Row 16: H(17); F(1); G(1); C(1); G(1); H(19); G(1); C(1); G(1); F(1); H(16)

Row 15: H(16); G(1); C(2); G(1); H(20); G(1); C(2); G(1); H(16)

Row 14: H(17); G(1); C(1); G(1); H(21); G(1); C(1); G(1); H(16)

Row 13: H(16); G(1); C(1); G(1); H(22); G(1); C(1); G(1); H(16)

Row 12: H(16); G(1); C(1); G(1); H(23); G(1); C(1); G(1); H(15)

Row 11: H(15); G(1); C(1); G(1); H(24); G(1); C(1); G(1); H(15)

Row 10: H(15); G(1); C(1); G(1); H(25); G(1); C(1); G(1); H(14)

Row 9: H(13); G(2); C(1); G(1); H(26); G(1); C(1); G(2); H(13)

Row 8: H(13); G(1); C(2); G(1); H(27); G(1); C(2); G(1); H(12)

Row 7: H(12); G(1); C(2); G(1); H(28); G(1); C(2); G(1); H(12)

Row 6: H(13); G(1); C(1); G(1); H(29); G(1); C(1); G(1); H(12)

Row 5: H(13); G(2); H(30); G(2); H(13)

Row 4: H(60)

Row 3: H(60)

Row 2: H(60)

Row 1: H(60)

CHINA SEA BAG

Materials

Size 11 Beads:

- color A: yellow;
  1,328 beads (13 grams)
- color B: mustard;
  3,258 beads (30 grams)
- color C: brown iris;
  578 beads (6 grams)
- color D: brown;
  4,804 beads (44 grams)

Note: These quantities allow you to string each row twice for double knitting.

size E silk thread; 110 yards
5 double-pointed needles,
size 0000

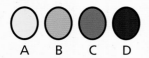

A   B   C   D

Optional (for finishing)

- lining material
- chain
- jump rings
- accent beads

Finished Size

5½" wide x 5½" long
(14 x 14 cm), exclusive
of strap

Knitting Instructions

- Cast on 104 stitches.
- Double-knit both sides without beads, using Eastern and Western knit stitch alternately (page 68).
- Separate the stitches to multiple needles, if desired, after the 10th row. Do this after a Western row to avoid empty stitches. If you choose to continue in double-knit stitch, pull the sides apart after each row to ensure that the rows are still separate.
- Row 1 begins with Eastern knit stitch.

Rows 1–14:

All odd (Eastern) rows: Make a new stitch after the first bead and another before the last bead of each half row. All even (Western) rows: Complete the increases from the previous row by knitting a bead onto each new stitch.

Rows 15–75:

Knit each row, alternating between Eastern and Western bead knitting.

Row 76:

Leave the first stitch empty and then every 10th and 11th stitch empty (indicated by the white spaces on the pattern).

Row 77:

Leave the first stitch empty and then every 9th through 11th stitch empty (indicated by the white spaces on the pattern).

Row 78:

Leave the first 3 stitches empty and then every 6th through 11th stitch empty (indicated by the white spaces on the pattern).

Divide the stitches, and work at least 2 rows without beads. End with a suspended bind-off.

Finishing Suggestions

Add crocheted eyelets, if desired. Line the bag and attach a strap.

Word Map

*String each row twice.

*All rows read left to right.

Row 78: D(1); A(1); D(1); A(1); D(2); A(1); D(1); A(1); D(2); A(1); D(1); A(1); D(2); A(1); D(1); A(1); D(2); A(1); D(1); A(1); D(2); A(1); D(1); A(1); D(1), *30 beads*

Row 77: D(1); A(1); D(1); A(2); D(1); A(1); D(2); A(1); D(1); A(2); D(1); A(1); D(2); A(1); D(1); A(2); D(1); A(1); D(2); A(1); D(1); A(2); D(1); A(1); D(2); A(1); D(1); A(2); D(1); A(1); D(1), *48 beads*

Row 76: A(1); D(1); A(1); D(1); A(1); D(1); A(1); D(1); A(1); D(1); A(1); D(1); A(1); A(1); D(1); A(1); D(1); A(1); D(1); A(1); D(1); A(1); A(1); D(1); A(1); D(1); A(1); D(1); A(1); D(1); A(1); A(1); D(1); A(1); D(1); A(1); D(1); A(1); D(1); A(1); A(1); D(1); A(1); D(1); A(1); D(1); A(1); D(1); A(1); D(1); A(1); D(1); A(1), *54 beads*

Row 75: D(1); A(1); D(1); A(1); D(2); A(1); D(1); A(1); D(1); A(1); D(1); A(1); D(1); A(1); D(2); A(1); D(1); A(1); D(1); A(1); D(1); A(1); D(2); A(1); D(1); A(1); D(2); A(1); D(1); A(1); D(1); A(1); D(1); A(1); D(2); A(1); D(1); A(1); D(1); A(1); D(1); A(1); D(2); A(1); D(1); A(1); D(1), *66 beads*

Row 74: A(1); D(1); A(1); D(5); A(1); D(1); A(2); D(1); A(1); D(5); A(1); D(1); A(2); D(1); A(1); D(5); A(1); D(1); A(2); D(1); A(1); D(5); A(1); D(1); A(2); D(1); A(1); D(5); A(1); D(1); A(2); D(1); A(1); D(5); A(1); D(1); A(1), *66 beads*

Row 73: A(1); D(2); B(4); D(2); A(3); D(2); B(4); D(2); A(3); D(2); B(4); D(2); A(3); D(2); B(4); D(2); A(3); D(2); B(4); D(2); A(3); D(2); B(4); D(2); A(2), *66 beads*

Row 72: D(2); B(7); D(4); B(7); D(4); B(7); D(4); B(7); D(4); B(7); D(4); B(7); D(2), *66 beads*

Row 71: B(66), *66 beads*

Row 70: B(66), *66 beads*

Row 69: B(2); C(2); D(1); B(10); C(1); D(1); B(4); C(1); D(1); B(4); C(1); D(1); B(4); C(1); D(1); B(4); C(1); D(1); B(4); C(1); D(1); B(5); D(2); B(12), *66 beads*

Row 68: B(2); C(1); B(1); D(2); B(9); C(1); D(2); B(3); C(1); D(2); B(3); C(1); D(2); B(3); C(1); D(2); B(3); C(1); D(2); B(3); C(1); D(2); B(4); D(3); B(11), *66 beads*

Row 67: B(1); C(1); B(1); C(1); D(1); B(10); C(1); B(5); C(1); B(5); C(1); B(5); C(1); B(5); C(1); B(5); C(1); B(2); D(9); B(9), *66 beads*

Row 66: B(2); C(1); B(3); D(2); B(8); C(1); B(1); D(2); B(2); C(1); B(1); D(2); B(2); C(1); B(1); D(2); B(2); C(1); B(1); D(2); B(2); C(1); B(1); D(2); B(1); D(4); B(8), 66 beads

Row 65: B(1); C(1); B(2); D(5); B(4); C(1); D(1); B(1); C(2); D(3); B(1); C(2); D(3); B(1); C(2); D(3); B(1); C(2); D(3); B(1); C(2); D(3); B(2); D(5); B(8), *66 beads*

Row 64: B(2); C(1); D(2); B(2); D(3); B(3); C(1); B(1); D(1); B(3); C(2); D(1); D(1); A(2); D(1); A(1); D(5); A(1); D(1); A(2); D(1); A(1); D(5); A(1); D(1); A(2); D(1); A(1); D(5); A(1); D(1); A(1), *66 beads*

Row 63: B(2); C(2); B(1); C(2); B(1); D(3); B(1); C(1); D(1); B(6); D(3); B(3); D(3); B(3); D(3); B(3); D(3); B(3); D(3); B(1); C(2); D(1); B(4); D(5); B(6), *66 beads*

Row 62: B(7); C(1); D(4); B(1); C(2); D(1); B(3); C(3); D(2); B(1); C(3); D(2); B(1); C(3); D(2); B(1); C(3); D(2); B(1); C(3); D(2); B(6); C(2); D(5); B(5), *66 beads*

Row 61: B(9); D(3); B(3); D(2); B(4); D(3); B(3); D(3); B(3); D(3); B(3); D(3); B(3); D(3); B(2); C(2); D(1); B(2); D(7); B(4), *66 beads*

Row 60: B(7); C(3); D(3); B(1); C(3); D(1); B(2); C(2); D(3); B(1); C(2); D(3); B(1); C(2); D(3); B(1); C(2); D(3); B(1); C(2); D(3); B(4); D(1); B(1); D(8); B(3), *66 beads*

Row 59: A(9); D(4); A(3); D(2); A(3); C(1); D(3); A(2); C(1); D(3); A(2); C(1); D(3); A(2); C(1); D(3); A(2); C(1); D(3); A(1); C(3); A(1); C(1); D(1); C(2); D(5); A(3), *66 beads*

Row 58: A(6); C(3); D(4); A(4); C(1); D(1); A(4); C(1); D(1); A(4); C(1); D(1); A(4); C(1); D(1); A(4); C(1); D(1); A(4); C(1); A(1); D(2); A(4); D(3); A(2), *66 beads*

Row 57: A(10); D(3); A(1); C(1); D(1); A(1); D(2); A(1); C(1); D(1); A(1); D(2); A(1); C(1); D(1); A(1); D(2); A(1); C(1); D(1); A(1); D(2); A(1); C(1); D(1); A(1); A(1); D(2); A(1); C(1); D(1); A(1); D(4); C(2); A(2); D(3); A(2), *66 beads*

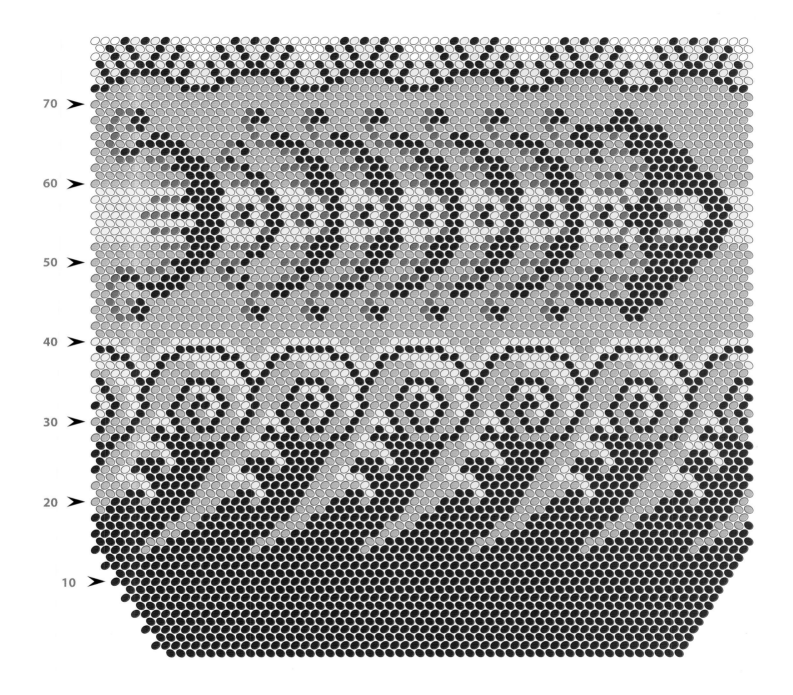

Row 56: A(5); C(3); D(5); A(1); C(1); D(1); A(1); C(1); D(1); A(1); C(1); D(1); A(1); C(1); D(1); A(1); C(1); D(1); A(1); C(1); D(1); A(1); C(1); D(1); A(1); C(1); D(1); A(1); C(1); D(1); A(1); C(1); D(1); A(1); C(1); D(1); A(1); C(1); D(1); A(1); C(1); D(4); A(4); D(2); A(2), *66 beads*

Row 55: A(10); D(3); A(1); C(1); D(1); A(1); D(2); A(1); C(1); D(1); A(1); D(2); A(1); C(1); D(1); A(1); D(2); A(1); C(1); D(1); A(1); D(2); A(1); C(1); D(1); A(1); D(2); A(1); C(1); D(1); A(1); D(4); C(2); A(2); D(3); A(2), *66 beads*

Row 54: A(6); C(3); D(4); A(4); C(1); D(1); A(4); C(1); D(1); A(4); C(1); D(1); A(4); C(1); D(1); A(4); C(1); D(1); A(4); C(1); D(1); A(4); C(1); A(1); D(2); A(4); D(3); A(2), *66 beads*

Row 53: A(9); D(4); A(3); D(2); A(3); C(1); D(3); A(2); C(1); D(3); A(2); C(1); D(3); A(2); C(1); D(3); A(2); C(1); D(3); A(1); C(3); A(1); C(1); D(1); C(2); D(5); A(3), *66 beads*

Row 52: B(7); C(3); D(3); B(1); C(3); D(1); B(2); C(2); D(3); B(1); C(2); D(3); B(1); C(2); D(3); B(1); C(2); D(3); B(1); C(2); D(3); B(4); D(1); B(1); D(8); B(3), *66 beads*

Row 51: B(9); D(3); B(3); D(2); B(4); D(3); B(3); D(3); B(3); D(3); B(3); D(3); B(3); D(3); B(2); C(2); D(1); B(2); D(7); B(4), *66 beads*

Row 50: B(7); C(1); D(4); B(1); C(2); D(1); B(3); C(3); D(2); B(1); C(3); D(2); B(1); C(3); D(2); B(1); C(3); D(2); B(1); C(3); D(2); B(6); C(2); D(5); B(5), *66 beads*

Row 49: B(2); C(2); B(1); C(2); B(1); D(3); B(1); C(1); D(1); B(6); D(3); B(3); D(3); B(3); D(3); B(3); D(3); B(3); D(3); B(1); C(2); D(1); B(4); D(5); B(6), *66 beads*

Row 48: B(2); C(1); D(2); B(2); D(3); B(3); C(1); B(1); D(1); B(3); C(2); D(1); B(3); C(2); D(1); B(3); C(2); D(1); B(3); C(2); D(1); B(3); C(2); D(1); B(3); C(2); D(1); B(4); D(1); B(1); C(2); D(6); B(6), *66 beads*

Row 47: B(1); C(1); B(2); D(5); B(4); C(1); D(1); B(1); C(2); D(3); B(1); C(2); D(3); B(1); C(2); D(3); B(1); C(2); D(3); B(1); C(2); D(3); B(1); C(2); D(3); B(2); D(5); B(8), *66 beads*

Row 46: B(2); C(1); B(3); D(2); B(8); C(1); B(1); D(2); B(2); C(1); B(1); D(2); B(2); C(1); B(1); D(2); B(2); C(1); B(1); D(2); B(2); C(1); B(1); D(2); B(4); D(4); B(8), *66 beads*

Row 45: B(1); C(1); B(1); C(1); D(1); B(10); C(1); B(5); C(1); B(5); C(1); B(5); C(1); B(5); C(1); B(5); C(1); B(2); D(9); B(9), *66 beads*

Row 44: B(2); C(1); B(1); D(2); B(9); C(1); D(2); B(3); C(1); D(2); B(3); C(1); D(2); B(3); C(1); D(2); B(3); C(1); D(2); B(3); C(1); D(2); B(3); C(1); D(1); B(3); C(2); D(3); B(11), *66 beads*

Row 43: B(2); C(2); D(1); B(10); C(1); D(1); B(4); C(1); D(1); B(4); C(1); D(1); B(4); C(1); D(1); B(4); C(1); D(1); B(4); C(1); D(1); B(4); C(1); D(2); B(12), *66 beads*

Row 42: B (66), *66 beads*

Row 41: B (66), *66 beads*

Row 40: A(3); B(5); A(6); B(5); A(6); B(5); A(6); B(5); A(6); B(5); A(6); B(5); A(3), *66 beads*

Row 39: D(2); A(2); B(2); A(2); D(5); A(2); B(2); A(2); D(5); A(2); B(2); A(2); D(5); A(2); B(2); A(2); D(5); A(2); B(2); A(2); D(5); A(2); B(2); A(2); D(3), *66 beads*

Row 38: A(2); D(2); A(1); B(1); A(1); D(2); A(4); D(2); A(1); B(1); A(1); D(2); A(4); D(2); A(1); B(1); A(1); D(2); A(4); D(2); A(1); B(1); A(1); D(2); A(4); D(2); A(1); B(1); A(1); D(2); A(2), *66 beads*

Row 37: A(3); D(1); A(2); D(1); B(3); A(4); D(1); A(2); D(1); B(3); A(4); D(1); A(2); D(1); B(3); A(4); D(1); A(2); D(1); B(3); A(4); D(1); A(2); D(1); B(3); A(1), *66 beads*

Row 36: B(2); A(2); D(1); A(1); D(1); B(6); A(2); D(1); A(1); D(1); B(6); A(2); D(1); A(1); D(1); B(6); A(2); D(1); A(1); D(1); B(6); A(2); D(1); A(1); D(1); B(4), *66 beads*

Row 35: D(1); B(1); A(2); D(2); B(3); D(3); B(1); A(2); D(2); B(3); D(3); B(1); A(2); D(2); B(3); D(3); B(1); A(2); D(2); B(3); D(3); B(1); A(2); D(2); B(3); D(2), *66 beads*

Row 34: A(1); D(1); B(2); A(1); D(1); B(3); D(1); A(2); D(1); B(2); A(1); D(1); B(3); D(1); A(2); D(1); B(2); A(1); D(1); B(3); D(1); A(2); D(1); B(2); A(1); D(1); B(3); D(1); A(2); D(1); B(2); A(1); D(1); B(3); D(1); A(2); D(1); B(2); A(1); D(1); B(3); D(1); A(1), *66 beads*

Row 33: A(1); D(1); B(1); A(1); D(1); B(3); D(1); B(1); D(1); A(1); D(1); B(1); A(1); D(1); B(3); D(1); B(1); D(1); A(1); D(1); B(1); A(1); D(1); B(3); D(1); B(1); D(1); A(1); D(1); B(3); D(1); B(1); D(1); A(1); D(1); B(1); A(1);

D(1); B(3); D(1); B(1); D(1); A(1); D(1);
B(1); A(1); D(1); B(3); D(1); B(1); D(1),
66 beads

Row 32: D(1); A(1); D(1); B(1); A(1);
D(1); B(2); D(1); B(1); D(2); A(1); D(1);
B(1); A(1); D(1); B(2); D(1); B(1); D(2);
A(1); D(1); B(1); A(1); D(1); B(2); D(1);
B(1); D(2); A(1); D(1); B(1); A(1); D(1);
B(2); D(1); B(1); D(2); A(1); D(1); B(1);
A(1); D(1); B(2); D(1); B(1); D(2); A(1);
D(1); B(1); A(1); D(1); B(2); D(1); B(1);
D(1), *66 beads*

Row 31: A(1); D(1); B(1); A(1); D(1);
B(1); A(1); D(1); B(1); D(1); B(2); D(1);
B(1); A(1); D(1); B(1); A(1); D(1); B(1);
D(1); B(2); D(1); B(1); A(1); D(1); B(1);
A(1); D(1); B(1); D(1); B(2); D(1); B(1);
A(1); D(1); B(1); A(1); D(1); B(1); D(1);
B(2); D(1); B(1); A(1); D(1); B(1); A(1);
D(1); B(1); D(1); B(2); D(1); B(1); A(1);
D(1); B(1); A(1); D(1); B(1); D(1); B(1),
66 beads

Row 30: B(1); D(1); B(2); D(1); B(1);
A(2); D(1); B(1); D(1); B(1); D(1); B(2);
D(1); B(1); A(2); D(1); B(1); D(1); B(1);
D(1); B(2); D(1); B(1); A(2); D(1); B(1);
D(1); B(1); D(1); B(2); D(1); B(1); A(2);
D(1); B(1); D(1); B(1); D(1); B(2); D(1);
B(1); A(2); D(1); B(1); D(1); B(1); D(1);
B(2); D(1); B(1); A(2); D(1); B(1); D(1),
66 beads

Row 29: D(1); B(2); D(1); B(3); A(1);
D(1); B(1); D(2); B(2); D(1); B(3); A(1);
D(1); B(1); D(2); B(2); D(1); B(3); A(1);
D(1); B(1); D(2); B(2); D(1); B(3); A(1);
D(1); B(1); D(2); B(2); D(1); B(3); A(1);
D(1); B(1); D(2); B(2); D(1); B(3); A(1);
D(1); B(1); D(1), *66 beads*

Row 28: B(2); D(2); B(1); A(1); D(4);
B(3); D(2); B(1); A(1); D(4); B(3); D(2);
B(1); A(1); D(4); B(3); D(2); B(1); A(1);
D(4); B(3); D(2); B(1); A(1); D(4); B(3);
D(2); B(1); A(1); D(4); B(1), *66 beads*

Row 27: D(2); B(2); A(3); D(6); B(2);
A(3); D(6); B(2); A(3); D(6); B(2); A(3);
D(6); B(2); A(3); D(6); B(2); A(3); D(4),
66 beads

Row 26: D(2); B(5); A(1); D(5); B(5);
A(1); D(5); B(5); A(1); D(5); B(5); A(1);
D(5); B(5); A(1); D(5); B(5); A(1); D(3),
66 beads

Row 25: D(1); B(3); D(3); A(1); D(4);
B(3); D(3); A(1); D(4); B(3); D(3); A(1);
D(4); B(3); D(3); A(1); D(4); B(3); D(3);
A(1); D(4); B(3); D(3); A(1); D(3),
66 beads

Row 24: D(1); B(2); A(1); D(3); B(1);
D(4); B(2); A(1); D(3); B(1); D(4); B(2);
A(1); D(3); B(1); D(4); B(2); A(1); D(3);
B(1); D(4); B(2); A(1); D(3); B(1); D(4);
B(2); A(1); D(3); B(1); D(3), *66 beads*

Row 23: B(2); A(3); D(6); B(2); A(3);
D(6); B(2); A(3); D(6); B(2); A(3); D(6);
B(2); A(3); D(6); B(2); A(3); D(6),
66 beads

Row 22: B(5); A(1); D(5); B(5); A(1);
D(5); B(5); A(1); D(5); B(5); A(1); D(5);
B(5); A(1); D(5); B(5); A(1); D(5),
66 beads

Row 21: B(3); D(2); A(1); D(4); B(4);
D(2); A(1); D(4); B(4); D(2); A(1);
D(4); B(4); D(2); A(1); D(4); B(4); D(2);
A(1); D(4); B(4); D(2); A(1); D(4); B(1),
66 beads

Row 20: B(2); D(3); B(1); D(4); B(3);
D(3); B(1); D(4); B(3); D(3); B(1); D(4);
B(3); D(3); B(1); D(4); B(3); D(3); B(1);
D(4); B(3); D(3); B(1); D(4); B(1),
66 beads

Row 19: B(1); D(8); B(3); D(8); B(3);
D(8); B(3); D(8); B(3); D(8); B(3); D(8);
B(2), *66 beads*

Row 18: B(2); D(7); B(4); D(7); B(4);
D(7); B(4); D(7); B(4); D(7); B(4); D(7);
B(2), *66 beads*

Row 17: D(7); B(3); D(8); B(3); D(8);
B(3); D(8); B(3); D(8); B(3); D(8); B(3);
D(1), *66 beads*

Row 16: D(7); B(3); D(8); B(3); D(8);
B(3); D(8); B(3); D(8); B(3); D(8); B(3);
D(1), *66 beads*

Row 15: D(5); B(2); D(9); B(2); D(9);
B(2); D(9); B(2); D(9); B(2); D(9); B(2);
D(4), *66 beads*

Row 14: D(5); B(1); D(10); B(1); D(10);
B(1); D(10); B(1); D(10); B(1); D(10);
B(1); D(5), *66 beads*

Row 13: D(64), *64 beads*
Row 12: D(64), *64 beads*
Row 11: D(62), *62 beads*
Row 10: D(62), *62 beads*
Row 9: D(60), *60 beads*
Row 8: D(60), *60 beads*
Row 7: D(58), *58 beads*
Row 6: D(58), *58 beads*
Row 5: D(56), *56 beads*
Row 4: D(56), *56 beads*
Row 3: D(54), *54 beads*
Row 2: D(54), *54 beads*
Row 1: D(52), *52 beads*

ANTIQUITY PURSE

Materials

Size 11 Beads:

- color A: white;
  2,996 beads (28 grams)
- color B: light gray;
  1,272 beads (12 grams)
- color C: dark gray;
  1,394 beads (13 grams)
- color D: black; 3,962
  beads (37 grams)

*Note: These quantities allow
you to string each row twice
for double knitting.*

size E silk thread; 106 yards

5 double-pointed needles,
  size 0000

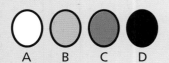

A   B   C   D

Optional (for finishing)

- lining material
- twisted cord
- jump rings
- accent beads

Finished Size

5½" wide x 6½" long
(14 x 16.5 cm), exclusive
of strap and fringe

Knitting Instructions

- Cast on 128 stitches.
- Double-knit both sides without beads using Eastern knit stitch (page 68).
- Separate the stitches to multiple needles, if desired, after the 10th row. Do this after a Western row to avoid empty stitches. If you choose to continue in double-knit stitch, pull the sides apart after each row to ensure that the rows are still separate.

Row 1:

Knit both sides with beads using Western knit stitch (page 68).

Rows 2–55:

All even (Eastern) rows: Make a new stitch after the first bead and another before the last bead of each row.
All odd (Western) rows: Complete the increases from the previous row by knitting a bead onto each new stitch.

Rows 56–93:

Bead knit each row, alternating between Eastern and Western knitting.

Divide the stitches, and work at least 2 rows without beads. End with a suspended bind-off.

Finishing Suggestions

Add crocheted eyelets, if desired. Line the bag, and attach a strap and fringe if you'd like.

Word Map

*String each row twice.
*All rows read left to right.

Row 93: A(68), *68 beads*
Row 92: A(68), *68 beads*
Row 91: A(1); B(1); A(1); B(1); A(1);
B(1); A(1); B(1); A(1); B(1); A(1); B(1);
A(1); B(1); A(1); B(1); A(1); B(1); A(1);
B(1); A(1); B(1); A(1); B(1); A(1); B(1);
A(1); B(1); A(1); B(1); A(1); B(1); A(1);
B(1); A(1); B(1); A(1); B(1); A(1); B(1);
A(1); B(1); A(1); B(1); A(1); B(1); A(1);
B(1); A(1); B(1); A(1); B(1); A(1); B(1);
A(1); B(1); A(1); B(1); A(1); B(1); A(1);
B(1); A(1); B(1); A(1); B(1); A(1); B(1),
68 beads

Row 90: A(1); B(1); A(1); B(1); A(1);
B(1); A(1); B(1); A(1); B(1); A(1); B(1);
A(1); B(1); A(1); B(1); A(1); B(1); A(1);
B(1); A(1); B(1); A(1); B(1); A(1); B(1);
A(1); B(1); A(1); B(1); A(1); B(1); A(1);
B(1); A(1); B(1); A(1); B(1); A(1); B(1);

A(1); B(1); A(1); B(1); A(1); B(1); A(1);
B(1); A(1); B(1); A(1); B(1); A(1); B(1);
A(1); B(1); A(1); B(1); A(1); B(1); A(1);
B(1); A(1); B(1); A(1); B(1); A(1); B(1),
68 beads

Row 89: A(1); B(1); A(1); B(1); A(1);
B(1); A(1); B(1); A(1); B(1); A(1); B(1);
A(1); B(1); A(1); B(1); A(1); B(1); A(1);
B(1); A(1); B(1); A(1); B(1); A(1); B(1);
A(1); B(1); A(1); B(1); A(1); B(1); A(1);
B(1); A(1); B(1); A(1); B(1); A(1); B(1);
A(1); B(1); A(1); B(1); A(1); B(1); A(1);
B(1); A(1); B(1); A(1); B(1); A(1); B(1);
A(1); B(1); A(1); B(1); A(1); B(1); A(1);
B(1); A(1); B(1); A(1); B(1); A(1); B(1),
68 beads

Row 88: A(1); B(1); A(1); B(1); A(1);
B(1); A(1); B(1); A(1); B(1); A(1); B(1);
A(1); B(1); A(1); B(1); A(1); B(1); A(1);
B(1); A(1); B(1); A(1); B(1); A(1); B(1);
A(1); B(1); A(1); B(1); A(1); B(1); A(1);
B(1); A(1); B(1); A(1); B(1); A(1); B(1);
A(1); B(1); A(1); B(1); A(1); B(1); A(1);
B(1); A(1); B(1); A(1); B(1); A(1); B(1);
A(1); B(1); A(1); B(1); A(1); B(1); A(1);
B(1); A(1); B(1); A(1); B(1); A(1); B(1),
68 beads

Row 87: C(1); B(1); C(1); B(1); C(1); B(1);
C(1); B(1); C(1); B(1); C(1); B(1); C(1);
B(1); C(1); B(1); C(1); B(1); C(1); B(1);
C(1); B(1); C(1); B(1); C(1); B(1); C(1);
B(1); C(1); B(1); C(1); B(1); C(1); B(1);
C(1); B(1); C(1); B(1); C(1); B(1); C(1);
B(1); C(1); B(1); C(1); B(1); C(1); B(1);
C(1); B(1); C(1); B(1); C(1); B(1); C(1);
B(1); C(1); B(1); C(1); B(1); C(1); B(1);
C(1); B(1); C(1); B(1); C(1); B(1),
68 beads

Row 86: C(1); B(1); C(1); B(1); C(1); B(1);
C(1); B(1); C(1); B(1); C(1); B(1); C(1);
B(1); C(1); B(1); C(1); B(1); C(1); B(1);
C(1); B(1); C(1); B(1); C(1); B(1); C(1);
B(1); C(1); B(1); C(1); B(1); C(1); B(1);
C(1); B(1); C(1); B(1); C(1); B(1); C(1);
B(1); C(1); B(1); C(1); B(1); C(1); B(1);
C(1); B(1); C(1); B(1); C(1); B(1); C(1);
B(1); C(1); B(1); C(1); B(1); C(1); B(1);
C(1); B(1); C(1); B(1); C(1); B(1),
68 beads

Row 85: C(1); B(1); C(1); B(1); C(1); B(1);
C(1); B(1); C(1); B(1); C(1); B(1); C(1);
B(1); C(1); B(1); C(1); B(1); C(1); B(1);
C(1); B(1); C(1); B(1); C(1); B(1); C(1);
B(1); C(1); B(1); C(1); B(1); C(1); B(1);
C(1); B(1); C(1); B(1); C(1); B(1); C(1);
B(1); C(1); B(1); C(1); B(1); C(1); B(1);
C(1); B(1); C(1); B(1); C(1); B(1); C(1);
B(1); C(1); B(1); C(1); B(1); C(1); B(1);
C(1); B(1); C(1); B(1); C(1); B(1),
68 beads

Row 84: C(1); B(1); C(1); B(1); C(1); B(1);
C(1); B(1); C(1); B(1); C(1); B(1); C(1);
B(1); C(1); B(1); C(1); B(1); C(1); B(1);
C(1); B(1); C(1); B(1); C(1); B(1); C(1);
B(1); C(1); B(1); C(1); B(1); C(1); B(1);
C(1); B(1); C(1); B(1); C(1); B(1); C(1);
B(1); C(1); B(1); C(1); B(1); C(1); B(1);
C(1); B(1); C(1); B(1); C(1); B(1); C(1);
B(1); C(1); B(1); C(1); B(1); C(1); B(1);
C(1); B(1); C(1); B(1); C(1); B(1),
68 beads

Row 83: C(1); D(1); C(1); D(1), *68 beads*

Row 82: C(1); D(1); C(1); D(1), *68 beads*

Row 81: C(1); D(1); C(1); D(1), *68 beads*

Row 80: C(1); D(1); C(1); D(1), *68 beads*

Row 79: D(68), *68 beads*

Row 78: D(30); A(2); D(4); A(2); D(30), *68 beads*

Row 77: D(21); B(3); D(4); A(6); D(1); A(6); D(4); B(3); D(20), *68 beads*

Row 76: D(19); A(1); C(1); B(3); C(1); D(1); A(16); D(1); C(1); B(3); C(1); A(1); D(19), *68 beads*

Row 75: D(18); A(2); C(1); B(2); C(1); D(1); A(9); C(1); A(9); D(1); C(1); B(2); C(1); A(2); D(17), *68 beads*

Row 74: D(17); A(2); D(1); C(1); B(1); C(1); D(1); A(9); D(2); A(9); D(1); C(1); B(1); C(1); D(1); A(2); D(17), *68 beads*

Row 73: D(17); A(2); D(1); C(3); D(1); A(9); C(1); B(1); C(1); A(9); D(1); C(3); D(1); A(2); D(16), *68 beads*

Row 72: D(16); A(3); D(1); C(3); D(1); A(8); B(4); A(8); D(1); C(3); D(1); A(3); D(16), *68 beads*

Row 71: D(17); A(3); D(4); A(9); C(1); B(1); C(1); A(9); D(4); A(3); D(16), *68 beads*

Row 70: D(16); A(6); D(2); A(9); C(2); A(9); D(2); A(6); D(16), *68 beads*

Row 69: D(17); A(7); D(1); A(1); B(1); A(7); C(1); A(7); B(1); A(1); D(1); A(7); D(16), *68 beads*

Row 68: D(17); A(2); B(1); A(4); D(1); A(1); B(3); A(4); D(2); A(4); B(3); A(1); D(1); A(4); B(1); A(2); D(17), *68 beads*

Row 67: D(19); A(1); B(1); A(4); D(1); A(2); B(4); A(2); D(1); A(2); B(4); A(2); D(1); A(4); B(1); A(1); D(18), *68 beads*

Row 66: D(17); B(2); A(1); B(3); A(2); D(1); A(2); B(2); A(3); D(2); A(3); B(2); A(2); D(1); A(2); B(3); A(1); B(2); D(17), *68 beads*

Row 65: D(15); A(3); B(1); C(1); A(2); B(2); A(2); D(1); A(5); D(1); A(1); D(1); A(1); D(1); A(5); D(1); A(2); B(2); A(2); C(1); B(1); A(3); D(14), *68 beads*

Row 64: D(14); A(1); D(2); B(2); C(1); A(3); B(1); A(2); D(2); B(2); C(2); D(1); A(2); D(1); C(2); B(2); D(2); A(2); B(1); A(3); C(1); B(2); A(3); D(14), *68 beads*

Row 63: D(14); A(1); B(3); C(4); A(4); D(2); B(1); C(2); D(2); A(3); D(2); C(2); B(1); D(2); A(4); C(4); B(3); A(1); D(13), *68 beads*

Row 62: D(13); A(1); B(1); D(8); B(1); C(1); D(2); B(1); C(1); D(2); A(2); B(2); A(2); D(2); C(1); B(1); D(2); C(1); B(1); D(8); B(1); A(1); D(13), *68 beads*

Row 61: D(13); A(1); B(1); D(1); C(5); A(2); B(1); C(1); D(1); A(1); B(1); C(1); D(1); A(2); B(5); A(2); D(1); C(1); B(1); A(1); D(1); C(1); B(1); A(2); C(5); D(1); B(1); A(1); D(12), *68 beads*

Row 60: D(12); A(2); D(1); C(1); B(4); A(1); C(3); D(1); A(1); B(1); C(1); D(1); A(2); B(6); A(2); D(1); C(1); B(1); A(1); D(1); C(3); A(1); B(4); C(1); D(1); A(2); D(12), *68 beads*

Row 59: D(12); A(2); D(1); C(1); B(1); A(4); B(1); C(1); D(2); A(1); B(1); C(1); D(1); A(2); B(7); A(2); D(1); C(1); B(1); A(1); D(2); C(1); B(1); A(4); B(1); C(1); D(1); A(2); D(11), *68 beads*

Row 58: D(12); A(1); D(1); C(1); B(1); A(4); D(1); C(1); D(1); A(3); B(1); C(1); D(1); A(1); B(8); A(1); D(1); C(1); B(1); A(3); D(1); C(1); D(1); A(4); B(1); C(1); D(1); A(1); D(12), *68 beads*

Row 57: D(12); A(1); D(1); C(1); B(1); A(3); B(2); C(1); D(1); A(3); B(1); C(1); D(1); A(1); B(9); A(1); D(1); C(1); B(1); A(3); D(1); C(1); B(2); A(3); B(1); C(1); D(1); A(1); D(11), *68 beads*

Row 56: D(12); A(1); D(1); C(1); B(1); A(2); B(2); C(1); D(1); A(3); B(1); C(1); D(1); A(2); C(1); B(6); C(1); A(2); D(1); C(1); B(1); A(3); D(1); C(1); B(2); A(2); B(1); C(1); D(1); A(1); D(12), *68 beads*

Row 55: D(12); A(1); D(1); B(2); A(3); B(2); C(1); D(1); A(3); B(1); C(1); D(1); A(1); D(1); C(1); B(2); C(1); B(2); C(1); D(1); A(1); D(1); C(1); B(1); A(3); D(1); C(1); B(2); A(3); B(2); D(1); A(1); D(11), *68 beads*

Row 54: D(11); A(1); D(1); B(1); A(5); B(1); C(1); D(1); A(2); B(1); C(1); D(1); A(1); D(2); C(6); D(2); A(1); D(1); C(1); B(1); A(2); D(1); C(1); B(1); A(5); B(1); D(1); A(1); D(11), *66 beads*

Row 53: D(12); A(1); B(1); A(5); B(1); C(1); D(1); A(2); B(1); C(1); D(2); A(1); D(9); A(1); D(2); C(1); B(1); A(2); D(1); C(1); B(1); A(5); B(1); A(1); D(11), *66 beads*

Row 52: D(11); A(1); B(1); A(5); C(2); D(1); A(1); B(1); C(3); D(1); A(1); D(2); A(4); D(2); A(1); D(1); C(3); B(1); A(1); D(1); C(2); A(5); B(1); A(1); D(11), *64 beads*

Row 51: D(12); A(2); D(3); A(1); D(3); A(1); B(1); C(4); D(1); A(9); D(1); C(4); B(1); A(1); D(3); A(1); D(3); A(2); D(11), *64 beads*

Row 50: D(16); A(4); B(1); C(2); B(2); C(1); D(1); A(8); D(1); C(1); B(2); C(2); B(1); A(4); D(16), *62 beads*

Row 49: D(17); A(2); B(2); C(1); A(3); B(2); C(1); A(7); C(1); B(2); A(3); C(1); B(2); A(2); D(16), *62 beads*

Row 48: D(17); B(3); D(1); A(3); B(2); C(2); A(4); C(2); B(2); A(3); D(1); B(3); D(17), *60 beads*

Row 47: D(22); A(3); B(2); D(1); C(5); D(1); B(2); A(3); D(21), *60 beads*

Row 46: D(21); A(2); B(1); D(3); C(1); B(2); C(1); D(3); B(1); A(2); D(21), *58 beads*

Row 45: D(22); A(1); B(1); D(4); B(1); A(1); B(1); D(4); B(1); A(1); D(21), *58 beads*

Row 44: D(21); A(1); D(5); A(2); D(5); A(1); D(21), *56 beads*

Row 43: D(22); A(1); D(4); A(3); D(4); A(1); D(21), *56 beads*

Row 42: D(26); A(2); D(26), *54 beads*

Row 41: C(1); D(1); C(1); D(1); C(1); D(1); C(1); D(1); C(1); D(1); C(1); D(1); C(1); D(1); C(1); D(1); C(1); D(1); C(1); D(1); C(1); D(1); C(1); D(1); A(3); D(1); C(1); D(1); C(1); D(1); C(1); D(1); C(1); D(1); C(1); D(1); C(1); D(1); C(1); D(1); C(1); D(1); C(1); D(1); C(1); D(1); C(1); D(1); C(1); D(1); C(1); D(1), *54 beads*

Row 40: D(1); C(1); D(1); C(1); D(1); C(1); D(1); C(1); D(1); C(1); D(1); C(1); D(1); C(1); D(1); C(1); D(1); C(1); D(1); C(1); A(2); D(1); C(1); D(1); C(1); D(1); C(1); D(1); C(1); D(1); C(1); D(1); C(1); D(1); C(1); D(1); C(1); D(1); C(1); D(1); C(1); D(1); C(1); D(1), *52 beads*

Row 39: D(1); C(1); D(1); C(1); D(1); C(1); D(1); C(1); D(1); C(1); D(1); C(1); D(1); C(1); D(1); C(1); D(1); C(1); D(1); C(1); D(1); C(1); A(3); D(1); C(1); D(1); C(1); D(1); C(1); D(1); C(1); D(1); C(1); D(1); C(1); D(1); C(1); D(1); C(1); D(1); C(1); D(1); C(1); D(1); C(1), *52 beads*

Row 38: C(1); D(1); C(1); D(1); C(1); D(1); C(1); D(1); C(1); D(1); A(5); D(1); C(1); D(1); C(1); D(1); C(1); D(1); C(1); D(1); A(2); D(1); C(1); D(1); C(1); D(1); C(1); D(1); C(1); D(1); A(5); D(1); C(1); D(7); C(1), *50 beads*

Row 37: C(9); A(8); C(7); A(3); C(7); A(8); C(8), *50 beads*

Row 36: C(1); B(1); C(1); B(1); C(1); B(1); C(1); A(3); D(4); A(4); C(1); A(1); C(1); B(1); C(1); A(2); C(1); B(1); C(1); A(1); C(1); A(4); D(4); A(3); C(1); B(1); C(1); B(1); C(1); B(1); C(1), *48 beads*

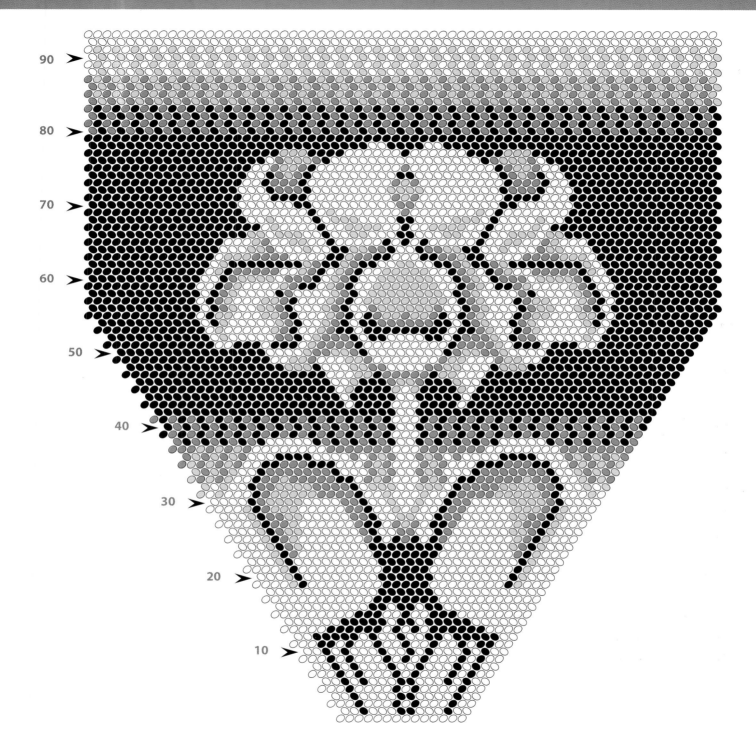

90
80
70
60
50
40
30
20
10

Row 35: C(1); B(1); C(1); B(1); C(1); B(1); C(1); A(2); D(2); C(3); D(3); A(3); C(1); B(1); C(1); A(3); C(1); B(1); C(1); A(3); D(3); C(3); D(2); A(2); C(1); B(1); C(1); B(1); C(1); B(1), *48 beads*

Row 34: B(1); C(1); B(1); C(1); B(1); A(2); D(1); C(7); D(1); A(3); C(1); B(1); C(1); A(2); C(1); B(1); C(1); A(3); D(1); C(7); D(1); A(2); B(1); C(1); B(1); C(1); B(1), *46 beads*

Row 33: B(1); C(1); B(1); C(1); B(1); A(2); D(1); C(2); B(1); C(5); D(2); A(1); C(1); B(1); C(1); A(3); C(1); B(1); C(1); A(1); D(2); C(5); B(1); C(2); D(1); A(2); B(1); C(1); B(1); C(1), *46 beads*

Row 32: B(1); A(1); B(1); A(2); D(1); C(2); B(4); C(4); D(1); A(1); B(3); A(2); B(3); A(1); D(1); C(4); B(4); C(2); D(1); A(2); B(1); A(1); B(1), *44 beads*

Row 31: B(1); A(1); B(1); A(3); D(1); C(1); B(5); C(4); D(1); A(2); B(1); A(3); B(1); A(2); D(1); C(4); B(5); C(1); D(1); A(3); B(1); A(1), *44 beads*

Row 30: A(4); D(1); C(1); B(4); A(4); C(2); D(1); A(2); B(1); A(2); B(1); A(2); D(1); C(2); A(4); B(4); C(1); D(1); A(4), *42 beads*

Row 29: A(4); B(1); D(1); C(1); B(3); A(5); C(2); D(1); A(2); B(1); A(1); B(1); A(2); D(1); C(2); A(5); B(3); C(1); D(1); B(1); A(3), *42 beads*

Row 28: A(3); B(1); D(1); C(2); B(2); A(5); C(2); D(1); A(2); B(2); A(2); D(1); C(2); A(5); B(2); C(2); D(1); B(1); A(3), *40 beads*

Row 27: A(4); B(1); D(1); C(2); B(1); A(6); C(1); D(2); A(1); C(1); B(1); C(1); A(1); D(2); C(1); A(6); B(1); C(2); D(1); B(1); A(3), *40 beads*

Row 26: A(3); B(1); D(1); C(1); B(2); A(6); C(1); D(1); A(2); C(2); A(2); D(1); C(1); A(6); B(2); C(1); D(1); B(1); A(3), *38 beads*

Row 25: A(4); B(1); D(1); C(1); B(1); A(7); C(1); D(1); A(1); D(1); C(1); D(1); A(1); D(1); C(1); A(7); B(1); C(1); D(1); B(1); A(3), *38 beads*

Row 24: A(3); B(1); D(1); C(1); B(1); A(7); D(8); A(7); B(1); C(1); D(1); B(1); A(3), *36 beads*

Row 23: A(4); B(1); D(1); C(1); A(8); D(7); A(8); C(1); D(1); B(1); A(3), *36 beads*

Row 22: A(3); B(1); D(1); A(9); D(6); A(9); D(1); B(1); A(3), *34 beads*

Row 21: A(4); B(1); D(1); A(9); D(5); A(9); D(1); B(1); A(3), *34 beads*

Row 20: A(3); B(1); D(1); A(8); D(6); A(8); D(1); B(1); A(3), *32 beads*

Row 19: A(4); B(1); D(1); A(8); D(5); A(8); D(1); B(1); A(3), *32 beads*

Row 18: A(12); D(6); A(12), *30 beads*
Row 17: A(12); D(7); A(11), *30 beads*
Row 16: A(10); D(2); A(1); D(2); A(1); D(2); A(10), *28 beads*
Row 15: A(9); D(3); A(2); D(1); A(2); D(3); A(8), *28 beads*
Row 14: A(6); D(5); A(1); D(2); A(1); D(5); A(6), *26 beads*

Row 13: A(5); D(6); A(1); D(1); A(1); D(1); A(1); D(6); A(4), *26 beads*
Row 12: A(2); D(5); A(1); D(2); A(1); D(1); A(2); D(2); A(1); D(5); A(2), *24 beads*
Row 11: A(3); D(2); A(1); D(1); A(2); D(1); A(2); D(1); A(2); D(1); A(2); D(1); A(1); D(2); A(2), *24 beads*
Row 10: A(2); D(1); A(1); D(1); A(3); D(1); A(2); D(1); A(1); D(1); A(3); D(1); A(1); D(1); A(2), *22 beads*
Row 9: A(3); D(1); A(1); D(1); A(3); D(1); A(1); D(1); A(1); D(1); A(3); D(1); A(1); D(1); A(2), *22 beads*
Row 8: A(2); D(1); A(1); D(1); A(3); D(1); A(2); D(1); A(3); D(1); A(1); D(1); A(2), *20 beads*
Row 7: A(3); D(1); A(1); D(1); A(3); D(1); A(1); D(1); A(3); D(1); A(1); D(1); A(2), *20 beads*
Row 6: A(2); D(1); A(1); D(1); A(3); D(2); A(3); D(1); A(1); D(1); A(2), *18 beads*
Row 5: A(3); D(1); A(4); D(1); A(1); D(1); A(4); D(1); A(2), *18 beads*
Row 4: A(2); D(1); A(4); D(2); A(4); D(1); A(2), *16 beads*
Row 3: A(3); D(1); A(3); D(1); A(1); D(1); A(3); D(1); A(2), *16 beads*
Row 2: A(2); D(1); A(3); D(2); A(3); D(1); A(2), *14 beads*
Row 1: A(14), *14 beads*

Chapter 7

Finishing Techniques

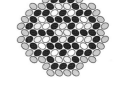

When you have finished your bead knitting, you might want to add some decorative details to give your project a finished look. Knitted and crocheted eyelets will also allow you to add a drawstring.

Choose quality materials, and give the finishing process the same time and careful consideration that you gave to your knitting. If you do, you will create a keepsake heirloom that you can enjoy and treasure for years.

 Knitted Eyelets

Knitted eyelets along the top edge of a bead knitted bag create a delicate, classic finish. Add a drawstring by weaving cord or chain in to and out of the holes in the eyelets.

Each eyelet occupies 4 stitches but you can add any number of stitches in between. Consider the total number of stitches on your needles, and try to arrange the eyelets evenly. Work several plain, unbeaded rows before beginning your eyelets. You will begin on a knit row.

Step 1: Start knitting the row. When you reach your first group of 4 stitches, slip the first stitch.

Step 2: Knit the next stitch, and then pass the slipped stitch over the knitted stitch and off the needle. Notice that you have decreased by 1 stitch.

Step 3: Create 2 new stitches by making a yarn over, followed by a second yarn over. To make the yarn over, bring the thread forward between the needles, and then

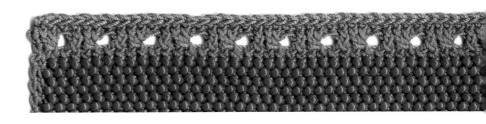

A.   B.   C.   D.

wrap it around the right-hand needle and between the needles again (A).

Step 4: With the thread in front of your work, slip the third stitch, and then knit the fourth (B). Pass the third stitch over and off the needle. Repeat this sequence to the end of the row.

Step 5: Turn over your work, and purl each stitch until you reach the first yarn over. Purl into the first elongated stitch (C). Without dropping the stitch from the needle in your left hand, take the thread between the needles to the back of your work, and knit into the front leg of the same stitch (D).

Step 6: Let both yarn overs drop from the needle in your right hand. This will leave a loose strand and a visible gap. Return the thread to the back of your work, and purl each stitch until you reach the next pair of yarn overs. Repeat this process to the end of the row.

Step 7: Knit the subsequent row as usual. Maintain good tension to firm up any loose stitches. Knit more rows if you want, then bind off (page 22).

Eyelets are made in the same way when knitting in the round, with one exception. When you reach the second (Western knit) row, simply reverse the order of the stitches when knitting the yarn overs. Knit into the front of the elongated stitch, bring the thread forward, and purl into the same stitch. Let both yarn overs drop, take the thread to the back, and continue knitting.

▶20 Crocheted Eyelets

You can add crocheted eyelets to any edge of a flat, bead knitted piece and to the top or the bottom of a piece worked in the round. These eyelets, sometimes called filet lace, are square in shape and yield a firmer, more tailored edge than knitted eyelets.

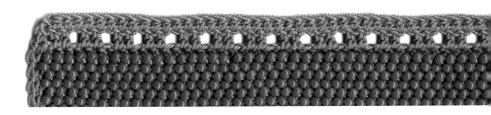

Step 1: Join a new thread end to the tail left after binding off (page 24). (If the tail is unavailable or not long enough, pull the new thread end through a stitch with a crochet hook, and tie a knot to secure it.) Wrap the thread two or three times around the pinky finger of your left hand for tension and hold the bead knitting in the same hand.

Step 2: With your right hand, insert the hook into the first stitch, catch the thread, and pull a loop through to the front of your knitting. Catch the thread again and pull a new loop through the starting loop (A). Repeat this step one more time to form a three-loop chain.

Step 3: Make a yarn over by wrapping the thread once around the hook in a clockwise direction. Then insert the hook into the next stitch (B).

Step 4: Catch the thread, and pull a loop through to the front. You should now have three loops on your needle. Catch the thread, and pull it through two loops (C). You should have two loops on your needle. Catch the thread, and pull it through two loops. You should have one loop on your needle. This is the first double crochet stitch.

Step 5: Begin the next stitch by making a yarn over and inserting the hook into the next stitch (D).

Step 6: Continue until you reach the point where you want to make the first eyelet.

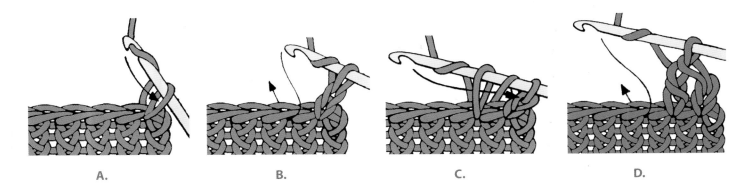

A.   B.   C.   D.

Step 7: To make the eyelet, simply chain once, make a yarn over, and insert the hook into the stitch after the next stitch. (You have skipped one.) Continue to work double crochet, adding eyelets at regular intervals.

Make as many crocheted rows as you would like. Complete a round row by inserting the hook into the top of the first stitch and pulling a loop through it. To begin a new row on a flat or round piece, chain twice after the join (this counts as the first double crochet).

▶21 Crocheted Fringe

You can also add a crocheted fringe to any edge of your bead knitting. The result is a looped fringe with a natural twist—my favorite type of fringe.

You have to do some advance planning because the beads must be prestrung.

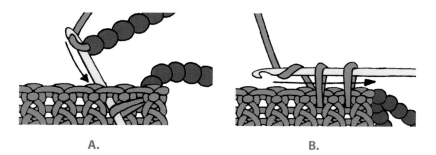

A.   **B.**

Complete one or two rows in double crochet before beginning to make the fringe.

Decide how many beads you want in each fringe before stringing your beads. Separate each segment of beads with a small piece of paper, just as you would when bead knitting (page 29).

Step 1: Attach the end of the thread to the beadwork to start your fringe. Insert the hook into the stitch nearest to the thread.

Step 2: Catch the thread, and pull a loop through to the front of the stitch. Insert the hook into the next stitch.

Step 3: Slide the first segment of beads to the top of the thread so that the first bead touches the beadwork. Wrap the thread around your pinky finger for tension. With the hook, catch the thread directly above the first segment of beads, and pull a loop through the stitch (A).

Step 4: You now have two loops on the hook. Make sure that the looped fringe is snug enough so that there is no empty thread showing through, but loose enough to swing freely. Catch the thread, and bring it through both loops on the hook (B). Insert the hook into the next stitch, and repeat to make a second loop of fringe.

More Fringe Styles

You can use a few basic beading techniques to add other styles of fringe to the edge of your bead knitting. You will need a beading needle and beading thread, but you will not need to prestring the beads.

The illustrations show examples of fringe made with seed beads—but be creative! You can vary the size and shape of your beads and the length of the fringe to suit your own style.

Thread a beading needle with approximately 5' (1.5 m) of thread. Sew through the corner of your bead knitting (or wherever you want to begin the fringe), and tie a knot to secure the end. When you complete the fringe, you can weave the thread tail into the work or hide it within the lining fabric.

A. Basic Fringe

String enough beads for the desired length of the fringe strand. Skip the last bead, and sew back through the rest of beads on the strand. Then sew through the edge of the bead knitting to begin the next strand.

Continue adding fringe as you want. To create a sparse fringe, make several small stitches in the edge of the work before beginning each strand.

B. Looped Fringe

Begin making the basic fringe, but form a loop at the end of the strand by skipping more than one bead before sewing through the rest of the beads on the strand.

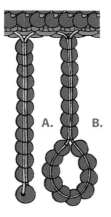

C. Branched Fringe

Begin making the basic fringe. Sew back through several beads, and then exit the strand. String more beads to create a "branch" protruding from the fringe. Skip the last branch bead, and sew back to the original strand. Repeat to make as many branches as you want along the length of the original strand.

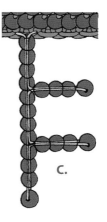

D. Netted Fringe

To make netted fringe, simply begin and end any of the previous types of fringe with a small section of additional beads. Space your stitches along the edge of the knitting to create a symmetrical Y shape at the top of the strand. Plan for enough beads to span several bead knitted stitches evenly.

To end your thread, sew into the bead knitting, and secure the tail with a knot.

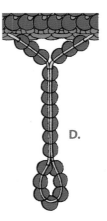

Chapter 8

Assembly and Lining

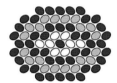

You can assemble bead knitted bags in three ways: You can double-knit the bag to form the finished shape (page 68). You can knit a flat piece of fabric and fold it in half to create the bag. You can stitch together two flat pieces of bead knitted fabric. No matter which type of bag you choose to make, you should add a lining.

You will prolong the life of your bead knitting by lining it with fabric. The fabric protects your work by preventing objects from rubbing or snagging the threads. A lining also lessens the wear and stress on the beadwork.

You can use any sort of fabric you prefer. My favorite is Ultrasuede because the edges do not unravel. If you choose to use a fabric that has a tendency to fray—such as silk or cotton—make sure to leave an extra hem allowance. Then you can turn the edges under and bind them with fusible tape before sewing the lining to your beadwork.

Assembling a Two-Piece Bag

To join two flat bead knitted pieces to make a bag, place the beaded sides together. Very carefully, pin the two pieces together at the bottom and side edges with straight pins.

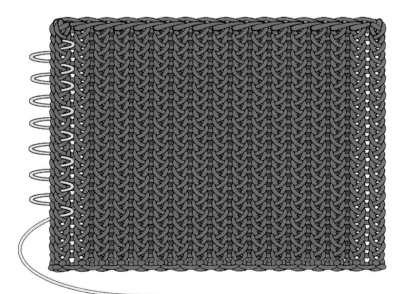

Sew into each knit stitch, beaded sides together.

With a needle and thread (single or double strand), sew through the corner of your beadwork and secure it with a knot. With a running stitch, sew into the first knit stitch of the edge row, through both pieces, exiting on the other side of the beadwork.

Sew into the next knit stitch, working on the side the thread exited, as shown in the illustration on the facing page. Sew into each knit stitch, or the fabric will pucker. Do not sew through any of the beads.

After joining all the edges—leaving an opening at the top—secure the thread, and turn the bag right side out.

Sew lining fabric with running stitches.

With small hand stitches, sew the lining fabric to the edges of your bead knitting. I prefer to use a running stitch so that I can easily control the tension.

Lining Flat Bead Knitting

After blocking the finished work (page 26), make a pattern by carefully tracing the shape onto a piece of paper. Draw a second line on the pattern approximately $\frac{1}{8}$" (3 mm) inside the original line. Cut the pattern along the new line.

Pin the pattern to your lining fabric and cut the fabric. (Leave a hem allowance if your lining fabric might fray.) Remove the paper and carefully pin the lining fabric to the back of your bead knitting.

Lining a Flat Bag

To line a flat, double knitted bag or a bag made by joining two flat pieces of bead knitting, make the inner lining separately, and then attach it to the bag.

After blocking the finished work (page 26), make a pattern by carefully tracing the shape onto a piece of paper. Draw a second line on the pattern approximately $\frac{1}{8}$" (3 mm) inside the original line. Cut the pattern along the new line.

Lining a Round Bag

The bags featured in this book are flat bags, but you may decide to work with increases and decreases to create a round bag. To line a round bag, you will need to create a fabric cylinder. Lay your bag flat, and measure the width of one side. Multiply this measurement by two. This number is the circumference of your bag—and also determines the width of the first fabric piece you will need for the lining. Measure the length of the bag, too.

Cut your lining fabric to the correct width and length, leaving a ½" (1.3 cm) seam allowance at the top, bottom, and both sides. Fold the lining fabric in half widthwise. Pin and sew the halves together at the side edge. This piece of fabric forms the sides of your cylinder.

Now you must determine the size for the bottom of the cylinder. Divide the circumference of the bag (which you calculated earlier) by 3.14 (pi). Divide this number in half to determine the radius of the circle. Add ½" (1.3 cm) for the seam allowance.

Set a compass to the radius measurement, and draw a circle on a piece of paper. Cut out the paper circle, and trace it onto your lining fabric.

Position the cylinder on top of the fabric circle, with the right side of the circle inside the cylinder. Sew the fabric circle to the bottom of the cylinder sides.

Make pleats, if necessary, by creating small folds along the top edge to fit the cylinder to the top of the bead knitted bag.

Fold the excess fabric at the top edge of the lining fabric to the wrong side to create a hem. Gently press the fold. Place the lining inside your bead knitted bag, and hand-sew together at the top edge.

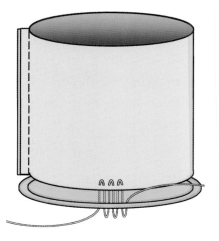

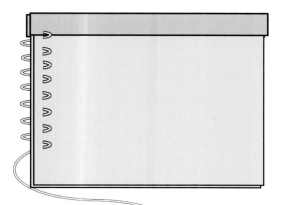

Sew the lining, right sides together.

Using the pattern as a guide, cut two identical shapes from your lining fabric, leaving approximately 1" (2.5 cm) of excess fabric at the top of the shape.

Fold the excess fabric over to the "wrong" side of the fabric so that the lining is the same length as your bead knitting. Gently press the fold for a crisp edge.

Place the two pieces of lining fabric, right sides together, and pin along the edges.

Working by hand or machine, sew the sides and the bottom of the lining fabric together.

Place the lining inside your bag—so that the wrong sides of the lining are smooth against the inside of the bag. Finish by hand, sewing the top edge of the lining fabric with small stitches along the top edge of the bag.

Attaching Straps

You might want to carry your bead knitted bag as a simple clutch purse, or you may prefer to attach a strap so you can wear the bag over your shoulder. You have many choices of length and style.

You can add a decorative chain, adding beads at intervals if you want. You could also make a strap from a braided silk cords or a narrow strip of flat, lined bead knitting. Experienced beaders may prefer to create a spiral beaded rope, and experienced knitters may choose a fancy I-cord. Be inventive!

If you added knitted or crocheted eyelets along the top edge of your bag, simply thread a drawstring or chain through the eyelet holes. The drawstring itself can serve as the strap. Or you can add large jump rings to the sides of the bag and attach a longer strap to the rings.

You might also want to sandwich the ends of a cord or a large jump ring between each of the two sides of a flat bag—or between the bag and lining fabric—before sewing it closed.

Chapter 9

Designing Your Own Patterns

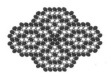

After you have had made one or more of the bead knitted bags in this book and have some experience reading patterns, you might try your hand at creating a few original designs of your own. Blank graph worksheets—for small and large bead sizes—are provided on pages 316 and 317. These graphs—and blank graphs for all the projects in the book—are also available as JPEGs and PDFs on the enclosed DVD. You can also download blank graph worksheets from my website, www.darkharebeadwork.com.

You can also convert needlepoint patterns and other types of bead patterns into bead knitting patterns. For example, a brick stitch pattern translates perfectly into bead knitting, although keep in mind that the image stretches vertically a bit. Use your imagination and have fun!

The chart at left contains all the information that you will need, and the formulas on the facing page are ready to use. I have included the formula for size 15 beads, too. None of the projects in this book calls for size 15 beads, but you can use them if you'd like. If you change bead sizes, the dimensions of the fabric—and the finished

	size	8	11	15
Beads	per inch (width)	9 beads	12 beads	16 beads
	per inch (length)	11 beads	15 beads	22 beads
	per square inch	99 beads	180 beads	352 beads
	per gram	40 beads	110 beads	272 beads
	grams per square inch	2.5	1.7	1.3
Thread	silk	size FF	size E	size D
	perle cotton	size 5	size 8	size 12
	crochet cotton	size 10	size 20	size 30
	inches per square inch	54	72	100
Needles	size	00	0000	00000

effect—will change, too. All measurements are approximate and may vary depending on your tension, the bead type, and the weight of the thread.

Here is an example of how you would use the chart and Formula 2 to create a 2" × 2" (5.1 × 5.1 cm) square with size 11 beads, size E thread, and size 0000 needles:

2" (5.1 cm) desired width × 12 beads =
   24 beads wide
2" (5.1 cm) desired length × 15 beads =
   30 beads long
24 beads wide × 30 beads long =
   720 beads total
720 beads ÷ 110 beads per gram =
   6.6 total grams
6.6 grams ÷ 1.7 grams per square inch =
   3.9 square inches
3.9 square inches × 72 inches per square inch = **281 inches of thread**
281 inches of thread ÷ 36 inches per yard =
   7.8 yards of thread

As you begin to increase and decrease, your pattern will no longer be rectangular, so you may need to count and/or estimate bead amounts for the irregular sections. Then add the section totals to the formula to calculate the project total.

Formula 1

Size 8 Beads:

___ (desired in. wide) x 9 beads = ___ beads wide
___ (desired in. long) x 11 beads = ___ beads long
___ beads wide x ___ beads long = ___ total bead count
___ (total bead count) ÷ 40 (beads per gr.) = ___ total gr.
___ (total gr.) ÷ 2.5 (gr. per square in.) = ___ square in.
___ (square in.) x 54 (in. per square in.) = ___ in. of thread
___ (in. of thread) ÷ 36 = ___ yd. of thread

Formula 2

Size 11 Beads:

___ (desired in. wide) x 12 beads = ___ beads wide
___ (desired in. long) x 15 beads = ___ beads long
___ beads wide x ___ beads long = ___ total bead count
___ (total bead count) ÷110 (beads per gr.) = ___ total gr.
___ (total gr.) ÷ 1.7 (gr. per square in.) = ___ square in.
___ (square in.) x 72 (in. per square in.) = ___ in. of thread
___ (in. of thread) ÷ 36 = ___ yd. of thread

Formula 3

Size 15 Beads:

___ (desired in. wide) x 16 beads = ___ beads wide
___ (desired in. long) x 22 beads = ___ beads long
___ beads wide x ___ beads long = ___ total bead count
___ (total bead count) ÷ 272 (beads per gr.) = ___ total gr.
___ (total gr.) ÷ 1.3 (gr. per square in.) = ___ square in.
___ (square in.) x 100 (in. per square in.) = ___ in. of thread
___ (in. of thread) ÷ 36 = ___ yd. of thread

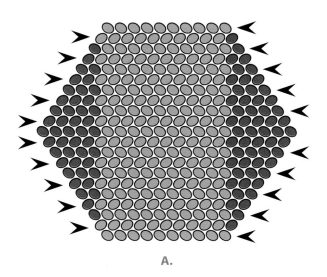

A.

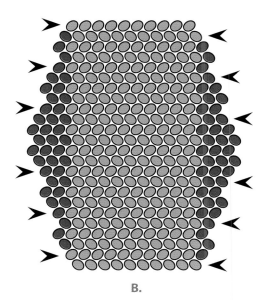

B.

Edge Increases and Decreases

An edge increase or decrease is made within a pair of rows. Although each increase will start at the beginning of a row, the actual bead will not be added until the end of the following row.

The beads shaded red in the illustrations indicate the increase and decrease shaping. The arrows indicate the direction in which you are knitting (right to left is a knit row; left to right is a purl row). Each arrow on the lower half of the graph shows where an increase begins. Notice that the new bead does not appear until the row above the increase.

Each arrow on the upper half of the graph shows where a decrease begins. The bead is omitted in the first row. The unbeaded stitch is bound off on the next row.

When designing a pattern with a rapid rate of increase, the beads follow the natural diagonal slope of the shaping (A). When designing a pattern with a slower rate of increase, the beads follow the diagonal only at the places where the increases actually occur (B). The rest of the rows are staggered.

Increases and Decreases within a Row

To design an increase within a row, you must first decide how many beads will be in the first row. This is the core of your pattern, shaded as gray beads in the illustration. To create a 2-bead increase, simply add 1 bead to each side of your core. You add a stitch on the knit row; you add the bead on the next purl row (C). For a faster increase, add 2 or more beads.

To keep your work flat, the first of the increases should occur 1 or 2 beads from the edges, with any additional increases separated by no more than 2 beads.

Remember that although increases always begin on a knit row, they will not appear until the subsequent purl row. The opposite is true when making edge decreases. The bead is omitted on the knit row. The unbeaded stitch is bound off on the purl row.

Always increase and decrease within the row when designing double bead knitting or bead knitting in the round (page 42). For double knitting, you will need to decrease on multiple needles (page 72).

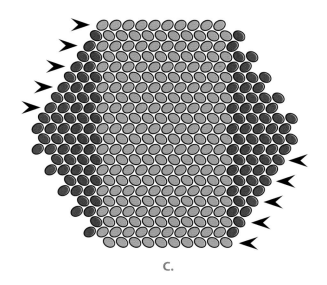

C.

PART 2: NECKLACES

Chapter 10

Getting Started

The designs for my beaded neckpieces are based on the ornate broadcollars worn by Egyptian royalty a millennium ago. Rather than try to recreate these ancient relics, I have adapted the basic elements for the modern beadworker. By repeating and combining just a few basic elements, you can create an elaborate piece of jewelry.

In the early chapters of this book you will learn two different ways to build the main component of a beaded neckpiece— the ladder. You'll also learn how to combine multiple ladders and how to add various structural and decorative elements.

In the second half of the book, there are detailed patterns and instruction for ten original designs. The projects range from beginner to advanced. Each provides an opportunity to combine a variety of techniques presented in the early chapters.

MATERIALS AND SUPPLIES

To make these beaded neckpieces, you will need the following materials and supplies. Each project includes a materials list with the specific materials for that project. Because correct sizing is so important, I have also provided the amount of beads you will need for each size in the range of sizes provided.

- Size 12 or smaller beading needles
- Strong bead thread (I use either 16 lb GSP fishing line or size 46 bonded nylon)
- Thin, sharp pins with a glass or plastic ball at the top
- Sharp, fine tipped scissors
- Tape measure with metric units
- Ruler with metric units
- Compass with metric units
- Calculator
- White paper, 8½"× 8½" (20.3 × 20.3 cm) or larger
- Foam board or a flat, sturdy cardboard box, 14" x 14" (35.5 × 35.5 cm) or larger
- Mechanical pencil for marking the template

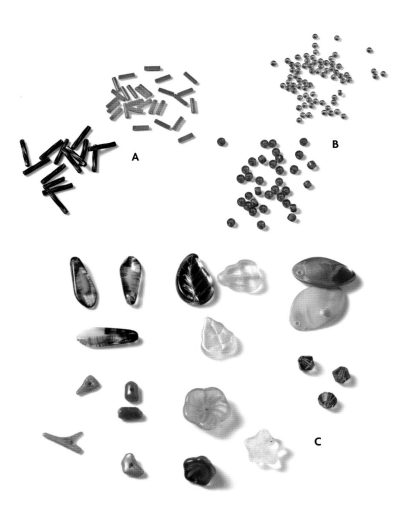

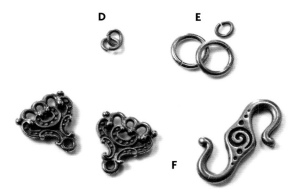

A 6mm × 2mm and 12mm × 2mm bugle beads
B 11° and 8° seed beads
C Dagger beads, crystals, stone chips, and other decorative beads
D 1.5cm to 3cm multistrand necklace reducers
E Jump rings
F Clasps or S hooks

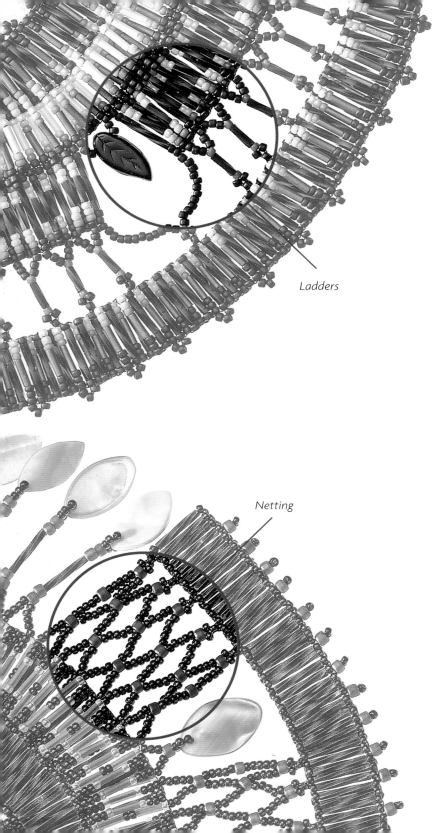

Ladders

Netting

ELEMENTS OF A BEADED NECKPIECE

When you make a beaded neckpiece, you have the creative freedom to combine several basic elements to make a unique design. You don't need to include every element in every collar, however. Here are some of the many elements you can choose from.

Ladders

Ladders make up the framework of the beaded neckpiece. A single ladder is made of multiple "bead units," each of which includes at least one bugle bead and at least one 11° seed bead on either end (to buffer the thread from the sharp edges of the bugle bead). You sew the units together, side by side, to make a long dense ribbon of beads. Then you pin the ladders to a template and join them to form circles. This concentric formation allows the neckpiece to hold its shape when you remove it from the template.

Netting

Netting is used to join ladders, and it also creates open areas, which provide visual interest in the design. You can create a light, airy feel by beading a row of netting between each ladder. Or you can add rows more sparingly—even a single row of netting will provide interesting contrast to the otherwise dense structure of several consecutive ladder rows. Your netting can be very complex and intricate, as in Trellis on page 204. Or it can be as simple as single spokes that span from one ladder to the next, as in Drab on page 158. Netted rows may include bugle beads, seed beads of varying sizes, crystals, pressed glass, or any other number of decorative elements.

Layering

In most cases, you will add new elements of the design to the edges of existing elements. You can, however, also work on the surface of your neckpiece to build layers, which will add depth and texture. One way to do this is by netting from the outside edge of a ladder to the inside edge of another, spanning one or more ladders in between.

Surface Embellishment

Surface embellishments add extra dimension to your beadwork, and sewing is a simple way to adorn the surface. Just stitch beads, pressed glass flowers, stone chips, or any other decoration at the juncture of two ladders. It's easiest to add these elements while you are weaving in and out of a ladder to join a subsequent row.

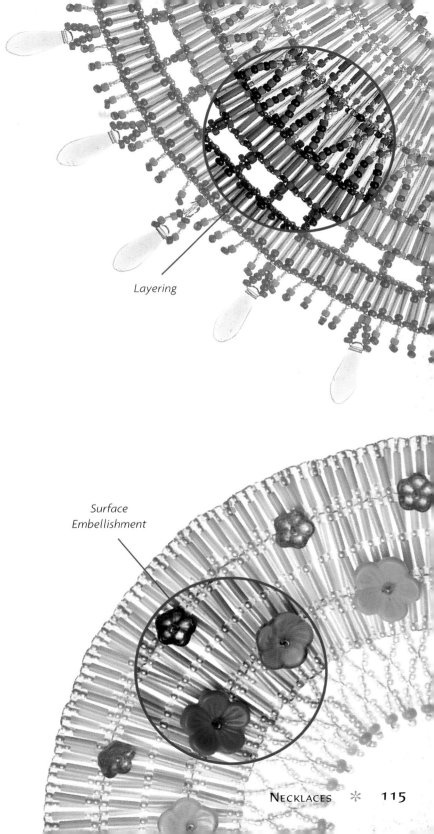

Layering

*Surface
Embellishment*

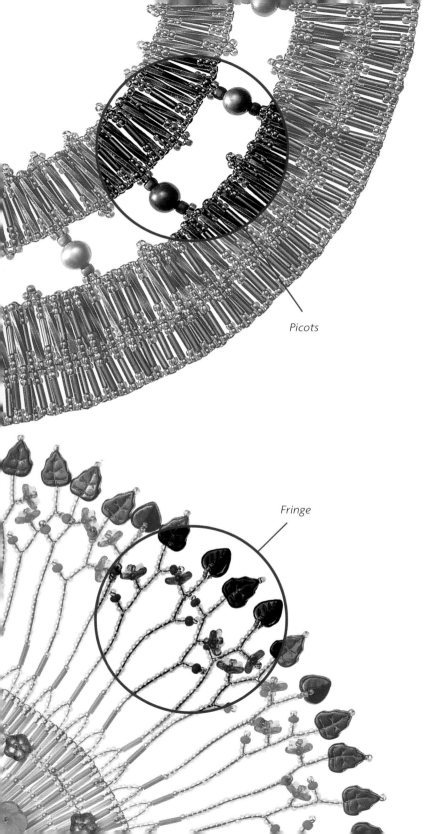

Picots

Fringe

Picots

Picots are small beaded loops along a beaded edge. Small picots, usually made with one to three beads, add texture to the straight edges of the beaded ladders. Most often, you'll add picots to the innermost or top ladder. You can also add them to the outer edge, within netted segments, or anywhere else within the neckpiece that you'd like extra embellishment.

Fringe

Fringe is basically an extended picot. Fringe adds drama and fluidity to the piece. You can create fringe that is long and straight, branched, looped, or layered. If you add daggers or other large beads along the bottoms of the strands, the fringe will sway with the wearer's every movement.

Closures

You'll add a closure to the back of each end of the neckpiece to clasp the neckpiece shut. You'll also add a metal finding to which you'll attach each closure. The metal findings should be broad enough to span at least one row (usually the initial ladder) to accommodate the weight of the neckpiece. Be sure they are securely attached. Metal reducers, which are often used for multistrand necklaces, are ideal findings for these projects.

Counterweights

Some neckpieces are asymmetrical from front to back—in other words, they may be heavier at the front, either by design or because there is a large amount of heavy fringe. To properly balance the neckpiece, you may need to add a counterweight at the back. A decorative coin with a center hole, a smooth stone decorated with beads, or a fishing weight are some of the many types of objects that work well as counterweights.

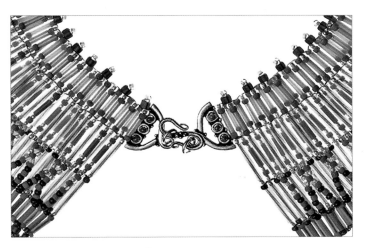

Closures

Counterweights

MEASURING AND MAKING A TEMPLATE

The first step to making a beaded neckpiece is to create a template. The template serves as the workspace on which you will secure your first row of beads, make measurements, add further rows, and make notations that will help you determine where to join additional elements.

Measuring for Circumference

Measure the base of your neck with a metric tape measure to find your neck circumference. The neckpiece will lie flat on your shoulders and breast plate, so be sure you measure your neck where it meets your body—not any higher. Add 2 cm to the measurement to allow for a comfortable fit. The total is the circumference of the first, innermost ladder of your neckpiece.

Now divide that number to find the diameter and then the radius of the circumference. You will then set your compass to the radius dimension to make the correct-size circle on your template. Here's the formula:

____ (circumference + 2 cm) ÷ 3.14 = ____ (diameter)
____ (diameter) ÷ 2 = ____ (radius)

Record and label each of these measurements. Metric measurements are standard for measuring beads, so you'll work with metric measurements throughout this book. You'll find it much easier to stick with metric than to convert millimeters to inches as you work.

Making the Template

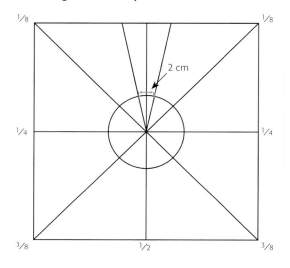

Before setting up your workspace, you need to prepare the template by drawing a few essential guidelines. It is important that your template is as square as possible so that these guidelines are accurate. Begin with a square sheet of paper that is at least 8½" x 8½" (21.6 × 21.6 cm).

Measure and mark the halfway point of each of the four edges of the square. Draw lines to connect the marks on opposite sides so that the paper is divided into four smaller squares. These lines will serve as markers as you create your neckpiece: the horizontal line is the ¼ marker, and the vertical line is the ½ marker.

Now draw a line from one corner of the square to the opposite corner. Repeat to connect the other two corners. These lines will serve as ⅜ markers. Your paper is now divided into eight triangles.

Set your compass to the radius you computed in the formula above. Place the point of the compass at the center of the template (where all four lines intersect). Draw a circle. The measurement of each line within the circle should be equal to the diameter in your formula.

Make two marks on either side of the vertical line that intersects the top edge of the circle. Each mark should be 1 cm from the line. You will leave the area between the marks free of beads so you can add the clasp there.

With tape or glue, adhere the template to the center of a sheet of foam board or a flat cardboard box. Now you have your work surface.

CHOOSING BEADS AND COLORS

The next step is to decide what the ladders will look like. There are only two rules you need to remember:

1. Every bugle bead must have a seed bead on each end.

2. Every bead unit within one ladder must be the same height.

Experiment with different combinations of beads. Stack them on straight pins and stand the pins side by side on your work surface. Think about the effect that you want to achieve. Do you want subtle colors that graduate from light to dark? Or do you want strong contrast in the colors of one unit and the next—or possibly even within one bead unit? Do you want every unit to be the same or do you want to create a rhythmic patterning with the ladder? How many different combinations do you want within a single ladder?

The drawings below show the combinations in the designs for the projects in this book. Refer to them as you think about the qualities you would like to have in your own designs.

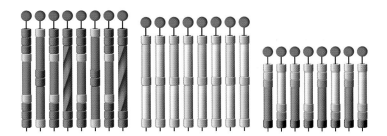

When you have finished experimenting, save the combinations that you like by making a "swatch library" of short ladders. Then work with these swatches to decide how you would like to combine the colors and the ladders. Once you've decided on several combinations you like, you're ready to begin making the long ladders for your neckpiece.

Chapter 11
Making Ladders

The ladders are the foundation of the neckpiece. They hold the piece together and, once they are joined, they give the piece its final shape and structure. You can build ladders with either the one-needle or the two-needle method. The main difference is in the way you string the beads. The resulting ladders are identical, so the method you choose is simply a matter of preference.

When building a ladder, the order in which you string the beads is important. With the one-needle technique, you will string a large number of beads before constructing the ladder. With the two-needle technique, you will add bead units one at a time and build the ladder gradually. Regardless of the technique you choose, you must always string the bead units from top to bottom and then from bottom to top, so the pattern is correct.

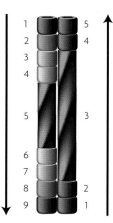

ONE-NEEDLE METHOD

String the beads for your first ladder in the correct order, as determined by your swatch library or as indicated in the instructions for the specific project you're making.

Begin with a piece of thread about 10' (3 m) long. To get the length you need, simply pull the thread from the spool twice, stretching your arms to their full length and measuring each length from fingertip to fingertip.

Thread a needle at one end and make a "stopper bead" by picking up a seed bead and sliding it to the center of your thread. Sew through this bead once more, making sure not to pierce the thread. The stopper bead should move back and forth along the thread with little effort, but the friction of the thread loop around the bead will keep it from moving too freely, keeping all the other beads from falling off the thread.

Referring to your sample swatch or the project instructions, string your first bead unit in order from bottom to top and string the second unit in order from top to bottom.

Continue to string beads this way until there are about 18" (46 cm) of thread remaining from the last bead to the needle. Slide the stopper bead so that it is about 18" (46 cm) from the far end of the thread. Slide the strung bead units to meet it, as shown in top drawing below.

Slide the first two bead units so that they are about two finger widths from the rest of the beads. Skip the first bead unit and sew into the far end of the second unit. The two units will fold the shared length of thread in half, causing the length of the second bead unit to lay parallel atop the length of the first bead unit, as shown in the bottom two drawings.

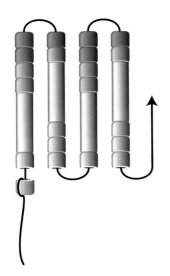

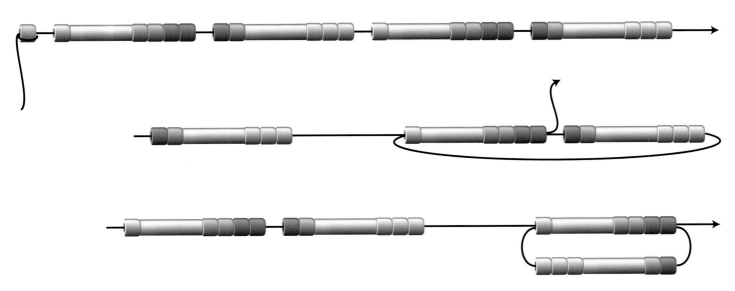

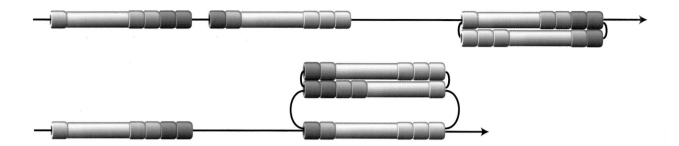

Pull the thread taut so that the first two units sit one above the next, as shown in the top drawing above.

Slide the next bead unit forward and sew into the far end of this unit. Pull taut, once again folding the shared thread in half. You should now have three parallel bead units, as shown in the bottom drawing above.

After joining several units, you will find that you are not able to slide any more bead units forward. When you reach this point, allow more space by sliding the stopper bead several inches along the thread.

Repeat the process and continue to build the ladder until there are 6" to 8" (15 to 20 cm) of thread free at each end.

TWO-NEEDLE METHOD

Begin with a piece of thread about 10' (3 m) long. To get the length you need, simply pull the thread from the spool twice, stretching your arms to their full length and measuring each length from fingertip to fingertip.

Add a needle to each end of the thread. String your first bead unit in order from top to bottom. String the second unit in order from bottom to top. Slide both units to the center of the length of thread.

With the needle that comes out of the second bead unit, sew into the far end of the first bead unit and exit the last bead of the same unit. The two units will fold the shared length of thread in half.

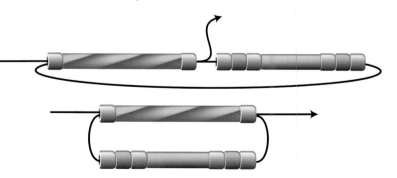

Pull the thread taut so that the first two units sit side by side.

Add a new bead unit, making sure to string the beads in the correct order. Sew into the far end of the new unit with the second needle and pull the thread taut.

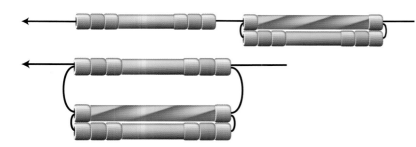

Repeat the process and continue to build the ladder until there are 6" to 8" (15 to 20 cm) of thread free at each end. You will need to end the ladder and then add more thread and beads to extend it to the length you want.

ENDING A LADDER

Before continuing the ladder, you need to tie off the thread extending from the ends of the top unit.

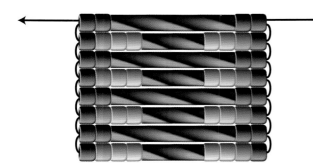

Remove the stopper bead from the end of the thread. If you are working with the one-needle method, you may find that several bead units remain on the thread, but the working end becomes too short to continue. Simply remove any remaining bead units. Sew into the next-to-last unit so that both thread ends are on the same side of the ladder.

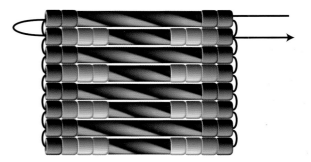

Secure the thread ends by tying them together twice, each time with an overhand knot. Pull the thread tight enough that the last two ladders do not separate—but not so tight that the end of the ladder buckles.

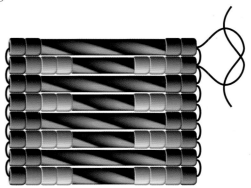

Remove the needle(s) and allow the thread ends to remain as they are. You will weave these ends into your work after the ladders are joined.

EXTENDING A LADDER

To extend a one-needle ladder, pull a new length of thread from your spool and, once again, "load" your thread so that half is strung with beads. Add the needle and sew through the last unit of your existing ladder, making sure to enter the proper side, as determined by your swatch or project instructions. Continue building the ladder until it is the desired length or until you run out of thread again.

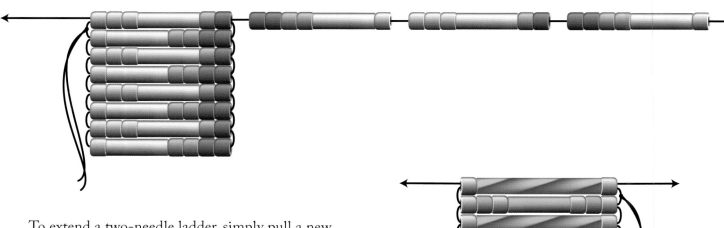

To extend a two-needle ladder, simply pull a new length of thread and add a needle to each end. Sew through the last bead unit of the existing ladder. Continue building that ladder until it is the desired length or until you run out of thread again.

ESTIMATING LADDER LENGTH

When planning your beaded neckpiece, it helps to know roughly how long each ladder needs to be. To estimate ladder length, you'll need to make a few simple calculations.

First you need to know the diameter of your neck opening. This is the diameter of the circle that you drew on your template. For subsequent ladders, measure the diameter of the circle from the outside edges of the outermost ladder (or points for netted rows) at the ¼-marker line on your template.

1. Find the circumference of the outer edge of the last row with this formula:

____ cm (diameter) x 3.14 = ____ cm (circumference)

This measurement is the circumference of the subsequent ladder.

2. Next you need to know how many bead units you need to span the circumference. One cm of the circle requires approximately 5.5 bead units.

____ cm (circumference) x 5.5 = ____ (units needed)

3. It's helpful to know the measurement of the ladder when it lies straight so you can estimate the length you'll need to have before you pin it to the template. One centimeter of a straight ladder requires approximately 4.7 bead units:

____ (units needed) ÷ 4.7 = ____ cm (straight ladder length)

Keep in mind that the ladder will be slightly shorter than your estimated length because you are leaving space free to accommodate the clasp.

You can get a more accurate estimate of the final length when the ladder is roughly halfway completed. Temporarily pin the ladder to the template from either clasp mark to the ½-marker line at the bottom of your template. Mark the halfway point on your ladder with a pin or a piece of string. Remove the ladder from the template. Lay the ladder straight and measure the distance from the beginning of the ladder to the halfway point. Multiply this number by two in order to find the total length you'll need.

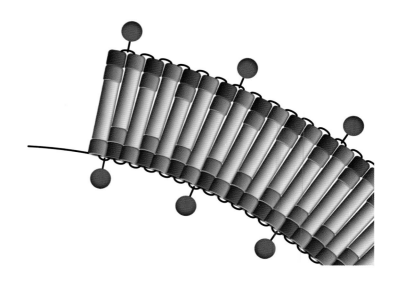

Chapter 12
Assembly

You only need to make one ladder at a time. When you have completed each ladder, you will pin it to the template and join it to the others. Once you begin designing your own neckpieces, however, you might want to make at least one segment of each ladder to help you plan the overall design.

PINNING LADDERS TO THE TEMPLATE

The first ladder is the most difficult to pin to the template because there are no other ladders to help you secure it. Carefully insert a straight pin through the small space at the inner (top) edge where the thread joins the first bead unit to the second bead unit. Make sure that you don't pierce the thread as this will weaken the ladder. Insert the pin into the template at one of the two marks that you made to accommodate the clasp.

Gently curve the ladder to conform to the shape of the circle, pinning both the inner and outer edges every couple of centimeters. Try not to stretch the outer edge of the ladder. Instead, allow the inner edge to rumple slightly, like a fan. Work all the way around to the second clasp mark.

You may need to readjust some of the pins to make sure that the bead units are evenly distributed.

The second and all subsequent ladders are considerably easier to pin to the template. Place the ladder on the template so that the first unit of the ladder is aligned with the first unit of the previous ladder—the idea is that they appear to be continuous units. Wrap the new ladder around the circle, pinning both edges enough to secure them, until you reach the opposite end. Readjust pins if necessary.

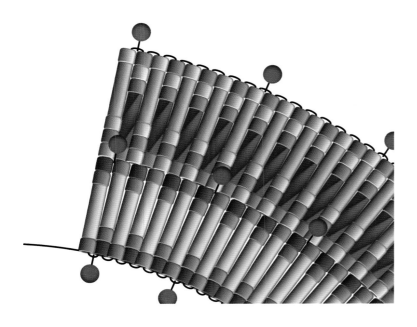

Each ladder in the project patterns contains more bead units than the preceding ladder in order to create concentric rings. As you join ladders, you'll see that each consecutive unit of the outer ladder is increasingly farther from the next unit of the inner ladder. With a bit of gentle manipulation, you can sew smoothly from one unit to the next, but eventually you will reach a point where you would have to stretch the outer ladder in order to meet the corresponding inner ladder. To keep the bead units evenly distributed without stretching the outer ladder, skip one bead unit in the outer ladder as you join it to the inner ladder. Make sure that you only skip one bead unit at a time to avoid leaving gaps in your beadwork.

JOINING THE FIRST TWO LADDERS

Now that you have pinned the second ladder to the template, you will join it to the first ladder. Begin by placing a stopper bead on a length of thread at least 5' (1.5 m) long. Thread a needle at one end. Sew through the outer edge of the first bead unit of the outermost ladder, then sew through the first unit of the previous ladder so that you exit the inside of the circle. Now work in the opposite direction, sewing through the second unit of each ladder until you exit the outer edge. Work back and forth in this way until you have joined several more units in each ladder.

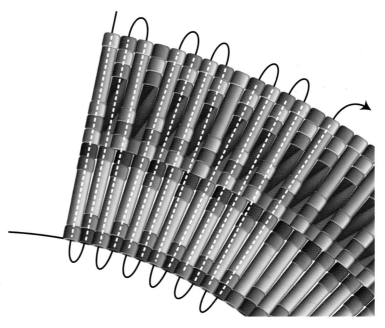

If you are unsure where in the ladder to skip a bead unit, make a "ray" to determine the best location. Place a straight pin at the center point of your template. Tie one end of a length of thread around the pin. Now lay the thread tautly across your neckpiece to find the most direct path from the unit of one ladder to a unit of the next.

ENDING AND BEGINNING THREADS

Eventually you will need to begin a new thread—usually when the thread you're working with is only about 6" (16 cm) long. Simply remove the needle and begin a new length of thread as before, adding a stopper bead and rethreading the needle. The ladders are secured to the template, so they'll stay in place even when the tension on the working thread is loose. Continue to join the ladders one unit at a time. When you have joined nine or ten units, the thread will be secure enough for you to remove the stopper bead and tie the two ends together with an overhand knot.

It's best to leave all thread ends hanging from your neckpiece until it is complete. This way, you won't clog a bead with doubled threads, which helps if you want to add elements through that bead later.

If you have so many hanging threads that it's hard to work, however, it's okay to finish some of them ahead of time—but only if you sew through bead units that you are positive you will not need later. Finish each loose end, one at a time, by weaving it through two or three bead units. Then cut the thread close to the beadwork with sharp scissors.

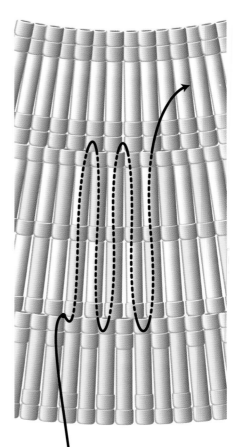

JOINING SUBSEQUENT LADDERS

The first two ladders are fairly easy to join because the needle always exits either at the inner or outer edge of the circle. To join the next ladders to the first two, you sew through the bead units of the new ladder and the ladder before it. As you exit the inner ladder, it gets a little tricky because the point of the needle will want to enter the outer edge of the adjoining ladder.

As you work around the circle, temporarily unpin a small section of both of the ladders you are working on and slide one or two fingers underneath, just enough to lift the inner ladder. Now you will have enough space for the needle to exit the inner edge. With your other hand, grasp the needle (with pliers, if necessary) to pull the thread through the bead unit. As you complete each section, replace the pins to secure the beadwork to the template.

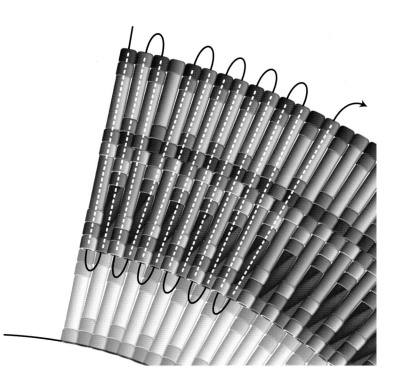

Chapter 13

Decorative Elements

The ladders give beaded neckpieces their shape, but the additional decorative elements—and how you arrange them—is what gives the piece its unique style and visual interest. For example, the netting in Spike on page 180 is layered on a ladder to add density. A similar style of netting creates open space in Chartreuse on page 152, to lighten the dense design.

PLANNING THREAD PASSES

Any ladder unit that is joined to ladders before and after it will contain four strands of thread: one to string the individual units, one to build the ladder, one to join the ladder to the ladder that precedes it, and one to join it to the ladder that follows.

The most important thing is to make sure that no bead becomes so clogged with thread that the needle cannot pass through it. When you're adding decorative elements, try to make the most of each pass of thread. As you plan, consider how you can combine steps to make efficient use of the small space within each bead. Here are some guidelines for planning the thread passes in projects with decorative elements.

NETTING

Netting is a way to join two ladders, but it is also a versatile decorative element. It can be as simple as singular netted spokes or as elaborate as wide, dense nets with multiple connections. A netted spike is a singular piece of netting with no connections other than those from one row to the next.

There are two ways to create decorative netting. You can edge it with lacy picots, which you can then use to attach the subsequent ladder. Or you can work the netting back and forth between ladders to create a decorative space between them.

You can also add netting at the inner edge of the top ladder to create a small "collar." The netting will gently rise up the slope of the wearer's neck. Netting also makes a great base for fringe at the outermost edge of the neckpiece.

PICOTS

Picots are a simple way to decorate an otherwise plain edge. You can add them to any open ladder. Picots usually consist of one to three beads. Each picot is a separate element, so you can add one at a time wherever you'd like—maybe in place of a netted spike or a strand of fringe. Picots are easy to make and they're extremely versatile. They set up accessible beads that you can use to attach netting, a subsequent ladder, or any number of other elements.

Netting and Surface Embellishment
Meadow (page 166)

As you add netting to the inner edge of the first ladder, also add pressed-glass flowers between the first and second ladders.

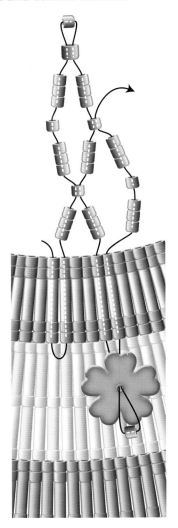

Netting and Picots
Chartreuse (page 152)

Add picots to the inner edge of the first ladder at the same time that you add netting to the outer edge of the same ladder.

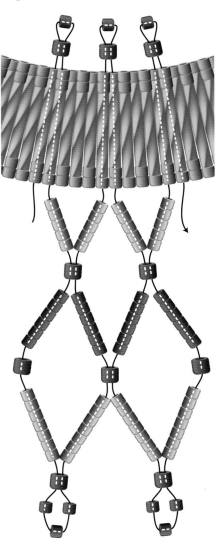

Joining Ladders and Picots
Gradient (page 188)

Add picots to the inner edge of the first ladder as you join the first and second ladders.

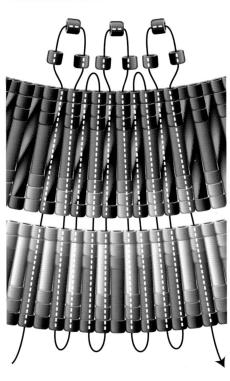

SURFACE EMBELLISHMENT

Surface embellishments provide easy ways to add extra dimension to your neckpiece. All you need is a small decorative element and a seed bead to hold it in place. You can add many types of embellishments to your beaded neckpiece—pressed glass, stone chips, or small crystal beads.

It's easiest to incorporate the embellishment into the neckpiece as you are adding other elements. For example, I added coral pieces to the surface of Ember on page 174 while making picots along the inner edge. I added the pressed-glass flowers in Meadow on page 166 while I was netting the inside edge and fringing the bottom one.

FRINGE

Fringe adds drama to a neckpiece. It also adds an appealing dynamic element, because the fringe moves as the wearer does. Fringe can vary in length, depending on the finished effect you want. It is also an excellent way to incorporate large decorative beads and other components into any neckpiece.

For example, a favorite bead or crystal strung on the center fringe strand makes a striking centerpiece. Intensely colored fringe beads will create strong contrast in a monochromatic piece. A branched fringe will add a touch of wild flair to the design. There are no rules with fringe (unlike the other elements in a beaded neckpiece), so use your imagination!

Layering and Picots
Spike (page 180)

Add a layer of netting over the third ladder as you make picots along the bottom edge of the fourth ladder.

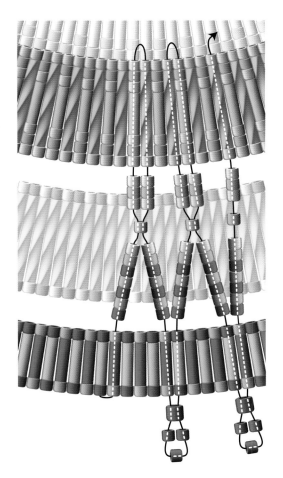

Picots and Surface Embellishment
Ember (page 174)

As you add picots to the inner edge of the first ladder, also add coral embellishments between the first and second ladders.

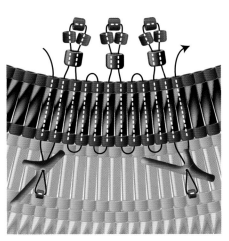

Fringe and Surface Embellishment
Trellis (page 204)

Add coral chips between the last two ladders as you add fringe to the outer edge of the neckpiece.

Chapter 14
Finishing

When you have completed the neckpiece, remove it from the template. Now you need to affix a clasp to the ends so that you can wear it! You have some choices as to how to close the ladder ends. For lightweight neckpieces, you can add a bead and loop closure, as shown below.

For a heavier neckpiece, you need a stronger closure, such as a sturdy clasp attached to a pair of metal reducers.

ATTACHING THE FINDING

The sturdiest way to close your neckpiece is to fit the ends of the innermost ladder(s) with a strong finding. You need one that can accommodate a jump ring for the clasp you'll add later. Metal reducers, which are often used for stringing multiple strands of beads, are excellent choices.

The most common types of reducers have three holes on one side and one hole on the other. They are usually about 15 mm wide from end to end. Hold the multiple-hole side against the innermost ladder of the neckpiece. Most likely, the reducer and the ladder will be the same height, so you can attach the top edge of the ladder to the first hole and the bottom edge to the last hole.

If the reducer is too long, simply attach the bottom edge of the ladder to a different hole or, if it is long enough, allow it to span two ladders.

Begin a new thread. Choose a thread color that matches the neckpiece, because this thread will be visible. It's best to weave it through a ladder other than the one that will hold the reducer. Exit the inner edge of an end bead unit. Sew through the first hole of the reducer and then back through the same bead unit. Sew through the hole on the opposite end of the reducer. Repeat these steps several times, securely attaching the reducer to each end of the bead unit.

Weave the thread into your beadwork to finish. Before you do, you can weave a bead into each hole of the reducer to give it a more finished appearance.

Eventually, you will run out of room for the thread within the bead unit. Reinforce the reducer by carefully weaving back and forth between the threads that connect the ladder until you reach the next unit into which you can sew. Sew back and forth until the reducer is securely attached.

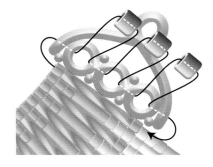

Repeat the entire process at the opposite end of the ladder, then weave the remaining thread ends into the neckpiece, as described on page 24.

ATTACHING THE CLASP

When you have finished the ends of your neckpiece, you can attach a clasp with one or more jump rings. Because these beaded neckpieces tend to be heavier than standard necklaces, be sure that the clasp is sturdy enough to hold a fair amount of weight. There are four types of clasps that work best: lobster-claw clasps, S hooks, toggles, and magnetic clasps.

Lobster-claw clasps include a lever that, when you pull it with your thumb, triggers a pin to open and close so that you can hook the jump ring on the opposite end of the neckpiece. With an S hook, you connect jump rings on either side of the neckpiece ends. Toggles have a small metal bar on one end that is inserted into a ring on the other end to close the neckpiece. Strong magnetic clasps firmly join the ends of the neckpiece and require little effort.

For extra security, you can also attach a safety chain to the closure by linking the jump ring on each end of the chain to the bottom holes of the metal reducers. The chain spans from one half of the reducer to the other. This way, if the clasp should open accidentally, the chain will hold the necklace in place until you can refasten it. Be sure the chain is long enough to allow the neck opening to fit over your head.

ATTACHING THE COUNTERWEIGHT

If your neckpiece is front-heavy—that is, if it has lots of beads, fringe, or other decorative elements that add weight to the front—you might want to add a counterweight at the back. Counterweights also add an elegant finish and a point of interest at the back of the piece. For example, because there is so much fringe on Eagle Feather, page 196, I added a beaded stone counterweight.

You can also add decorative metal coins or a metal fishing weight. Just link the element to one or both of the reducers or to the center of the safety chain, using jump rings or loops of beads or chain, as shown in the drawings at right.

Chapter 15

The Projects

These ten projects are arranged in order of complexity, from the simplest to the most advanced. Before you begin the project you'd like to make, read through the instructions and, if necessary, review the discussion of the techniques presented in the early chapters.

FINDING YOUR SIZE

At the beginning of each project you will find a list of materials. Notice that there are three different bead amounts indicated for each component. The amounts you use depend on the diameter of the circle you've drawn on your template, which corresponds to the size of your neckpiece.

Check your measurements to find which size to follow:

size A: for a circle less than 13 cm in diameter
size B: for a circle from 13.1 to 16 cm in diameter
size C: for a circle from 16.1 to 19 cm in diameter

HELPFUL TIPS

Here are some guidelines to refer to as you make any of the projects in this book. They will also help you when you are making neckpieces that you design yourself.

- Sometimes, you may not be able to find the drop beads or perfectly match the colors of bugle and seed beads recommended for the projects. Don't worry. Just substitute beads with the colors and shapes that you like.

- Unless the directions say otherwise, pin every first ladder onto the template from clasp mark to clasp mark. Pin every subsequent ladder from one end of the previous row to the other end of that row.

- Avoid having extra thread ends by working with a double length of thread and placing a stopper bead half-way along the doubled length. When you have completed the first half of the netting, remove the stopper bead and work the second half of the netting with the long thread tail. To prevent tangles, coil the end and tape it underneath your work surface until you need it.

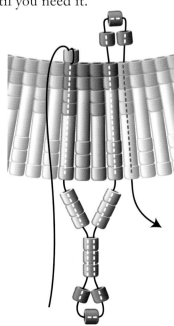

- At times, when joining a ladder to netting or picots, the center point of the net or picot will not align with the right bead unit. You can usually slightly readjust the ladder or the netting to correct the problem. If you can't, simply sew into the next unit, then reverse direction and sew backward to catch the point you missed. When the net or picot is in place, continue sewing in the original direction.

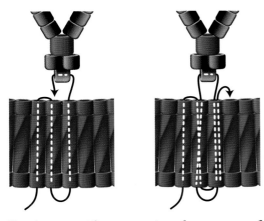

- Don't worry if your netting does not perfectly correspond with the number of bead units at either end of the ladder. When you reach the last unit, simply adjust the number of skipped beads between the top netted points so that the end of the last net joins with the last unit, as shown in the top drawing at right. Omit or add a bead or two if necessary, as shown in the bottom drawing at right.

- When adding decorative elements, always begin in the center of the ladder. Working from this starting point will help you create a strong symmetrical design.

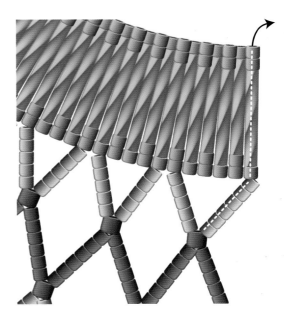

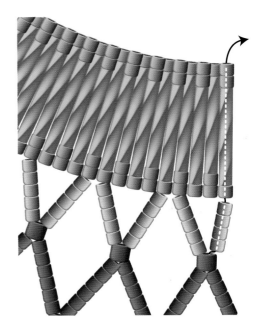

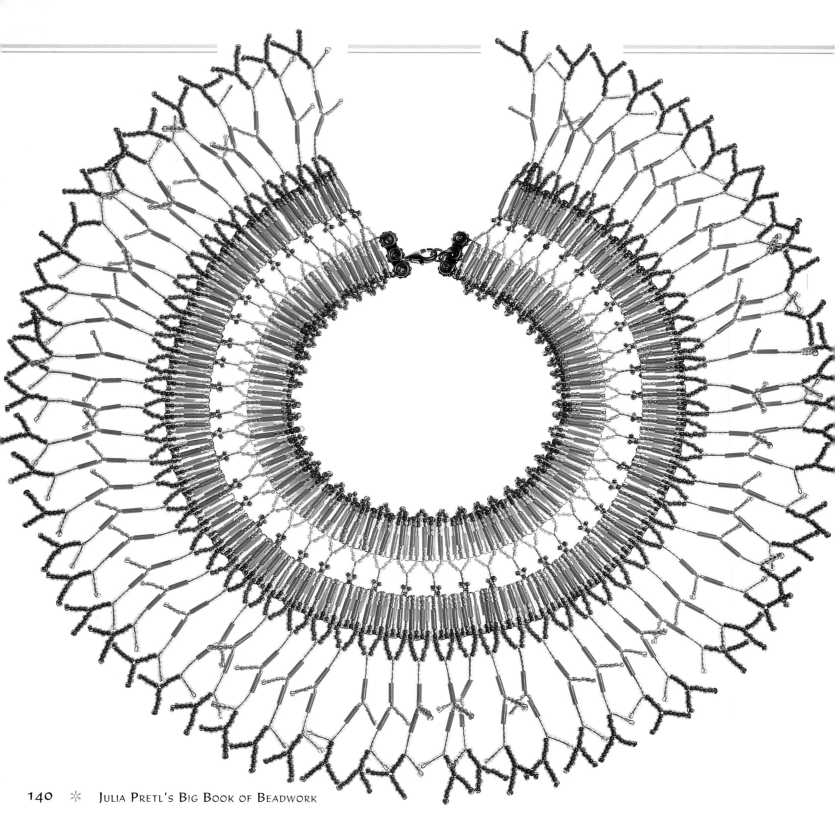

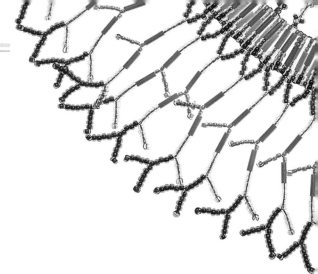

Urchin

This delicate collar combines branched fringe and open spaces for an airy feel.

BEAD KEY

6mm untwisted white bugles
size A = 20 g; size B = 23 g;
size C = 27 g

11° white seeds
size A = 18 g; size B = 22 g;
size C = 25 g

11° light pink seeds
size A = 20 g; size B = 23 g;
size C = 27 g

11° dark pink seeds
size A = 29 g; size B = 34 g;
size C = 39 g

Step A: Ladder 1

Unit 1 (top to bottom)

- 11° dark pink seeds x 2
- 11° light pink seeds x 2
- 6mm untwisted white bugle x 1
- 11° white seed x 1

Unit 2 (bottom to top)

- 11° white seeds x 3
- 6mm untwisted white bugle x 1
- 11° light pink seed x 1
- 11° dark pink seed x 1

Build ladder 1 and pin it to the template.

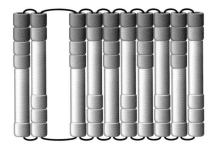

Step B: Netting and Inner Picot

Begin at the center of ladder 1 and work from left to right. Find the two units nearest to the halfway point. Count one unit outward on both sides for a total of four bead units. Sew through the first of the four units, exiting the outside of ladder 1.

Pick up:

- 11° white seeds x 3
- 11° light pink seeds x 3
- 11° dark pink seeds x 3

Sew back up through the three 11° light pink seeds, making sure not to split the thread. Pick up three 11° white seeds and sew through the last of the four bead units, skipping the two center units and exiting the inside of ladder 1. This is your first net.

Pick up three 11° dark pink seeds. Moving to the right, sew through the next unit, exiting the outside of ladder 1. This is your first picot.

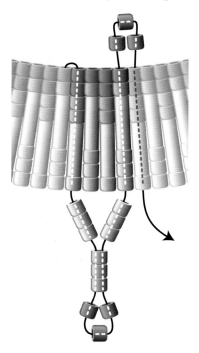

Repeat these steps to the end of the ladder. Remove the stopper bead from the tail and place a needle on the end. Add netting and picots to the remainder of the ladder. Pin all of the netted ends in place so that they are stretched taut and evenly distributed.

Step C: Ladder 2

Unit 1 (top to bottom)

- 11° white seed x 1
- 6mm untwisted white bugle x 1
- 11° light pink seeds x 2
- 11° dark pink seeds x 2

Unit 2 (bottom to top)

- 11° dark pink seed x 1
- 11° light pink seed x 1
- 6mm untwisted white bugle x 1
- 11° white seeds x 3

Ladder 2 will wrap around the outer points of the netting from the previous row. The first unit and the last unit will extend from the first to the last netted point.

Build ladder 2 and pin it to the template.

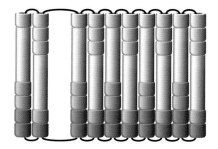

Sew through the first unit of ladder 2, exiting the inside edge, and then through the 11° dark pink seed at the bottom center of the first net. Sew through the next unit, exiting the outside edge. Weave in and out

through the ladder until you reach the next netted point. Sew through this point. Continue to the end of the ladder, joining net points as you reach them.

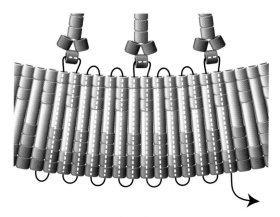

Step D: Branched Fringe

Begin at the center of ladder 2 and work from left to right. Find the unit nearest to the halfway point. Count two units outward on both sides for a total of five bead units. Sew through the first of the five units, exiting the outside of ladder 2.

Pick up:

- 11° dark pink seeds x 5
- 11° light pink seeds x 5
- 6mm untwisted white bugle bead x 1
- 11° white seeds x 2
- 6mm untwisted white bugle bead x 1
- 11° light pink seeds x 5
- 11° dark pink seeds x 11

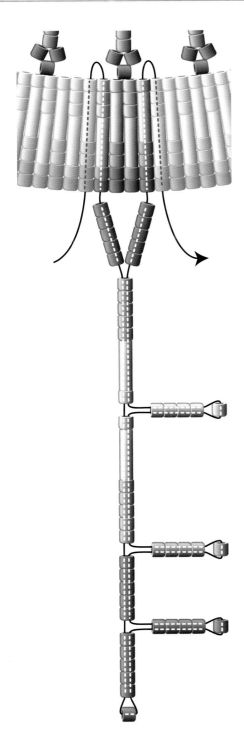

Skip the last bead and sew back through the next five beads. String five 11° dark pink seeds, skip the last bead, and sew through the next four beads to complete the first branch.

Sew through the next five 11° dark pink seeds. String five 11° light pink seeds, skip the last bead, and sew through the next four beads to complete the second branch.

Sew through the next seven beads, exiting the first of two 11° white seeds. String five 11° white seeds, skip the last bead, and sew through the next four beads to complete the last branch.

Sew through the next seven beads. Pick up five 11° dark pink seeds.

Enter the outside of ladder 2 through the unit that is three units away from the one that you last exited (you will have skipped two bead units).

Sew through the next unit, exiting the outside of ladder 2, and begin the next strand of branched fringe. Work to the end of the ladder. Repeat for the second half of the neckpiece.

Step E: Finishing

Add a closure to the open ends of the neckpiece. Weave in the thread ends. Attach a clasp. If necessary, refer to the finishing technique instructions on pages 134–136.

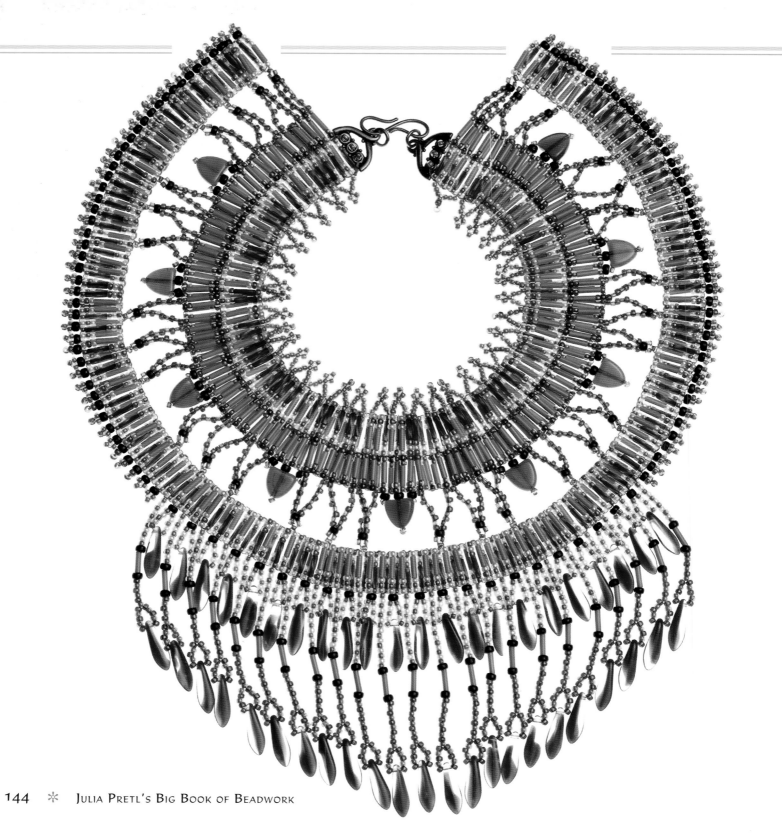

New Mexico

The bold colors and rhythmic patterns of this design evoke the landscape of the American Southwest.

BEAD KEY

6mm twisted dark red bugles
size A = 9 g; size B = 11 g;
size C = 12 g

6mm untwisted orange bugles
size A = 9 g; size B = 11 g;
size C = 12 g

6mm untwisted lavender bugles
size A = 9 g; size B = 10 g;
size C = 11 g

11° dark red seeds
size A = 9 g; size B = 10 g;
size C = 11 g

11° dusty rose seeds
size A = 33 g; size B = 38 g;
size C = 43 g

11° white seeds
size A = 13 g; size B = 15 g;
size C = 17 g

8° purple seeds
size A = 8 g; size B = 9 g;
size C = 10 g

**6mm x 8mm purple drops
(vertical hole)**
size A = 13 beads; size B = 16 beads;
size C = 19 beads

Large rust-colored daggers
All sizes = 45 beads

Step A: Ladder 1

Unit 1 (top to bottom)
- 11° dusty rose seed x 1
- 6mm twisted dark red bugle x 1
- 11° dusty rose seed x 1
- 11° white seed x 1
- 11° dusty rose seed x 1

Unit 2 (bottom to top)
- 11° white seed x 1
- 6mm untwisted orange bugle x 1
- 11° white seed x 1
- 11° dusty rose seed x 1
- 11° white seed x 1

Build ladder 1 and pin it to the template.

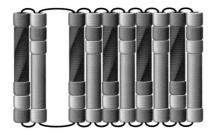

Step B: Top Netting

Begin at the center of ladder 1 and work from left to right. Find the bead unit nearest to the halfway point. Count two units outward on both sides for a total of five bead units. Sew through the first of the five units, exiting the inside of ladder 1.

Pick up seven 11° dusty rose seeds. Skip the last three beads and sew through the fourth bead, making sure not to split the thread.

Pick up three 11° dusty rose seeds and sew through the last of the five bead units, skipping the three center units and exiting the outside

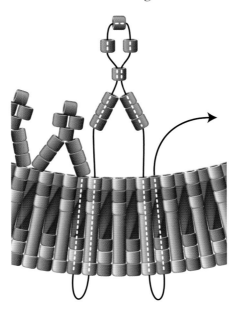

of ladder 1. Pull snug so that no thread is exposed. This is your first net.

Sew up through the next bead unit of ladder 1, exiting the inside edge. Continue to make nets to the end of the ladder. Repeat to build the remaining half of ladder 1.

Step C: Ladder 2

Unit 1 (top to bottom)
- 11° dark red seed x 1
- 11° dusty rose seed x 1
- 6mm untwisted lavender bugle x 1
- 11° dusty rose seed x 1

Unit 2 (bottom to top)
- 11° dark red seed x 1
- 11° dusty rose seed x 1
- 6mm untwisted lavender bugle x 1
- 11° dusty rose seed x 1

Build ladder 2 and pin it to the template.

Join ladder 1 and ladder 2.

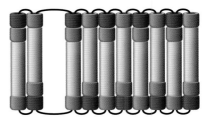

Step D: Picots, Drops, and Netting

Begin at the center of ladder 2 and work from left to right. Find the two bead units nearest to the halfway point. Count two units outward on both sides for a total of six bead units. Sew through the first of the six units, exiting the outside of ladder 2.

Pick up one 8° purple seed and one 11° dusty rose seed. Skip the 11° seed and sew up through the 8° seed and the next unit of ladder 2, making sure not to split the thread. This is your first picot. Sew back down through the next unit of ladder 2, exiting the outside edge.

Pick up one 8° purple seed, one purple drop, and one 11° dusty rose

seed. Skip the last bead and sew up through the other two. Sew up through the next unit of ladder 2, exiting the inside edge, and then back out through the subsequent unit. Add one more picot to the other side of the drop.

Each net will occupy a total of five bead units.

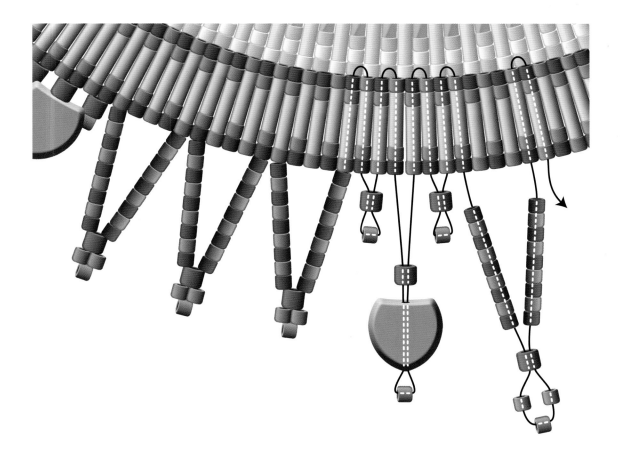

Pick up:

- 11° dark red seed x 1
- 11° dusty rose seed x 1
  (repeat four times)
- 11° dark red seed x 1
- 8° purple seed x 1
- 11° dusty rose seeds x 3

Skip the last three beads and sew up through the 8° purple seed, making sure not to split the thread.

Pick up:

- 11° dark red seed x 1
- 11° dusty rose seed x 1
  (repeat four times)
- 11° dark red seed x 1

Sew through the last of the five bead units, skipping the three center units and exiting the inside of ladder 2. Pull snug so that no thread is exposed. This is your first net.

Sew through the next bead unit of ladder 2, exiting the outside edge. Make two more net segments.

Continue this pattern, making a picot, a drop, a picot, and then three net segments to the end of the ladder. Be sure to end the ladder with a net segment, even if it means ending with more than three net segments. Repeat for the remaining half of ladder 2, beginning with three net segments.

Pin all of the netted ends in place so that they are stretched taut and evenly distributed.

Step E: Ladder 3

Ladder 3 will wrap around the outer points of the netting from the previous row. The first unit and the last unit will extend from the first to the last netted point.

Unit 1 (top to bottom)

- 11° dusty rose seed x 1
- 11° white seed x 1
- 11° dusty rose seed x 1
- 6mm twisted dark red bugle x 1
- 11° dusty rose seed x 1

Unit 2 (bottom to top)

- 11° white seed x 1
- 11° dusty rose seed x 1
- 11° white seed x 1
- 6mm untwisted orange bugle x 1
- 11° white seed x 1

Build ladder 3 and pin it to the template.

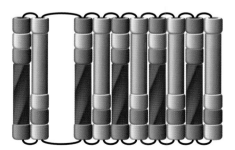

Sew through the first unit of ladder 3, exiting the inside edge, and then through the 11° dusty rose seed at the bottom center of the first net. Sew through the next unit, exiting the outside edge. Weave in and out through the ladder until you reach the next netted point. Sew through this point. Continue to the end of the ladder, joining net points as you reach them.

The fringe for this neckpiece contains forty-five strands and occupies ninety bead units. The remainder of the bottom edge of ladder 3 is lined with picots. Find the two bead units nearest to the halfway point. Sew through the first of the two bead units, exiting the outside edge.

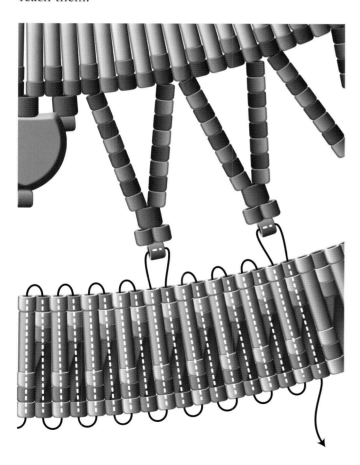

Step F: Long Fringe

Pick up:
- 11° dusty rose seed x 1
- 11° white seed x 1
  (repeat five more times)
- 11° dusty rose seed x 1
- 8° purple seed x 1
- 6mm untwisted lavender bugle x 1
- 8° purple seed x 1
- 11° dark red seed x 1
- 11° dusty rose seed x 1
- 11° dark red seed x 1
  (repeat four more times)
- Large rust-colored dagger x 1
- 11° dark red seed x 1
- 11° dusty rose seed x 1
- 11° dark red seed x 1
- 11° dusty rose seed x 1
- 11° dark red seed x 1

Skip five seed beads on either side of the dagger and sew up through the remainder of the strand. Then sew through the second of the two center units, exiting the inside of ladder 3. Turn and sew through the subsequent bead unit.

Step G: Short Dagger Loop

Pick up:
- 8° purple seed x 1
- 11° dusty rose seed x 1
- 11° white seed x 1
- 11° dusty rose seed x 1
- 11° white seed x 1
- 11° dusty rose seed x 1
- Large rust dagger x 1
- 11° dusty rose seed x 1
- 11° white seed x 1
- 11° dusty rose seed x 1
- 11° white seed x 1
- 11° dusty rose seed x 1

Sew up through the 8° purple seed and then through the next bead unit, exiting the inside of ladder 3. Turn and sew through the subsequent bead unit.

Repeat this process, alternating between long fringe strands and short dagger loops to the ⅜ mark on your template.

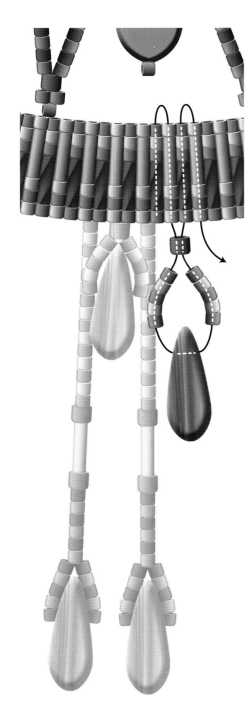

Step H: Picots

Pick up one 8° purple seed and three 11° dusty rose seeds. Skip the rose seeds and sew through the purple seed and then up through the next bead unit. This is your first picot. Turn and exit the outside edge of ladder one.

Continue to add a picot between every two bead units, working to the end of the ladder. Repeat this entire process to complete the remaining half of ladder 3.

Step I: Finishing

Add a closure to the open ends of the neckpiece. Weave in the thread ends. Attach a clasp. If necessary, refer to the finishing technique instructions on pages 134–136.

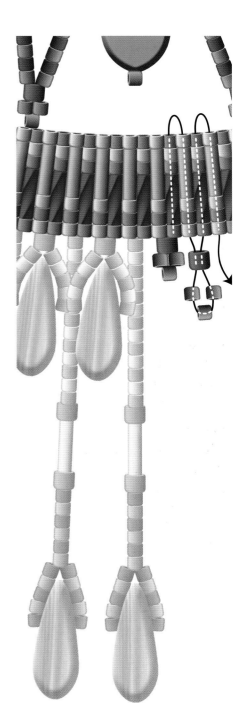

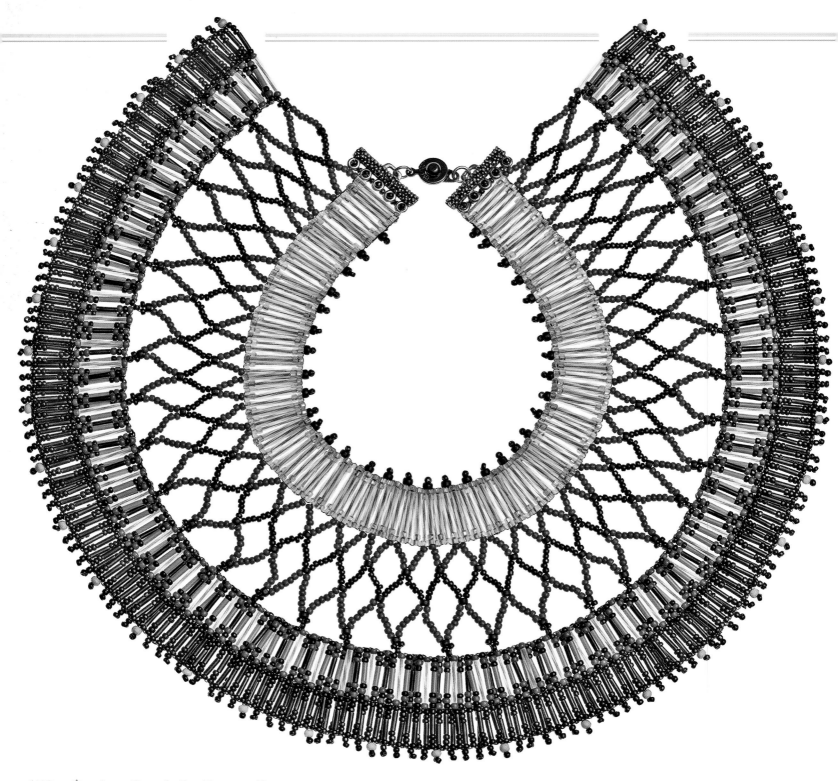

Chartreuse

This bold design combines techniques to create broad netting and picoted fringe.

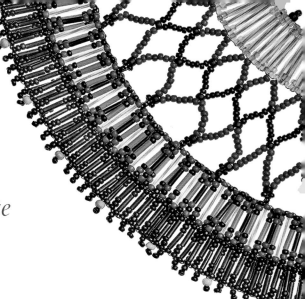

BEAD KEY

12mm twisted chartreuse bugles
size A = 20 g; size B = 23 g;
size C = 27 g

6mm untwisted purple bugles
size A = 16 g; size B = 17 g;
size C = 19 g

6mm untwisted lavender bugles
size A = 6 g; size B = 7 g;
size C = 7 g

11° purple seeds
size A = 36 g; size B = 41 g;
size C = 46 g

11° lavender seeds
size A = 19 g; size B = 23 g;
size C = 26 g

11° chartreuse seeds
size A = 7 g; size B = 8 g;
size C = 9 g

8° purple seeds
size A = 5 g; size B = 6 g;
size C = 7 g

8° chartreuse seeds
size A = 2 g; size B = 2 g;
size C = 2 g

Step A: Ladder 1

Unit 1 (top to bottom)
- 11° chartreuse seeds x 2
- 12mm twisted chartreuse bugle x 1
- 11° chartreuse seed x 1

Unit 2 (bottom to top)
- 11° chartreuse seeds x 2
- 12mm twisted chartreuse bugle x 1
- 11° chartreuse seed x 1

Build ladder 1 and pin it to the template.

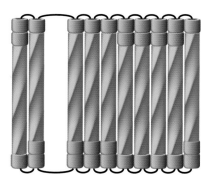

Step B: Picots and Netting

Begin at the center of ladder 1 and work from left to right. Find the two bead units nearest to the halfway point. Count two units outward on both sides for a total of six bead units. Sew through the first unit, exiting the inside of ladder 1.

Pick up one 8° purple seed and one 11° purple seed. Skip the last seed and sew through the 8° seed and then through the next bead unit, exiting the outside edge of ladder 1. This is your first picot.

Pick up:
- 11° lavender seed x 5
- 8° purple seed x 1
- 11° purple seeds x 6
- 8° purple seed x 1
- 11° lavender seeds x 7
- 8° purple seed x 1
- 11° purple seeds x 3

Skip the last three beads and sew through the next 8° seed. Pick up seven 11° lavender seeds, one 8° seed, and six purple seeds, then sew through the first 8° added for the netting. Pick up five 11° lavender seeds, skip three bead units, and sew through the last of the bead units, exiting the inside edge of ladder 1. This is your first net.

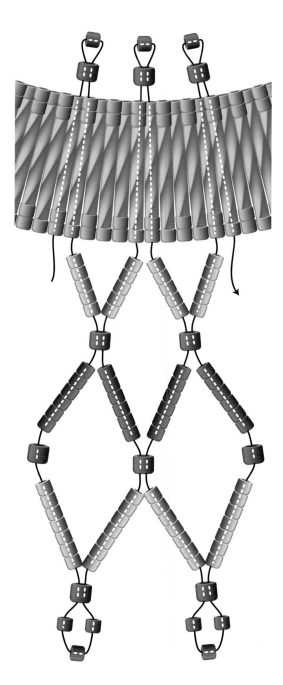

Make another picot and sew through the next bead unit, exiting the outside of ladder 1. Begin the next segment.

Pick up:
- 11° lavender seeds x 5
- 8° purple seed x 1
- 11° purple seeds x 6

Sew through the first open 8° purple seed. Complete this net segment as you did the previous one. Continue to add picots and netting to the end of the ladder. Complete the remaining half of the ladder in the same manner.

Step C: Ladder 2

Ladder 2 will wrap around the outer points of the netting from the previous row. The first unit and the last unit will extend from the first to the last netted point.

Unit 1 (top to bottom)
- 11° lavender seed x 1
- 12mm twisted chartreuse bugle x 1
- 11° lavender seed x 1

Unit 2 (bottom to top)
- 11° purple seed x 1
- 11° lavender seed x 1
- 11° purple seed x 1
- 6mm untwisted lavender bugle x 1
- 11° purple seed x 1
- 11° lavender seed x 1
- 11° purple seed x 1

Unit 3 (top to bottom)
- 11° lavender seed x 1
- 11° purple seed x 1
- 11° lavender seed x 1
- 6mm untwisted purple bugle x 1
- 11° lavender seed x 1
- 11° purple seed x 1
- 11° lavender seed x 1

Unit 4 (bottom to top)
- 11° purple seed x 1
- 11° lavender seed x 1
- 11° purple seed x 1
- 6mm untwisted lavender bugle x 1
- 11° purple seed x 1
- 11° lavender seed x 1
- 11° purple seed x 1

Build ladder 2 and pin it to the template.

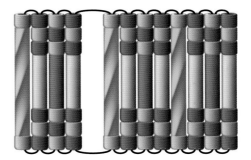

Sew through the first unit of ladder 2, exiting the inside edge, and then through the 11° purple seed at the bottom center of the first net. Sew through the next unit, exiting the outside edge. Weave in and out through the ladder until you reach the next netted point. Sew through this point. Continue to the end of the ladder, joining net points as you reach them.

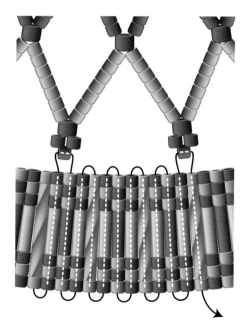

Step D: Ladder 3

Unit 1 (top to bottom)

- 11° purple seed x 1
- 6mm untwisted purple bugle x 1
- 11° purple seeds x 3

Unit 2 (bottom to top)

- 11° purple seed x 1
- 6mm untwisted purple bugle x 1
- 11° purple seeds x 3

Build ladder 3 and pin it to the template. Join ladder 2 and ladder 3.

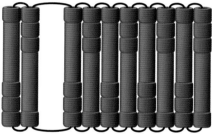

Step E: Short Fringe and Picots

Begin at the center of ladder 3 and work from left to right. Find the two bead units nearest to the halfway point. Sew through the first of the two units, exiting the outside of ladder 3.

Pick up one 8° chartreuse seed and one 11° purple seed. Skip the last seed and sew through the 8° seed and then through the next bead unit, exiting the inside edge of ladder 3. This is your first picot.

Turn and sew through the next bead unit to exit the outside of ladder 3. Pick up three 11° purple seeds. Skip the last seed and sew up through the other two and then through the next bead unit, exiting the inside of ladder 3. Repeat this step three more times until you have four short fringe strands.

Make another picot.

Continue to make four short fringe strands for every picot as you work to the end of the ladder. Repeat the steps to complete the remaining half of the ladder.

Step F: Finishing

Add a closure to the open ends of the neckpiece. Weave in the thread ends. Attach a clasp. If necessary, refer to the finishing technique instructions on pages 134–136.

Drab

Subtle color changes give this neckpiece an air of simple elegance.

BEAD KEY

12mm twisted brown metallic bugles
size A = 21 g; size B = 24 g;
size C = 28 g

6mm untwisted dark green metallic bugles
size A = 22 g; size B = 26 g;
size C = 29 g

11° dark green luster seeds
size A = 72 g; size B = 83 g;
size C = 94 g

8° brown matte metallic seeds
size A = 3 g; size B = 4 g;
size C = 4 g

6mm assorted color pearls
size A = 17 pearls; size B = 24 pearls;
size C = 28 pearls

Step A: Ladder 1

Unit 1 (top to bottom)

- 11° dark green luster seed x 1
- 12mm twisted brown metallic bugle x 1
- 11° dark green luster seed x 1

Unit 2 (bottom to top)

- 11° dark green luster seeds x 3
- 6mm untwisted dark green metallic bugle x 1
- 11° dark green luster seeds x 3

Build ladder 1 and pin it to the template.

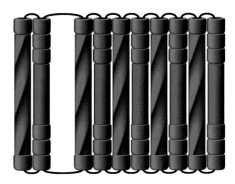

Step B: Ladder 2 and Netting

In this neckpiece, ladder 2 does *not* wrap around ladder 1. Instead, measure 1.5 cm from the outside edge of ladder 1 and mark it on the halfway line. Make a new circle by setting your compass from the center of the template to the 1.5 cm mark on the halfway marker line. You'll use this circle as a guide when pinning ladder 2 to the template. The netting will span the distance between the two ladders.

Unit 1 (top to bottom)

- 11° dark green luster seed x 1
- 12mm twisted brown metallic bugle x 1
- 11° dark green luster seed x 1

Unit 2 (bottom to top)

- 11° dark green luster seeds x 3
- 6mm untwisted dark green metallic bugle x 1
- 11° dark green luster seeds x 3

Build ladder 2 and pin it to the template.

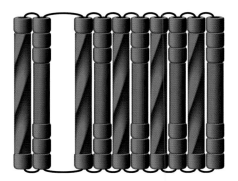

Begin at the center of ladder 1 and work from left to right. Find the two units nearest to the halfway point. Sew through the unit first of the two units, exiting the outside of ladder 1.

Pick up:

- 11° dark green luster seed x 1
- 8° brown matte metallic seed x 1
- 6mm pearl x 1
- 8° brown matte metallic seed x 1
- 11° dark green luster seed x 1

Make a ray by extending a length of thread from the center point of the template and between the two center units of ladder 1 to the corresponding pair of bead units for ladder 2. For the first net, the ray will be on the vertical centerline of the template. Sew through the first unit, exiting the outside of ladder 2. Sew through the next unit, exiting the inside of the ladder.

Pick up one 11° dark green luster seed. Skip the first 11° bead of the net and sew through the next three beads. Pick up one 11° dark green luster seed and sew through the next bead unit of ladder 1. This is your first net.

Sew down and then up through the next two bead units. Pick up three 11° dark green luster seeds and sew down through the next bead unit. This is your first picot.

Sew up and then down through the next two bead units. Pick up three 11° dark green luster seeds and sew up through the next bead unit to make a picot at the outside edge of ladder 1.

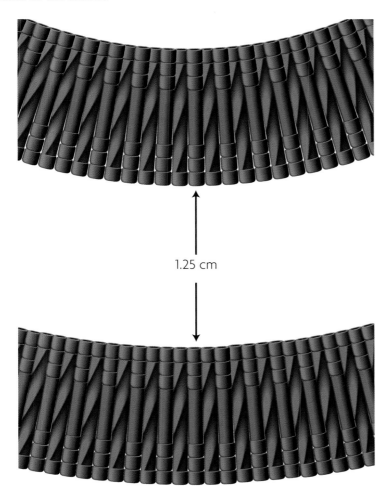

1.25 cm

Sew down and then up through the next two bead units. Pick up three 11° dark green luster seeds and sew up through the next bead unit to make a second picot at the inside edge of ladder 1.

Sew up and then down through the next two bead units and begin a new net. Continue to the end of the ladder.

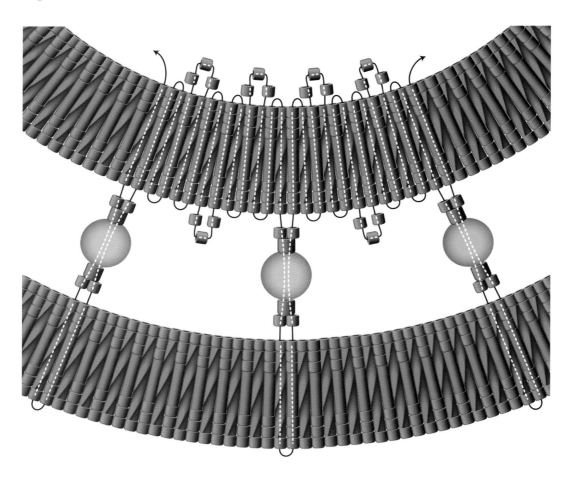

Ideally, both halves of ladder 1 will end with a net, which will ensure that ladder 2 is supported. If not, continue until you have three units remaining. Exit either the outside edge of ladder 1 or the inside of ladder 2, depending on the location of the last picot or net you made. Pick up a strand (usually 9 to 10 beads) of 11° dark green luster seeds. Sew through the corresponding bead unit so that the strand bridges the two ladders. Sew through the next unit and repeat this process two more times.

Step C: Ladder 3 and Picots

Unit 1 (top to bottom)

- 11° dark green luster seeds x 2
- 6mm untwisted dark green metallic bugle x 1
- 11° dark green luster seed x 1

Unit 2 (bottom to top)

- 11° dark green luster seeds x 2
- 6mm untwisted dark green metallic bugle x 1
- 11° dark green luster seed x 1

Build ladder 3 and pin it to the template.

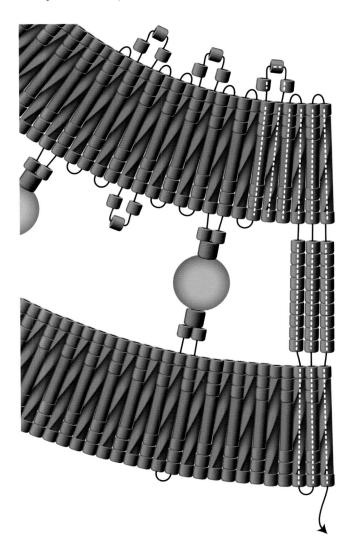

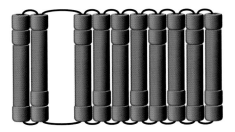

Join ladder 2 and ladder 3. Each time you exit the inside edge of ladder 2 at the midpoint between two nets, pick up three 11° dark green luster seeds to make a picot.

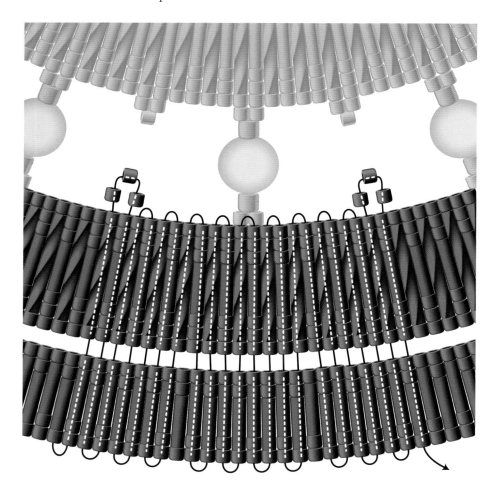

Step D: Fringe

Begin at the center of ladder 3 and work from left to right. Find the two bead units nearest to the halfway point. Sew through the first of the two units, exiting the outside of ladder 3.

Pick up:

- 8° brown matte metallic seed x 1
- 11° dark green luster seeds x 5
- 12mm twisted brown metallic bugle x 1
- 11° dark green luster seeds x 5
- 6mm untwisted dark green metallic bugle x 1
- 11° dark green luster seeds x 50
- 6mm untwisted dark green metallic bugle x 1
- 11° dark green luster seeds x 5
- 12mm twisted brown metallic bugle x 1
- 11° dark green luster seeds x 5

Sew back up through the 8° seed and the second center bead unit, forming a loop with the rest of the strand. Turn and sew through the next unit, exiting the outside of ladder 3.

To make the next fringe loop, pick up the same bead sequence as you did for the previous—but this time pick up forty-nine 11° dark green luster seeds instead of fifty.

Continue to make fringe loops, reducing the large group of beads by one bead each time, until you are working with twenty-five beads. Making no further reductions, continue making fringe loops until you reach the ⅜ line of your template.

Repeat this process to complete the remaining half of the bottom fringe.

Step E: Finishing

Add a closure to the open ends of the neckpiece. Weave in the thread ends. Attach a clasp. If necessary, refer to the finishing technique instructions on pages 134–136.

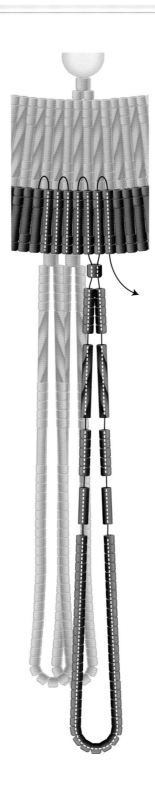

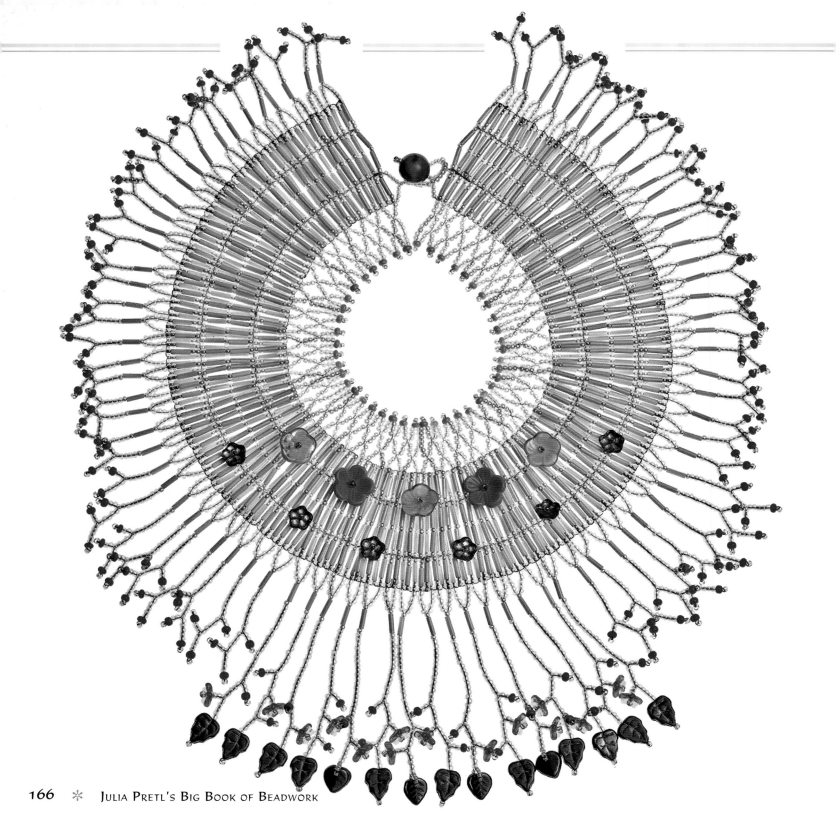

Meadow

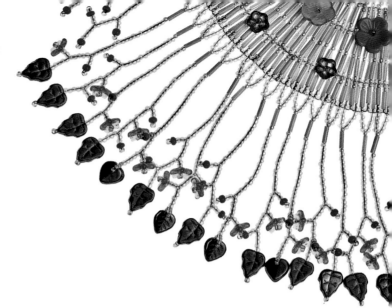

Meadow combines brightly colored ladders and pressed-glass flowers to create the look and feel of springtime.

BEAD KEY

6mm untwisted cream bugles
size A = 8 g; size B = 9 g;
size C = 11 g

6mm untwisted yellow bugles
size A = 20 g; size B = 23 g;
size C = 26 g

11° pale yellow seeds
size A = 30 g; size B = 36 g;
size C = 42 g

11° pale green seeds
size A = 33 g; size B = 37 g;
size C = 42 g

8° yellow seeds
size A = 2 g; size B = 2 g;
size C = 3 g

8° pale blue seeds
size A = 8 g; size B = 9 g;
size C = 10 g

Small green pressed-glass flowers (6)

Small yellow pressed-glass flowers (15)

Large yellow pressed-glass flowers (3)

Large blue pressed-glass flowers (2)

Pressed-glass green leaves, with vertical hole (15)

Step A: Ladder 1

Unit 1 (top to bottom)

- 11° pale yellow seeds x 2
- 6mm untwisted cream bugle x 1
- 11° pale yellow seed x 1

Unit 2 (bottom to top)

- 11° pale yellow seeds x 2
- 6mm untwisted cream bugle x 1
- 11° pale yellow seed x 1

Build ladder 1 and pin it to the template.

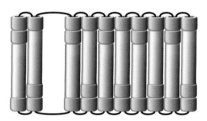

Step B: Ladder 2

Unit 1 (top to bottom)

- 11° pale yellow seed x 1
- 6mm untwisted yellow bugle x 1
- 11° pale yellow seed x 1
- 6mm untwisted cream bugle x 1
- 11° pale yellow seed x 1

Unit 2 (bottom to top)

- 11° pale yellow seed x 1
- 6mm untwisted yellow bugle x 1
- 11° pale yellow seed x 1
- 6mm untwisted cream bugle x 1
- 11° pale yellow seed x 1

Build ladder 2 and pin it to the template. Join ladder 1 and ladder 2.

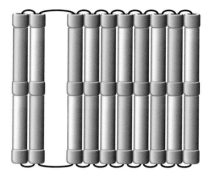

Step C: Ladder 3

Unit 1 (top to bottom)

- 11° pale yellow seed x 1
- 6mm untwisted yellow bugle x 1
- 11° pale green seeds x 2

Unit 2 (bottom to top)

- 11° pale green seed x 1
- 6mm untwisted yellow bugle x 1
- 11° pale yellow seeds x 2

Build ladder 3 and pin it to the template. Join ladder 2 and ladder 3.

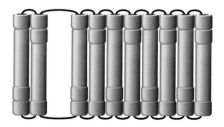

Step D: Top Netting and Surface Embellishment

Arrange the pressed glass flowers on the completed ladders in two rows: one row between ladders 1 and 2; the other between ladders 2 and 3. Very carefully pin each large yellow, large blue, and small green pressed-glass flower between the ladders, following the layout diagram on page 169 (or create your own design).

Begin the netting at the center of ladder 1 and work from left to right. Find the two bead units nearest to the halfway point. Sew through the second of the two units, exiting the inside of ladder 1.

Pick up:

- 11° pale yellow seeds x 3
- 11° pale green seed x 1
- 11° pale yellow seeds x 3
- 11° pale green seed x 1
- 11° pale yellow seeds x 3
- 8° yellow seed x 1
- 11° pale yellow seed x 1

Skip the last bead and sew through the 8° yellow seed.

Pick up:

- 11° pale yellow seeds x 3
- 11° pale green seed x 1
- 11° pale yellow seeds x 3

Skip the next seven beads and sew through the corresponding 11° pale green seed. String three 11° pale yellow seeds, skip two bead units from where you began, and sew through the next bead unit, exiting the outside of ladder 1. You may have to temporarily remove one or more pressed-glass flowers to perform this step. Sew back up through the next unit to continue the netting.

Whenever you reach a pressed-glass flower between the first and second ladders, sew through the back of the flower and pick up one 11° pale green seed. Sew back through the flower and then through the next bead unit, exiting the inside of ladder 1.

Pick up:

- 11° pale yellow seeds x 3
- 11° pale green seed x 1
- 11° pale yellow seeds x 3

Skip the first seven beads of the previous net segment and sew through the corresponding 11° pale green seed. Complete this net segment as you did the previous segment.

Continue to the end of ladder, netting the inside edge of ladder 1 and attaching pressed-glass flowers where necessary. Repeat this process to complete the netting on the remaining half of the ladder.

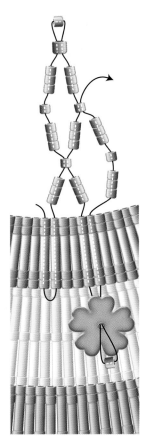

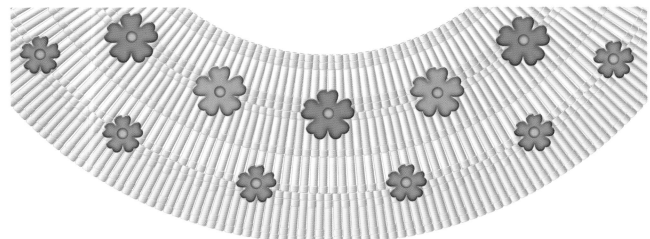

Step E: Fringe and Surface Embellishment

As you add strands of fringe to the outside edge of ladder 3, attach the remaining pressed-glass flowers to the neckpiece, as you did for the netting.

Begin the fringe at the center of ladder 3 and work from left to right. Find the bead unit nearest to the halfway point and count outward by one unit on each side for a total of three units. Sew through the first of the three units, exiting the outside of ladder 3.

The center section alternates between a three-branch fringe strand and a two-branch fringe strand.

Three-Branch Fringe Strand

Pick up:

- 11° pale green seeds x 5
- 11° pale yellow seed x 1
- 6mm untwisted yellow bugle x 1
- 11° pale yellow seed x 1
- 11° pale green seeds x 30
- pressed-glass green leaf x 1
- 11° pale green seed x 1

Skip the last seed and sew back through the leaf bead and the next five seed beads.

Pick up:

- 11° pale green seeds x 2
- 8° pale blue seed x 1
- 11° pale green seed x 1

Skip the last bead and sew through the remaining three to complete the first branch.
Sew through the next five 11° pale green seeds.

Pick up:

- 11° pale green seeds x 2
- small yellow pressed-glass flower x 1
- 11° pale green seed x 1

Skip the last bead and sew through the remaining three to complete the second branch.
Sew through the next five 11° pale green seeds.

Pick up:

- 11° pale green seeds x 2
- 8° pale blue seed x 1
- 11° pale green seed x 1

Skip the last bead and sew through the remaining three to complete the third branch.

Sew through the next eighteen beads, stopping before the last five 11° pale green seeds. Pick up five 11° pale green seeds and sew through the last of the three bead units, exiting the inside of ladder 3. Attach a pressed-glass flower if necessary and sew through the next unit, exiting the outside edge of ladder 3.

Two-Branch Fringe Strand

Pick up:

- 11° pale green seeds x 5
- 11° pale yellow seed x 1
- 6mm untwisted yellow bugle x 1
- 11° pale yellow seed x 1
- 11° pale green seeds x 30
- pressed-glass green leaf x 1
- 11° pale green seed x 1

Skip the last seed and sew back through the leaf bead and the next five seed beads.

Pick up:

- 11° pale green seeds x 2
- small yellow pressed-glass flower x 1
- 11° pale green seed x 1

Skip the last bead and sew through the remaining three to complete the first branch. Sew through the next five 11° pale green seeds.

Pick up:

- 11° pale green seeds x 2
- 8° pale blue seed x 1
- 11° pale green seed x 1

Skip the last bead and sew through the remaining three to complete the second branch.
Sew through the next twenty-three beads, stopping before the last five 11° pale green seeds. Pick up five 11° pale green seeds and sew through the last of the three bead units, exiting on the inside of ladder 3. Attach a pressed-glass flower if necessary and sew through the next unit, exiting the outside edge of ladder 3.

Alternate between three- and two-branch fringe strands to make a total of eight strands. Next, you'll begin two levels of short branched fringe.

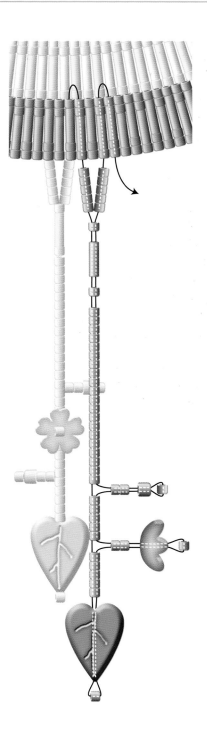

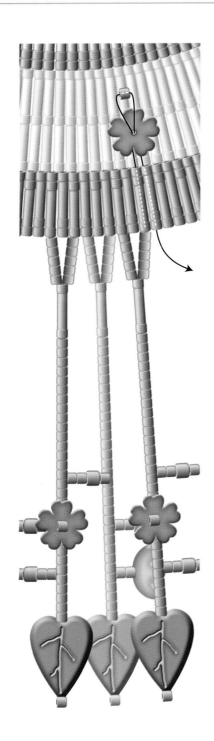

First Level (repeat eight times)

Pick up:

- 11° pale green seeds x 5
- 11° pale yellow seed x 1
- 6mm untwisted yellow bugle x 1
- 11° pale yellow seed x 1
- 11° pale green seeds x 20
- 8° pale blue seed x 1
- 11° pale green seed x 1

Skip the last seed and sew back through the 8° pale blue seed and the next five seed beads.

Pick up:

- 11° pale green seeds x 2
- 8° pale blue seed x 1
- 11° pale green seed x 1

Skip the last bead and sew through the remaining three to complete the first branch.

Sew through the next five 11° pale green seeds.

Pick up:

- 11° pale green seeds x 2
- 8° pale blue seed x 1
- 11° pale green seed x 1

Skip the last bead and sew through the remaining three to complete the second branch.

Sew through the next thirteen beads, stopping before the last five 11° pale green seeds. Pick up five 11° pale green seeds and sew through the last of the three bead units, exiting the inside of ladder 3. Attach a pressed-glass flower if necessary and sew through the next unit, exiting the outside edge of ladder 3.

Second Level (repeat to the end of the ladder)

Pick up:

- 11° pale green seeds x 5
- 11° pale yellow seed x 1
- 6mm untwisted yellow bugle x 1
- 11° pale yellow seed x 1
- 11° pale green seeds x 10
- 8° pale blue seed x 1
- 11° pale green seed x 1

Skip the last seed and sew back through the 8° pale blue seed and the next five seed beads.

Pick up:

- 11° pale green seeds x 2
- 8° pale blue seed x 1
- 11° pale green seed x 1

Skip the last bead and sew through the remaining three to complete the second branch.

Sew through the next eight beads, stopping before the last five 11° pale green seeds. Pick up five 11° pale green seeds and sew through the last of the three bead units, exiting the inside of ladder 3. Attach a pressed-glass flower if necessary and sew through the next unit, exiting the outside edge of ladder 3.

Repeat these steps to complete the remaining half of the ladder.

Step F: Finishing

Add a closure to the open ends of the neckpiece. Weave in the thread ends. Attach a clasp. If necessary, refer to the finishing technique instructions on pages 134–136.

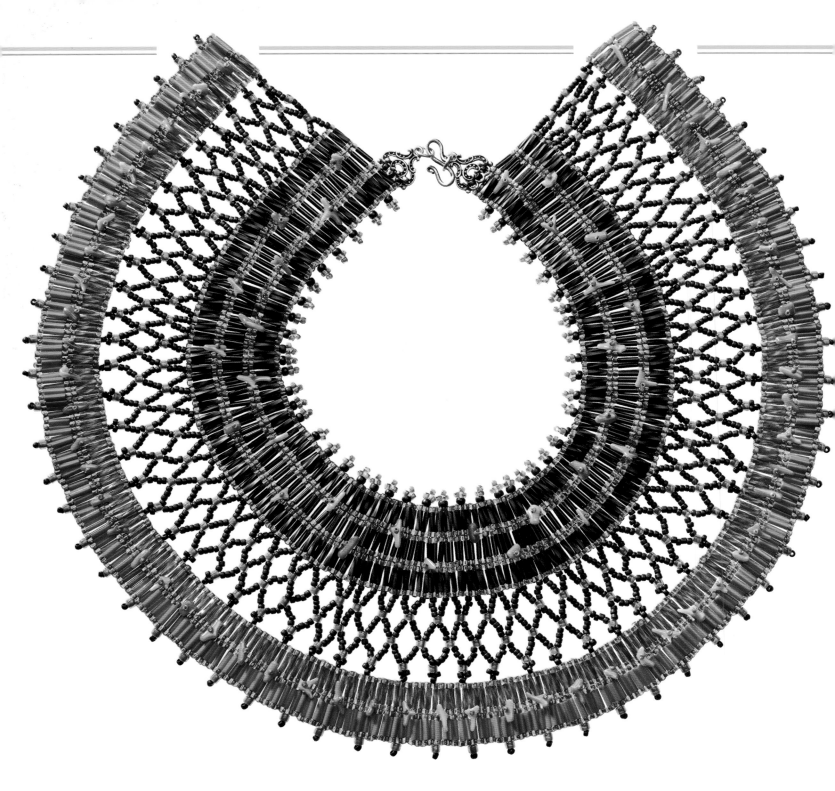

Ember

This fiery neckpiece has strong contrasting colors and tightly woven netting.

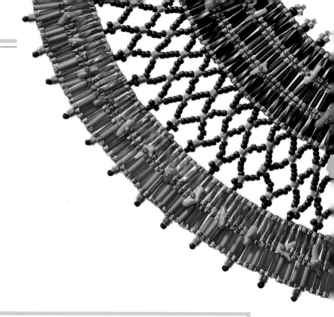

BEAD KEY

6mm twisted black matte bugles
size A = 16 g; size B = 19 g;
size C = 22 g

6mm untwisted black bugles
size A = 8 g; size B = 9 g;
size C = 10 g

6mm twisted red bugles
size A = 13 g; size B = 14 g;
size C = 16 g

6mm untwisted red bugles
size A = 13 g; size B = 14 g;
size C = 16 g

11° black seeds
size A = 19 g; size B = 22 g;
size C = 25 g

11° red seeds
size A = 3 g; size B = 3 g; size C = 4 g

8° black seeds
size A = 2 g; size B = 2 g; size C = 3 g

8° red seeds
size A = 2 g; size B = 3 g;
size C = 3 g

Small coral pieces
size A = 87 beads; size B = 123
beads; size C = 137 beads

Step A: Ladder 1

All Units

- 11° red seed x 1
- 6mm twisted black matte bugle x 1
- 11° red seed x 1

Build ladder 1 and pin it to the template.

Step B: Ladder 2

All Units

- 11° red seed x 1
- 6mm untwisted black bugle x 1
- 11° red seed x 1

Build ladder 2 and pin it to the template. Join ladder 1 and ladder 2.

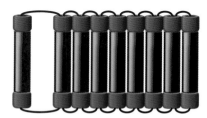

Step C: Ladder 3

All Units

- 11° red seed x 1
- 6mm twisted black matte bugle x 1
- 11° red seed x 1

Build ladder 3 and pin it to the template. Join ladder 2 and ladder 3.

Step D: Top Picots and Surface Embellishment

Begin at the center of ladder 1 and work from left to right. Find the two bead units nearest to the halfway point. Sew through the first of the two units, exiting the inside of ladder 1.

Pick up one 8° black seed and three 11° red seeds. Skip the red seeds and sew through the black one and then through the second bead unit of the two-unit group, exiting the outside of ladder 1. Weave up, down, and up through the next three bead units and make a second picot.

When you have exited the outside edge of ladder 1, pick up one coral piece and one 11° red seed. Sew back through the coral piece and up through the next bead unit. Weave down and then up through the next two bead units and make another picot.

Continue in this manner, attaching a coral piece after every third picot, until you reach the end of the ladder. Repeat to complete the remaining half of ladder 1.

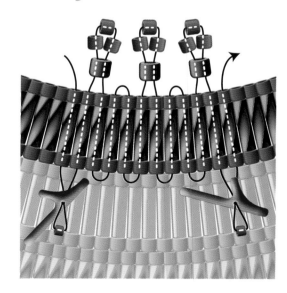

Step E: Netting and Surface Embellishment

Begin at the center of ladder 3 and work from left to right. Find the two bead units nearest the halfway point and count outward by one unit on each side for a total of four bead units. Sew through the first of the two units, exiting the outside of ladder 3.

Pick up:

- 11° black seeds x 4
- 8° red seed x 1
- 11° black seeds x 4
- 8° red seed x 1
- 11° black seeds x 4
- 8° red seed x 1
- 11° black seeds x 3

Skip the last three beads and sew through the 8° red seed.

Pick up:

- 11° black seeds x 4
- 8° red seed x 1
- 11° black seeds x 4

Skip the next nine beads and sew through the top 8° red seed. String four 11° black seeds and sew through the last bead unit in the four-unit group. Pick up one coral piece and one 11° red seed. Sew back through the coral piece and down through the next bead unit, exiting the outside of ladder 3. Now begin the next net segment.

Pick up:

- 11° black seeds x 4
- 8° red seed x 1
- 11° black seeds x 4

Sew through the middle 8° red seed. Complete this net segment as you did the first.

Continue in this manner, attaching a coral piece after every fourth net segment, until you reach the end of the ladder. Repeat to complete the remaining half of ladder 3.

Pin all of the netted ends in place so that they are taut and evenly distributed.

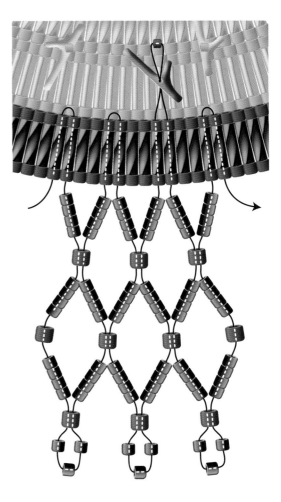

Step F: Ladder 4

All Units
- 11° red seed x 1
- 6mm twisted red bugle x 1
- 11° red seed x 1

Ladder 4 will wrap around the outer points of the netting from the previous row. The first unit and the last unit will extend from the first to the last netted point.

Build ladder 4 and pin it to the template.

Sew through the first unit of ladder 4, exiting the inside edge, and then through the 11° black seed at the bottom center of the first net. Sew through the next unit, exiting the outside edge. Weave in and out through the ladder until you reach the next netted point. Sew through this point. Continue to the end of the ladder, joining net points as you reach them.

Step G: Ladder 5

All Units

- 11° red seed x 1
- 6mm untwisted red bugle x 1
- 11° red seed x 1

Build ladder 5 and pin it to the template.

Step H: Bottom Picots and Surface Embellishment

Begin at the center of ladder 5 and work from left to right. Find the two bead units nearest to the halfway point. Sew through the first of the two units, exiting the outside of ladder 5.

Pick up one 8° red seed and one 11° black seed. Skip the black seed and sew through the red one and then through the second bead unit of the two-unit group, exiting the inside of ladder 5.

Pick up one coral piece and one 11° red seed. Sew back through the coral piece and down through the next bead unit. Weave up, down, up, and down through the next four bead units and make another picot.

Continue in this manner, attaching a coral piece after every picot, until you reach the end of the ladder. Repeat to complete the remaining half of ladder 3.

Step I: Finishing

Add a closure to the open ends of the neckpiece. Weave in the thread ends. Attach a clasp. If necessary, refer to the finishing technique instructions on pages 134–136.

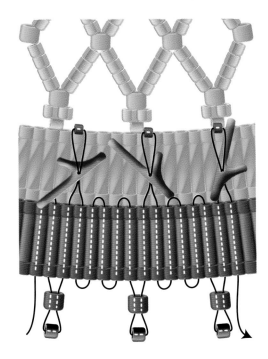

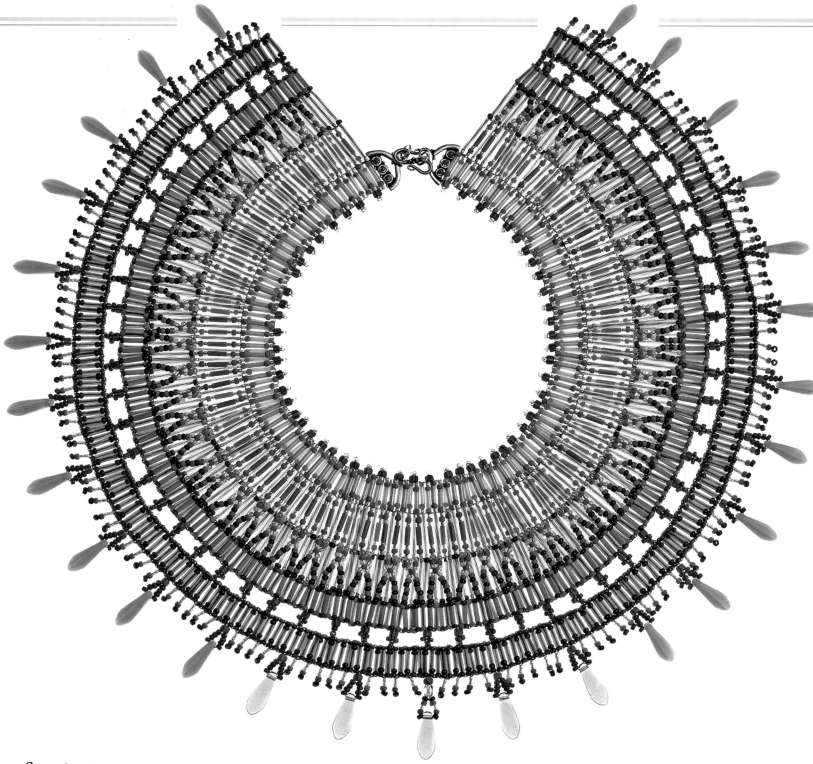

Spike

This striking collar combines layering and spiked fringe.

BEAD KEY

12mm twisted,
chartreuse bugles
size A = 27 g; size B = 13 g;
size C = 36 g

6mm untwisted,
dark turquoise bugles
size A = 17 g; size B = 19 g;
size C = 21 g

6mm untwisted,
light turquoise bugles
size A = 9 g; size B = 11 g;
size C = 12 g

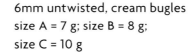

6mm untwisted, cream bugles
size A = 7 g; size B = 8 g;
size C = 10 g

11° dark turqoise seeds
size A = 25 g; size B = 28 g; size C = 31 g

11° light turquoise seeds
size A = 21 g; size B = 24 g; size C = 27 g

11° white seeds
size A = 20 g; size B = 24 g; size C = 27 g

8° dark turquoise seeds
size A = 5 g; size B = 5 g; size C = 6 g

Large turquoise and
chartreuse daggers
size A = 39; size B = 44; size C = 49

Step A: Ladder 1

Unit 1 (top to bottom)

- 11° white seed x 1
- 11° light turquoise seed x 1
- 6mm untwisted white bugle x 1
- 11° light turquoise seed x 1

Unit 2 (bottom to top)

- 11° white seed x 1
- 11° light turquoise seed x 1
- 6mm untwisted white bugle x 1
- 11° light turquoise seed x 1

Build ladder 1 and pin it to the template.

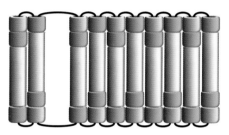

Step B: Ladder 2 and Inside Picots

Unit 1 (top to bottom)

- 11° white seed x 1
- 12mm twisted chartreuse bugle x 1
- 11° white seed x 1

Unit 2 (bottom to top)

- 11° white seed x 1
- 11° light turquoise seed x 1
- 11° white seed x 1
- 6mm untwisted light turquoise bugle x 1
- 11° white seed x 1
- 11° light turquoise seed x 1
- 11° white seed x 1

Build ladder 2 and pin it to the template.

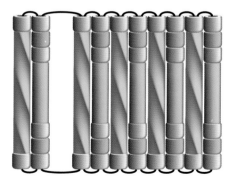

Join ladder 1 and ladder 2. Every other time that you exit the inside of ladder 1, pick up one 8° dark turquoise seed and one 11° white seed. Sew back through the 8° dark turquoise seed and then through the next bead unit to complete a picot.

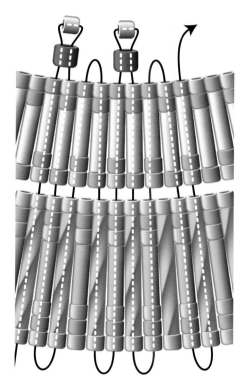

Step C: Ladder 3

Unit 1 (top to bottom)

- 11° dark turquoise seed x 1
- 12mm twisted chartreuse bugle x 1
- 11° white seed x 1

Unit 2 (bottom to top)

- 11° dark turquoise seed x 1
- 12mm twisted chartreuse bugle x 1
- 11° white seed x 1

Build ladder 3 and pin it to the template. Join ladder 2 and ladder 3.

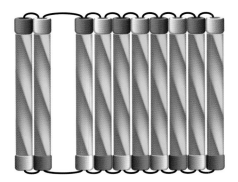

Step D: Ladder 4

Unit 1 (top to bottom)

- 11° light turquoise seed x 1
- 6mm untwisted dark turquoise bugle x 1
- 11° light turquoise seed x 1

Unit 2 (bottom to top)

- 11° dark turquoise seed x 1
- 6mm untwisted light turquoise bugle x 1
- 11° dark turquoise seed x 1

Build ladder 3 and pin it to the template. Join ladder 3 and ladder 4.

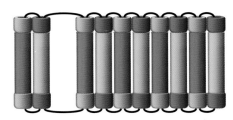

Step E: Net Overlay and Outside Picots

This netting spans from the inside of ladder 4 to the outside of ladder 2, overlaying ladder 3.

Begin at the center of ladder 4 and work from left to right. Find the unit nearest to the halfway point. Count two units outward on both sides for a total of five bead units. Sew through the first unit of the five units, exiting the inside of ladder 4.

Pick up:

• 11° dark turquoise seed x 1
• 11° light turquoise seed x 1
• 11° dark turquoise seed x 1
• 11° light turquoise seed x 1
• 11° dark turquoise seed x 1
• 11° light turquoise seed x 1
• 11° white seed x 1
• 11° light turquoise seed x 1
• 11° white seed x 1
• 11° light turquoise seed x 1
• 11° white seed x 1

Make a ray to the center of the template by extending a length of thread from the center of ladder 4's five-bead unit to the center point of the template. For the first net, this

ray will be on the vertical center-line of the template. Find the two units of ladder 2 that are closest to the ray and sew through first unit, exiting the inside of the ladder. Sew through the next unit, exiting the outside of the ladder.

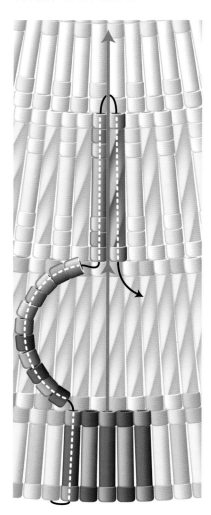

Pick up:

• 11° white seed x 1
• 11° light turquoise seed x 1
• 11° white seed x 1

Sew down through the fourth bead from the top, making sure not to split the thread.

Pick up:

• 11° white seed x 1
• 11° light turquoise seed x 1
• 11° dark turquoise seed x 1
• 11° light turquoise seed x 1
• 11° dark turquoise seed x 1
• 11° light turquoise seed x 1
• 11° dark turquoise seed x 1

Skip three bead units and sew through the last of the five units, exiting the outside of ladder 4.

Pick up one 8° dark turquoise seed and three 11° dark turquoise seeds. Skip the last three beads and sew back through the 8° dark turquoise seed to complete a picot and then up through the next unit, exiting the inside of ladder 4. Begin a new net and repeat this process, making netting and picots, to the end of the ladder. Tie off the thread and then work in the opposite direction with the tail thread.

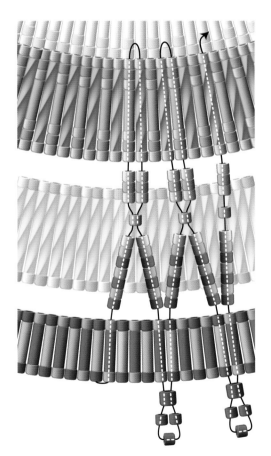

Step F: Ladder 5

Unit 1 (top to bottom)

- 11° dark turquoise seeds x 2
- 6mm untwisted dark turquoise bugle x 1
- 11° dark turquoise seed x 1

Unit 2 (bottom to top)

- 11° dark turquoise seeds x 2
- 6mm untwisted dark turquoise bugle x 1
- 11° dark turquoise seed x 1

Build ladder 3 and pin it to the template.

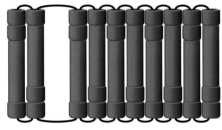

Sew through the first unit of ladder 5, exiting the inside edge, and then through the center bead of the first picot. Sew through the next unit, exiting the outside edge. Weave in and out through the ladder until you reach the next picot. Sew through the center bead. Continue to the end of the ladder, joining picot points as you reach them.

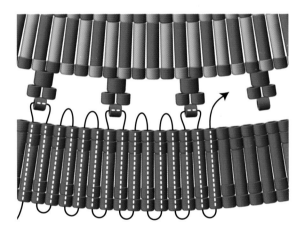

Step G: Fringe and Daggers

Begin at the center of ladder 5 and work from left to right. Find the two units nearest to the vertical centerline. Sew through the unit to the left, exiting the outside of ladder 5.

This neckpiece has two types of fringe—dagger fringe and short fringe.

For the dagger fringe, pick up:

• 8° dark turquoise seed x 1
• 11° dark turquoise seeds x 4
• large dagger bead x 1
• 11° dark turquoise seeds x 4

Optional: Make the center fringe stand out by substituting the above with this sequence:

• 8° dark turquoise seed x 1
• 4mm green crystal bead x 1
• 11° dark turquoise seed x 1
• 11° light turquoise seed x 1
• 11° white seed x 1
• large dagger bead x 1
• 11° white seed x 1
• 11° light turquoise seed x 1
• 11° dark turquoise seed x 1

Sew back through the size 8 dark turquoise seed (and the crystal as well if using the above sequence). Sew back through the next unit of ladder 5, exiting the inside edge of the ladder.

For the short fringe, pick up:

• 11° white seeds x 2
• 11° light turquoise seed x 1
• 11° dark turquoise seed x 1

Skip the last seed and sew through the strand. Sew back through the next unit of ladder 5, exiting the inside of the ladder.

Make five short fringes between every dagger fringe. Continue to both ends of the ladder. Tie off the thread.

Step H: Finishing

Add a closure to the open ends of the neckpiece. Weave in the thread ends. Attach a clasp. If necessary, refer to the finishing technique instructions on pages 134–136.

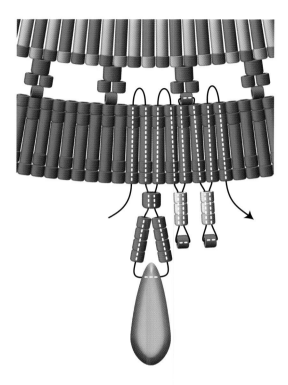

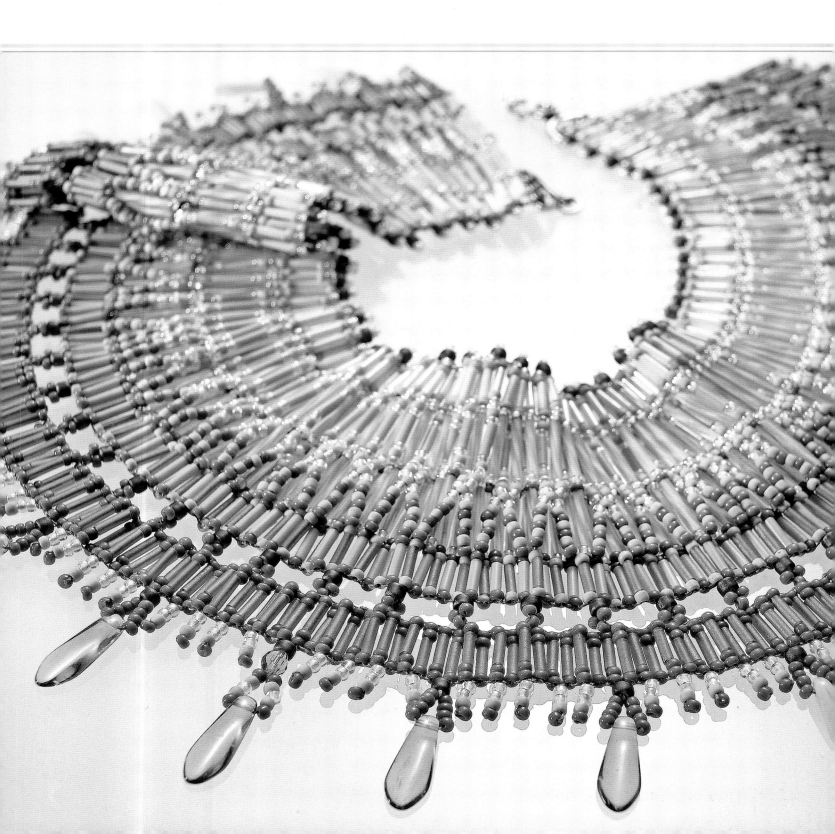

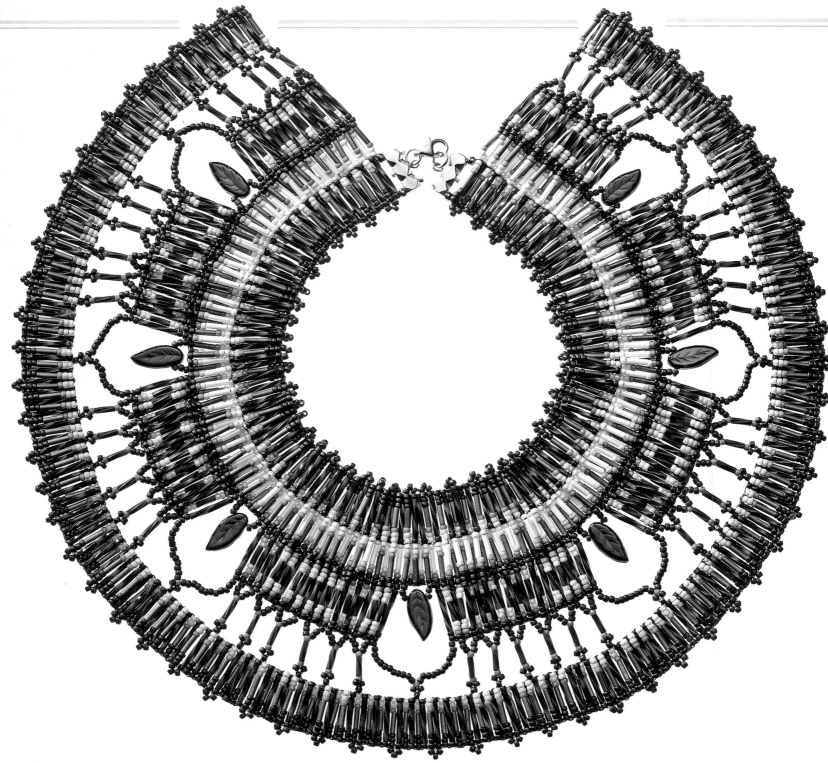

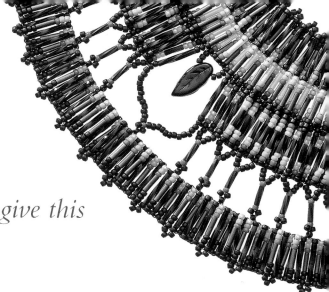

Gradient

Gradual color changes and dangling leaves give this unusual piece its unique style.

BEAD KEY

12mm twisted black bugles
size A = 28 g; size B = 33 g;
size C = 37 g

6mm twisted black bugles
size A = 7 g; size B = 8 g;
size C = 9 g

6mm untwisted dark gray bugles
size A = 14 g; size B = 16 g;
size C = 18 g

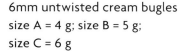

6mm untwisted cream bugles
size A = 4 g; size B = 5 g;
size C = 6 g

11° black seeds
size A = 31 g; size B = 37 g; size C = 41 g

11° medium gray seeds
size A = 10 g; size B = 12 g; size C = 13 g

11° light gray seeds
size A = 9 g; size B = 10 g; size C = 11 g

11° cream seeds
size A = 15 g; size B = 17 g;
size C = 19 g

15mm flat black leaves, with
horizontal hole (7)

Step A: Ladder 1

Unit 1 (top to bottom)

- 11° black seeds x 3
- 6mm untwisted black bugle x 1
- 11° medium gray seed x 1
- 11° light gray seed x 1
- 11° cream seed x 1

Unit 2 (bottom to top)

- 11° black seed x 1
- 12mm twisted black bugle x 1
- 11° black seed x 1

Build ladder 1 and pin it to the template.

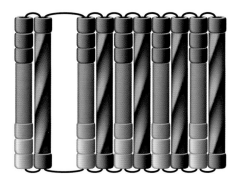

Step B: Ladder 2 and Top Picots

Unit 1 (top to bottom)

- 11° cream seed x 1
- 11° light gray seed x 1
- 11° medium gray seed x 1
- 6mm untwisted black bugle x 1
- 11° black seed x 1

Unit 2 (bottom to top)

- 11° black seed x 1
- 11° medium gray seed x 1
- 11° light gray seed x 1
- 6mm untwisted cream bugle x 1
- 11° cream seed x 1

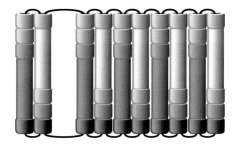

Build ladder 2 and pin it to the template. Join ladder 1 and ladder 2. Every other time that you exit the inside edge of ladder 1, string three 11° black seeds to form a picot.

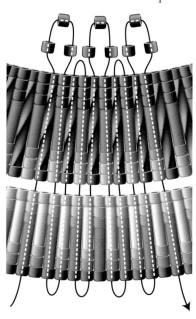

Step C: Ladder 3 and Leaf Drops

Unit 1 (top to bottom)

- 11° black seeds x 2
- 12mm twisted black bugle x 1
- 11° black seeds x 2

Unit 2 (bottom to top)

- 11° black seed x 1
- 11° medium gray seed x 1
- 11° light gray seed x 1
- 11° cream seed x 1
- 6mm twisted black bugle x 1
- 11° cream seed x 1
- 11° light gray seed x 1
- 11° medium gray seed x 1
- 11° black seed x 1

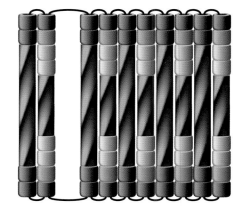

Unlike the first two ladders, ladder 3 has eight separate ladder segments. To find the correct length of each segment, locate each of the ⅛ lines on your template (not counting the top center line). Find the bead unit of ladder 2 nearest to each line. Count three units outward on each side for a total of seven bead units. Mark these units on the template.

Make a ladder segment of the appropriate length to extend from the last bead unit of a seven-unit group to the first bead unit of the next seven-unit group. Count the number of bead units in this ladder segment and make five more identical segments.

The two end segments will span from the last bead unit of a seven-unit group to each of the end units of ladder 2. Pin each ladder segment to the template. Make sure that there are five exposed bead units of ladder 2 at each ⅛ line.

Join the first segment of ladder 3 to ladder 2. Ideally, your needle will be positioned so that it exits the first of the five exposed bead units at the outside edge of ladder 2 to begin the leaf segment. If not, work around until you can exit the correct unit.

Pick up:

• 11° black seeds x 3
• 15mm flat black leaf x 1
• 11° black seeds x 3

Sew through the last bead unit of the five-unit group, exiting the inside edge of ladder 2. Sew through the next unit and begin to join the next segment of ladder 3. Repeat this process until you have joined all eight ladder sections and added all seven leaf beads.

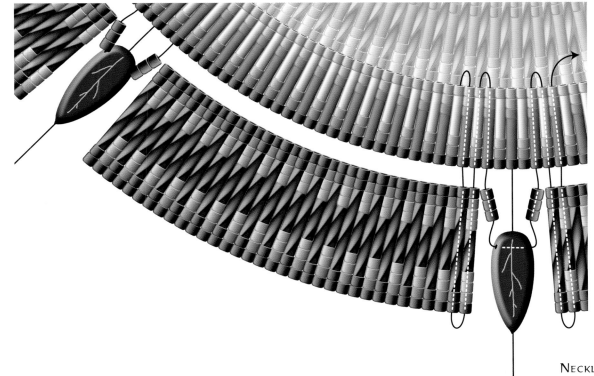

Step D: Netted Spokes

For this design, you will add netted spokes to the outside edge of the segments of ladder 3. You'll also add a larger net span between segments. Each net will occupy a four-unit group, with an extra unit on either end of each segment to accommodate the larger net span. So you'll need to work with a multiple of four units for each spoke and one extra unit on each end of the ladder segment (4 + 2).

The actual ladder segment will vary in length (and number of bead units), depending on the size of the neckpiece. You always need a free unit on each end, but depending on the size of the segment, you may need to make some adjustments. If so, here are some guidelines.

If your ladder segment consists of a multiple of 4 + 0 extra units, two of the netted spokes (preferably at the ends of the segment) will occupy a five-unit group.

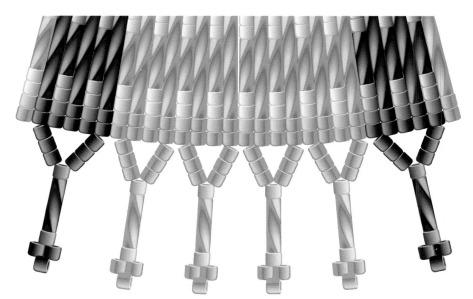

If your ladder segment consists of a multiple of 4 + 1 extra unit, one of the netted spokes (preferably in the middle of the segment) will occupy a three-unit group.

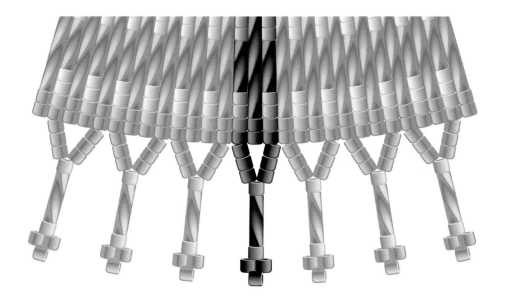

If your ladder segment consists of a multiple of 4 + 3 extra units, one of the netted spokes (preferably in the middle of the segment) will occupy a five-unit group.

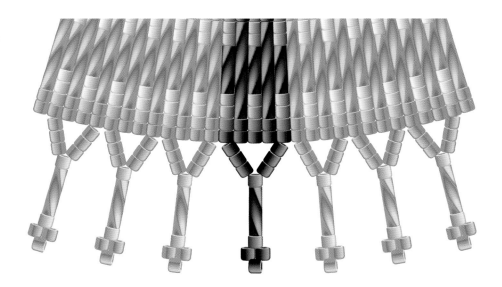

Sew through the last bead unit to the left of the halfway line, exiting the outside edge of ladder 3.

Pick up:

- 11° black seeds x 12
- 11° medium gray seed x 1
- 11° black seeds x 3

Skip the last three beads and sew through the 11° medium gray seed. Pick up twelve 11° black seeds and sew up through the first bead unit of the next ladder segment, exiting the inside edge. Sew through the next bead unit of ladder 3, exiting the outside edge.

Pick up:

- 11° black seeds x 3
- 11° medium gray seed x 1
- 6mm twisted black bugle x 1
- 11° black seeds x 3

Skip the last three beads and sew through the next three beads. Pick up three 11° black seeds and sew up through last unit of the four-unit group (take into account any adjustments you've made in the ladder segment), exiting the inside edge. Sew through the next bead unit of ladder 3, exiting the outside edge. Add netted spikes to the remainder of the ladder.

Continue this process until you reach the end of ladder 3, adding netted spikes and nets that extend from one ladder segment to the next. Complete the remaining half of the ladder. Pin all of the netted ends in place so that they are taut and evenly distributed.

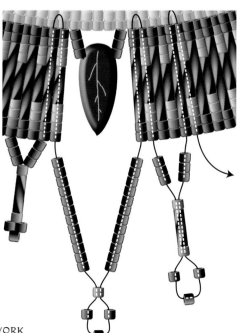

Step E: Ladder 4

Ladder 4 will wrap around the outer points of the netting from the previous row. The first unit and the last unit will extend from the first to the last netted point.

Unit 1 (top to bottom)

- 11° cream seed x 1
- 11° light gray seed x 1
- 11° medium gray seed x 1
- 6mm untwisted black bugle x 1
- 11° black seeds x 3

Unit 2 (bottom to top)

- 11° black seed x 1
- 12mm twisted black bugle x 1
- 11° black seed x 1

Build ladder 4 and pin it to the template.

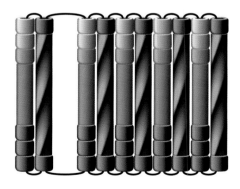

Sew through the first unit of ladder 4, exiting the inside edge, and then through the 11° black seed at the bottom center of the first net. Sew through the next unit, exiting the outside edge. Weave in and out through the ladder until you reach the next netted point. Sew through this point. Continue to the end of the ladder, joining net points as you reach them.

Step F: Bottom Picots

Begin at the center of ladder 3 and work from left to right. Find the two bead units nearest to the halfway point. Sew through the first of the two units, exiting the outside of ladder 4. Pick up three 11° black seeds and sew up, down, up, down, up, down through the next six bead units. Begin the next picot.

Continue this process to the end of ladder 3. Complete the remaining half of the ladder.

Step G: Finishing

Add a closure to the open ends of the neckpiece. Weave in the thread ends. Attach a clasp. If necessary, refer to the finishing technique instructions on pages 134–136.

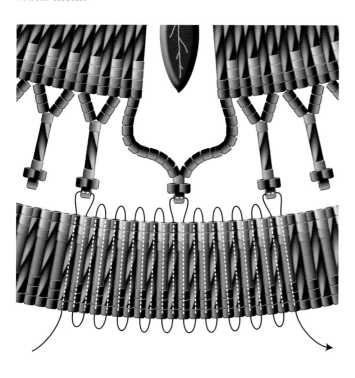

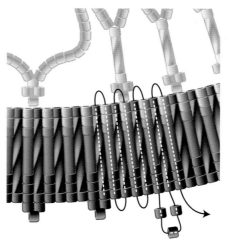

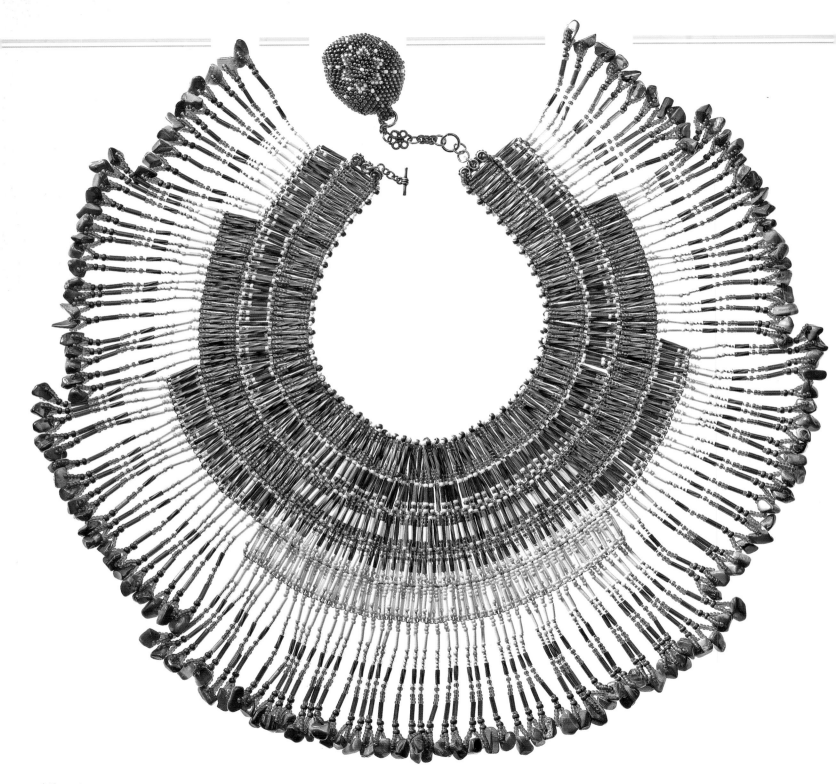

Eagle Feather

Inspired by Native American imagery, this neckpiece is built with multiple ladders and dense fringe.

BEAD KEY

12mm twisted iridescent blue bugles
size A = 28 g; size B = 33 g;
size C = 38 g

6mm twisted iridescent blue bugles
size A = 13 g; size B = 15 g;
size C = 17 g

6mm untwisted brown bugles
size A = 11 g; size B = 12 g;
size C = 14 g

6mm untwisted cream bugles
size A = 11 g; size B = 12 g;
size C = 14 g

11° brown seeds
size A = 49 g; size B = 57 g;
size C = 65 g

11° pale blue seeds
size A = 16 g; size B = 19 g;
size C = 21 g

11° cream seeds
size A = 23 g; size B = 26 g;
size C = 29 g

8° purple seeds
size A = 12 g; size B = 13 g;
size C = 15 g

Tigereye nuggets
size A = 147; size B = 204;
size C = 229

Step A: Ladder 1

Unit 1 (top to bottom)

- 11° brown seed x 1
- 12mm twisted iridescent blue bugle x 1
- 11° brown seed x 1

Unit 2 (bottom to top)

- 11° brown seeds x 3
- 6mm twisted iridescent blue bugle x 1
- 11° brown seeds x 3

Build ladder 1 and pin it to the template.

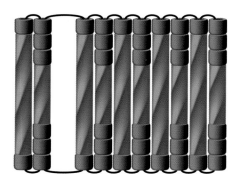

Step B: Top Picots

Begin at the center of ladder 1 and work from left to right. Find the unit nearest to the halfway point. Count one unit outward on both sides for a total of three bead units. Sew through the first of the three units, exiting the inside of ladder 1.

Pick up:

- 11° cream seed x 1
- 8° purple seed x 1
- 11° cream seed x 1

Sew through the third unit of the three-unit group, exiting the outside edge. Sew through the next unit and begin a new picot. Repeat until you reach the end of ladder 1. Complete the remaining half of the ladder.

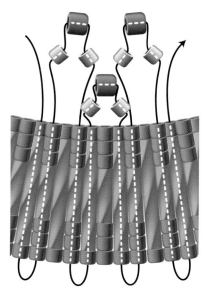

Step C: Ladder 2

Unit 1 (top to bottom)

11° pale blue seed x 1

12mm twisted iridescent blue bugle x 1

11° pale blue seed x 1

Unit 2 (bottom to top)

- 11° brown seed x 1
- 11° cream seed x 1
- 11° brown seed x 1
- 11° cream seed x 1
- 6mm untwisted brown bugle x 1
- 11° cream seed x 1
- 11° brown seed x 1

Build ladder 2 and pin it to the template. Join ladder 1 and ladder 2.

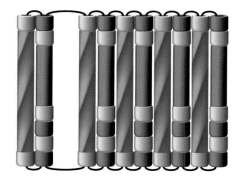

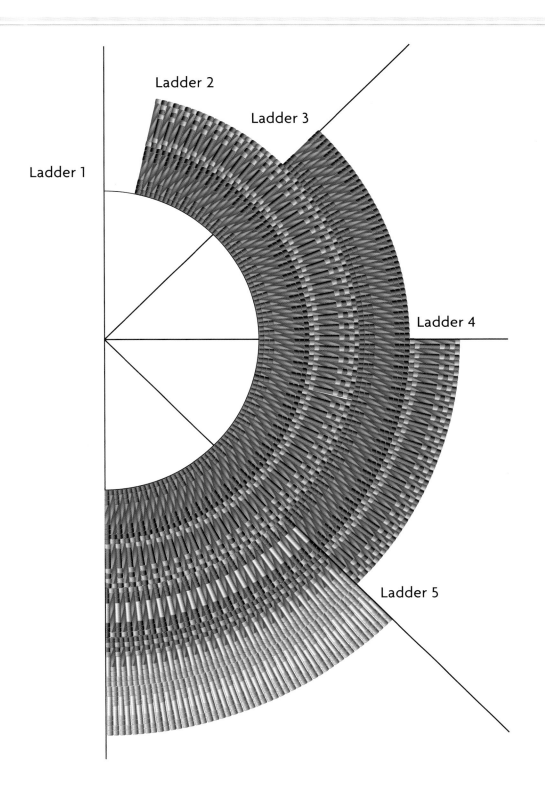

Ladder 1

Ladder 2

Ladder 3

Ladder 4

Ladder 5

Step D: Ladder 3

Ladder 3 will begin and end at each of the ⅛ lines on your template. The ladder is made up of three connected segments.

Ladder Segment 1

(⅛ line to ⅜ line)

Unit 1 (top to bottom)

- 11° brown seed x 1
- 12mm twisted iridescent blue bugle x 1
- 11° brown seed x 1

Unit 2 (bottom to top)

- 11° brown seeds x 3
- 6mm twisted iridescent blue bugle x 1
- 11° brown seeds x 3

Build ladder segment 1. Stop when you reach the ⅜ line on your template. Do not end the thread. Continue by picking up the bead-unit sequence for ladder segment 2.

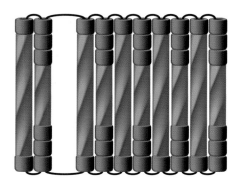

Ladder Segment 2

(⅜ line to ⅜ line)

Unit 1 (top to bottom)

- 11° brown seeds x 3
- 6mm untwisted cream bugle x 1
- 11° brown seeds x 3

Unit 2 (bottom to top)

- 11° cream seed x 1
- 12mm twisted iridescent blue bugle x 1
- 11° cream seed x 1

Build ladder segment 2. Stop when you reach the next ⅜ line. Do not end the thread. Continue by picking up the bead-unit sequence for ladder segment 3.

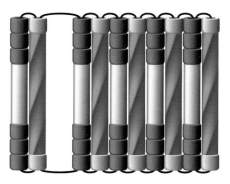

Ladder Segment 3

(⅜ line to ⅛ line)

Unit 1 (top to bottom)

- 11° brown seed x 1
- 12mm twisted iridescent blue bugle x 1
- 11° brown seed x 1

Unit 2 (bottom to top)

- 11° brown seeds x 3
- 6mm twisted iridescent blue bugle x 1
- 11° brown seeds x 3

Build ladder segment 3. Stop when you reach the ⅛ line. Pin ladder 3 to the template so that it reaches from one ⅛ line to the other. Join ladder 2 and ladder 3.

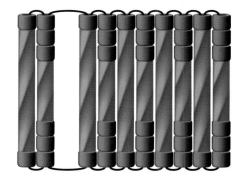

Step E: Ladder 4

Ladder 4 will begin and end at ¼ lines. It is made up of three connected segments.

Ladder Segment 1

(¼ line to ⅜ line)

Unit 1 (top to bottom)

- 11° pale blue seed x 1
- 12mm twisted iridescent blue bugle x 1
- 11° pale blue seed x 1

Unit 2 (bottom to top)

- 11° brown seed x 1
- 11° cream seed x 1
- 11° brown seed x 1
- 11° cream seed x 1
- 6mm untwisted brown bugle x 1
- 11° cream seed x 1
- 11° brown seed x 1

Build ladder segment 1. Stop when it reaches the ⅜ line. Do not end the thread. Continue by picking up the bead-unit sequence for ladder segment 2.

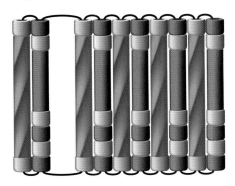

Ladder Segment 2

(⅜ line to ⅜ line)

Unit 1 (top to bottom)

- 11° brown seed x 1
- 11° pale blue seed x 1
- 11° brown seed x 1
- 11° pale blue seed x 1
- 6mm untwisted cream bugle x 1
- 11° cream seeds x 2

Unit 2 (bottom to top)

- 11° cream seed x 1
- 11° pale blue seed x 1
- 11° cream seed x 1
- 11° pale blue seed x 1
- 6mm twisted iridescent blue bugle x 1
- 11° brown seeds x 2

Build ladder segment 2. Stop when you reach the next ⅜ line. Do not end the thread. Continue by picking up the bead-unit sequence for ladder segment 3.

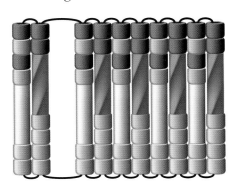

Ladder Segment 3

(⅜ line to ¼ line)

Unit 1 (top to bottom)

- 11° pale blue seed x 1
- 12mm twisted iridescent blue bugle x 1
- 11° pale blue seed x 1

Unit 2 (bottom to top)

- 11° brown seed x 1
- 11° cream seed x 1
- 11° brown seed x 1
- 11° cream seed x 1
- 6mm untwisted brown bugle x 1
- 11° cream seed x 1
- 11° brown seed x 1

Build ladder segment 3. Stop when it reaches the ¼ line. Pin ladder 4 to the template so that it reaches from one ¼ line to the other. Join ladder 3 and ladder 4.

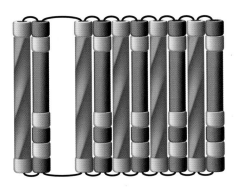

Step F: Ladder 5

Ladder 5 will begin and end at each of the ⅜ lines.

Unit 1 (top to bottom)

- 11° cream seeds x 4
- 6mm untwisted cream bugle x 1
- 11° cream seeds x 2

Unit 2 (bottom to top)

- 11° pale blue seed x 1
- 11° cream seed x 1
- 11° pale blue seed x 1
- 11° cream seed x 1
- 6mm untwisted cream bugle x 1
- 11° cream seeds x 2

Pin ladder 5 to the template so that it reaches from one ⅜ line to the other. Join ladder 4 and ladder 5.

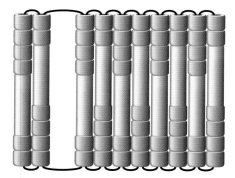

Step G: Fringe

Begin at the center of ladder 5 and work from left to right. Find the two units nearest to the halfway point. Sew through the unit first of the two units, exiting the outside of ladder 5.

Pick up:

- 11° cream seeds x 3
- 6mm untwisted cream bugle x 1
- 11° cream seed x 1
- 11° pale blue seed x 1
- 11° cream seed x 1
- 11° pale blue seeds x 3
- 6mm twisted iridescent blue bugle x 1
- 11° pale blue seed x 1
- 11° brown seed x 1
- 11° pale blue seed x 1
- 11° brown seeds x 3
- 6mm untwisted brown bugle x 1
- 11° brown seed x 1
- 8° purple seed x 1
- 11° brown seed x 1
- 8° purple seed x 1
- 11° brown seeds x 5
- tigereye nugget x 1
- 11° brown seeds x 5

Skip the last eleven beads. Sew up through the remainder of the strand and then through the second bead unit in the two-unit group, exiting the inside edge. Sew through the next bead unit and begin another fringe strand.

Work to the end of ladder 5. If you end on an odd-numbered bead unit, simply complete the last strand of fringe and sew back up through the same unit that you exited.

Sew up through the adjoining bead unit of ladder 4, exiting the inside edge. Sew back through the next bead unit, exiting the outside edge, and begin a new fringe strand.

Repeat to the end of the neckpiece. Complete the remaining half.

Step E: Finishing

Add a closure to the open ends of the neckpiece. Weave in the thread ends. Attach a clasp. If necessary, refer to the finishing technique instructions on pages 134–136.

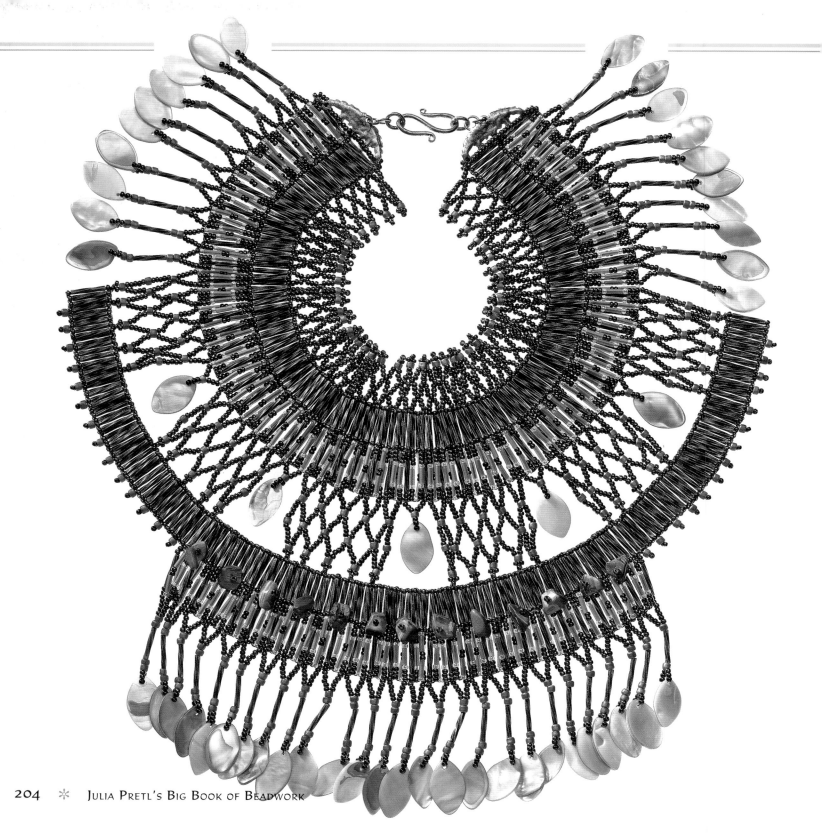

Trellis

This fascinating collar features sectioned netting and tiered fringe.

BEAD KEY

12mm twisted bronze bugles
size A = 39 g; size B = 46 g;
size C = 52 g

6mm untwisted dark
turquoise bugles
size A = 12 g; size B = 14 g;
size C = 16 g

11° bronze seeds
size A = 59 g; size B = 69 g;
size C = 79 g

11° pale green seeds
size A = 6 g; size B = 7 g; size C = 8 g

8° dark turquoise seeds
size A = 11 g; size B = 13 g; size C = 14 g

Tigereye nuggets
size A = 13; size B = 21; size C = 23

20mm flat mother-of-pearl drops,
with front-to-back hole
size A = 51; size B = 80; size C = 90

Step A: Ladder 1

All Units

- 11° bronze seed x 1
- 12mm twisted bronze bugle x 1
- 11° bronze seed x 1

Build ladder 1 and pin it to the template.

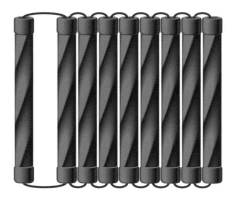

Step B: Top Netting

Begin at the center of ladder 1 and work from left to right. Find the two units nearest to the halfway point and count outward by one unit on each side for a total of four units. Sew through the first unit of the four units, exiting the inside of ladder 1.

Pick up:

- 11° bronze seeds x 11
- 8° dark turquoise seed x 1
- 11° bronze seeds x 3

Skip the last three beads and sew through the 8° dark turquoise seed. Pick up seven 11° bronze seeds. Skip the next seven beads and sew through the eighth bead. Pick up three 11° bronze seeds and sew through the last bead unit in the four-unit group. Sew up through the next bead unit, exiting the inside edge of ladder 1, to begin the next net segment.

Pick up seven 11° bronze seeds. Skip the first seven beads of the first netted segment and sew through the next bead.

Pick up:

- 11° bronze seeds x 3
- 8° dark turquoise seed x 1
- 11° bronze seeds x 3

Complete this net segment as you did the first. Repeat to the end of ladder 1. Complete the remaining half of the ladder.

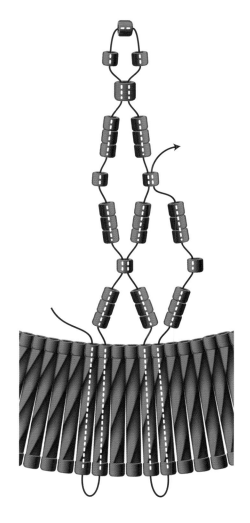

Step C: Ladder 2

Unit 1 (top to bottom)

- 11° bronze seed x 2
- 12mm twisted bronze bugle x 1
- 11° bronze seed x 2

Unit 2 (bottom to top)

- 11° bronze seeds x 3
- 11° pale green seed x 1
- 6mm untwisted dark turquoise bugle x 1
- 11° pale green seed x 1
- 11° bronze seeds x 3

Unit 3 (top to bottom)

- 11° pale green seed x 1
- 6mm untwisted dark turquoise bugle x 1
- 11° bronze seeds x 2
- 6mm untwisted dark turquoise bugle x 1
- 11° pale green seed x 1

Unit 4 (bottom to top)

- 11° bronze seeds x 3
- 11° pale green seed x 1
- 6mm untwisted dark turquoise bugle x 1
- 11° pale green seed x 1
- 11° bronze seeds x 3

Build ladder 1 and pin it to the template. Join ladder 1 and ladder 2.

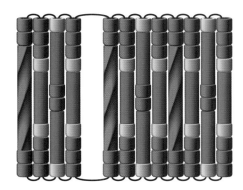

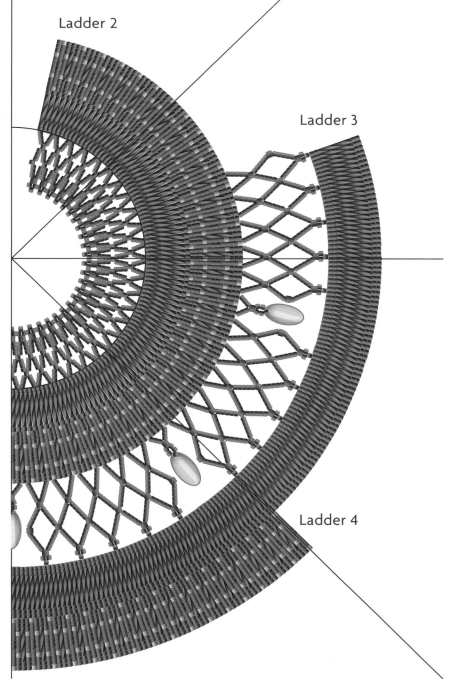

Ladder 1

Ladder 2

Ladder 3

Ladder 4

Step D: Netting and Drops

Begin at the center of ladder 1 and work from left to right. Find the unit nearest the halfway point. Count outward by two units on each side for a total of five units. Sew through the first of the five units, exiting the outside of ladder 2.

Pick up:

• 11° bronze seeds x 3
• 8° dark turquoise seed x 1
• 11° bronze seeds x 3
• 20mm flat mother-of-pearl drop x 1
• 11° bronze seeds x 3

Skip the next seven beads and sew up through the 8° dark turquoise bead. Pick up three 11° bronze seeds. Sew through the last bead unit of the five-unit group. The drop should straddle the center unit.

Sew through the next bead unit, exiting the outside edge of ladder 2. Each segment of netting will span a five-unit group.

Pick up:

• 11° bronze seeds x 5
• 8° dark turquoise seed x 1
• 11° bronze seeds x 5
• 8° dark turquoise seed x 1
• 11° bronze seeds x 5
• 8° dark turquoise seed x 1
• 11° bronze seeds x 3

Skip the last three beads and sew through the 8° dark turquoise seed.

Pick up:

• 11° bronze seeds x 5
• 8° dark turquoise seed x 1
• 11° bronze seeds x 5

Skip the next eleven beads and sew through the 8° dark turquoise seed. Pick up five 11° bronze seeds and sew through the last bead unit of the five-unit group. Sew through the next unit, exiting the outside edge of ladder 2, to begin the next net segment.

Pick up:

• 11° bronze seeds x 5
• 8° dark turquoise seed x 1
• 11° bronze seeds x 5

Skip the first eleven beads of the first net segment and go through the next 8° dark turquoise seed.

Pick up:

• 11° bronze seeds x 5
• 8° dark turquoise seed x 1
• 11° bronze seeds x 3

Complete this net segment as you did the last. Repeat until you have completed five full nets (each net will terminate with a three-bead picot).

Repeat this entire process, alternating drop and netting, until you reach the ¼ line. If necessary, work beyond this line until the last five-net section is complete. Bead the remaining half of ladder 2 in the same way.

Pin all of the netted ends in place so that they are taut and evenly distributed.

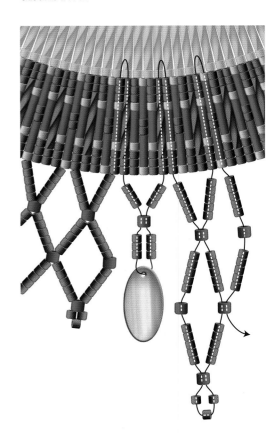

Step E: Ladder 3

All Units
- 11° bronze seed x 1
- 12mm twisted bronze bugle x 1
- 11° bronze seed x 1

Ladder 3 will wrap around the outer points of the netting from the previous row. The first unit and the last unit will extend from the first to the last netted point.

Build ladder 3 and pin it to the template.

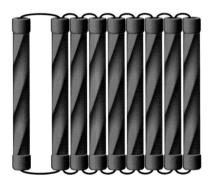

Sew through the first unit of ladder 3, exiting the inside edge, and then through the 11° brown seed at the bottom center of the first net. Sew through the next unit, exiting the outside edge. Weave in and out through the ladder until you reach the next netted point. Sew through this point. Continue to the end of the ladder, joining net points as you reach them.

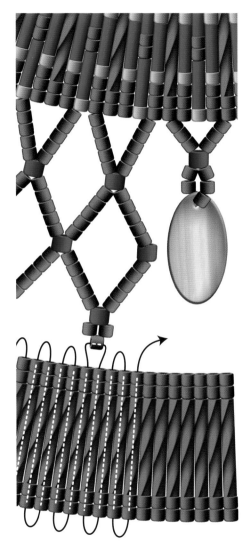

Step F: Ladder 4

Ladder 4 will extend from one ⅜ line to the other ⅜ line.

Unit 1 (top to bottom)
- 11° bronze seeds x 2
- 12mm twisted bronze bugle x 1
- 11° bronze seeds x 2

Unit 2 (bottom to top)
- 11° bronze seeds x 3
- 11° pale green seed x 1
- 6mm untwisted dark turquoise bugle x 1
- 11° pale green seed x 1
- 11° bronze seeds x 3

Unit 3 (top to bottom)
- 11° pale green seed x 1
- 6mm untwisted dark turquoise bugle x 1
- 11° bronze seeds x 2
- 6mm untwisted dark turquoise bugle x 1
- 11° pale green seed x 1

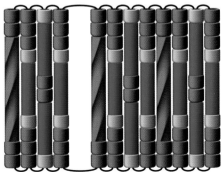

Unit 4 (bottom to top)

- 11° bronze seeds x 3
- 11° pale green seed x 1
- 6mm untwisted dark turquoise bugle x 1
- 11° pale green seed x 1
- 11° bronze seeds x 3

Build ladder 4 and pin it to the template. Join ladder 3 and ladder 4.

Step G: Fringe, Surface Embellishment, and Picots

Begin at the center of ladder 4 and work from left to right. Find the two units nearest to the halfway point and count outward by one unit on each side for a total of four units. Sew through the first of the four units, exiting the outside of ladder 4.

Pick up:

- 11° bronze seeds x 5
- 8° dark turquoise seeds x 2
- 12mm twisted bronze bugle x 1
- 8° dark turquoise seeds x 2
- 11° bronze seeds x 3
- 20mm flat mother-of-pearl drop x 1
- 11° bronze seeds x 3

Skip the last seven beads and sew through the strand until only the first five bronze seeds remain. Pick

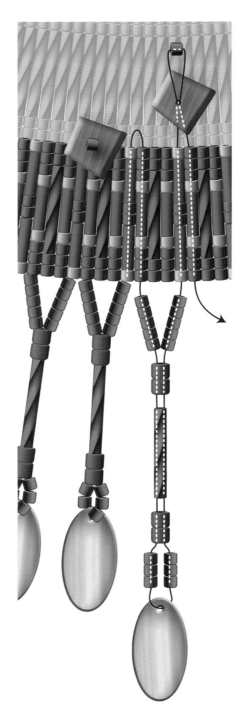

up five 11° bronze seeds and sew through the last bead unit of the four-unit group, exiting the inside edge of ladder 4.

Pick up one tigereye nugget and one 11° bronze seed. Skip the last bead and sew back through the tigereye nugget and then through the next bead unit, exiting the outside of ladder 4. Repeat to the end of ladder 4, adding surface embellishment after every other fringe strand. Don't worry if there are not enough remaining bead units to span the usual four units—simply sew up through the final unit after completing the last strand of fringe.

Sew up through the adjoining bead unit of ladder 3 and then down through the next unit to begin a series of picots. Pick up one 8° dark turquoise seed and one 11° bronze seed. Skip the last bead and sew through the 8° dark turquoise seed and then through the next bead unit, exiting the inside edge. Sew down, up, and down through the next three units and make another picot. Repeat to the end of ladder 3. Work up through the last leg of the end net and then through the adjoining unit of ladder 2. Sew back

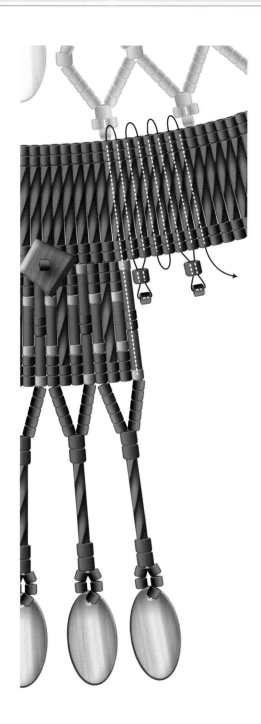

through the next unit, exiting the outside edge of ladder 2. Complete another section of fringe as you did for ladder 4, but without adding surface embellishment.

Repeat to complete the remaining half of the neckpiece.

Step H: Finishing

Add a closure to the open ends of the neckpiece. Weave in the thread ends. Attach a clasp. If necessary, refer to the finishing technique instructions on pages 134–136.

PART 3: BOXES

Chapter 16

Getting Started

My little boxes are self-supporting, peyote-stitched vessels, woven with cylinder beads. I developed this technique by applying to beadwork the same principles that are used to increase in crochet. These boxes may be as small as 1" (2.5 cm) wide—or as large as your patience (and tension) will allow.

The process of making a box has many steps. As you complete each step, write down what you have done in case you need to refer back later in the project.

Before you begin a new step, read through that section carefully. There are several instances in which the instructions differ for different types of boxes. There may also be important or helpful notes to help you work.

Study the diagrams carefully, and make sure that your beadwork structure conforms to the diagram before you proceed to the next row.

There are patterns and instructions for twelve boxes, three of each of the four shapes: triangle, hexagon, pentagon, and square. There are also instructions for two oblong variations. The patterns and instruction sections have been arranged from the easiest box to build (triangle) to the more complex (square), but you may begin with any of the four box shapes. Whichever you choose, you will begin making each box at the center of the base.

Tools and Materials

To make bead boxes, you'll need the following materials and supplies. Each project in the book has its own materials list, which will give you the number and size of the beads for that project. Each box is made with multiple colors (coded in the instructions as color A, B, C, D, and so on). All bead counts are approximate, so it's a good idea to buy extra.

- Size 11 cylinder beads (I use Miyuki Delicas)
- Size 12 or smaller beading needles
- Bead thread (such as Silamide or GSP fishing line)
- Large, decorative beads (for the feet and finials)
- Size 11 round seed beads
- Needle-nose pliers

When I first began teaching, I strongly encouraged my students to work with Silamide, a bonded nylon thread, and I used it for every box I made. Since then I have fallen in love with the new GSP fishing lines, such as Fireline, Powerpro, and Spiderwire. Every class I teach inevitably has at least one diehard Nymo user. I finally stopped arguing and learned that, although Nymo will not allow for the amount of tension I like to have in my own boxes, it will still result in a lovely box.

I sometimes like to double my thread so that if one strand breaks, I can make repairs with the piece still intact. I suggest using a thinner thread if you plan to double it and a thicker thread (or fishing line) if you plan to use a single strand. Begin each box with at least 5' (1.5 m) of thread.

Matte cylinder beads (especially black ones) and metallic cylinder beads are much more fragile than coated (shiny) ones. To avoid breakage, I suggest that you use the more durable, coated beads for your first project.

The Basic Parts of the Box

Before you begin to bead, it helps to have an overview of the basic parts and to visualize the steps involved in building each one.

The Base

The first step is making the base, or bottom. There are four different base shapes: triangular, hexagonal, pentagonal, and square. Generally, the base will be relatively

a. Flat lid fits
inside box

b. Lid fits
over sides

c. Flat lid fits
in recessed top

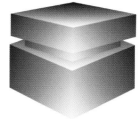

d. Lid fits over
recessed top

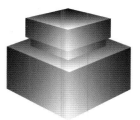

e. Small lid over
recessed top

flat, but, depending on the shape you are making and the tension as you work, the base may have a tendency to peak in the center.

The hexagonal base has a pronounced peak. When the base is inverted—so that the peak is inside the box—the six corners of the box base and body are sharp. The hexagonal peaked base also can be used, peak side out, as a domed lid. The bases of pentagonal boxes always lie perfectly flat. The bases of triangle and square boxes can vary.

The Sides

The next step in building a box is making the sides. The sides consist of a single straight tube of beadwork that is built up directly from the base.

As the sides of your box approach the desired height, you have the option of creating two different types of top edges: straight or recessed. A straight top is simply an extension of the sides of the box. A recessed top is a bit more complicated, but the result is especially attractive.

To decide which type of top edge to make, it is important to understand the relationship between the tops of the box sides and the box lid. The two styles of box top—straight or recessed—accommodate different styles of lids.

A straight top is designed to accommodate:

- A flat lid with inner walls that fit inside the box (a)
- A lid with sides that fit over the sides of the box (b)

A recessed top is designed to accommodate:

- A flat lid that is smaller than the base of the box with inner walls that fit inside the inner column (the recessed portion of the sides) (c)
- A lid that is the same width as the box with sides that fit over the inner column (d)
- A lid that is smaller than the box with sides that fit over the inner column (e)

The Hem

To finish both straight and recessed tops, you need to create a hem. The hem is a narrow strip of peyote stitch added just inside the top edge of the box. It will eventually "zip" to the outer layer, creating the appearance of a continuous fabric. The hem is truly the most important aspect of this technique. It defines the corners and helps the box to keep its shape.

The Lid

After the body of the box is complete, you will make the lid. There are two types of lids: flat lids (a, c) and lids with sides (b, d, e).

Lids will vary in size, depending on the size of the box and the style of the lid.

Glossary of Terms

Here is a list of some basic terms you will encounter as you work through the instructions to create your box.

Corner bead: The bead that forms a point in the base or lid, created by making consistent increases at the outer edges of each base or lid segment. For example, a triangle base has three corner beads; a square base has four corner beads.

Down bead: Every bead in the row prior to the working row. Down beads will recede into the edges of the beadwork.

Hem: A second layer of beads built into the top edge of the sides to add stability and shape to the box.

Inner column: A tube of peyote stitch made after decreasing the sides of the box. The inner column is narrower than the box sides and often helps to seat the lid.

Inner walls: An unhemmed tube of beadwork, built from the underside of a flat box lid. The inner walls slide into the sides of the box to keep the lid securely seated on the box.

Stepping up: The process of sewing again into the last bead from the previous row to begin a new row.

Up bead: Every bead in the working row. Up beads will protrude from the edges of the beadwork.

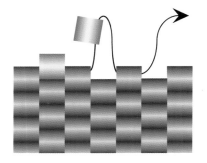

New bead added
between up beads

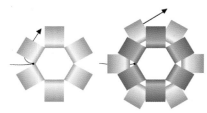

Circular peyote stitch

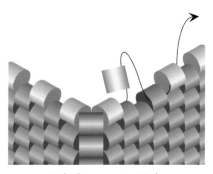

Tubular peyote stitch

Chapter 17

Building the Base

To build the boxes, you will work with variations on peyote stitch. Peyote stitch is a popular beadwork technique that has several variations. A more descriptive name for the stitch is "one-bead netting," because technically it is a netted stitch with "up" beads—the beads that protrude from the row—and "down" beads—the beads that recede into the row. The working row is always built from the up beads. The netting contains one bead per stitch, so the result is a solid fabric of beads.

To make the boxes, you will work with two basic beadwork variations on peyote stitch: circular peyote stitch and tubular peyote stitch. You don't need to have experience with these beadwork stitches. By following the written instructions and drawings provided, you will be learning these techniques naturally.

Circular peyote stitch begins at a center point and increases symmetrically, allowing each row to have a greater number of beads than the row before it, so that the beadwork radiates outward. The planned increases create segments in the beadwork and give each box shape its specific number of sides.

Tubular peyote stitch begins at a top or a bottom edge and creates a beaded tube. Box sides are formed with tubular peyote stitch. If you begin tubular peyote with an odd number of beads, the rows of beadwork spiral. If you begin with an even number of beads, the first bead in a row is also the last bead, so you need to "step up"—or sew again into the last bead—to begin the next row.

To make the base, you will work with the variation on circular peyote. To get comfortable with the technique, you'll want to practice first. Here are the instructions for making the base for each of the four box shapes. Choose the shape you'd like to try first as your practice piece, and follow the instructions for that box shape.

Begin with a length of thread approximately 5' (1.5 m) long and about 5 grams of beads in one or more colors that you like. I prefer to double my thread (10' [3 m] long before doubling) so that if one strand breaks, I can make repairs with the piece still intact—but do whatever is comfortable for you. I suggest that you use a thinner thread if you plan to double it and a thicker thread if you plan to use a single strand.

Triangle Box

STARTUP ROWS

Row 1: String 3 beads, and tie in an overhand knot (as if you are beginning to tie a shoestring), leaving an 8" (20.3 cm) tail. Grasp the tail tightly in the hand that is not holding the needle until you have established several rows. Sew through the next bead.

Row 2: String 2 new beads, and proceed through the next bead to form a V. Continue adding 2 beads after each bead in the previous row until you reach the end of the row. You will now have 9 beads. "Step up" to begin the next row. (Note: When you step up, you will sew through only the first of the 2 beads, coming out in the center of the V.)

Row 3: String 2 beads, and sew through the second of the 2 beads from the previous row. You should now have a second V inside the first one. String 1 bead, and sew through the next up bead. Pull firmly so that this bead snaps into place.

Continue this process, sewing 2 beads over each corner bead and then 1 bead between each 2 up beads, until you reach the end of the row. Step up to begin the next row. (Note: When you step up, you will sew through only the first of the 2 beads, coming out in the center of the V.)

Startup rows for triangle base

Row 1

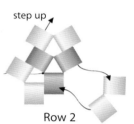

step up

Row 2

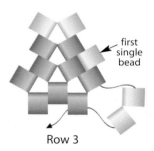

first single bead

Row 3

Making a bead box is a high-tension project. Pull firmly on the thread (not the needle!) after every stitch.

INCREASE CYCLE

By now you have noticed that the base portion of the triangle box is made up of two parts: three corners (where the increases occur) and three straight sides (beaded in typical peyote stitch). After the startup row, each row will increase the triangle by 3 beads (1 bead per side). Continue to add 2 beads to each corner—each V inside the one from the previous row—until your triangle reaches the desired size (about 1" to 1½" [2.5 cm to 3.8 cm] for your practice piece).

Last Row: String 1 bead, and sew through the second of the 2 beads, making sure that it sits snugly inside the V. This bead establishes the corner of the triangle. Sew 1 bead between the up beads until you come out in the center of the next V. Add a bead for the second corner. Continue until you reach the end of the row.

When you have finished the increase cycles, begin making the sides (page 228).

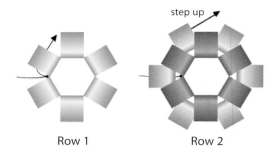

Startup rows for hexagon base

step up

Row 1   Row 2

Hexagon Box

STARTUP ROWS

Row 1: String 6 beads, and tie in an overhand knot (as if you are beginning to tie a shoestring), leaving an 8" (20.3 cm) tail. Grasp the tail tightly in the hand not holding the needle until you have established several rows. Sew through the next bead.

Row 2: String 1 new bead, and proceed through the next bead. You may need to pull the thread firmly to get the new bead to snap between the 2 beads in the previous row.

Continue adding a bead after each bead in the previous row until you reach the end of the row. You will now have 12 beads. Step up to begin the next row.

Row 3: Repeat row 2. You will now have 18 beads. Step up to begin the next row.

Row 4: String 2 beads, and sew through the next bead. This should form a V. String 2 more beads, and sew through the next bead. Continue adding 2 beads after each bead in the previous row until you reach the end of the row. Step up to begin the next row. (Note: When you step up, you will sew through only the first of the 2 beads, coming out in the center of the V.)

Row 5: String 1 bead, and sew through the second of the 2 beads, making sure that it sits snugly inside the V. This bead establishes the corner of the hexagon. String 1 bead, and then sew through the next up bead. Pull firmly so that this bead snaps into place. Add a bead for the second corner. Continue until you reach the end of the row. Step up to begin the next row. (Note: The last bead of the row will be the first leg of the first V, and you will step up to the adjacent corner bead.)

Each time you begin or end a thread, weave the tail into the beadwork by stitching diagonally through adjacent beads. When weaving in the tail, avoid sewing through the corner beads and the beads adjacent to the corner beads. They are the most difficult to repair when broken. You'll find tips for replacing broken beads on page 236.

INCREASE CYCLE

The base portion of the hexagon box is made up of two parts: six corners (where the increases occur) and six straight sides (beaded in flat peyote stitch). As you proceed, the corners increase in cycles. The hexagon box has an increase cycle of three rows, as follows:

Row 1: Bead around the hexagon as usual with 1 bead between every 2 up beads (including the corner bead).

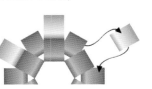
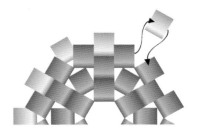

Row 3   Row 4   Row 5

Row 2: Add 2 beads to each corner to form a V.

Row 3: Add 1 bead to each corner, inside the V.

After the startup rows, each cycle will increase the hexagon by 6 beads (1 bead per side). Continue this cycle until your hexagon reaches the desired size (about 2" [5.1 cm] for your practice piece).

When you have finished the increase cycles, begin making the sides (page 228).

Startup rows for
pentagon base

step up

Row 1

Row 2

Row 3

Row 4

Pentagon Box

STARTUP ROWS

Row 1: String 5 beads and tie in an overhand knot (as if you are beginning to tie a shoestring), leaving an 8" (20.3 cm) tail. Grasp the tail tightly in the hand that is not holding the needle until you have established several rows. Sew through the next bead.

Row 2: String 1 new bead, and proceed through the next bead. You may need to pull the thread firmly to get the new bead to snap between the 2 beads in the previous row. Continue adding a bead after each bead in the previous row until you reach the end of the row. You will now have 10 beads. Step up to begin the next row.

Row 3: String 2 beads, and sew through the next bead. This should form a V. String 2 more beads, and sew through the next bead. Continue adding 2 beads after each bead in the previous row until you reach the end of the row. Step up to begin the next row. (Note: When you step up, you will sew through only the first of the 2 beads, coming out in the center of the V.)

Row 4: String 1 bead, and sew through the second of the 2 beads, making sure that it sits snugly inside the V. This bead establishes the corner of the pentagon. String 1 bead, and then sew through the next up bead. Pull firmly so that this bead snaps into place. Add a bead for the second corner. Continue until you reach the end of the row. Step up to begin the next row. (Note: The last bead of the row will be the first leg of the first V, and you will step up to the adjacent corner bead.)

INCREASE CYCLE

The base portion of the pentagon box is made up of two parts: five corners (where the increases occur) and five straight sides (beaded in flat peyote stitch). As you proceed, the corners increase in cycles. The pentagon box has an increase cycle of four rows, as follows:

Row 1: Bead around the pentagon as usual with 1 bead between every 2 up beads (including the corner bead).

Row 2: This row is new; it is not included in the startup rows. String 3 beads, and proceed through the next bead. The middle bead of these 3 beads should lie directly on top of the

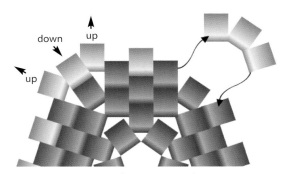

Increase row for pentagon base

one below it. Pull up the side beads, with your fingernails if necessary, to seat the middle one. Continue adding 3 beads to each corner. Step up to begin the next row. (Note: When you step up, you will sew through only the first of the 3 beads.)

Row 3: Add 2 beads to each corner, skipping the middle bead, to form a V.

Row 4: Add 1 bead to each corner, inside the V.

After the startup rows, each cycle will increase the pentagon by 10 beads (2 beads per side). Continue this cycle until your pentagon reaches the desired size (about 2" [5.1 cm] for your practice piece).

When you have finished the increase cycles, begin making the sides (page 228).

Square Box

STARTUP ROWS

Row 1: String 4 beads, and tie in an overhand knot (as if you are beginning to tie a shoestring), leaving an 8" (20.3 cm) tail. Grasp the tail tightly in the hand that is not holding the needle until you have established several rows. Sew through the next bead.

Row 2: String 1 new bead, and proceed through the next bead. Continue adding a bead after each bead in the previous row until you reach the end of the row. You will now have 8 beads. Step up to begin the next row.

Row 3: String 3 beads, and proceed through the next bead. The middle bead of these 3 should lie directly on top of the one below it. Pull up the side beads, with your fingernails if necessary, to seat the middle one. Continue adding 3 beads after each bead in the previous row until you reach the end of the row. Step up to begin the next row. (Note: When you step up, you will sew through only the first of the 3 beads.)

Row 4: String 2 beads, and sew through the third bead of the three-bead set from the previous row, skipping the middle bead to form a V. String 1 bead, and sew through the next up bead. Pull firmly so that this bead snaps into place. Continue this process—sewing 2 beads over each corner bead and then 1 bead between every two up beads—until you reach the end of the row. Step up to begin the next row. (Note: When you step up, you will sew through only the first of the 2 beads, coming out in the center of the V.)

Row 5: String 2 beads, and sew through the second of the two beads from the previous row. You should now have a second V sitting inside the first one. Sew 1 bead between the up beads until you come out in the center of the next V. Add 2 beads for the second corner. Continue until you reach the end of the row. Step up to begin the next row.

Startup rows for square base

Row 1

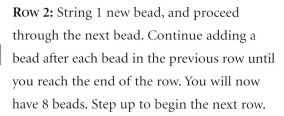

step up

Row 2

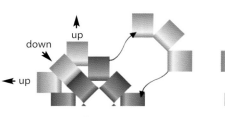

down

up

up

Row 3

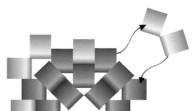

Row 4

(Note: When you step up, you will sew through only the first of the two beads, coming out in the center of the V.)

Row 6: String 1 bead, and sew through the second of the two beads, making sure that it sits snugly inside the V. This bead establishes the corner of the square. Sew 1 bead between the up beads until you come out in the center of the next V. Add a bead for the second corner. Continue until you reach the end of the row. Step up to begin the next row. (Note: The last bead of the row will be the first leg of the first V, and you will step up to the adjacent corner bead.)

INCREASE CYCLE

By now you have noticed that the base portion of the square box is made up of two parts: four corners (where the increases occur) and four straight sides (which have no increases). As you proceed, the corners increase in cycles. The square box has an increase cycle of five rows, as follows:

Row 1: Bead around the square as usual, with 1 bead between every 2 up beads (including the corner bead).

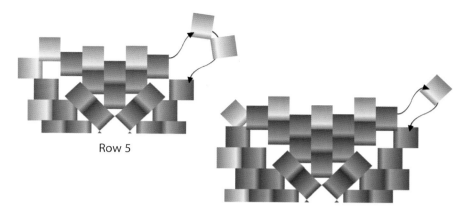

Row 5

Row 6

Row 2: Add 3 beads to each corner, making sure that the middle bead touches the bead below it.

Row 3: Add 2 beads to each corner, skipping the middle bead, to form a V.

Row 4: Add 2 beads to each corner, forming a second V inside the first one.

Row 5: Add 1 bead to each corner, inside the second V.

After the startup rows, each cycle will increase the square by 12 beads (3 beads per side). Continue this cycle until your square reaches the desired size (about 2" [5.1 cm] for your practice piece).

When you have finished the increase cycles, begin making the sides (page 228).

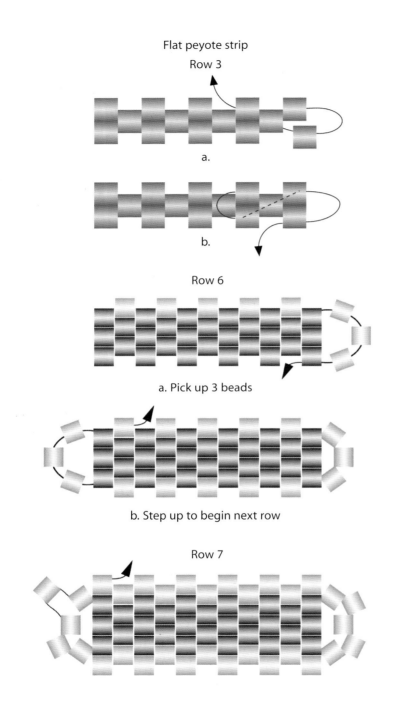

Flat peyote strip

Row 3

a.

b.

Row 6

a. Pick up 3 beads

b. Step up to begin next row

Row 7

Oblong Variations

You can also build an oblong box, working with the square or hexagon base and creating two elongated sides. The sides can be as long as you want.

When making the base for an oblong box, you will work in a variation on peyote stitch called flat peyote stitch. Flat peyote stitch may be even count, which means you begin with an even number of beads, or it may be odd count, which means you begin with an odd number of beads. Even-count peyote is naturally asymmetrical, and odd-count peyote is symmetrical from side to side. To make an oblong box, you will work a strip of flat, odd-count peyote stitch.

Rows 1 and 2: String an odd number of beads, as determined by your desired box length. This string of beads will make up the first two rows of the flat peyote strip.

Row 3: Pick up 1 more bead. Skip the last bead, and sew into the next-to-the-last bead. Skip the next bead in the string, and sew the one that comes after it. Continue this way until you reach the end of the string. This process is identical to tubular peyote stitch. Notice that there is 1 bead remaining. To complete the row, pick up 1 bead, and sew into what is now the last bead in the second row and the next-to-last bead in the first row (a).

Turn the needle 180 degrees to sew into the next-to-last bead of the third row. Then sew through rows 2 and 1 so that the needle exits the last bead of the first row.

Turn the needle again and sew into the last bead of row 3 (b). You are now ready to bead row 4.

ROWS 4 AND 5: Bead by adding 1 bead to each space. Pick up a bead, and sew into the last up bead to begin row 5. Add 1 bead to each space, and finish the row as you did for row 3 (a, b).

ROW 6: Make a sixth row that completely encircles the strip. (Do not turn to begin a seventh row.)

Pick up 3 beads, and sew into the corner bead on the opposite side of the flat edge (a).

Bead a row along the working side of the strip, and add 3 more beads to the remaining flat end. Step up to begin row 7 (b).

Row 7: Bead around the entire edge, this time adding 1 bead between each of the 3 end beads. (You will add a total of 2 beads to each end of the strip.) Step up and follow the instruction for either the hexagon or square variation.

Oblong Hexagon Variation

To make corners on each end for a hexagon box, add 2 beads to each of the three end spaces to establish the increase corners. Bead along the second long side, and repeat this process on the far end. Step up to begin the next row, following the increase cycles for the hexagon box (page 220).

Oblong Square Variation

To make two corners on each end for a square box, add 3 beads to the first end space to establish an increase corner. Add 1 bead to the second end space to establish the short side of the rectangle, and then add 3 more beads to the third end space for the second increase corner. Bead along the second long side; repeat this process for the far end. Step up to begin the next row, following the increase cycles for the square box (page 224).

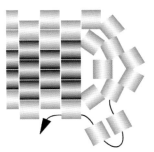

Oblong hexagon variation

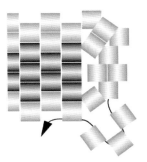

Oblong square variation

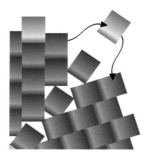

Tubular peyote stitch

Chapter 18
Building the Sides

When you are satisfied with the size of the base of your box, continue to bead around the edges without increasing (every space gets only one bead). Remember to step up as you complete each row—you are now working with tubular peyote stitch.

After a few rows, you will find that the edges are beginning to curl upward. Keep your tension firm and, as you round the corners, carefully pinch the corner into shape. This is especially important when making a triangle box because the fewer the number of sides, the sharper the corner angle will be.

Straight and Recessed Tops

Depending on the style of the box lid you choose, the sides of your box will be either straight or recessed at the top.

To bead a box that has straight sides from bottom to top, continue until your box is two rows short of the desired height. The last row should have an up bead at the corners. Now you can simply begin to make the hem (page 30).

To bead a box with sides that are recessed at the top, continue until your box is the desired height (about 2" [5.1 cm] for your practice piece). Make one or more decrease cycles, depending on the shape of the box (see sidebar on facing page). A decrease cycle is the opposite of an increase cycle but is identical in appearance.

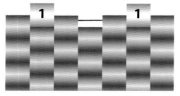

Row 1

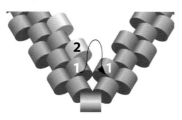

Row 2

A complete triangle box decrease cycle is:

Row 1:
Skip the corner bead.

Decreasing for a Triangle Box

The decrease cycle for a triangle box is simple. After you have completed the first row, every subsequent row is the same.

Row 1: Make sure you have finished the sides of your box with an up bead on either side of the corner bead. For the next row, bead the sides as usual. When you come to a corner, omit the corner bead, and sew directly from the first up bead into the next.

Pull firmly on the thread as you sew the first few beads following the skipped bead so that as little thread as possible shows. When you complete this row, the corners of the box will be more defined, and the sides will begin

Row 2: Bead the next row as you did the first. When you come to a corner, you will notice that the 2 corner beads from the previous row are practically touching. Sew through the first bead and then the next without adding a bead in between. Bead the remaining sides in the same way, skipping a bead as you round each corner. Step up to begin the next row.

When you have finished the required number of decrease cycles for your style of lid, begin making the inner column (page 233).

Decrease Cycles for Sides

Here's an overview of the guidelines to follow when finishing the sides of the box. Each box style will have a different decrease cycle, depending on the style of the lid.

- **For a flat lid that is smaller than the base of the box:**

  All box shapes: Subtract the number of lid increase cycles from the number of base increase cycles. This is the number of decrease cycles you will make.

- **For a lid with sides that are flush with the sides of the box:**

  Triangle box: Complete four decrease cycles.
  Hexagon box: Complete two decrease cycles.
  Pentagon box: Complete one decrease cycle.
  Square box: Complete one decrease cycle.

- **For a lid with sides that are smaller than the base of the box:**

  All box shapes: Subtract the number of lid increase cycles from the number of base increase cycles. This is the number of decrease cycles you will make. Next, follow the directions above for a lid with sides that are flush with the sides of the box.

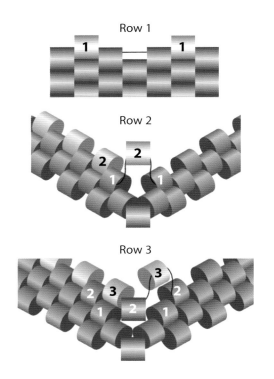

Row 1

Row 2

Row 3

A complete hexagon box decrease cycle is:

Row 1:
Skip the corner bead.

Row 2:
Bead as usual (add the corner bead).

Row 3:
Bead as usual.

that as little thread as possible shows. When you complete this row, the corners of the box will be more defined, and the sides will begin to curl inward. Step up to begin the next row.

Row 2: Bead this row as usual, with a bead between every pair of up beads.

Row 3: Bead as usual with a bead between every pair of up beads (including those on either side of the corner bead). You have now completed the decrease cycle for the

When you have finished the required number of decrease cycles for your style of lid, begin making the inner column (page 233).

Decreasing for a Pentagon Box

The decrease cycle for a pentagon box includes four rows.

Row 1: Make sure you have finished the sides of your box with an up bead on either side of the corner bead. For the next row, bead the sides as usual. When you come to

Decreasing for a Hexagon Box

The decrease cycle for a hexagon box includes three rows.

Row 1: Make sure you have finished the sides of your box with an up bead on either side of the corner bead. For the next row, bead the sides as usual. When you come to a corner, omit the corner bead, and sew directly from the first up bead into the next.

Pull firmly on the thread as you sew the first few beads after the skipped bead so a corner, omit the corner bead, and sew directly from the first up bead into the next.

Pull firmly on the thread as you sew the first few beads following the skipped bead so that as little thread as possible shows. When you complete this row, the corners of the box will be more defined, and the sides will begin to curl inward. Step up to begin the next row.

Row 2: Bead this row as usual, with a bead between every pair of up beads.

Row 3: Bead the sides of this row as usual, with a bead between every pair of up beads. When you reach a corner, do not sew into the new corner bead from the previous row.

Row 4: Bead as usual with a bead between every pair of up beads (including those on either side of the corner bead). You have now completed the decrease cycle for the pentagon box.

When you have finished the required number of decrease cycles for your style of lid, begin making the inner column (page 233).

Row 1

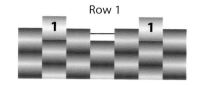

Row 2

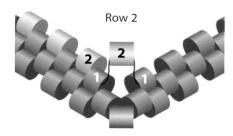

Row 3

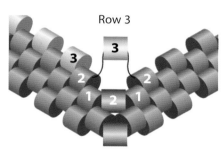

Row 4

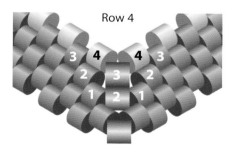

A complete pentagon box decrease cycle is:

Row 1:
Skip the corner bead.

Row 2:
Bead as usual (add the corner bead).

Row 3:
Bead as usual (add the corner bead; do not sew into the corner bead from the previous row).

Row 4:
Bead as usual.

Row 1

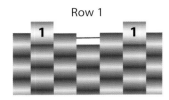

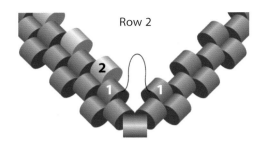

Row 2

A complete square box decrease cycle is:

Row 1:
Skip the corner bead.

Row 2:
Skip the corner bead.

Row 3:
Bead as usual (add the corner bead).

Row 4:
Bead as usual (add the corner bead; do not sew into the corner bead from the previous row).

Row 5:
Bead as usual.

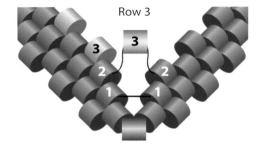

Row 3

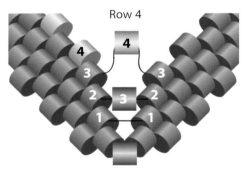

Row 4

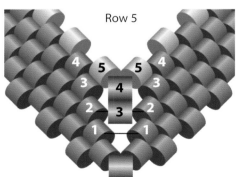

Row 5

Decreasing for a Square Box

The decrease cycle for a square box includes five rows.

Row 1: Make sure you have finished the sides of your box with an up bead on either side of the corner bead. For the next row, bead the sides as usual. When you come to a corner, omit the corner bead, and sew directly from the first up bead into the next.

Pull firmly on the thread as you sew the first few beads following the skipped bead so that as little thread as possible shows. When you complete this row, the corners of the box will be more defined, and the sides will begin to curl inward. Step up to begin the next row.

Row 2: Bead the next row as you did the first. When you come to a corner, sew through the first bead and then the next without adding a bead in between. There will probably be some thread visible between the two beads—that's okay. Bead the remaining sides in the same way, skipping a bead as you round each corner. Step up to begin the next row.

Row 3: Bead this row as usual, with a bead between every pair of up beads, including the corner beads.

Row 4: Bead the sides of this row as usual, with a bead between every pair of up beads. When you reach a corner, do not sew into the new corner bead from the previous row.

Row 5: Bead as usual with a bead between every pair of up beads (including those on either side of the corner bead). You have now completed the decrease cycle for the square box.

When you have finished the required number of decrease cycles for your style of lid, begin making the inner column.

The Inner Column

After you have made the appropriate number of decreases, you will begin the inner column. Bead the next row with tubular peyote stitch, with a bead between every pair of up beads, including the corner beads (a).

(The drawing below shows a recessed top for a hexagon lid, but the inner columns for all the box shapes work the same way.)

The bead rows will begin to curl upward. Continue until the column is two rows short of the desired height. The last row should end with an up bead at each corner (b).

Now you are ready to make the hem.

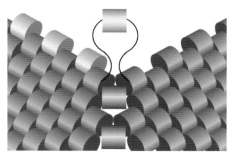

a.

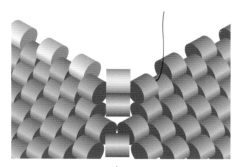

b.

The Hem

Before completing the last two rows of the box, you need to complete four hem rows. To build the first hem row, step back down through the adjacent bead of the previous row so that the needle exits inside the box. Pick up a bead. Sew into the next bead of the same row (a). (This will be much easier to do if you sew diagonally so that the needle exits the outside of the box.)

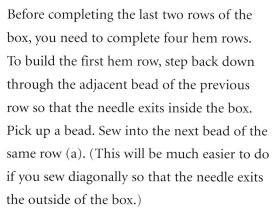

a.

b.

Pull the thread tightly so that the bead sits inside the box and adjacent to the corresponding bead of the last row. Pull the thread so that it slides between the beads and is once again positioned inside the box (b).

Continue to bead around the inside of the box. When you reach the corner, sew into the corner bead of the box and then back down into the adjacent bead without adding a hem bead (c). Repeat this process for each side/corner until you reach the first hem

c.

d.

e.

bead. Sew into this bead to step up for the next hem row.

Add a second row to the hem, filling in each corner space with a single bead (d). Pull the thread tightly as you round each corner to decrease the amount of visible thread—this will sharply define the corner of the box.

Step up and bead a third hem row (e). Step up to bead the last hem row. Add 2 beads to each corner space. When this row is complete, weave through the hem beads until you are able to sew back into the last row of the body to the outside of the box. Complete the body by beading the last two rows (f).

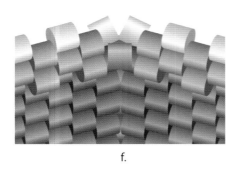

f.

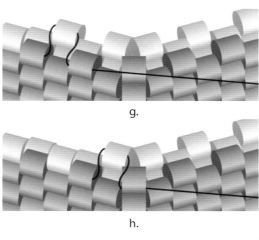

g.

h.

i. The completed hem

You will now "zip"—or interlock—the last row of the body and the last row of the hem. Look at the space where the thread has exited. Behind this space, there will be an up hem bead. Sew into this bead and then into the next up bead of the body of the box (g). Pull the thread tightly so that the hem bead fills the space.

When you reach the corner of the box, sew into only the first of the doubled hem beads and then into the corner bead of the body of the box (h). Pull tight so that the hem bead fills the space beside the corner bead. Sew into the second doubled hem bead, and proceed as usual.

When the hem and the body of the box are completely zipped (i), finish by weaving the thread into the box.

Replacing Broken Beads

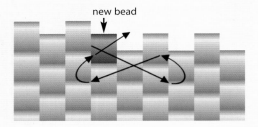

new bead

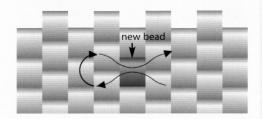

new bead

Because making a beaded box is a high-tension project, inevitably you will encounter the problem of broken beads. Although broken beads are frustrating, you can replace them.

As you are beading, if you break a bead in the previous row, string a new bead (preferably one slightly smaller than the space), and sew diagonally through the two adjacent beads in the previous two rows. Exit inside the box to hide the thread.

Next, sew into the bead directly above the bead that you exited and then diagonally through the two adjacent beads in the two previous rows, again exiting inside the box. Sew back into the new bead, and continue beading the row you are working.

If you break a bead when weaving into the beadwork to begin or end a thread, string a new bead (preferably one slightly smaller than the space occupied by the broken bead). Then sew through the bead in the row adjacent to the broken bead. Exit inside the box to hide the thread. Next, sew through the bead directly above the one that you just exited, and then sew back into the new bead. Continue weaving the thread into the beadwork.

When beading a box base or lid, a broken corner bead or a bead beside a corner is nearly impossible to replace. As you are beading a new row, if you break a corner bead in the previous row, take out all the beads until you reach the broken bead. Replace the bead, and bead the row again. (To be on the safe side, do not weave thread ends through the corners of the bead-work when you are beginning or ending a thread.)

Chapter 19
Lids, Finials, and Feet

The final step in making a box is to top it with a lid. There are two lid variations: a flat lid and a lid with sides. A flat lid may be the same width as the top of the box or it can extend beyond the edges. A lid with sides may overlap the sides of the box or sit on top.

Flat Lid

A flat lid has an inner wall that fits inside the hem of the box. Bead the top of the lid in the same way as you beaded the base of the box. For a box with a straight top, use the exact same number of increase cycles. For a box with a recessed top, subtract the number of decrease cycles at the top from the number of increase cycles that you made for the base (see sidebar, page 229).

Inner Wall

As you work, check the size of the lid. When the lid no longer clears the edges of the box hem—but before it reaches its full size—you will not step up to begin the next row. Instead, pick up a bead, and sew into the next bead of this same row (just as you did when you added the hem to the body of the box), as shown in the drawing. Again, this is easiest to do if you sew diagonally through each bead so that you exit on the "wrong" side, or underside, of the lid and then bring the thread back to the right side (top side) again.

Continue to add beads in this way until you reach a corner.

There are two types of corners that you will encounter: a corner with a corner bead and a corner without a corner bead, depending on the arrangement of beads in the last row of your increase cycle.

Beading the inner wall

Corner with a Bead

When your needle exits the last bead of the side of the lid, you may find that this row has a bead in the corner. Pick up a bead, sew into the first bead of the next segment of the lid and continue as before (a). When the row is complete, step up to the first inner-wall bead to begin a second row. Bead the second row as usual (b).

Corner without a Bead

When your needle exits the last bead of the side of the lid, you may find that this row has no bead in the corner. Sew into the first bead of the next segment, and continue as before (a). When the row is complete, step up to the first inner wall bead to begin a second row.

Bead the second row as usual. When you exit the last bead of a segment, pick up

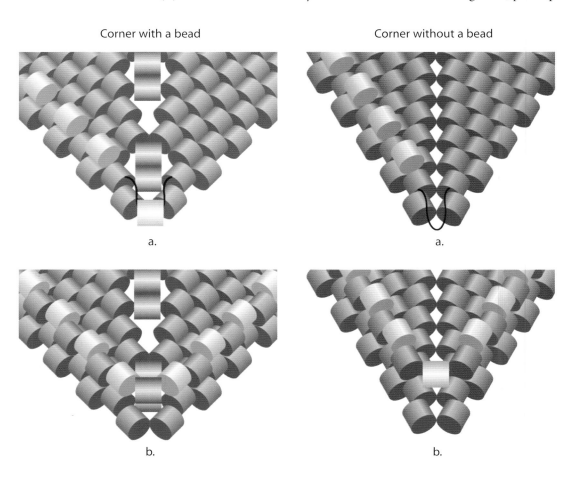

Corner with a bead

a.

b.

Corner without a bead

a.

b.

1 bead, and sew into the first bead of the next segment. Bead the rest of the row, adding a bead to each corner (b).

Finishing the Lid

Continue to bead in tubular peyote stitch until the inner wall is approximately ¼" (6 mm) deep—it should seat securely in the box top. If you find that the inner wall is catching the side of your box, taper it slightly by skipping each corner space when you bead the last row or by completing the final row with size 15 seed beads. Weave your thread back down to the last lid row. Complete the last two rows.

Lid with Sides

A lid with sides is designed to fit over the opening of a straight top or over the inner column of a box with a recessed top. A lid with sides is beaded in exactly the same way as the body of a box that has a straight top, although the lid usually has shorter sides.

If the lid is to fit over a box with a straight top, make the top of the lid the same size as the base of the box, and then bead:

- Four additional increase cycles for a triangle box

Lid with sides that fit over straight top of pentagon box

- Two additional increase cycles for a hexagon box
- One additional increase cycle for a pentagon box
- One additional increase cycle for a square box

If the sides of the lid are to be flush with the sides of the body of your box, make the same number of increases in the top of the lid as you did in the base of the box (pages 218–225).

Lid with sides smaller than body of square box with recessed top

a.

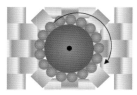

b.

If the lid is to be smaller than the body of your box, subtract one or more full increase cycles for the lid from the number of increase cycles used for the base of the box. This number should correspond to the number of decrease cycles used when making a recessed top (page 229).

Finials

To finish the lid of your box, you may want to add a large, decorative bead to make a knob, or finial. Begin a new thread so that it exits a bead in the center of the top of the lid. String the large bead, and then string a smaller bead. Sew back into the large bead, and exit through the center of the underside of the lid. Sew through another center bead, up through the large bead, and through the center bead again (a).

Repeat this process until you have sewn through each center bead at least once or until the finial is securely attached to the lid. Push the needle back through to the top of the lid, but do not sew through the large bead.

Wind the thread around the base of the large bead several times. The thread should be sandwiched between the large bead and the top of the lid. String enough beads to encircle the base of the large bead, and wrap the thread around it. (I find that round seed beads are much more attractive than cylinder beads here.) Wind the thread around the large bead several more times so that it vanishes between the circle of beads and the top of the lid (b). Weave the thread into the lid to finish.

Feet

To make decorative feet for your box, select 3 or 4 larger beads, depending on the shape of your box. Begin a new thread so that it exits about $\frac{1}{4}$" (6 mm) from one corner of the underside of the box, through a space

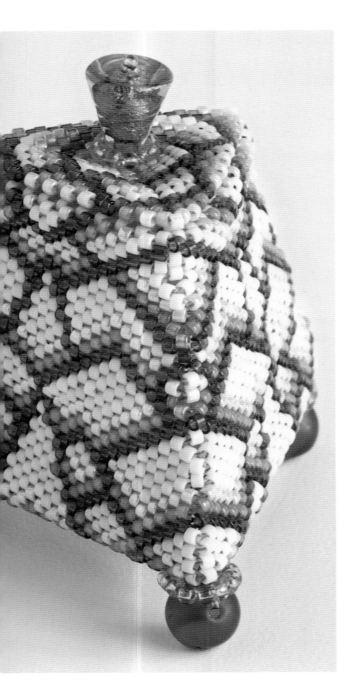

You may find it easier to attach
the feet to the base of the box before
you begin to construct the sides.

Foot

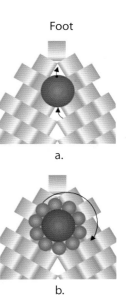

a.

b.

created when you made your increases.
String one of the large beads, and then insert
the needle through an increase space that is
closer to the corner of the box (a). Working
from inside the box, push the needle back
through the increase space that you originally
exited. Repeat this process several times.

As you did with the finial, wind the
thread around the base of the large bead
several times. The thread should be
sandwiched between the large bead and the
base of the box. String enough beads to
encircle the base of the large bead, and wrap
the string around it. (Again, I prefer round
seed beads here.) Wind the thread several
more times so that it vanishes between the
circle of beads and the base of the box (b).
Weave the thread into the lid to finish. Add
the rest of the feet to the box in the same way.

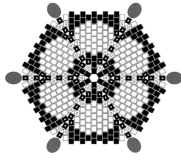

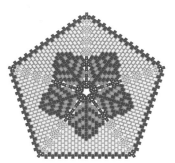

Chapter 20
Patterns and Word Maps

In the pattern instructions on pages 248–308, you will find all the information you'll need to make twelve miniature bead boxes—three in each shape: three-sided, four-sided, five-sided, and six-sided. The boxes are arranged by level of complexity—from easiest (triangle box) to most challenging (square box).

The photographs, colored patterns, and coded word maps provide all the information you need to build each box. There's also a list of the materials you'll need and a key so you can easily find the page numbers for the techniques you'll need to refer to as you work.

Pages 309–315 contain blank graph worksheets for each box shape, which you can copy and color to design your own box patterns. You can also download copies of all of the blank graph worksheets from my website, www.darkharebeadwork.com.

Reading Patterns

At first sight, a box pattern can be a bit daunting, but it is not as difficult as it seems. Here are several tips to help you as you read a box pattern.

Box Sides and Lid Sides

Each side of the box is identical, so only one side is shown. Repeat the pattern for each side of the box. Any deviations from this rule are included within the specific pattern.

Side patterns are read from left to right.

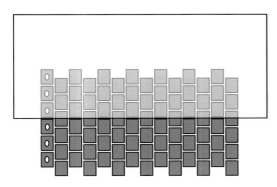

Locating the working row

Choose a side pattern and align the edge of a piece of paper with the top line of one row of beads within the pattern. Notice that the "beads" are staggered. In other words, every other whole bead sits below the edge of the paper. These whole beads constitute the working row. The alternating beads that are cut off at the halfway point belong to the subsequent row.

In the left-hand column of each row of the side pattern is a dotted bead. The dotted bead indicates the corner of the box. (Remember that because peyote stitch is staggered, only every other row has a corner bead.)

Each box-side pattern is read from the bottom row of the graph. You actually begin beading at the bottom row of the box side and will also view your beadwork this way.

Recessed Top

The bottom six rows of the graph at right are tubular peyote, so the corner of every other row receives a bead. The top eight rows, which form the recessed top, contain two decrease cycles. The dotted corner beads represent the new corners created by the decreases. This sample graph is for the side of a pentagon box with a recessed top.

Row 1: Skip the corner bead.

Row 2: Bead as usual (add the corner bead).

Row 3: Bead as usual (add the corner bead; do not sew into the corner bead from the previous row).

Row 4: Bead as usual (no corner bead).

Repeat rows 1 through 4.

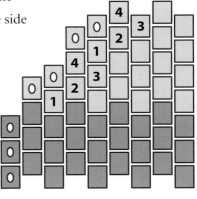

Pentagon box side
with recessed top

Bases and Lids

The graphed pattern for the base and the lid of the box begins at the center of the shape. As you increase the number of beads in each segment increases, you read the beads from left to right. As you move to each new

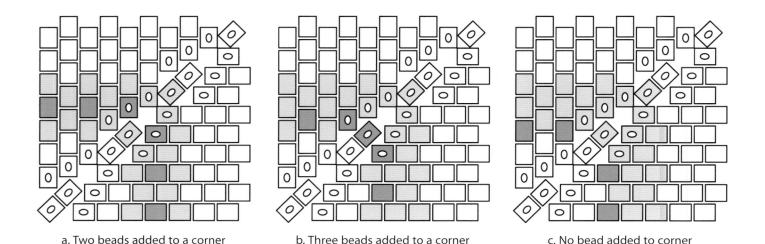

a. Two beads added to a corner   b. Three beads added to a corner   c. No bead added to corner

segment, read around the pattern in a clockwise direction.

In most of the box patterns presented in this book, each segment is identical. In these cases, you do not have to turn the pattern as you work. Simply repeat each graphed segment as many times as the box design requires.

The dotted beads refer to the corner increases. With the exception of the increases, each segment of a base or lid pattern is read in the same way as a box-side pattern.

When you add 2 beads to a corner, the first bead becomes the *last* bead of the segment that you just beaded, and the second bead becomes the *first* bead of the segment that you will bead next (a).

Similarly, when you add 3 beads to a corner, the first bead becomes the *last* bead of the segment that you just beaded, the second bead becomes a *corner* bead, and the third bead becomes the *first* bead of the segment that you will bead next (b).

Finally, notice that for the first row of every increase cycle (except for the triangle box) you will sew through the corner bead in the center of the V from the previous row. No beads are added to the corner (c).

All Patterns

Although every row of the pattern begins at a corner, every row of your beadwork does not. Every time you step up to begin a new row, you are actually sewing through the first bead of the previous row for a second time. For this reason, not only will you move up one pattern row, but also you will move one row to the right. It may be helpful to draw a line that begins with your first bead and moves diagonally up the pattern, as shown in the drawing at right, to keep track of your starting bead on each row.

Reading Word Maps

As a visual person, I have always shunned the idea of word maps. Out of curiosity, I decided to put one of my more complex patterns into text form before I beaded it. I quickly learned how much easier it is to work when you have a pattern in both graphic and written form.

With practice, reading a box pattern will become second nature. Until then, working with both the pattern and the word map together is extremely helpful.

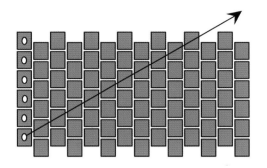

Word maps contain the row number, the bead color (coded as A, B, C, and so on), and the number of beads in that color in the row. Repeats of color combinations are indicated with an x and the number of repeats. For example: 1. **C(1)** ... x3 means you will bead one bead of color C three times in row 1.

Here are several tips to help you as you read a word map. Spend some time reading through this section, while referring to your box pattern, before actually beginning to bead.

1. All word maps are read from left to right and top to bottom.
2. The first line of the word map for a box side corresponds to the bottom row of the pattern.
3. The first line of the word map for a base/lid corresponds to the center of the pattern.

When you are building a box, the most important thing to remember is the sequence of the increase cycle for the box that you are beading. This way, you will always know how many beads to add (if any) to each corner.

Sample word map

(for base of triangle box)

1. **C(1)** ... x3
2. **C(2)** ... x3
3. **C(2)**; C(1) ... x3
4. **C(2)**; A(1); B(1) ... x3
5. **C(2)**; A(1); C(1); B(1) ... x3
6. **C(2)**; A(2); B(2) ... x3
7. **C(2)**; A(2); C(1); B(2) ... x3
8. **C(2)**; A(3); B(3) ... x3
9. **C(2)**; A(3); C(1); B(3) ... x3
10. **C(2)**; A(4); B(4) ... x3

4. For most box patterns, the sides are identical, so you may start at any corner. (For patterns in which one or more sides are different, such as the New School box on page 270, the specific instructions for the sides are included.)

5. Each row of a base/lid word map begins at the corner of the box—but, because the actual beadwork progresses by one bead per row, you will not always begin a row at the corner. Use the corners as reference points to complete the first partial side of your box. Then continue reading the word map from the corner to the end of the row.

6. Letters describing corner beads are in boldface type and are found at the beginning of the row.

7. When there is more than one corner bead, an increase row is indicated, and all beads listed are to be picked up at the same time. For example, a square base row that begins with C(3) is always an increase row. To bead the corner space, you would pick up 3 beads instead of 1, just as you did when increasing for the corner of your practice square (page 224–225).

8. The abbreviation "nc" means "no corner." For rows beginning with "nc," you are sewing into the previous row, which contains a corner bead, so the row on which you are working will have no corner bead.

9. The abbreviation "sc" means "skip corner." This notation indicates a decrease row—so you will sew from the last bead of one side into the first bead of the next without adding a corner bead.

Chapter 21
Patterns for Triangle Boxes

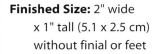 # Kaleidoscope

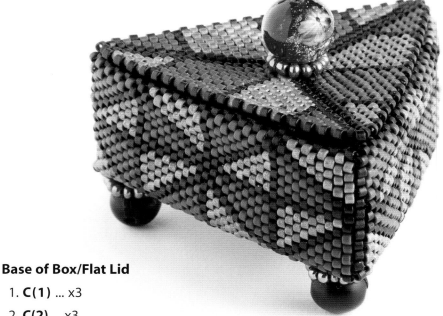

Finished Size: 2" wide
x 1" tall (5.1 x 2.5 cm)
without finial or feet

A = Light Blue; Delica #747;
584 beads (3 grams)

B = Royal Blue; Delica #726;
480 beads (3 grams)

C = Black; Delica #10;
1,140 beads (6 grams)

Hem/Inner Wall = Any color;
582 beads (3 grams)

   A   **B**   **C**

Construction Techniques

For the Base: pages 219–220

For the Sides: pages 228–229

For the Flat Lid: pages 237–239

Base of Box/Flat Lid

1. **C(1)** … x3
2. **C(2)** … x3
3. **C(2)**; C(1) … x3
4. **C(2)**; A(1); B(1) … x3
5. **C(2)**; A(1); C(1); B(1) … x3
6. **C(2)**; A(2); B(2) … x3
7. **C(2)**; A(2); C(1); B(2) … x3
8. **C(2)**; A(3); B(3) … x3
9. **C(2)**; A(3); C(1); B(3) … x3
10. **C(2)**; A(4); B(4) … x3
11. **C(2)**; A(4); C(1); B(4) … x3
12. **C(2)**; A(5); B(5) … x3
13. **C(2)**; C(1); A(4); C(1); B(4); C(1) … x3
14. **C(2)**; B(1); A(5); B(5); A(1) … x3

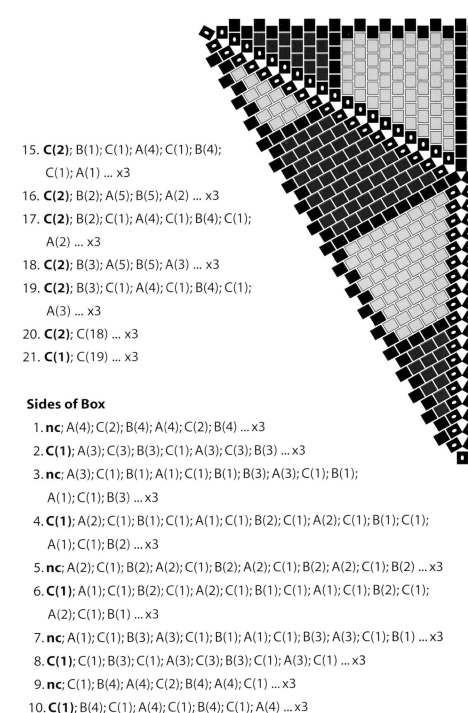

15. **C(2)**; B(1); C(1); A(4); C(1); B(4); C(1); A(1) ... x3

16. **C(2)**; B(2); A(5); B(5); A(2) ... x3

17. **C(2)**; B(2); C(1); A(4); C(1); B(4); C(1); A(2) ... x3

18. **C(2)**; B(3); A(5); B(5); A(3) ... x3

19. **C(2)**; B(3); C(1); A(4); C(1); B(4); C(1); A(3) ... x3

20. **C(2)**; C(18) ... x3

21. **C(1)**; C(19) ... x3

Sides of Box

1. **nc**; A(4); C(2); B(4); A(4); C(2); B(4) ... x3

2. **C(1)**; A(3); C(3); B(3); C(1); A(3); C(3); B(3) ... x3

3. **nc**; A(3); C(1); B(1); A(1); C(1); B(1); B(3); A(3); C(1); B(1); A(1); C(1); B(3) ... x3

4. **C(1)**; A(2); C(1); B(1); C(1); A(1); C(1); B(2); C(1); A(2); C(1); B(1); C(1); A(1); C(1); B(2) ... x3

5. **nc**; A(2); C(1); B(2); A(2); C(1); B(2); A(2); C(1); B(2); A(2); C(1); B(2) ... x3

6. **C(1)**; A(1); C(1); B(2); C(1); A(2); C(1); B(1); C(1); A(1); C(1); B(2); C(1); A(2); C(1); B(1) ... x3

7. **nc**; A(1); C(1); B(3); A(3); C(1); B(1); A(1); C(1); B(3); A(3); C(1); B(1) ... x3

8. **C(1)**; C(1); B(3); C(1); A(3); C(3); B(3); C(1); A(3); C(1) ... x3

9. **nc**; C(1); B(4); A(4); C(2); B(4); A(4); C(1) ... x3

10. **C(1)**; B(4); C(1); A(4); C(1); B(4); C(1); A(4) ... x3

11. **nc**; C(20) ... x3

12. **C(1)**; C(19) ... x3

13. **nc**; C(1); A(4); B(4); C(2); A(4); B(4); C(1) ... x3

14. **C(1)**; C(1); A(3); C(1); B(3); C(3); A(3); C(1); B(3); C(1) ... x3

15. **nc**; B(1); C(1); A(3); B(3); C(1); A(1); B(1); C(1); A(3); B(3); C(1); A(1) ... x3

16. **C(1)**; B(1); C(1); A(2); C(1); B(2); C(1); A(1); C(1); B(1); C(1); A(2); C(1);
    B(2); C(1); A(1) ... x3

17. **nc**; B(2); C(1); A(2); B(2); C(1); A(2); B(2); C(1); A(2); B(2); C(1); A(2) ... x3

18. **C(1)**; B(2); C(1); A(1); C(1); B(1); C(1); A(2); C(1); B(2); C(1); A(1); C(1);
    B(1); C(1); A(2) ... x3

19. **nc**; B(3); C(1); A(1); B(1); C(1); A(3); B(3); C(1); A(1); B(1); C(1); A(3) ... x3

20. **C(1)**; B(3); C(3); A(3); C(1); B(3); C(3); A(3) ... x3

21. **nc**; B(4); C(2); A(4); B(4); C(2); A(4) ... x3

22. **C(1)**; B(4); C(1); A(4); C(1); B(4); C(1); A(4) ... x3

BEGIN HEM

23. **nc**; C(20) ... x3

24. **C(1)**; C(19) ... x3

◢◣◥ Egypt

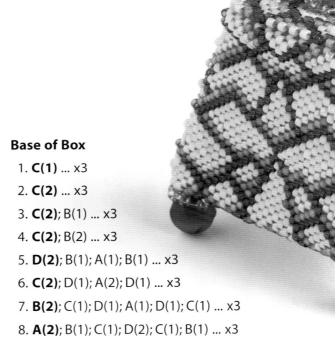

Finished Size: 2" wide
x 1¹⁄₂" tall (5.1 x 3.8 cm)
without finial or feet

A = Cream; Delica #157;
507 beads (3 grams)

B = Yellow; Delica #205;
546 beads (3 grams)

C = Mustard; Delica #272;
576 beads (3 grams)

D = Brown; Delica #709;
795 beads (3 grams)

Hem/Inner Wall = Any color;
279 beads (2 grams)

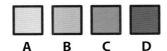

Construction Techniques

For the Base: pages 219–220

For the Sides: pages 228–229

For the Flat Lid: pages 237–239

Base of Box

1. **C(1)** ... x3
2. **C(2)** ... x3
3. **C(2)**; B(1) ... x3
4. **C(2)**; B(2) ... x3
5. **D(2)**; B(1); A(1); B(1) ... x3
6. **C(2)**; D(1); A(2); D(1) ... x3
7. **B(2)**; C(1); D(1); A(1); D(1); C(1) ... x3
8. **A(2)**; B(1); C(1); D(2); C(1); B(1) ... x3
9. **D(2)**; A(1); B(1); D(3); B(1); A(1) ... x3
10. **C(2)**; D(1); A(1); D(1); C(2); D(1); A(1); D(1) ... x3
11. **B(2)**; C(1); D(2); C(3); D(2); C(1) ... x3
12. **A(2)**; B(1); C(1); D(1); B(4); D(1); C(1); B(1) ... x3
13. **D(2)**; A(1); B(1); C(1); D(1); B(3); D(1); C(1); B(1); A(1) ... x3
14. **C(2)**; D(1); A(1); B(1); C(1); D(1); A(2); D(1); C(1); B(1); A(1); D(1) ... x3
15. **B(2)**; C(1); D(1); A(1); B(1); C(1); D(1); A(1); D(1); C(1); B(1); A(1);
    D(1); C(1) ... x3
16. **A(2)**; B(1); C(1); D(1); A(1); B(1); D(4); B(1); A(1); D(1); C(1); B(1) ... x3
17. **D(2)**; A(1); B(1); D(2); A(1); D(1); C(1); D(1); C(1); D(1); A(1); D(2); B(1); A(1) ... x3
18. **C(2)**; D(1); A(1); D(1); C(1); D(2); C(4); D(2); C(1); D(1); A(1); D(1) ... x3

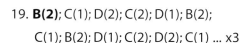

19. **B(2)**; C(1); D(2); C(2); D(1); B(2);
    C(1); B(2); D(1); C(2); D(2); C(1) ... x3

20. **A(1)**; B(1); C(1); D(1); C(1); B(1); C(1);
    D(1); B(4); D(1); C(1); B(1); C(1); D(1);
    C(1); B(1) ... x3

Sides of Box

21. **nc**; A(1); B(1); C(2); B(2); C(1); B(1); A(1); B(1); A(1);
    B(1); C(1); B(2); C(2); B(1); A(1) ... x3

22. **A(1)**; A(1); B(1); D(1); B(1); A(1); B(1); D(1); A(4); D(1);
    B(1); A(1); B(1); D(1); B(1); A(1) ... x3

23. **nc**; A(2); D(2); A(2); D(2); A(3); D(2); A(2); D(2); A(2) ... x3

24. **A(1)**; A(1); D(1); C(1); D(1); A(1); D(1); C(1); A(4); C(1); D(1);
    A(1); D(1); C(1); D(1); A(1) ... x3

25. **nc**; A(1); D(1); C(2); D(2); C(1); D(1); A(3); D(1); C(1); D(2); C(2); D(1);
    A(1) ... x3

26. **sc**; D(1); C(1); B(1); C(1); D(1); C(2); D(1); A(2); D(1); C(2); D(1); C(1); B(1); C(1); D(1) ... x3

27. **D(1)**; C(1); B(2); C(2); B(2); A(3); B(2); C(2); B(2); C(1) ... x3

28. **nc**; C(1); B(1); A(1); B(1); D(1); B(2); D(1); A(2); D(1); B(2); D(1); B(1); A(1); B(1); C(1) ... x3

29. **C(1)**; B(1); A(2); B(1); D(1); A(2); D(1); A(1); D(1); A(2); D(1); B(1); A(2); B(1) ... x3

30. **nc**; B(1); A(3); B(1); D(1); A(1); D(1); A(2); D(1); A(1); D(1); B(1); A(3); B(1) ... x3

31. **sc**; A(4); D(4); A(1); D(4); A(4) ... x3

32. **A(1)**; **A(3)**; D(1); C(1); D(1); C(1); **D(2)**; C(1); D(1); C(1); D(1); A(3) ... x3

33. **nc**; A(3); D(1); C(4); A(1); C(4); D(1); A(3) ... x3

34. **A(1)**; A(2); D(1); C(1); B(1); C(1); B(1); D(2); B(1); C(1); B(1); C(1); D(1); A(2) ... x3

35. **nc**; A(2); D(1); C(1); B(4); D(1); B(4); C(1); D(1); A(2) ... x3

36. **sc**; A(1); D(1); C(1); B(1); A(1); B(1); A(1); B(2); A(1); B(1); A(1); B(1); C(1); D(1); A(1) ... x3

37. **A(1)**; D(1); C(1); B(1); A(4); D(1); A(4); B(1); C(1); D(1) ... x3

38. **nc**; D(1); C(1); B(1); A(4); D(2); A(4); B(1); C(1); D(1) ... x3

39. **D(1)**; D(1); B(1); A(4); D(1); C(1); D(1); A(4); B(1); D(1) ... x3

40. **nc**; C(1); D(1); A(4); D(1); C(2); D(1); A(4); D(1); C(1) ... x3

41. **sc**; C(1); D(1); A(3); D(1); C(1); B(1); C(1); D(1); A(3); D(1); C(1) ... x3

42. **B(1)**; D(2); A(2); D(1); C(1); B(2); C(1); D(1); A(2); D(2) ... x3

43. **nc**; B(1); C(1); D(1); A(1); D(2); B(1); A(1); B(1); D(2); A(1); D(1); C(1); B(1) ... x3

44. **A(1)**; D(1); C(1); D(2); C(1); D(1); A(2); D(1); C(1); D(2); C(1); D(1) ... x3

45. **nc**; D(1); B(1); C(1); D(1); C(1); B(1); A(3); B(1); C(1); D(1); C(1); B(1); D(1) ... x3

46. **sc**; A(1); B(1); C(2); B(1); D(1); A(2); D(1); B(1); C(2); B(1); A(1) ... x3

47. **D(1)**; A(1); B(1); C(1); B(1); A(1); D(1); A(1); D(1); A(1); B(1); C(1); B(1); A(1) ... x3

48. **nc**; D(1); A(1); B(2); A(6); B(2); A(1); D(1) ... x3

49. **C(1)**; D(1); A(1); B(1); A(2); D(1); A(1); D(1); A(2); B(1); A(1); D(1) ... x3

50. **nc**; C(1); D(1); A(4); D(2); A(4); D(1); C(1) ... x3

51. **sc**; C(1); D(1); A(3); D(1); A(1); D(1); A(3); D(1); C(1) ... x3

52. **B(1)**; C(1); D(1); A(2); D(4); A(2); D(1); C(1) ... x3

53. **nc**; B(1); C(1); D(1); A(1); D(1); C(1); D(1); C(1); D(1); A(1); D(1); C(1); B(1) ... x3

54. **A(1)**; B(1); C(1); D(2); C(4); D(2); C(1); B(1) ... x3

55. **nc;** A(1); B(1); C(1); D(1); C(1); B(3); C(1); D(1); C(1); B(1); A(1) ... x3

56. **sc;** A(1); B(1); D(2); B(4); D(2); B(1); A(1) ... x3

57. **A(1);** A(1); D(1); A(1); D(1); A(1); D(1); A(1); D(1); A(1); D(1); A(1) ... x3

58. **nc;** A(1); D(1); A(1); B(1); D(4); B(1); A(1); D(1); A(1) ... x3

59. **A(1);** D(1); A(1); B(1); C(1); D(1); A(1); D(1); C(1); B(1); A(1); D(1) ... x3

BEGIN HEM

60. **nc;** D(1); A(1); B(1); C(1); D(1); A(2); D(1); C(1); B(1); A(1); D(1) ... x3

61. **D(1);** A(1); B(1); C(1); D(1); B(3); D(1); C(1); B(1); A(1) ... x3

Flat Lid

1. **A(1);** B(1); C(1) ... x3

2. **C(2)** ... x3

3. **C(2);** B(1) ... x3

4. **C(2);** B(2) ... x3

5. **D(2);** B(1); A(1); B(1) ... x3

6. **C(2);** D(1); A(2); D(1) ... x3

7. **B(2);** C(1); D(1); A(1); D(1); C(1) ... x3

8. **A(2);** B(1); C(1); D(2); C(1); B(1) ... x3

9. **D(2);** A(1); B(1); D(3); B(1); A(1) ... x3

10. **C(2);** D(1); A(1); D(1); **C(2);** D(1); A(1); D(1) ... x3

11. **B(2);** C(1); D(2); C(3); D(2); C(1) ... x3

12. **A(2);** B(1); C(1); D(1); B(4); D(1); C(1); B(1) ... x3

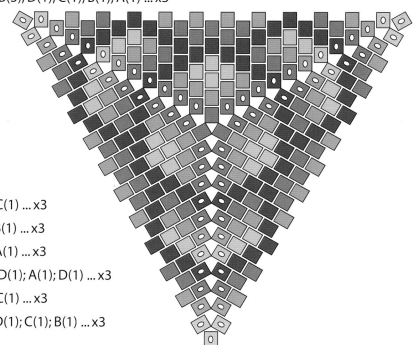

▼ Red Knot

Finished Size: 2¼" wide
x 1¾" tall (5.7 x 4.5 cm)
without finial or feet

A = White; Delica #352;
237 beads (2 grams)

B = Light Cream; Delica #353;
492 beads (3 grams)

C = Medium Cream; Delica
#205; 261 beads (2 grams)

D = Dark Cream; Delica #621;
1,125 beads (6 grams)

E = Red; Delica #162;
1,578 beads (8 grams)

F = Brown; Delica #769;
1,638 beads (9 grams)

Hem/Inner Wall = Any color;
852 beads (5 grams)

| A | B | C | D | E | F |

Construction Techniques

For the Base: pages 219–220

For the Sides: pages 228–229

For the Flat Lid: pages 237–239

Base of Box/Flat Lid

1. **E(1)** … x3
2. **E(2)** … x3
3. **E(2)**; E(1) … x3
4. **F(2)**; E(2) … x3
5. **C(2)**; E(3) … x3
6. **F(2)**; F(1); E(2); F(1) … x3
7. **E(2)**; D(1); F(1); E(1); F(1); C(1) … x3
8. **E(2)**; F(1); D(1); F(1); E(1); F(2) … x3
9. **E(2)**; E(1); F(1); D(1); F(1); E(1); F(1); E(1) … x3
10. **E(2)**; E(2); F(1); D(1); F(1); E(3) … x3

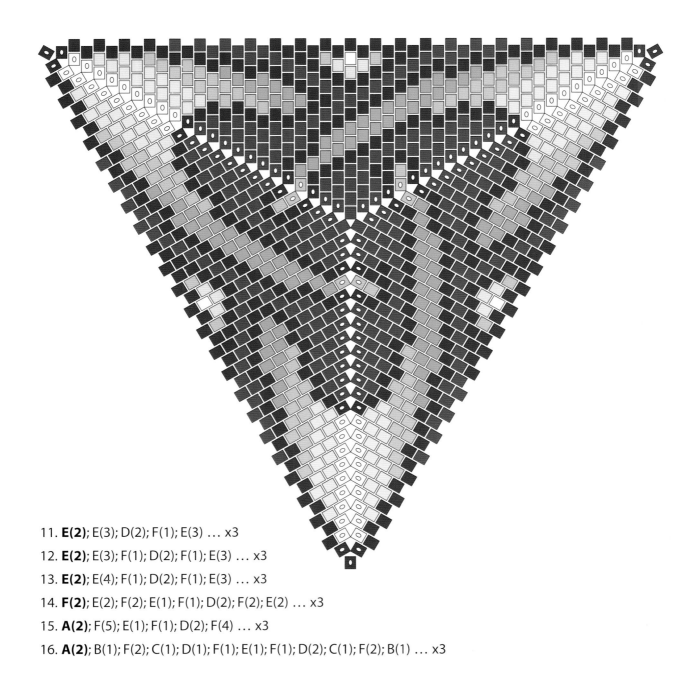

11. **E(2)**; E(3); D(2); F(1); E(3) … x3

12. **E(2)**; E(3); F(1); D(2); F(1); E(3) … x3

13. **E(2)**; E(4); F(1); D(2); F(1); E(3) … x3

14. **F(2)**; E(2); F(2); E(1); F(1); D(2); F(2); E(2) … x3

15. **A(2)**; F(5); E(1); F(1); D(2); F(4) … x3

16. **A(2)**; B(1); F(2); C(1); D(1); F(1); E(1); F(1); D(2); C(1); F(2); B(1) … x3

17. **A(2)**; B(2); C(2); D(2); F(1); E(1); F(1); D(2); C(2); B(2) … x3

18. **A(2)**; B(2); C(2); D(2); F(1); E(2); F(1); D(2); C(2); B(2) … x3

19. **A(2)**; B(2); C(2); D(2); F(1); E(1); F(1); E(1); F(1); D(2); C(2); B(2) … x3

20. **A(2)**; B(2); C(2); D(2); F(1); E(1); F(2); E(1); F(1); D(2); C(2); B(2) … x3

21. **A(2)**; B(2); C(2); D(1); F(2); E(1); F(1); B(1); F(1); E(1); F(2); D(1); C(2); B(2) … x3

22. **A(2)**; B(2); C(2); F(3); E(1); F(1); B(2); F(1); E(1); F(3); C(2); B(2) … x3

23. **A(2)**; B(2); C(1); F(3); E(2); F(1); C(1); A(1); C(1); F(1); E(2); F(3); C(1); B(2) … x3

24. **F(2)**; F(5); E(3); F(6); E(3); F(5) … x3

25. **F(1)**; F(4); E(4); F(7); E(4); F(4) … x3

Sides of Box

1. **nc**; D(3); C(3); B(3); A(6); B(3); C(3); D(3) … x3

2. **F(1)**; F(2); C(3); B(4); A(5); B(4); C(3); F(2) … x3

3. **nc**; F(3); C(3); B(3); A(6); B(3); C(3); F(3) … x3

4. **E(1)**; E(2); F(1); C(2); B(4); A(2); F(1); A(2); B(4); C(2); F(1); E(2) … x3

5. **nc**; E(3); F(1); C(2); B(3); A(2); F(2); A(2); B(3); C(2); F(1); E(3) … x3

6. **E(1)**; E(3); F(1); C(1); B(4); A(1); F(1); E(1); F(1); A(1); B(4); C(1); F(1); E(3) … x3

7. **nc**; E(4); F(1); C(1); B(3); A(1); F(1); E(2); F(1); A(1); B(3); C(1); F(1); E(4) … x3

8. **F(1)**; F(2); E(2); F(1); B(4); F(1); E(3); F(1); B(4); F(1); E(2); F(2) … x3

9. **nc**; F(3); E(2); F(1); B(3); F(1); **E(4)**; F(1); B(3); F(1); E(2); F(3) … x3

10. **E(1)**; F(1); D(1); F(1); E(2); F(1); B(2); F(1); E(2); F(1); E(2); F(1); B(2); F(1); E(2); F(1); D(1); F(1) … x3

11. **nc**; E(1); F(1); D(1); F(1); E(2); F(1); B(1); F(1); E(2); F(2); E(2); F(1); B(1); F(1); E(2); F(1); D(1); F(1); E(1) … x3

12. **E(1)**; E(1); F(1); C(1); F(1); E(2); F(2); E(2); F(3); E(2); F(2); E(2); F(1); C(1); F(1); E(1) … x3

13. **nc**; E(2); F(1); C(1); F(1); E(2); F(1); E(2); F(4); E(2); F(1); E(2); F(1); C(1); F(1); E(2) … x3

14. **F(1)**; E(2); F(1); C(1); F(1); E(2); F(1); E(1); F(2); E(1); F(2); E(2); F(1); E(1); F(1); C(1); F(1); E(2) … x3

15. **nc**; F(1); E(2); F(1); C(1); F(1); E(2); F(3); E(2); F(2); E(2); F(2); C(1); F(1); E(2); F(1) … x3

16. **F(1)**; F(1); E(2); F(1); C(1); F(1); E(2); F(2); E(3); F(2); E(2); F(1); C(1); F(1); E(2); F(1) … x3

17. **nc**; F(2); E(2); F(3); E(2); F(1); E(4); F(2); E(2); F(2); E(2); F(2) … x3

18. **E(1)**; F(2); E(2); F(1); E(1); F(1); E(1); F(1); E(2); F(1); E(1); F(1); E(1); F(1); E(2); F(1); E(2); F(2) … x3

19. **nc**; E(1); F(2); E(1); F(1); E(2); F(2); E(2); F(3); E(2); F(1); E(1); F(1); E(2); F(2); E(1) … x3

20. **E(1)**; E(1); F(3); E(2); F(2); E(2); F(1); A(1); F(1); E(2); F(3); E(2); F(2); E(1) … x3

21. **nc**; E(2); F(2); E(2); F(2); E(2); F(3); E(2); F(3); E(2); F(2); E(2) … x3

22. **F(1)**; E(2); F(1); E(2); F(2); E(2); F(1); E(1); F(1); E(2); F(1); E(1); F(1); E(2); F(2); E(2) … x3

23. **nc**; F(1); E(2); F(1); E(1); F(1); E(1); F(1); E(1); F(1); E(2); F(1); E(1); F(1); E(2); F(1); E(1); F(1); E(1); F(1); E(1); F(1) … x3

24. **D(1)**; F(1); E(2); F(2); E(2); F(3); E(2); F(3); E(2); F(2); E(2); F(2) … x3

25. **nc(1)**; D(1); F(1); E(2); F(2); E(2); F(1); A(1); F(1); E(2); F(1); A(1); F(1); E(2); F(2); E(2); F(1); D(1) … x3

26. **D(1)**; F(2); E(2); F(2); E(2); F(3); E(2); F(3); E(2); F(2); E(2); F(1) … x3

27. **nc**; F(1); E(1); F(1); E(1); F(1); E(1); F(1); E(2); F(1); E(1); F(1); E(2); F(1); E(1); F(1); E(1); F(1); E(1); F(1); E(2); F(1) … x3

28. **F(1)**; E(2); F(2); E(2); F(1); E(1); F(1); E(2); F(1); E(1); F(1); E(2); F(2); E(2); F(1); E(2) … x3

29. **nc**; E(2); F(2); E(2); F(3); E(2); F(3); E(2); F(2); E(2); F(2); E(2) … x3

30. **E(1)**; E(1); F(2); E(2); F(3); E(2); F(1); A(1); F(1); E(2); F(2); E(2); F(3); E(1) … x3

31. **nc**; E(1); F(2); E(2); F(1); E(1); F(1); E(2); F(3); E(2); F(2); E(2); F(1); E(1); F(2); E(1) … x3

32. **E(1)**; F(2); E(2); F(1); E(2); F(1); E(1); F(1); E(1); F(1); E(2); F(1); E(1); F(1); E(1); F(1); E(2); F(2) … x3

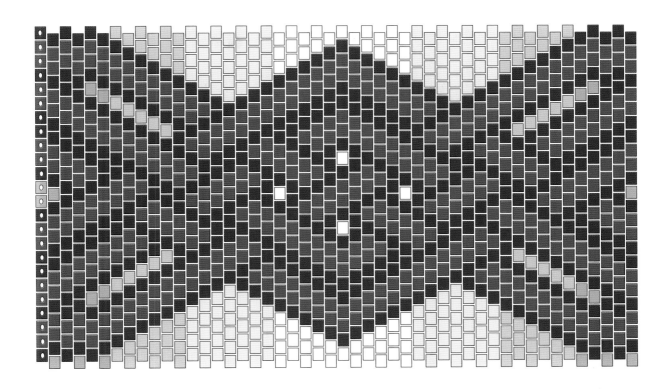

33. **nc**; F(2); E(2); F(2); E(2); F(2); E(4); F(1); E(2); F(3); E(2); F(2) … x3

34. **F(1)**; F(1); E(2); F(1); C(1); F(1); E(2); F(2); E(3); F(2); E(2); F(1); C(1); F(1); E(2); F(1) … x3

35. **nc**; F(1); E(2); F(1); C(1); F(2); E(2); F(2); E(2); F(3); E(2); F(1); C(1); F(1); E(2); F(1) … x3

36. **F(1)**; E(2); F(1); C(1); F(1); E(1); F(1); E(2); F(2); E(1); F(2); E(1); F(1); E(2); F(1); C(1);

    F(1); E(2) … x3

37. **nc**; E(2); F(1); C(1); F(1); E(2); F(1); E(2); F(4); E(2); F(1); E(2); F(1); C(1); F(1); E(2) … x3

38. **E(1)**; E(1); F(1); C(1); F(1); E(2); F(2); E(2); F(3); E(2); F(2); E(2); F(1); C(1); F(1); E(1) … x3

39. **nc**; E(1); F(1); D(1); F(1); E(2); F(1); B(1); F(1); E(2); F(2); E(2); F(1); B(1); F(1); E(2); F(1);

    D(1); F(1); E(1) … x3

40. **E(1)**; F(1); D(1); F(1); E(2); F(1); B(2); F(1); E(2); F(1); E(2); F(1); B(2); F(1); E(2); F(1); D(1); F(1) … x3

41. **nc**; F(3); E(2); F(1); B(3); F(1); E(4); F(1); B(3); F(1); E(2); F(3) … x3

42. **F(1)**; F(2); E(2); F(1); B(4); F(1); E(3); F(1); B(4); F(1); E(2); F(2) … x3

43. **nc**; E(4); F(1); C(1); B(3); A(1); F(1); E(2); F(1); A(1); B(3); C(1); F(1); E(4) … x3

44. **E(1)**; E(3); F(1); C(1); B(4); A(1); F(1); E(1); F(1); A(1); B(4); C(1); F(1); E(3) … x3

45. **nc**; E(3); F(1); C(2); B(3); A(2); F(2); A(2); B(3); C(2); F(1); E(3) … x3

46. **E(1)**; E(2); F(1); C(2); B(4); A(2); F(1); A(2); B(4); C(2); F(1); E(2) … x3

BEGIN HEM

47. **nc**; F(3); C(3); B(3); A(6); B(3); C(3); F(3) … x3

48. **F(1)**; F(2); C(3); B(4); A(5); B(4); C(3); F(2) … x3

Chapter 22

Patterns for
Hexagon
Boxes

✶ Tuffet

Finished Size: 1³⁄₄" wide x 1¹⁄₄" tall (4.5 x 3.2 cm) without feet

A = White; Delica #157;
414 beads (3 grams)

B = Lavender; Delica #158;
480 beads (3 grams)

C = Purple; Delica #884;
462 beads (3 grams)

D = Black; Delica #310;
1,308 beads (7 grams)

Hem/Inner Wall = Any color;
288 beads (2 grams)

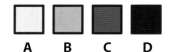

| A | B | C | D |

Construction Techniques

For the Base: pages 222–223

For the Sides: pages 230–231

Lid with Sides: pages 239–240

Base of Box

1. **nc**; C(1) ... x6
2. **B(1)** ... x6
3. **nc**; B(1) ... x6
4. **A(2)** ... x6
5. **A(1)**; D(1) ... x6
6. **nc**; D(2) ... x6
7. **D(2)**; C(1) ... x6
8. **D(1)**; C(2) ... x6
9. **nc**; C(1); B(1); C(1) ... x6
10. **D(2)**; B(2) ... x6
11. **C(1)**; B(1); A(1); B(1) ... x6
12. **nc**; D(1); A(2); D(1) ... x6
13. **C(2)**; D(1); A(1); D(1) ... x6
14. **B(1)**; C(1); D(2); C(1) ... x6
15. **nc**; B(1); D(3); B(1) ... x6
16. **A(2)**; D(1); C(2); D(1) ... x6
17. **A(1)**; B(1); C(1); B(1); C(1); B(1) ... x6
18. **nc**; D(2); B(2); D(2) ... x6
19. **D(2)**; D(1); B(1); A(1); B(1); D(1) ... x6
20. **D(1)**; C(1); D(1); A(2); D(1); C(1) ... x6
21. **nc**; C(2); D(1); A(1); D(1); C(2) ... x6
22. **C(2)**; B(1); C(1); D(2); C(1); B(1) ... x6
23. **C(1)**; B(2); C(1); D(1); C(1); B(2) ... x6

24. **nc**; B(1); A(1); B(1); D(2); B(1); A(1); B(1) ... x6

25. **D(2)**; A(2); D(1); C(1); D(1); A(2) ... x6

26. **D(1)**; D(1); A(1); D(1); C(2); D(1); A(1); D(1) ... x6

Sides of Box

27. **nc**; C(1); D(2); C(1); B(1); C(1); D(2); C(1) ... x6

28. **B(1)**; C(1); D(1); C(1); B(2); C(1); D(1); C(1) ... x6

29. **nc**; B(1); C(2); B(1); A(1); B(1); C(2); B(1) ... x6

30. **A(1)**; B(1); D(1); B(1); A(2); B(1); D(1); B(1) ... x6

31. **nc**; A(1); B(2); A(3); B(2); A(1) ... x6

32. **A(1)**; A(1); D(1); A(4); D(1); A(1) ... x6

33. **nc**; A(1); D(2); A(3); D(2); A(1) ... x6

34. **A(1)**; D(1); C(1); D(1); A(2); D(1); C(1); D(1) ... x6

35. **nc**; D(1); C(2); D(1); A(1); D(1); C(2); D(1) ... x6

36. **D(1)**; C(1); B(1); C(1); D(2); C(1); B(1); C(1) ... x6

37. **nc**; D(1); B(2); D(3); B(2); D(1) ... x6

38. **sc**; D(1); A(1); D(1); C(2); D(1); A(1); D(1) ... x6

39. **D(1)**; D(2); C(1); B(1); C(1); D(2) ... x6

40. **nc**; D(3); B(2); D(3) ... x6

41. **sc**; D(3); A(1); D(3) ... x6

42. **D(1)**; D(6) ... x6

43. **nc**; D(7) ... x6

44. **sc**; D(6) ... x6

45. **D(1)**; D(5) ... x6

46. **nc**; D(6) ... x6

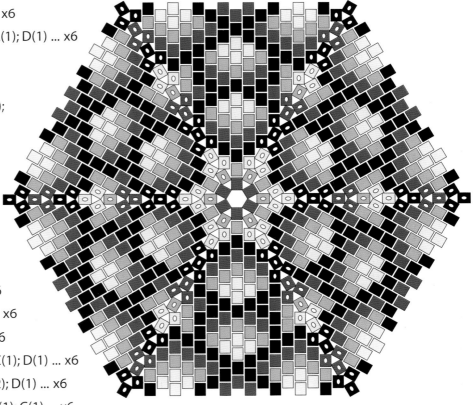

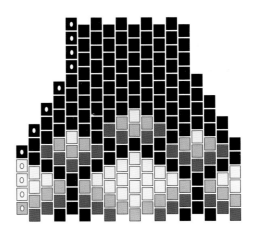

47. **sc**; D(5) ... x6

48. **D(1)**; D(4) ... x6

49. **nc**; D(5) ... x6

50. **D(1)**; D(4) ... x6

51. **nc**; D(5) ... x6

52. **D(1)**; D(4) ... x6

BEGIN HEM

53. **nc**; D(5) ... x6

54. **D(1)**; D(4) ... x6

Lid with Sides

1. **nc**; C(1) ... x6

2. **B(1)** ... x6

3. **nc**; B(1) ... x6

4. **A(2)** ... x6

5. **A(1)**; D(1) ... x6

6. **nc**; D(2) ... x6

7. **D(2)**; C(1) ... x6

8. **D(1)**; C(2) ... x6

9. **nc**; C(1); B(1); C(1) ... x6

10. **D(2)**; B(2) ... x6

11. **C(1)**; B(1); A(1); B(1) ... x6

12. **nc**; D(1); A(2); D(1) ... x6

13. **C(2)**; D(1); A(1); D(1) ... x6

14. **B(1)**; C(1); D(2); C(1) ... x6

15. **nc**; B(1); D(3); B(1) ... x6

16. **A(2)**; D(1); C(2); D(1) ... x6

17. **A(1)**; B(1); C(1); B(1); C(1); B(1) ... x6

18. **nc**; D(2); B(2); D(2) ... x6

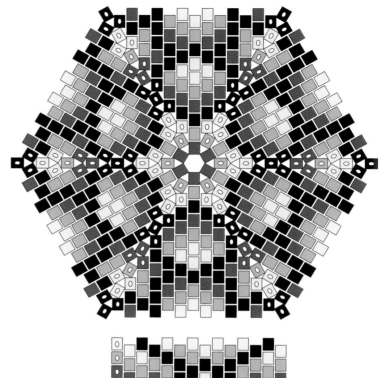

19. **D(2)**; D(1); B(1); A(1); B(1); D(1) ... x6

20. **D(1)**; C(1); D(1); A(2); D(1); C(1) ... x6

Sides of Lid

21. **nc**; C(2); D(1); A(1); D(1); C(2) ... x6

22. **C(1)**; B(2); D(2); B(2) ... x6

23. **nc**; B(2); D(3); B(2) ... x6

24. **B(1)**; A(1); D(1); B(2); D(1); A(1) ... x6

BEGIN HEM

25. **nc**; A(1); D(1); B(1); A(1); B(1); D(1); A(1) ... x6

26. **A(1)**; D(1); A(4); D(1) ... x6

Deco Pagoda

This box is a little different in that it has a tiered structure. You begin each new tier (except the bottom one) with the same method used to make a hem, but you make decreases to complete the tier. The roofs are extensions of the top row of each tier. This structure becomes clear as you follow the word map.

Base of Box

1. **nc**; B(1) ... x6
2. **A(1)** ... x6
3. **nc**; B(1) ... x6
4. **B(2)** ... x6
5. **B(1)**; B(1) ... x6
6. **nc**; B(2) ... x6
7. **A(2)**; A(1) ... x6
8. **B(1)**; A(2) ... x6
9. **nc**; A(3) ... x6
10. **A(2)**; A(2) ... x6
11. **B(1)**; A(3) ... x6
12. **nc**; A(4) ... x6
13. **B(2)**; A(3) ... x6
14. **B(1)**; A(4) ... x6
15. **nc**; B(1); A(3); B(1) ... x6
16. **A(2)**; B(1); A(2); B(1) ... x6
17. **B(1)**; B(5) ... x6
18. **nc**; A(1); B(4); A(1) ... x6
19. **A(2)**; B(5) ... x6

20. **B(1)**; A(1); B(1); A(2); B(1); A(1) ... x6

21. **nc**; A(1); B(1); A(3); B(1); A(1) ... x6

22. **A(2)**; A(2); B(2); A(2) ... x6

23. **B(1)**; A(1); B(5); A(1) ... x6

24. **nc**; A(8) ... x6

25. **A(2)**; A(1); B(5); A(1) ... x6

26. **B(1)**; A(3); B(2); A(3) ... x6

27. **nc**; B(3); A(3); B(3) ... x6

28. **A(2)**; B(3); A(2); B(3) ... x6

29. **B(1)**; B(9) ... x6

Bottom Tier

1. **nc**; A(1); B(3); A(2); B(3); A(1) ... x6

2. **A(1)**; B(4); A(1); B(4) ... x6

3. **nc**; A(1); B(3); A(2); B(3); A(1) ... x6

4. **B(1)**; B(9) ... x6

5. **nc**; A(1); B(3); A(2); B(3); A(1) ... x6

6. **A(1)**; A(1); B(2); A(3); B(2); A(1) ... x6

7. **nc**; B(1); A(3); B(2); A(3); B(1) ... x6

8. **B(1);** B(1); A(2); B(3); A(2); B(1) ... x6

9. **nc**; B(10) ... x6

10. **B(1)**; B(1); A(2); B(3); A(2); B(1) ... x6

11. **nc**; B(2); A(1); B(4); A(1); B(2) ... x6

12. **B(1)**; B(1); A(2); B(3); A(2); B(1) ... x6

13. **nc**; B(10) ... x6

14. **B(1);** B(1); A(2); B(3); A(2); B(1) ... x6

15. **nc**; B(1); A(3); B(2); A(3); B(1) ... x6

16. **A(1)**; A(1); B(2); A(3); B(2); A(1) ... x6

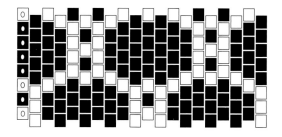

Bottom Tier

Middle Tier

Bead row 1 exactly as you would bead the first hem row. The skipped corner is considered an "**sc.**"

  1. **sc**; A(9) ... x6

The next five rows use Steps 2, 3, 1, 2, and 3 of a hexagon box decrease cycle (page 230).

You then resume tubular peyote stitch.

  2. **A(1)**; A(1); B(1); A(4); B(1); A(1) ... x6

  3. **nc**; A(1); B(1); A(2); B(1); A(2); B(1); A(1) ... x6

  4. **sc**; B(1); A(2); B(2); A(2); B(1) ... x6

  5. **B(1)**; B(1); A(1); B(1); C(1); B(1); A(1); B(1) ... x6

  6. **nc**; A(1); B(6); A(1) ... x6

  7. **A(1)**; A(1); B(1); A(1); B(1); A(1); B(1); A(1) ... x6

  8. **nc**; A(2); B(1); A(2); B(1); A(2) ... x6

  9. **B(1)**; A(2); B(1); A(1); B(1); A(2) ... x6

 10. **nc**; B(1); A(2); B(2); A(2); B(1) ... x6

 11. **C(1)**; B(1); A(2); B(1); A(2); B(1) ... x6

 12. **nc**; B(2); A(1); B(2); A(1); B(2) ... x6

 13. **B(1)**; A(1); B(2); C(1); B(2); A(1) ... x6

 14. **nc**; A(2); B(4); A(2) ... x6

 15. **A(1)**; A(1); B(1); A(1); B(1); A(1); B(1); A(1) ... x6

 16. **nc**; A(1); B(1); A(4); B(1); A(1) ... x6

 17. **A(1)**; B(1); A(5); B(1) ... x6

 18. **nc**; B(1); A(6); B(1) ... x6

 19. **B(1)**; A(7) ... x6

Top Tier

Bead row 1 exactly as you would bead the first hem row.

The skipped corner is considered an "**sc.**"

  1. **sc**; B(7) ... x6

Middle Tier

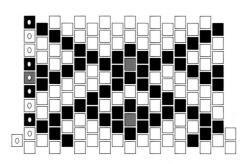

Top Tier

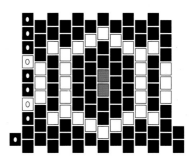

The next five rows use Steps 2, 3, 1, 2, and 3 of a hexagon box decrease cycle (pages 230–231). You then resume tubular peyote stitch.

2. **B(1)**; B(6) ... x6

3. **nc**; B(3); A(1); B(3) ... x6

4. **sc**; B(2); A(2); B(2) ... x6

5. **B(1)**; A(2); B(1); A(2) ... x6

6. **nc**; B(1); A(1); B(2) ... x6

7. **A(1)**; B(5) ... x6

8. **nc**; A(2); B(2); A(2) ... x6

9. **B(1)**; B(2); C(1); B(2) ... x6

10. **nc**; A(2); B(2); A(2) ... x6

11. **B(1)**; B(2); C(1); B(2) ... x6

12. **nc**; A(2); B(2); A(2) ... x6

13. **A(1)**; B(5) ... x6

14. **nc**; B(1); A(1); B(2); A(1); B(1) ... x6

15. **B(1)**; A(2); B(1); A(2) ... x6

16. **nc**; B(2); A(2); B(2) ... x6

17. **B(1)**; B(2); A(1); B(2) ... x6

BEGIN HEM

18. **nc**; B(6) ... x6

19. **B(1)**; B(5) ... x6

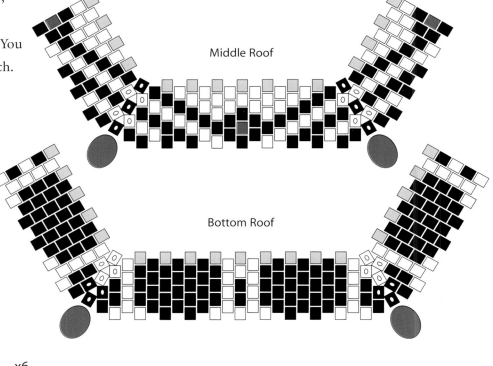

Middle Roof

Bottom Roof

You will now add first the middle roof and then the bottom roof. Begin a new thread, and weave through the appropriate tier until your needle exits the last (top) row of the tier. (This row is indicated by the grey beads in the diagram.) You will then add one row without increasing (the corner will be a down bead) and then perform two and one-half hexagon-box increase cycles.

Begin the third cycle in the usual way, but in the second step of the increase—where you would usually add two corner beads—add one "D" bead. This row will be the final row of the roof. Read the graph from the top row downward. (The graph shows a full roof side with partial sides adjoining. The partial sides are for reference only.)

Middle Roof

1. **nc**; B(1); A(6); B(1) ... x6

2. **A(2)**; B(1); A(5); B(1) ... x6

3. **B(1)**; A(1); B(1); A(4); B(1); A(1) ... x6

4. **nc**; B(1); A(1); B(1); A(1); B(1); A(1); B(1); A(1); B(1) ... x6

5. **A(2)**; B(1); A(1); B(4); A(1); B(1) ... x6

6. **B(1)**; A(1); B(1); A(1); B(1); C(1); B(1); A(1); B(1); A(1) ... x6

7. **nc**; B(1); A(1); B(1); A(1); B(2); A(1); B(1); A(1); B(1) ... x6

8. **D(1)**; B(3); A(1); B(1); A(1); B(3) ... x6

Bottom Roof

1. **nc**; A(1); B(3); A(2); B(3); A(1) ... x6

2. **A(2)**; B(9) ... x6

3. **B(1)**; A(1); B(3); A(2); B(3); A(1) ... x6

4. **nc**; B(5); A(1); B(5) ... x6

5. **B(2)**; A(1); B(3); A(2); B(3); A(1) ... x6

6. **B(1)**; B(11) ... x6

7. **nc**; B(1); A(1); B(3); A(2); B(3); A(1); B(1) ... x6

8. **D(1)**; A(2); B(2); A(3); B(2); A(2) ... x6

Flat Lid

1. **nc**; B(1) ... x6

2. **A(1)** ... x6

3. **nc**; B(1) ... x6

4. **B(2)** ... x6

5. **B(1)**; B(1) ... x6

6. **nc**; B(2) ... x6

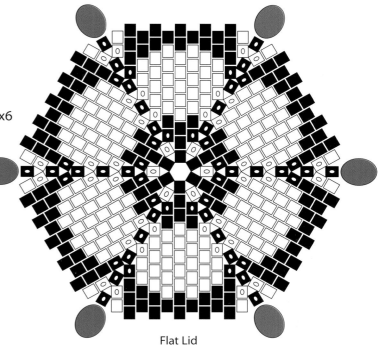

Flat Lid

7. **A(2)**; A(1) ... x6

8. **B(1)**; A(2) ... x6

9. **nc**; A(3) ... x6

10. **A(2)**; A(2) ... x6

11. **B(1)**; A(3) ... x6

12. **nc**; A(4) ... x6

13. **B(2)**; A(3) ... x6

14. **B(1)**; A(4) ... x6

15. **nc**; B(1); A(3); B(1) ... x6

16. **A(2)**; B(1); A(2); B(1) ... x6

17. **B(1)**; B(5) ... x6

18. **nc**; A(1); B(4); A(1) ... x6

19. **D(1)**; B(5) ... x6

 # New School

Finished Size: 3" wide x
2¼" tall (7.6 x 5.7 cm)
without finial or feet

A = Dark Cream; Delica #907;
1,494 beads (8 grams)

B = Yellow; Delica #124;
418 beads (3 grams)

C = Pale Pink; Delica #728;
96 beads (1 gram)

D = Turquoise; Delica #217;
284 beads (2 grams)

E = Green; Delica #859;
776 beads (4 grams)

F = Purple; Delica #884;
584 beads (3 grams)

G = Black; Delica #10;
3,238 beads (17 grams)

Hem/Inner Wall = Any color;
684 beads (4 grams)

A   B   C   D   E   F   G

Construction Techniques

For the Base: pages 222–223

For the Sides: pages 230–231

For the Flat Lid: pages 239–240

Base of Box

Flat strip (indicated on the graph by ovals inside of squares)

1 and 2. G(1); D(1); G(2); E(1); G(2); D(1); G(2); E(1); G(2); D(1); G(2); E(1); G(2); D(1); G(1) ... x1

3. D(2); G(1); D(2); G(1); D(2); G(1); D(2) ... x1

4. D(1); G(2); D(1); G(2); D(1); G(2); D(1) ... x1

5. G(2); E(1); G(2); E(1); G(2); E(1); G(2) ... x1

Add end beads.

6. G(1); E(2); G(1); E(2); G(1); E(2); G(1); **G(3)** (end beads) ... x2

7. G(2); E(1); G(2); E(1); G(2); E(1); G(2); G(1) (between end beads); G(1) (between end beads) ... x2

8. F(1); G(2); F(1); G(2); F(1); G(2); F(1); **G(2)**; **F(2)**; **G(2)** ... x2

Begin hexagon increase cycles. From this point on, read the word map as usual, beginning with corner beads. The long sides will be first.

9. **G(1)**; F(2); G(1); F(2); G(1); F(2); G(1); F(2); G(1); F(1); F(1); F(1) ...x2

10. **nc**; G(1); F(1); G(2); F(1); G(2); F(1); G(4); nc; G(1); F(1); nc; F(1); G(1) ...x2

11. **C(2)**; G(2); B(1); G(2); C(1); G(2); E(1); G(2); C(2); G(1); F(2); G(1) ...x2

12. **C(1)**; C(1); G(1); B(2); G(1); C(2); G(1); E(1); G(1); A(1); G(1); C(1); C(1); G(1); F(1); G(2) ...x2

13. **nc**; C(1); G(2); B(2); G(1); C(1); G(3); A(1); G(2); nc; C(1); G(2); nc; G(3) ...x2

14. **G(2)**; G(1); E(1); B(3); G(2); D(1); G(1); A(1); G(1); E(1); G(2); G(1); E(1); G(2); G(1); E(1) ...x2

15. **G(1)**; G(1); E(1); G(1); B(3); G(1); D(1); G(1); A(1); G(1); E(1); G(1); G(1); G(1); E(1); G(1); G(1); G(1); E(1); G(1) ...x2

16. **nc**; G(1); E(2); G(1); B(3); G(2); A(1); G(1); E(2); G(1); nc; G(1); E(2); G(1); nc; G(1); E(2); G(1) ...x2

17. **G(2)**; E(3); G(1); B(2); G(2); A(1); G(1); E(3); G(2); E(3); G(2); E(3) ...x2

18. **E(1)**; E(4); G(1); B(1); G(2); A(1); G(1); E(4); E(1); E(4); E(1); E(4) ...x2

19. **nc**; E(5); G(2); A(2); G(1); E(5); **nc;** E(5); **nc**; E(5) ... x2

20. **E(2)**; E(5); G(1); A(2); G(1); E(5); **E(2)**; E(4); **E(2)**; E(4) ... x2

21. **E(1)**; E(6); A(3); E(6); **E(1)**; E(5); **E(1)**; E(5) ... x2

22. **nc**; E(6); G(1); A(2); G(1); E(6); **nc**; E(6); **nc**; E(6) ... x2

23. **G(2)**; E(5); G(2); A(2); G(1); E(5); **G(2)**; E(5); **G(2)**; E(5) ... x2

24. **B(1)**; G(1); E(4); G(1); B(1); G(2); A(1); G(1); E(4); G(1); **B(1)**; G(1); E(4); G(1); **B(1)**; G(1); E(4); G(1) ... x2

25. **nc**; A(1); G(1); E(3); G(1); B(2); G(2); A(1); G(1); E(3); G(1); B(1); **nc**; A(1); G(1); E(3); G(1); B(1); **nc**; A(1); G(1); E(3); G(1); B(1) ...x2

26. **B/G**; A(1); G(1); E(2); G(1); B(3); F(1); G(1); A(1); G(1); E(2); G(1); B(1); **B/G**; A(1); G(1); E(2); G(1); B(1); **B/G**; A(1); G(1); E(2); G(1); B(1) ... x2

27. **G(1)**; G(1); A(1); G(1); E(1); G(1); B(3); G(1); F(1); G(1); A(1); G(1); E(1); G(1); B(2); **G(1)**; G(1); A(1); G(1); E(1); G(1); B(2); **G(1)**; G(1); A(1); G(1); E(1); G(1); B(2) ... x2

28. **nc**; F(1); G(1); A(1); G(1); E(1); B(3); G(1); F(2); G(1); A(1); G(1); E(1); B(3); **nc**; F(1); G(1); A(1); G(1); E(1); B(3); **nc**; F(1); G(1); A(1); G(1); E(1); B(3) ... x2

29. **G/F**; F(1); G(1); A(1); G(2); B(2); G(1); F(3); G(1); A(1); G(2); B(2); **G/F**; F(1); G(1); A(1); G(2); B(2); **G/F**; F(1); G(1); A(1); G(2); B(2) ... x2

30. **F(1)**; F(2); G(1); A(1); G(2); B(1); G(1); F(4); G(1); A(1); G(2); B(1); G(1); **F(1)**; F(2); G(1); A(1); G(2); B(1); G(1); **F(1)**; F(2); G(1); A(1); G(2); B(1); G(1) ... x2

31. **nc**; F(3); G(1); A(2); G(2); F(5); G(1); A(2); G(2); F(1); **nc**; F(3); G(1); A(2); G(2); F(1); **nc**; F(3); G(1); A(2); G(2); F(1) ... x2

32. **F(2)**; F(3); G(1); A(2); G(1); F(6); G(1); A(2); G(1); F(1); **F(2)**; F(3); G(1); A(2); G(1); F(1); **F(2)**; F(3); G(1); A(2); G(1); F(1) ... x2

33. **F(1)**; F(4); A(3); F(7); A(3); F(2); **F(1)**; F(4); A(3); F(2); **F(1)**; F(4); A(3); F(2) ... x2

Sides of Box

Everyone beads differently, depending sometimes on which hand is dominant or on natural tendency. Some people will prefer to bead the base in a clockwise direction, and others will bead counterclockwise. Because the pattern is read clockwise, the side of the beadwork that is facing you may or may not be a mirror image of the graphed pattern.

Similarly, some beaders will naturally work the sides of the box away from their bodies (with the underside of the box facing toward them). Others will work the sides of the box toward their bodies (with the inside of the box facing them). Work whichever way is most comfortable for you, but, after adding the first few beads for the sides, look closely at your beadwork. The dark lines of the pattern should align from the base to the sides. If they do not, remove the beads from this row, and turn the base so that the opposite side of the box faces you. You will need to weave through a few beads to reorient the needle so that it is traveling in the right direction. Rework the row so that the pattern lines on the side and the base align.

1. **nc**; F(2); G(1); A(2); G(1); F(6); G(1); A(2); G(1); F(4); **nc**; F(2); G(1); A(2); G(1); F(4); **nc**; F(2); G(1); A(2); G(1); F(4) ... x2

2. **F(1)**; F(1); G(2); A(2); G(1); F(5); G(2); A(2); G(1); F(3); **F(1)**; F(1); G(2); A(2); G(1); F(3); **F(1)**; F(1); G(2); A(2); G(1); F(3) ... x2

3. **nc**; F(1); G(1); B(1); G(2); A(1); G(1); F(4); G(1); B(1); G(2); A(1); G(1); F(3); **nc**; F(1); G(1); B(1); G(2); A(1); G(1); F(3); **nc**; F(1); G(1); B(1); G(2); A(1); G(1); F(3) ... x2

4. **F(1)**; G(2); B(1); G(2); A(1); G(1); F(3); G(2); B(1); G(2); A(1); G(1); F(2); **F(1)**; G(2); B(1); G(2); A(1); G(1); F(2); **F(1)**; G(2); B(1); G(2); A(1); G(1); F(2) ... x2

5. **nc**; G(1); B(1); G(1); B(1); E(1); G(1); A(1); G(1); F(2); G(1); B(1); G(1); B(1); E(1); G(1); A(1); G(1); F(2); **nc**; G(1); B(1); G(1); B(1); E(1); G(1); A(1); G(1); F(2); **nc**; G(1); B(1); G(1); B(1); E(1); G(1); A(1); G(1); F(2) ... x2

6. **G(1)**; G(1); B(1); G(4); A(1); G(1); F(1); G(2); B(1); G(4); A(1); G(1); F(1); **G(1)**; G(1); B(1); G(4); A(1); G(1); F(1); **G(1)**; G(1); B(1); G(4); A(1); G(1); F(1) ... x2

7. **nc**; B(1); G(1); B(1); G(4); A(1); G(1); F(1); B(1); G(1); B(1); G(4); A(1); G(1); F(1); **nc**; B(1); G(1); B(1); G(4); A(1); G(1); F(1); **nc**; B(1); G(1); B(1); G(4); A(1); G(1); F(1) ... x2

8. **G(1)**; B(1); G(3); D(1); G(2); A(1); G(2); B(1); G(3); D(1); G(2); A(1); G(1); **G(1)**; B(1); G(3); D(1); G(2); A(1); G(1); **G(1)**; B(1); G(3); D(1); G(2); A(1); G(1) ... x2

9. **nc**; G(1); B(1); G(1); E(1); D(2); E(1); G(1); A(1); G(2); B(1); G(1); E(1); D(2); E(1); G(1); A(1); G(1); **nc**; G(1); B(1); G(1); E(1); D(2); E(1); G(1); A(1); G(1); **nc**; G(1); B(1); G(1); E(1); D(2); E(1); G(1); A(1); G(1) ... x2

10. **A(1)**; G(4); D(1); G(1); E(1); G(1); A(2); G(4); D(1); G(1); E(1); G(1); A(1); **A(1)**; G(4); D(1); G(1); E(1); G(1); A(1); **A(1)**; G(4); D(1); G(1); E(1); A(1) ... x2

11. **nc**; A(1); G(1); D(1); G(3); E(2); G(1); A(2); G(1); D(1); G(3); E(2); G(1); A(1); **nc**; A(1); G(1); D(1); G(3); E(2); G(1); A(1); **nc**; A(1); G(1); D(1); G(3); E(2); G(1); A(1) ... x2

12. **A(1)**; A(1); D(2); E(1); G(1); E(1); G(1); E(1); A(3); D(2); E(1); G(1); E(1); G(1); E(1); A(1); **A(1)**; A(1); D(2); E(1); G(1); E(1); G(1); E(1); A(1); **A(1)**; A(1); D(2); E(1); G(1); E(1); G(1); E(1); A(1) ... x2

13. **nc**; A(1); G(1); D(1); G(3); E(2); G(1); A(2); G(1); D(1); G(3); E(2); G(1); A(1); **nc**; A(1); G(1); D(1); G(3); E(2); G(1); A(1); **nc**; A(1); G(1); D(1); G(3); E(2); G(1); A(1) ... x2

14. **A(1)**; G(4); D(1); G(1); E(1); G(1); A(2); G(4); D(1); G(1); E(1); G(1); A(1); **A(1)**; G(4); D(1); G(1); E(1); G(1); A(1); **A(1)**; G(4); D(1); G(1); E(1); G(1); A(1) ... x2

15. **nc**; G(1); B(1); G(1); E(1); D(2); E(1); G(1); A(1); G(2); B(1); G(1); E(1); D(2); E(1); G(1); A(1); G(1); **nc**; G(1); B(1); G(1); E(1); D(2); E(1); G(1); A(1); G(1); **nc**; G(1); B(1); G(1); E(1); D(2); E(1); G(1); A(1); G(1) ... x2

16. **G(1)**; B(1); G(3); D(1); G(2); A(1); G(2); B(1); G(3); D(1); G(2); A(1); G(1); **G(1)**; B(1); G(3); D(1); G(2); A(1); G(1); **G(1)**; B(1); G(3); D(1); G(2); A(1); G(1) ... x2

17. **nc**; B(1); G(1); B(1); G(4); A(1); G(1); C(1); B(1); G(1); B(1); G(4); A(1); G(1); C(1); **nc**; B(1); G(1); B(1); G(4); A(1); G(1); C(1); **nc**; B(1); G(1); B(1); G(4); A(1); G(1); C(1) ... x2

18. **G(1)**; G(1); B(1); G(4); A(1); G(4); B(1); G(4); A(1); G(2); **G(1)**; G(1); B(1); G(4); A(1); G(2); **G(1)**; G(1); B(1); G(4); A(1); G(2) ... x2

19. **nc**; G(1); B(1); G(1); B(1); E(1); G(1); A(1); G(4); B(1); G(1); B(1); E(1); G(1); A(1); G(3); **nc**; G(1); B(1); G(1); B(1); E(1); G(1); A(1); G(3); **nc**; G(1); B(1); G(1); B(1); E(1); G(1); A(1); G(3) ... x2

20. **G(1)**; G(2); B(1); G(2); A(1); G(2); F(1); G(3); B(1); G(2); A(1); G(2); F(1); **G(1)**; G(2); B(1); G(2); A(1); G(2); F(1); **G(1)**; G(2); B(1); G(2); A(1); G(2); F(1) ... x2

21. **nc**; E(1); G(1); B(1); G(2); A(1); G(1); C(1); F(2); E(1); G(1); B(1); G(2); A(1); G(1); C(1); F(2); **nc**; E(1); G(1); B(1); G(2); A(1); G(1); C(1); F(2); **nc**; E(1); G(1); B(1); G(2); A(1); G(1); C(1); F(2) ... x2

22. **G(1)**; G(3); A(2); G(1); C(1); G(1); F(1); G(4); A(2); G(1); C(1); G(1); F(1); **G(1)**; G(3); A(2); G(1); C(1); G(1); F(1); **G(1)**; G(3); A(2); G(1); C(1); G(1); F(1) ... x2

23. **nc**; G(1); F(1); G(1); A(2); G(1); C(2); G(3); F(1); G(1); A(2); G(1); C(2); G(2); **nc**; G(1); F(1); G(1); A(2); G(1); C(2); G(2); **nc**; G(1); F(1); G(1); A(2); G(1); C(2); G(2) ... x2

24. **C(1)**; F(2); A(3); C(1); G(1); C(1); G(1); C(1); F(2); A(3); C(1); G(1); C(1); G(1); **C(1)**; F(2); A(3); C(1); G(1); C(1); G(1); **C(1)**; F(2); A(3); C(1); G(1); C(1); G(1) ... x2

25. **nc**; G(1); F(1); G(1); A(2); G(1); C(2); G(3); F(1); G(1); A(2); G(1); C(2); G(2); **nc**; G(1); F(1); G(1); A(2); G(1); C(2); G(2); **nc**; G(1); F(1); G(1); A(2); G(1); C(2); G(2) ... x2

26. **G(1)**; G(3); A(2); G(1); C(1); G(1); F(1); G(4); A(2); G(1); C(1); G(1); F(1); **G(1)**; G(3); A(2); G(1); C(1); G(1); F(1); **G(1)**; G(3); A(2); G(1); C(1); G(1); F(1) ... x2

27. **nc**; E(1); G(1); B(1); G(2); A(1); G(1); C(1); F(2); E(1); G(1); B(1); G(2); A(1); G(1); C(1); F(2); **nc**; E(1); G(1); B(1); G(2); A(1); G(1); C(1); F(2); **nc**; E(1); G(1); B(1); G(2); A(1); G(1); C(1); F(2) ... x2

28. **G(1)**; G(2); B(1); G(2); A(1); G(2); F(1); G(3); B(1); G(2); A(1); G(2); F(1); **G(1)**; G(2); B(1); G(2); A(1); G(2); F(1); **G(1)**; G(2); B(1); G(2); A(1); G(2); F(1) ... x2

29. **nc**; G(1); B(1); G(1); B(1); E(1); G(1); A(1); G(4); B(1); G(1); B(1); E(1); G(1); A(1); G(3); **nc**; G(1); B(1); G(1); B(1); E(1); G(1); A(1); G(3); **nc**; G(1); B(1); G(1); B(1); E(1); G(1); A(1); G(3) ... x2

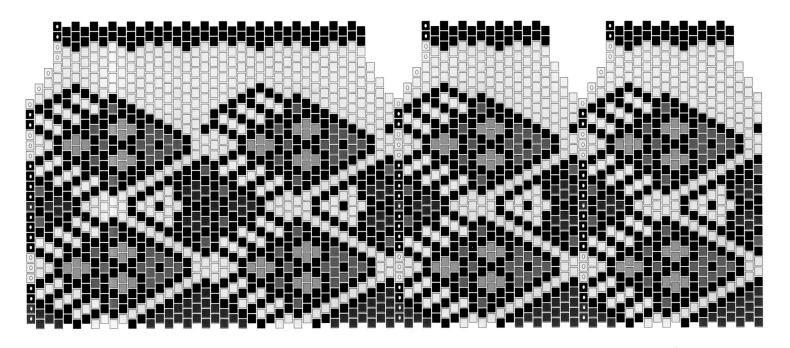

30. **G(1)**; G(1); B(1); G(4); A(1); G(4); B(1); G(4); A(1); G(2); **G(1)**; G(1); B(1); G(4); A(1); G(2); **G(1)**; G(1); B(1); G(4); A(1); G(2) ... x2

31. **nc**; B(1); G(1); B(1); G(4); A(1); G(1); C(1); B(1); G(1); B(1); G(4); A(1); G(1); C(1); **nc**; B(1); G(1); B(1); G(4); A(1); G(1); C(1); **nc**; B(1); G(1); B(1); G(4); A(1); G(1); C(1) ... x2

32. **G(1)**; B(1); G(3); D(1); G(2); A(1); G(2); B(1); G(3); D(1); G(2); A(1); G(1); **G(1)**; B(1); G(3); D(1); G(2); A(1); G(1); **G(1)**; B(1); G(3); D(1); G(2); A(1); G(1) ... x2

33. **nc**; G(1); B(1); G(1); E(1); D(2); E(1); G(1); A(1); G(2); B(1); G(1); E(1); D(2); E(1); G(1); A(1); G(1); **nc**; G(1); B(1); G(1); E(1); D(2); E(1); G(1); A(1); G(1); **nc**; G(1); B(1); G(1); E(1); D(2); E(1); G(1); A(1); G(1) ... x2

34. **A(1)**; G(4); D(1); G(1); E(1); G(1); A(2); G(4); D(1); G(1); E(1); G(1); A(1); **A(1)**; G(4); D(1); G(1); E(1); G(1); A(1); **A(1)**; G(4); D(1); G(1); E(1); G(1); A(1) ... x2

35. **nc**; A(1); G(1); D(1); G(3); E(2); G(1); A(2); G(1); D(1); G(3); E(2); G(1); A(1); **nc**; A(1); G(1); D(1); G(3); E(2); G(1); A(1); **nc**; A(1); G(1); D(1); G(3); E(2); G(1); A(1) ... x2

36. **A(1)**; A(1); D(2); E(1); G(1); E(1); G(1); E(1); A(3); D(2); E(1); G(1); E(1); G(1); E(1); A(1); **A(1)**; A(1); D(2); E(1); G(1); E(1); G(1); E(1); A(1); **A(1)**; A(1); D(2); E(1); G(1); E(1); G(1); E(1); A(1) ... x2

37. **nc**; A(1); G(1); D(1); G(3); E(2); G(1); A(2); G(1); D(1); G(3); E(2); G(1); A(1); **nc**; A(1); G(1); D(1); G(3); E(2); G(1); A(1); **nc**; A(1); G(1); D(1); G(3); E(2); G(1); A(1) ... x2

38. **A(1)**; G(4); D(1); G(1); E(1); G(1); A(2); G(4); D(1); G(1); E(1); G(1); A(1); **A(1)**; G(4); D(1); G(1); E(1); G(1); A(1); **A(1)**; G(4); D(1); G(1); E(1); G(1) ... x2

39. **nc**; G(1); B(1); G(1); E(1); D(2); E(1); G(1); A(1); G(2); B(1); G(1); E(1); D(2); E(1); G(1); A(1); G(1); **nc**; G(1); B(1); G(1); E(1); D(2); E(1); G(1); A(1); G(1); **nc**; G(1); B(1); G(1); E(1); D(2); E(1); G(1); A(1); G(1) ... x2

40. **G(1)**; B(1); G(3); D(1); G(2); A(2); G(1); B(1); G(3); D(1); G(2); A(2); **G(1)**; B(1); G(3); D(1); G(2); A(2); **G(1)**; B(1); G(3); D(1); G(2); A(2) ... x2

41. **nc**; B(1); G(1); B(1); G(4); A(3); B(1); G(1); B(1); G(4); A(3); **nc**; B(1); G(1); B(1); G(4); A(3); **nc**; B(1); G(1); B(1); G(4); A(3) ... x2

42. **G(1)**; G(1); B(1); G(4); A(3); G(2); B(1); G(4); A(3); **G(1)**; G(1); B(1); G(4); A(3); **G(1)**; G(1); B(1); G(4); A(3) ... x2

43. **nc**; G(1); B(1); G(1); B(1); E(1); G(1); A(4); G(1); B(1); G(1); B(1); E(1); G(1); A(4); **nc**; G(1); B(1); G(1); B(1); E(1); G(1); A(4); **nc**; G(1); B(1); G(1); B(1); E(1); G(1); A(4) ... x2

44. **A(1)**; G(2); B(1); G(2); A(5); G(2); B(1); G(2); A(4); **A(1)**; G(2); B(1); G(2); A(4); **A(1)**; G(2); B(1); G(2); A(4) ... x2

The separations in the pattern are for illustrative purposes to indicate the corner decreases that begin on the following row. They do not occur in the actual beadwork.

45. **nc**; A(1); G(1); B(1); G(2); A(6); G(1); B(1); G(2); A(5); **nc**; A(1); G(1); B(1); G(2); A(5); **nc**; A(1); G(1); B(1); G(2); A(5) ... x2

46. **sc**; A(1); G(2); A(8); G(2); A(6); **sc**; A(1); G(2); A(6); **sc**; A(1); G(2); A(6) ... x2

47. **A(1)**; A(1); G(1); A(9); G(1); A(6); **A(1)**; A(1); G(1); A(6); **A(1)**; A(1); G(1); A(6) ... x2

48. **nc**; A(19); **nc**; A(9); **nc**; A(9) ... x2

49. **sc**; A(18); **sc**; A(8); **sc**; A(8) ... x2

50. **A(1)**; A(17); **A(1)**; A(7); **A(1)**; A(7) ... x2

51. **nc**; A(18); **nc**; A(8); **nc**; A(8) ... x2

52. **sc**; A(17); **sc**; A(7); **sc**; A(7) ... x2

53. **A(1)**; A(16); **A(1)**; A(6); **A(1)**; A(6) ... x2

54. **nc**; A(17); **nc**; A(7); **nc**; A(7) ... x2

55. **A(1)**; G(1); A(2); G(1); A(2); G(1); A(3); G(1); A(2); G(1); A(2); **A(1)**; G(1); A(2); G(1); A(2); **A(1)**; G(1); A(2); G(1); A(2) ... x2

56. **nc**; G(17); **nc**; G(7); **nc**; G(7) ... x2

57. **G(1)**; G(16); **G(1)**; G(6); **G(1)**; G(6) ... x2

BEGIN HEM

58. **nc**; G(17); **nc**; G(7); **nc**; G(7) ... x2

59. **G(1)**; G(16); **G(1)**; G(6); **G(1)**; G(6) ... x2

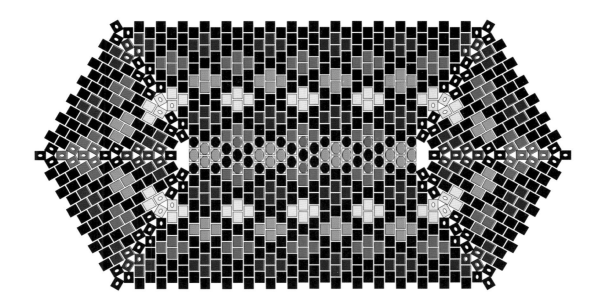

Flat Lid

Flat strip (indicated on the graph as ovals inside
of squares)

1 and 2. G(1); D(1); G(2); E(1); G(2); D(1); G(2); E(1);
G(2); D(1); G(2); E(1); G(2); D(1); G(1) ... x1

3. D(2); G(1); D(2); G(1); D(2); G(1); D(2) ... x1

4. D(1); G(2); D(1); G(2); D(1); G(2); D(1) ... x1

5. G(2); E(1); G(2); E(1); G(2); E(1); G(2) ... x1

Add end beads.

6. G(1); E(2); G(1); E(2); G(1); E(2); G(1); **G(3)** (end
beads) ... x2

7. G(2); E(1); G(2); E(1); G(2); E(1); G(2); G (between
end beads); G(1) (between end beads) ... x2

8. F(1); G(2); F(1); G(2); F(1); G(2); F(1); **G(2)**; **F(2)**;
G(2) ... x2

Begin hexagon increase cycles. From this point on,
read the word map as usual, beginning with the
corner beads. The long sides will be first.

9. **G(1)**; F(2); G(1); F(2); G(1); F(2); G(1); F(2); **G(1)**;
F(1); **F(1)**; F(1) ... x2

10. **nc**; G(1); F(1); G(2); F(1); G(2); F(1); G(2); F(1); G(1);
nc; G(1); F(1); **nc**; F(1); G(1) ... x2

11. **C(2)**; G(2); C(1); G(2); C(1); G(2); C(1); G(2); **C(2)**;
G(1); **F(2)**; G(1) ... x2

12. **C(1)**; C(1); G(1); C(2); G(1); C(2); G(1); C(2); G(1);
C(1); **C(1)**; C(1); G(1); **F(1)**; G(1); C(1) ... x2

13. **nc**; C(1); G(2); C(1); G(2); C(1); G(2); C(1); G(2);
C(1); **nc**; C(1); G(2); **nc**; G(2); C(1) ... x2

14. **G(2)**; G(1); D(1); G(2); D(1); G(2); D(1); G(2); D(1);
G(1); **G(2)**; G(1); D(1); **G(2)**; D(1); G(1) ... x2

15. **G(1)**; G(1); D(2); G(1); D(2); G(1); D(2); G(1); D(2); G(1); **G(1)**; G(1); D(2); **G(1)**; D(2); G(1) ... x2

16. **nc**; G(2); D(1); G(2); D(1); G(2); D(1); G(2); D(1); G(2); **nc**; G(2); D(1); G(1); **nc**; G(1); D(1); G(2) ... x2

17. **G(2)**; E(1); G(2); E(1); G(2); E(1); G(2); E(1); G(2); E(1); **G(2)**; E(1); G(2); **E(2)**; G(2); E(1) ... x2

18. **G(1)**; E(2); G(1); E(2); G(1); E(2); G(1); E(2); G(1); E(2); **G(1)**; E(2); G(1); E(1); **E(1)**; E(1); G(1); E(2) ... x2

19. **nc**; G(1); E(1); G(2); E(1); G(2); E(1); G(2); E(1); G(2); E(1); G(1); **nc**; G(1); E(1); G(2); E(1); **nc**; E(1); G(2); E(1); G(1) ... x2

20. **F(2)**; G(2); F(1); G(2); F(1); G(2); F(1); G(2); F(1); G(2); **F(2)**; G(2); F(1); G(1); **E(2)**; G(1); F(1); G(2) ... x2

21. **F(1)**; F(1); G(1); F(2); G(1); F(2); G(1); F(2); G(1); F(2); G(1); F(1); **F(1)**; F(1); G(1); F(2); G(1); **E(1)**; G(1); F(2); G(1); F(1) ... x2

22. **nc**; F(1); G(2); F(1); G(2); F(1); G(2); F(1); G(2); F(1); G(2); F(1); **nc**; F(1); G(2); F(1); G(2); **nc**; G(2); F(1); G(2); F(1) ... x2

23. **G(2)**; G(15); **G(2)**; G(5); **G(2)**; G(5) ... x2

24. **G(1);** G(16); **G(1)**; G(6); **G(1)**; G(6) ... x2

Chapter 23

Patterns for
Pentagon
Boxes

 # Star

Finished Size: 1½" wide x
1¼" tall (3.8 cm x 3.2 cm)
without feet

A = Cream; Delica #205;
370 beads (2 grams)

B = Light Green; Delica #374;
390 beads (2 grams)

C = Dark Green; Delica #859;
385 beads (2 grams)

D = Metalic Brown; Iris #007;
1,890 beads (10 grams)

Hem/Inner Wall = Any color;
360 beads (2 grams)

A   B   C   D

Construction Techniques

For the Base: pages 222–223

For the Sides: pages 228; 230–231

For the Lid with Sides:
pages 239–240

Base of Box/Lid with Sides

1. **D(1)** ... x5
2. **nc**; C(1) ... x5
3. **C(2)** ... x5
4. **D(1)**; B(1) ... x5
5. **nc**; B(2) ... x5
6. **BDB**; A(1) ... x5
7. **D(2)**; A(2) ... x5
8. **C(1)**; D(1); A(1); D(1) ... x5
9. **nc**; D(4) ... x5
10. **CBC**; C(1); D(1); C(1) ... x5
11. **B(2)**; D(1); C(2); D(1) ... x5
12. **A(1)**; D(1); B(1); C(1); B(1); D(1) ... x5
13. **nc**; D(1); A(1); B(2); A(1); D(1) ... x5

14. **DAD**; D(1); A(1); B(1); A(1); D(1) ... x5

15. **D(2)**; C(1); D(1); A(2); D(1); C(1) ... x5

16. **D(1)**; C(2); D(1); A(1); D(1); C(2) ... x5

17. **nc**; B(1); A(1); B(1); D(2); B(1); A(1); B(1) ... x5

18. **BDB**; A(2); B(1); D(1); B(1); A(2) ... x5

19. **D(2)**; D(8) ... x5

20. **D(1)**; D(9) ... x5

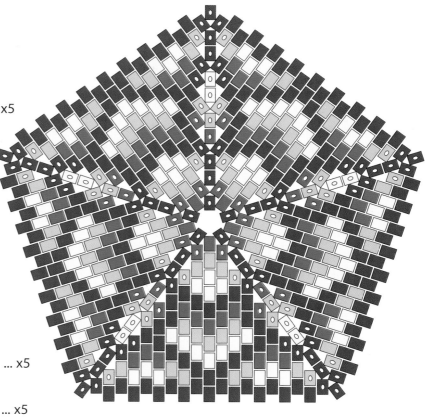

Sides of Box

21. **nc**; D(10) ... x5

22. **D(1)**; D(9) ... x5

23. **nc**; D(10) ... x5

24. **A(1)**; D(4); A(1); D(4) ... x5

25. **nc**; A(1); D(3); A(2); D(3); A(1) ... x5

26. **B(1)**; D(1); A(2); D(1); B(1); D(1); A(2); D(1) ... x5

27. **nc**; D(1); A(3); D(2); A(3); D(1) ... x5

28. **D(1)**; A(1); B(2); A(1); D(1); A(1); B(2); A(1) ... x5

29. **nc**; A(1); B(3); A(2); B(3); A(1) ... x5

30. **D(1)**; B(1); C(2); B(1); D(1); B(1); C(2); B(1) ... x5

31. **nc**; D(1); C(3); D(2); C(3); D(1) ... x5

32. **C(1)**; D(4); C(1); D(4) ... x5

33. **nc**; C(1); D(3); C(2); D(3); C(1) ... x5

34. **B(1)**; C(1); D(2); C(1); B(1); C(1); D(2); C(1) ... x5

35. **nc**; B(1); C(1); D(1); C(1); B(2); C(1); D(1); C(1); B(1) ... x5

36. **A(1)**; B(1); C(2); B(1); A(1); B(1); C(2); B(1) ... x5

37. **nc**; B(1); C(1); D(1); C(1); B(2); C(1); D(1); C(1); B(1) ... x5

38. **B(1)**; C(1); D(2); C(1); B(1); C(1); D(2); C(1) ... x5

39. **nc**; C(1); D(1); B(1); D(1); C(2); D(1); B(1); D(1); C(1) ... x5

40. **C(1)**; D(1); A(2); D(1); C(1); D(1); A(2); D(1) ... x5

41. **nc**; D(2); A(1); D(4); A(1); D(2) ... x5

42. **D(1)**; D(9) ... x5

43. **nc**; D(10) ... x5

44. **D(1)**; D(9) ... x5

45. **nc**; D(10) ... x5

46. **sc**; D(9) ... x5

47. **D(1)**; D(8) ... x5

48. **D(1)**; D(7) ... x5

49. **nc**; D(8) ... x5

50. **D(1)**; D(7) ... x5

51. **nc**; D(8) ... x5

52. **D(1)**; D(7) ... x5

BEGIN HEM

53. **nc**; D(8) ... x5

54. **D(1)**; D(7) ... x5

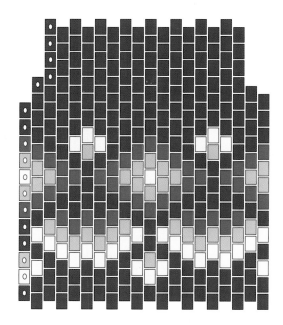

Sides of Lid

21. **nc**; D(10) ... x5

22. **B(1)**; D(4); B(1); D(4) ... x5

23. **nc**; A(1); D(3); A(2); D(3); A(1) ... x5

24. **A(1)**; D(4); A(1); D(4) ... x5

BEGIN HEM

25. **nc**; D(10) ... x5

26. **D(1)**; D(9) ... x5

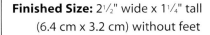 # Flower

Finished Size: 2½" wide x 1¼" tall
(6.4 cm x 3.2 cm) without feet

A = White; Delica #353; 235 beads
(2 grams)

B = Pale Pink; Delica #206;
215 beads (2 grams)

C = Medium Pink; Delica #106;
205 beads (2 grams)

D = Rose; Delica #779; 165 beads
(1 gram)

E = Light Green; Delica #371;
530 beads (3 grams)

F = Green; Delica #327; 1,340 beads
(7 grams)

G = Light Cream; Delica #621;
2,280 beads (12 grams)

H = Dark Cream; Delica #102;
1,280 beads (7 grams)

Hem/Inner Wall = Any color;
660 beads (4 grams)

A   B   C   D   E   F   G   H

Construction Techniques

For the Base: pages 222–223

For the Sides: pages 228; 230–231

For the Lid with Sides: pages 239–240

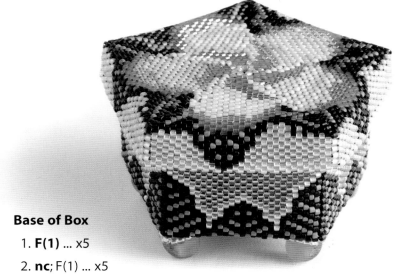

Base of Box

1. **F(1)** ... x5
2. **nc**; F(1) ... x5
3. **F(2)** ... x5
4. **F(1)**; F(1) ... x5
5. **nc**; E(2) ... x5
6. **EFE**; F(1) ... x5
7. **E(2)**; F(2) ... x5
8. **F(1)**; F(3) ... x5
9. **nc**; F(1); E(2); F(1) ... x5
10. **F(3)**; E(1); F(1); E(1) ... x5
11. **F(2)**; E(1); F(2); E(1) ... x5
12. **F(1)**; E(1); F(3); E(1) ... x5
13. **nc**; F(2); E(2); F(2) ... x5
14. **G(3)**; F(1); E(1); F(1); E(1); F(1) ... x5
15. **G(2)**; G(1); F(4); G(1) ... x5
16. **G(1)**; G(2); F(3); G(2) ... x5
17. **nc**; G(2); F(1); E(2); F(1); G(2) ... x5

18. **G(3)**; G(2); F(3); G(2) ... x5

19. **G(2)**; G(3); F(2); G(3) ... x5

20. **G(1)**; G(4); F(1); G(4) ... x5

21. **nc**; G(10) ... x5

22. **G(3)**; G(9) ... x5

23. **G(2)**; G(10) ... x5

24. **G(1)**; G(11) ... x5

25. **nc**; G(12) ... x5

26. **G(3)**; G(11) ... x5

27. **F(2)**; F(12) ... x5

28. **F(1)**; F(13) ... x5

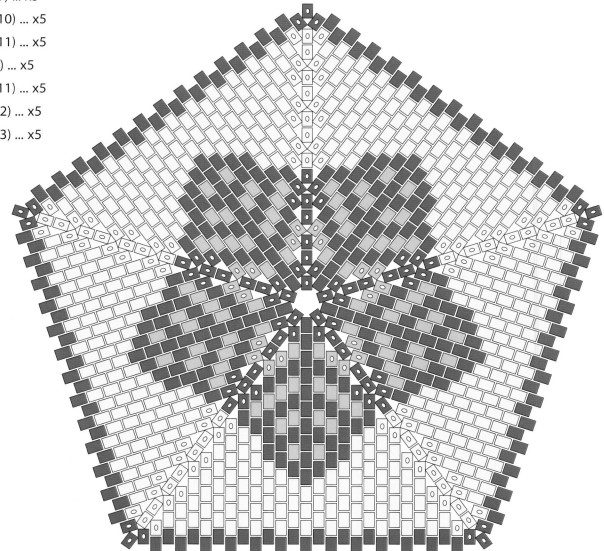

Sides of Box

1. **nc**; E(1); F(1); E(1); F(1); E(1); F(1); E(2); F(1); E(1); F(1); E(1); F(1); E(1) … x5

2. **F(1)**; E(1); F(1); E(1); F(2); E(1); F(1); E(1); F(2); E(1); F(1); E(1) … x5

3. **nc**; F(1); E(1); F(3); E(1); F(2); E(1); F(3); E(1); F(1) … x5

4. **F(1)**; F(1); E(1); F(1); G(1); E(1); F(3); E(1); G(1); F(1); E(1); F(1) … x5

5. **nc**; E(1); F(1); E(1); F(3); E(2); F(3); E(1); F(1); E(1) … x5

6. **F(1)**; E(1); F(1); E(1); G(1); F(1); E(1); F(1); E(1); F(1); G(1); E(1); F(1); E(1) … x5

7. **nc**; F(1); E(1); F(2); G(1); F(4); G(1); F(2); E(1); F(1) … x5

8. **F(1)**; F(1); E(1); F(1); G(2); F(3); G(2); F(1); E(1); F(1) … x5

9. **nc**; E(1); F(2); G(1); H(1); F(1); E(2); F(1); H(1); G(1); F(2); E(1) … x5

10. **F(1)**; E(1); F(1); G(1); H(2); F(3); H(2); G(1); F(1); E(1) … x5

11. **nc**; F(1); E(1); F(1); H(2); G(1); F(2); G(1); H(2); F(1); E(1); F(1) … x5

12. **F(1)**; F(1); E(1); G(1); H(2); G(1); F(1); G(1); H(2); G(1); E(1); F(1) … x5

13. **nc**; E(1); F(2); H(3); G(2); H(3); F(2); E(1) … x5

14. **F(1)**; E(1); F(1); G(1); H(3); G(1); H(3); G(1); F(1); E(1) … x5

15. **nc**; F(2); G(1); H(8); G(1); F(2) … x5

16. **F(1)**; F(1); G(1); H(9); G(1); F(1) … x5

17. **nc**; E(1); F(1); H(10); F(1); E(1) … x5

18. **F(1)**; F(1); G(1); H(9); G(1); F(1) … x5

19. **nc**; F(1); G(1); H(10); G(1); F(1) … x5

20. **F(1)**; G(1); H(11); G(1) … x5

21. **nc**; G(1); H(12); G(1) … x5

22. **G(1)**; H(13) … x5

23. **nc**; H(14) … x5

24. **H(1)**; H(13) … x5

25. **nc**; H(14) … x5

26. **H(1)**; H(13) … x5

27. **nc**; H(14) … x5

28. **H(1)**; H(13) … x5

29. **nc**; H(14) … x5

30. **H(1)**; H(13) … x5

31. **nc**; H(14) … x5

32. **H(1)**; H(13) … x5

BEGIN HEM

33. **nc**; G(14) … x5

34. **G(1)**; G(13) … x5

Lid with Sides

1. **G(1) ...** x5
2. **nc**; G(1) ... x5
3. **DG ...** x5
4. **D(1)**; D(1) ... x5
5. **nc**; A(1); D(1) ... x5
6. **DCA**; D(1) ... x5
7. **CA**; D(2) ... x5

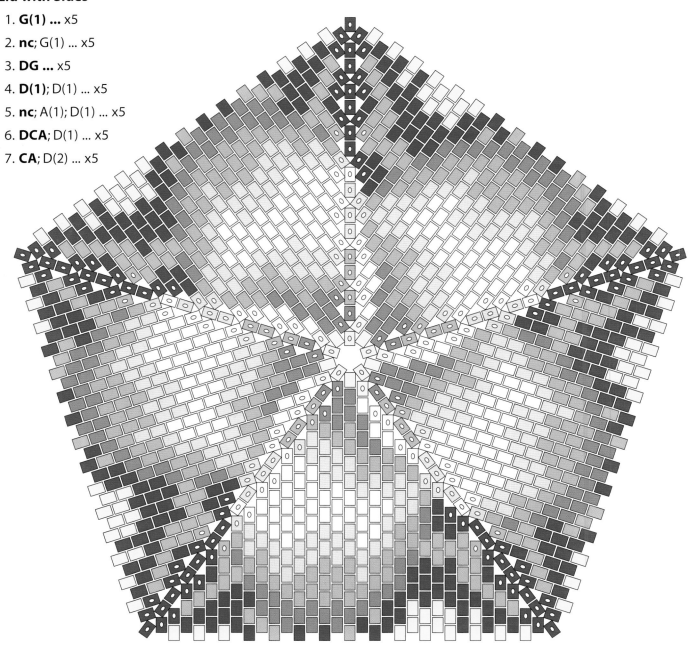

8. **C(1)**; A(1); C(2) ... x5

9. **nc**; A(1); D(1); C(1); B(1) ... x5

10. **BCA**; D(1); C(1); B(1) ... x5

11. **A(2)**; C(2); B(2) ... x5

12. **B(1)**; C(2); B(2); A(1) ... x5

13. **nc**; C(3); B(1); A(2) ... x5

14. **ABB**; B(4); A(1) ... x5

15. **AB**; B(3); A(3) ... x5

16. **B(1)**; C(1); B(1); A(5) ... x5

17. **nc**; F(1); B(1); A(6) ... x5

18. **AAF**; D(1); B(1); A(5) ... x5

19. **BF**; F(1); C(1); B(1); A(5) ... x5

20. **F(1)**; F(1); D(1); C(1); A(1); B(2); A(2); B(1) ... x5

21. **nc**; E(2); C(1); B(1); A(1); B(2); A(1); B(1); C ... x5

22. **EFE**; E(2); C(1); B(6) ... x5

23. **F(2)**; E(2); D(1); C(1); B(4); C(1); D(1) ... x5

24. **F(1)**; E(1); F(2); D(1); C(3); B(2); C(1); E(1) ... x5

25. **nc**; F(1); E(1); F(2); C(1); B(1); C(2); B(1); C(1);
    E(1); F(1) ... x5

26. **F(3)**; E(1); F(2); D(1); C(5); D(1); E(1) ... x5

27. **F(2)**; E(1); F(3); D(1); C(4); D(1); F(1); E(1) ... x5

28. **F(1)**; E(1); F(4); D(1); C(3); D(1); F(2); E(1) ... x5

29. **nc**; E(1); F(2); G(2); F(1); D(5); F(2); E(1) ... x5

30. **F(3)**; F(1); G(3); F(1); E(1); D(4); E(1); F(2) ... x5

31. **F(2)**; F(3); G(2); F(2); D(3); E(1); F(3) ... x5

32. **F(1)**; G(6); F(1); E(1); F(2); E(1); F(1); G(3) ... x5

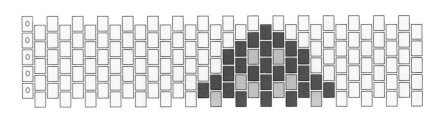

Sides of Lid

1. **nc**; G(7); E(1); F(3); E(1); G(4) ... x5

2. **G(1)**; G(6); F(2); E(2); F(2); G(3) ... x5

3. **nc**; G(7); F(1); E(1); F(1); E(1); F(1); G(4) ... x5

4. **G(1)**; G(7); F(4); G(4) ... x5

5. **nc**; G(8); F(3); G(5) ... x5

6. **G(1)**; G(7); F(1); E(2); F(1); G(4) ... x5

7. **nc**; G(8); F(3); G(5) ... x5

8. **G(1)**; G(8); F(2); G(5) ... x5

BEGIN HEM

9. **nc**; G(9); F(1); G(6) ... x5

10. **G(1)**; G(15) ... x5

 # Dragon

Finished Size: 1½" wide x 1¼" tall (3.8 cm x 3.2 cm) without feet

A = Pea Green; Delica #371; 171 beads (1 grams)

B = Mint Green; Delica #373; 539 beads (3 grams)

C = Teal; Delica #859; 767 beads (4 grams)

D = Purple; Delica #782; 1,829 beads (10 grams)

E = Lavender; Delica #158; 893 beads (5 grams)

F = Pale Yellow; Delica #621; 1,276 beads (7 grams)

G = White; Delica #211; 14 beads

Hem/Inner Wall = Any color; 475 beads (3 grams)

A   B   C   D   E   F   G

Construction Techniques

For the Base: pages 222–223

For the Sides: pages 228; 230–231

For the Flat Lid: pages 239–240

Base of Box/Flat Lid

1. **F(1)** ... x5
2. **nc**; F(1) ... x5
3. **F(2)** ... x5
4. **F(1)**; D(1) ... x5
5. **nc**; D(2) ... x5
6. **DFD**; E(1) ... x5
7. **D(2)**; E(2) ... x5
8. **D(1)**; E(1); D(1); E(1) ... x5
9. **nc**; E(1); D(2); E(1) ... x5
10. **E(3)**; E(2); D(1) ... x5
11. **D(2)**; D(1); E(1); D(2) ... x5
12. **D(1)**; D(3); C(1); D(1) ... x5
13. **nc**; C(2); D(1); C(3) ... x5
14. **CCB**; C(3); B(1); C(1) ... x5
15. **CB**; B(2); C(1); B(3) ... x5
16. **B(1)**; A(1); B(1); C(1); B(1); A(1); B(1); C(1) ... x5
17. **nc**; A(2); C(1); B(1); A(2); C(1); B(1) ... x5
18. **B(3)**; A(1); B(1); C(1); B(1); A(1); B(1); C(1) ... x5
19. **BC**; B(3); C(1); B(3); C(1) ... x5
20. **C(1)**; C(1); B(1); C(3); B(1); C(3) ... x5
21. **nc**; D(1); C(3); D(1); C(3); D(1); C(1) ... x5
22. **CDD**; D(1); C(1); D(3); C(1); D(3) ... x5
23. **D(2)**; E(1); D(3); E(1); D(3); E(1); D(1) ... x5
24. **E(1)**; E(2); D(1); E(3); D(1); E(3); D(1) ... x5

25. **nc**; E(1); D(2); E(2); D(2); E(2); D(2); E(1) ... x5

26. **DED**; E(1); D(1); E(1); D(1); E(1); D(1); E(1); D(1); E(1); D(1); E(1) ... x5

27. **D(2)**; D(1); E(2); D(2); E(2); D(2); E(2); D(1) ... x5

28. **D(1)**; F(1); D(1); E(1); D(1); F(1); D(1); E(1); D(1); F(1); D(1); E(1); D(1); F(1) ... x5

29. **nc**; F(2); D(2); F(2); D(2); F(2); D(2); F(2) ... x5

30. **DDF**; D(3); F(1); D(3); F(1); D(3); F(1); D(1) ... x5

31. **F(2)**; F(1); D(1); F(3); D(1); F(3); D(1); F(3); D(1) ... x5

32. **F(1)**; F(15) ... x5

Sides of Box

This pattern is a little different. Although the box has five sides, there is only one dragon. The first word map/pattern "side" actually accounts for one side of the box (the dragon's head) and will be beaded only one time per row. The next four sides (the dragon's body) are identical and will be beaded four times per row. Make sure to bead the "head" on the same side of the box for each row. The lid and base of the box are simply beaded as a pentagon lid and base with identical segments.

1. **nc**; F(16) ... x1

   nc; F(16) ... x4

2. **F(1)**; F(15) ... x1

   F(1); F(15) ... x4

3. **nc**; F(10); D(3); F(3) ... x1

   nc; F(16) ... x4

4. **F(1)**; F(10); D(3); F(2) ... x1

   F(1); F(15) ... x4

5. **nc**; F(1); D(1); F(7); D(1); F(1); E(2); D(1); F(2) ... x1

   nc; F(1); D(1); F(3); D(1); F(3); D(1); F(3); D(1); F(2) ... x4

6. **F(1)**; D(2); F(5); D(4); E(2); D(2) ... x1

   F(1); D(3); F(1); D(3); F(1); D(3); F(1); D(3) ... x4

7. **nc**; F(7); D(2); E(1); D(3); E(1); D(2) ... x1

   nc; F(2); D(2); F(2); D(2); F(2); D(2); F(2); D(2) ... x4

8. **D(1)**; F(1); D(1); F(4); D(1); G(1); E(2); D(2); E(3) ... x1

   D(1); F(1); D(1); E(1); D(1); F(1); D(1); E(1); D(1); F(1); D(1); E(1); D(1); F(1); D(1); E(1) ... x4

9. **nc**; D(2); F(3); D(2); G(1); D(1); E(2); D(2); E(3) ... x1

   nc; D(2); E(2); D(2); E(2); D(2); E(2); D(2); E(2) ... x4

10. **E(1)**; D(1); F(4); D(1); G(1); D(1); E(1); D(1); E(3); D(2) ... x1

    E(1); D(1); E(1); D(1); E(1); D(1); E(1); D(1); E(1); D(1); E(1); D(1); E(1); D(1); E(1); D(1) ... x4

11. **nc**; E(1); F(5); G(2); E(1); D(2); E(2); D(3) ... x1

    nc; E(2); D(2); E(2); D(2); E(2); D(2); E(2); D(2) ... x4

12. **D(1)**; F(1); D(1); F(3); D(3); E(4); D(1); C(2) ... x1

    D(1); E(3); D(1); E(3); D(1); E(3); D(1); E(3) ... x4

13. **nc**; F(1); D(2); F(2); D(1); G(1); D(1); E(1); D(1); E(2); D(1); C(3) ... x1

    nc; D(2); E(1); D(3); E(1); D(3); E(1); D(3); E(1); D(1) ... x4

14. **C(1)**; D(1); E(1); F(1); D(3); G(1); E(1); C(1); D(3); C(1); B(2) ... x1

    C(1); D(3); C(1); D(3); C(1); D(3); C(1); D(3) ... x4

15. **nc**; F(1); E(1); D(3); C(1); D(2); C(2); D(2); C(1); B(3) ... x1

    nc; C(2); D(1); C(3); D(1); C(3); D(1); C(3); D(1); C(1) ... x4

16. **F(1)**; D(2); E(1); C(1); B(1); C(1); D(1); C(1); B(1); C(3); B(1); A(2) ... x1

    B(1); C(3); B(1); C(3); B(1); C(3); B(1); C(3) ... x4

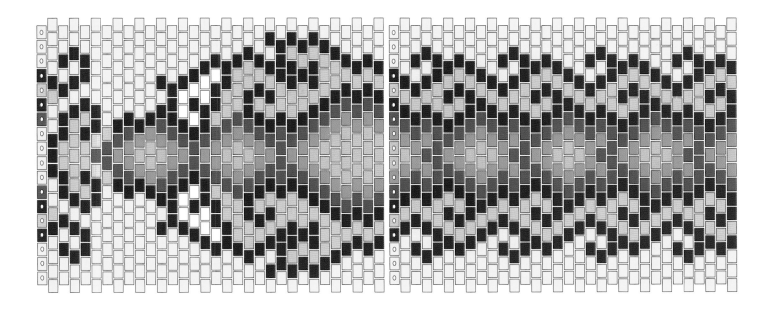

17. **nc**; D(1); E(2); C(1); B(2); C(2); B(2); C(2); B(1);
    A(3) ... x1

    nc; B(2); C(1); B(3); C(1); B(3); C(1); B(3); C(1);
    B(1) ... x4

18. **F(1)**; E(2); C(1); B(1); A(1); B(1); C(1); B(1); A(1);
    B(1); C(1); B(1); A(3) ... x1

    A(1); B(1); C(1); B(1); A(1); B(1); C(1); B(1); A(1);
    B(1); C(1); B(1); A(1); B(1); C(1); B(1) ... x4

19. **nc**; D(1); E(1); C(1); B(1); A(2); B(2); A(2); B(2);
    A(4) ... x1

    nc; A(1); C(1); B(1); A(2); C(1); B(1); A(2); C(1); B(1);
    A(2); C(1); B(1); A(1) ... x4

20. **F(1)**; E(2); C(1); B(1); A(1); B(1); C(1); B(1); A(1);
    B(1); C(1); B(1); A(3) ... x1

    A(1); B(1); C(1); B(1); A(1); B(1); C(1); B(1); A(1); B(1);
    C(1); B(1); A(1); B(1); C(1); B(1) ... x4

21. **nc**; D(1); E(2); C(1); B(2); C(2); B(2); C(2); B(1); A(3) ... x1
    nc; B(2); C(1); B(3); C(1); B(3); C(1); B(3); C(1); B(1) ... x4

22. **F(1)**; D(2); E(1); C(1); B(1); C(1); D(1); C(1); B(1); C(3);
    B(1); A(2) ... x1

    B(1); C(3); B(1); C(3); B(1); C(3); B(1); C(3) ... x4

23. **nc**; F(1); E(1); D(3); C(1); D(2); C(2); D(2); C(1); B(3) ... x1
    nc; C(2); D(1); C(3); D(1); C(3); D(1); C(3); D(1); C(1) ... x4

24. **C(1)**; D(1); E(1); F(1); D(3); G(1); E(1); C(1); D(3); C(1);
    B(2) ... x1

    C(1); D(3); C(1); D(3); C(1); D(3); C(1); D(3) ... x4

25. **nc**; F(1); D(2); F(2); D(1); G(1); D(1); E(1); D(1); E(2);
    D(1); C(3) ... x1

nc; D(2); E(1); D(3); E(1); D(3); E(1); D(3); E(1); D(1) ... x4

26. **D(1)**; F(1); D(1); F(3); D(3); E(4); D(1); C(2) ... x1

    D(1); E(3); D(1); E(3); D(1); E(3); D(1); E(3) ... x4

27. **nc**; E(1); F(5); G(2); E(1); D(2); E(2); D(3) ... x1

    nc; E(2); D(2); E(2); D(2); E(2); D(2); E(2); D(2) ... x4

28. **E(1)**; D(1); F(4); D(1); G(1); D(1); E(1); D(1); E(3);

        D(2) ... x1

    E(1); D(1); E(1); D(1); E(1); D(1); E(1); D(1); E(1);

        D(1); E(1); D(1); E(1); D(1); E(1); D(1) ... x4

29. **nc**; D(2); F(3); D(2); G(1); D(1); E(2); D(2); E(3) ... x1

    nc(1); D(2); E(2); D(2); E(2); D(2); E(2); D(2); E(2) ... x4

30. **D(1)**; F(1); D(1); F(4); D(1); G(1); E(2); D(2); E(3) ... x1

    D(1); F(1); D(1); E(1); D(1); F(1); D(1); E(1); D(1);

        F(1); D(1); E(1); D(1); F(1); D(1); E(1) ... x4

31. **nc**; F(7); D(2); E(1); D(3); E(1); D(2) ... x1

    nc; F(2); D(2); F(2); D(2); F(2); D(2); F(2); D(2) ... x4

32. **F(1)**; D(2); F(5); D(4); E(2); D(2) ... x1

    F(1); D(3); F(1); D(3); F(1); D(3); F(1); D(3) ... x4

33. **nc**; F(1); D(1); F(7); D(1); F(1); E(2); D(1); F(2) ... x1

    nc; F(1); D(1); F(3); D(1); F(3); D(1); F(3); D(1); F(2) ... x4

34. **F(1)**; F(10); D(3); F(2) ... x1

    F(1); F(15) ... x4

BEGIN HEM

35. **nc**; F(10); D(3); F(3) ... x1

    nc; F(16) ... x4

36. **F(1)**; F(15) ... x1

    F(1); F(15) ... x4

Chapter 24

Patterns for
Square
Boxes

Tempest

Finished Size: 1½" wide x 1¼" tall (3.8 cm x 3.2 cm) without finial or feet

A = White; Delica # 351; 520 beads (3 grams)

B = Light Blue; Delica # 730; 560 beads (3 grams)

C = Royal Blue; Delica # 864; 664 beads (4 grams)

D = Dark Blue; Delica # 377; 1,148 beads (6 grams)

Hem/Inner Wall = Any color; 428 beads (3 grams)

A B C D

Construction Techniques

For the Base: pages 224–225

For the Sides: pages 228; 232–233

For the Flat Lid: pages 237–239

Base of Box/Flat Lid

1. **D(1)** ... x4
2. **nc**; C(1) ... x4
3. **C(3)** ... x4
4. **B(2)**; B(1) ... x4
5. **D(2)**; B(2) ... x4
6. **C(1)**; A(3) ... x3
7. **nc**; D(1); A(2); D(1) ... x4
8. **CBC**; D(1); A(1); D(1) ... x4
9. **B(2)**; C(1); D(2); C(1) ... x4
10. **A(2)**; B(1); D(3); B(1) ... x4
11. **A(1)**; A(1); D(1); C(2); D(1); A(1) ... x4
12. **nc**; D(2); B(1); C(1); B(1); D(2) ... x4
13. **D(3)**; D(1); A(1); B(2); A(1); D(1) ... x4
14. **D(2)**; C(1); D(1); A(1); B(1); A(1); D(1); C(1) ... x4
15. **D(2)**; C(2); D(1); A(2); D(1); C(2) ... x4
16. **D(1)**; C(1); B(1); C(1); D(1); A(1); D(1); C(1); B(1); C(1) ... x4
17. **nc**; C(1); B(2); C(1); D(2); C(1); B(2); C(1) ... x4
18. **CDC**; B(1); A(1); B(1); C(1); D(1); C(1); B(1); A(1); B(1) ... x4
19. **C(2)**; B(1); A(2); B(1); C(2); B(1); A(2); B(1) ... x4
20. **D(2)**; D11 ... x4
21. **D(1)**; D12 ... x4

Sides of Box

22. **nc**; D(1); B(1); A(1); D(1); A(1); B(1); D(1); B(1); A(1); D(1); A(1); B(1); D(1) ... x4

23. **A(1)**; C(1); B(1); A(2); B(1); C(2); B(1); A(2); B(1); C(1) ... x4

24. **nc**; D(1); C(1); B(1); A(1); B(1); C(1); D(1); C(1); B(1); A(1); B(1); C(1); D(1) ... x4

25. **A(1)**; D(1); C(1); B(2); C(1); D(2); C(1); B(2); C(1); D(1) ... x4

26. **nc**; B(1); D(1); C(1); B(1); C(1); D(1); A(1); D(1); C(1); B(1); C(1); D(1); B(1) ... x4

27. **B(1)**; B(1); D(1); C(2); D(1); B(2); D(1); C(2); D(1); B(1) ... x4

28. **nc**; B(1); C(1); D(1); C(1); D(1); C(1); B(1); C(1); D(1); C(1); D(1); C(1); B(1) ... x4

29. **B(1)**; C(1); D(4); C(2); D(4); C(1) ... x4

30. **nc**; C(1); D(1); A(1); D(1); A(1); D(1); C(1); D(1); A(1); D(1); A(1); D(1); C(1) ... x4

31. **C(1)**; D(1); B(1); A(2); B(1); D(2); B(1); A(2); B(1); D(1) ... x4

32. **nc**; D(1); C(1); B(1); A(1); B(1); C(1); D(1); C(1); B(1); A(1); B(1); C(1); D(1) ... x4

33. **D(1)**; D(1); C(1); B(2); C(1); D(2); C(1); B(2); C(1); D(1) ... x4

34. **nc**; A(1); D(1); C(1); B(1); C(1); D(1); A(1); D(1); C(1); B(1); C(1); D(1); A(1) ... x4

35. **A(1)**; A(1); D(1); C(2); D(1); A(2); D(1); C(2); D(1); A(1) ... x4

36. **nc**; A(1); B(1); D(1); C(1); D(1); B(1); A(1); B(1); D(1); C(1); D(1); B(1); A(1) ... x4

37. **A(1)**; A(1); C(1); D(2); C(1); A(2); C(1); D(2); C(1); A(1) ... x4

38. **nc**; A(1); B(1); D(3); B(1); A(1); B(1); D(3); B(1); A(1) ... x4

39. **A(1)**; B(1); C(1); A(2); C(1); B(2); C(1); A(2); C(1); B(1) ... x4

40. **nc**; A(1); C(1); D(1); A(1); D(1); C(1); A(1); C(1); D(1); A(1); D(1); C(1); A(1) ... x4

41. **A(1)**; B(1); D(1); A(2); D(1); B(2); D(1); A(2); D(1); B(1) ... x4

42. **nc**; B(1); C(1); A(3); C(1); B(1); C(1); A(3); C(1); B(1) ... x4

43. **A(1)**; C(1); D(1); A(2); D(1); C(2); D(1); A(2); D(1); C(1) ... x4

44. **nc**; B(1); D(1); A(3); D(1); B(1); D(1); A(3); D(1); B(1) ... x4

45. **B(1)**; C(1); B(1); A(2); B(1); C(2); B(1); A(2); B(1); C(1) ... x4

46. **nc**; C(1); D(1); B(1); A(1); B(1); D(1); C(1); D(1); B(1); A(1); B(1); D(1); C(1) ... x4

47. **B(1)**; D(1); C(1); B(2); C(1); D(2); C(1); B(2); C(1); D(1) ... x4

48. **nc**; C(1); D(1); C(1); B(1); C(1); D(1); C(1); D(1); C(1); B(1); C(1); D(1); C(1) ... x4

49. **C(1)**; D(2); C(2); D(4); C(2); D(2) ... x4

50. **nc**; D(3); C(1); D(5); C(1); D(3) ... x4

51. **C(1)**; D(12) ... x4

BEGIN HEM

52. **nc**; D(13) ... x4

53. **D(1)**; D(12) ... x4

 # Tomcat

Finished Size: 2" wide x
2¹⁄₂" tall (5.1 cm x 6.4 cm)
without feet

A = White; Delica #352;
1,296 beads (7 grams)

B = Cream; Delica #205;
357 beads (2 grams)

C = Mustard; Delica #181;
717 beads (4 grams)

D = Auburn; Delica #773;
1,381 beads (7 grams)

E = Brown; Delica #769;
945 beads (5 grams)

F = Turquoise; Delica #861;
123 beads (2 grams)

G = Green; Delica #274;
16 beads

Hem/Inner Wall = Any color;
464 beads (3 grams)

| A | B | C | D | E | F | G |

Construction Techniques

For the Base: pages 224–225

For the Sides: pages 228; 232–233

For the Lid with Sides:
pages 237–239

Base of Box

1. **B(1)** … x4
2. **nc**; B(1) … x4
3. **CBC** … x4
4. **C(2)**; C(1) … x4
5. **C(2)**; C(2) … x4
6. **C(1)**; C(3) … x4
7. **nc**; D(4) … x4
8. **D(3)**; D(3) … x4
9. **D(2)**; D(4) … x4
10. **D(2)**; D(5) … x4
11. **E(1)**; E(6) … x4
12. **nc**; E(7) … x4
13. **AEA**; A(6) … x4
14. **A(2)**; A(7) … x4
15. **A(2)**; A(8) … x4
16. **A(1)**; A(9) … x4
17. **nc**; A(10) … x4
18. **A(3)**; A(9) … x4
19. **A(2)**; A(10) … x4
20. **A(2)**; A(11) … x4

21. **A(1)**; A(12) ... x4

22. **nc**; A(13) ... x4

23. **A(3)**; A(12) ... x4

24. **A(2)**; A(13) ... x4

25. **A(2)**; A(14) ... x4

26. **A(1)**; A(15) ... x4

27. **nc**; A(16) ... x4

28. **A(3)**; A(15) ... x4

29. **A(2)**; A(16) ... x4

30. **A(2)**; A(17) ... x4

31. **A(1)**; A(18) ... x4

Sides of Box

1. **nc**; A(19) ... x4

2. **A(1)**; A(15); E(1);
   A(2) ... x4

3. **nc**; A(15); E(2);
   A(2) ... x4

4. **A(1)**; A(14); E(1); B(1);
   E(1); A(1) ... x4

5. **nc**; A(5); E(4); A(3);
   E(1); A(1); E(1); B(2);
   E(1); A(1) ... x4

6. **A(1)**; A(1); E(14); B(2); A(1) ... x4

7. **nc**; A(1); E(4); D(4); E(3); B(1); E(1); B(1); E(1); B(1); E(1); A(1) ... x4

8. **A(1)**; E(1); F(2); E(1); D(6); E(1); B(6); E(1) ... x4

9. **nc**; A(1); F(2); E(1); D(7); E(1); C(1); E(1); C(1); E(1); B(1); E(1); A(1) ... x4

10. **A(1)**; E(1); F(1); E(1); D(8); E(1); C(5); E(1) ... x4

11. **nc**; A(1); F(1); E(1); D(3); E(3); D(3); E(4); C(1); E(1); A(1) … x4

12. **A(1)**; E(2); D(3); E(5); D(2); E(3); C(2); E(1) … x4

13. **nc**; A(1); E(1); D(3); E(1); C(1); B(2); E(2); D(4); C(2); E(1); A(1) … x4

14. **A(1)**; E(1); D(3); E(1); C(1); B(4); E(1); D(4); C(1); E(2) … x4

15. **nc**; A(1); E(1); D(2); E(1); C(1); B(5); E(1); D(4); E(1); F(1); A(1) … x4

16. **A(1)**; E(1); D(2); E(1); C(2); B(5); E(1); D(3); E(3) … x4

17. **nc**; A(1); D(2); E(1); C(2); B(6); E(4); C(1);
E(1); A(1) … x4

18. **A(1)**; E(1); D(1); E(1); C(2); B(7); E(3);
B(1); D(1); E(1) … x4

19. **nc**; E(1); D(2); C(3); B(10); C(1);
E(1); A(1) … x4

20. **A(1)**; D(2); E(1); C(2); B(9);
C(2); D(1); E(1) … x4

21. **nc**; E(1); D(2); C(3); B(8);
C(2); D(1); E(1); A(1) … x4

22. **A(1)**; D(2); E(1); C(3); B(6); E(1);
C(1); E(1); D(2); E(1) … x4

23. **nc**; E(1); D(2); C(3); B(3); E(1);
B(2); E(4); D(1); E(2) … x4

24. **A(1)**; D(3); C(3); B(3); E(1);
B(1); E(1); B(1); E(1); B(1);
E(1); D(1); E(1) … x4

25. **nc**; E(1); D(3); C(3); B(1);
E(1); B(1); E(1); B(5); D(1);
E(1); A(1) … x4

26. **A(1)**; D(3); C(5); E(1); B(1);
E(2); B(1); E(1); B(1); E(3) … x4

27. **nc**; E(1); D(3); C(5); E(1); B(1); E(1); B(1); E(2); B(1); E(1); F(1); E(1) … x4

28. **A(1)**; D(4); C(5); E(2); B(1); E(1); D(1); E(1); B(1); E(2) … x4

29. **nc**; E(1); D(5); C(4); E(1); B(2); D(2); B(2); E(1); A(1) … x4

30. **A(1)**; D(7); C(1); D(2); C(1); B(1); E(1); D(1); E(1); B(1); C(1); E(1) … x4

31. **nc**; E(1); D(9); E(1); C(1); B(1); D(2); B(1); C(1); E(1); A(1) … x4

32. **A(1)**; D(9); E(1); C(1); E(2); D(1); E(2); C(1); E(1) … x4

33. **nc**; E(1); D(9); C(1); E(2); D(2); E(2); C(1); A(1) … x4

34. **A(1)**; E(1); D(8); E(4); D(1); E(4) … x4

35. **nc**; A(1); D(9); E(1); G(2); D(2); G(2); E(1); A(1) … x4

36. **A(1)**; E(1); D(8); E(4); D(1); E(4) … x4

37. **nc**; A(1); D(10); E(2); D(2); E(2); D(1); A(1) … x4

38. **A(1)**; E(1); D(8); E(1); D(7); E(1) … x4

39. **nc**; A(1); E(1); D(16); A(1) … x4

40. **A(1)**; E(1); D(8); E(1); D(7); E(1) … x4

41. **nc**; A(1); E(1); D(16); A(1) … x4

42. **A(1)**; E(2); D(7); E(1); D(7); E(1) … x4

43. **nc**; A(1); F(1); E(1); D(6); E(1); D(2); E(1); D(2); E(1); D(2); A(1) … x4

44. **A(1)**; E(1); F(1); E(2); D(3); E(3); D(1); E(5); D(1); E(1) … x4

45. **nc**; A(1); F(2); E(6); F(1); D(2); E(3); F(1); D(2); A(1) … x4

46. **A(1)**; E(1); F(3); E(3); F(2); E(1); D(1); E(1); A(1); F(2); E(1); D(1); E(1) … x4

47. **nc**; A(1); F(4); E(2); F(3); D(1); E(3); F(2); E(1); D(1); A(1) … x4

48. **A(1)**; E(1); F(4); A(1); F(3); E(2); F(1); A(1); F(3); E(2) … x4

49. **nc**; A(1); E(9); D(1); E(6); D(1); A(1) … x4

50. **A(1)**; E(5); A(1); E(6); A(1); E(5) … x4

51. **nc**; A(10); E(1); A(6); E(1); A(1) … x4

52. **sc**; E(1); A(8); E(1); A(7); E(1) … x4

53. **sc**; E(17) … x4

54. **E(1)**; E(4); A(1); E(6); A(1); E(4) … x4

55. **A(1)**; C(3); E(2); D(5); E(2); C(3) … x4

56. **nc**; C(4); A(1); D(6); A(1); C(4) … x4

57. **sc**; C(3); E(2); D(5); E(2); C(3) … x4

58. **sc**; C(3); A(1); D(6); A(1); C(3) … x4

59. **C(1)**; C(2); E(2); D(5); E(2); C(2) … x4

60. **C(1)**; C(2); A(1); D(6); A(1); C(2) … x4

61. **nc**; C(2); E(2); D(5); E(2); C(2) … x4

62. **C(1)**; C(2); A(1); D(6); A(1); C(2) … x4

63. **nc**; C(2); E(2); D(5); E(2); C(2) … x4

64. **C(1)**; C(2); A(1); D(6); A(1); C(2) … x4

BEGIN HEM

65. **nc**; C(2); E(2); D(5); E(2); C(2) … x4

66. **C(1)**; C(2); A(1); D(6); A(1); C(2) … x4

Lid with Sides

1. **B(1)** ... x4
2. **nc**; B(1) ... x4
3. **CBC** ... x4
4. **C(2)**; C(1) ... x4
5. **C(2)**; C(2) ... x4
6. **C(1)**; C(3) ... x4
7. **nc**; D(4) ... x4
8. **D(3)**; D(3) ... x4
9. **D(2)**; D(4) ... x4
10. **D(2)**; D(5) ... x4
11. **E(1)**; E(6) ... x4
12. **nc**; E(7) ... x4
13. **AEA**; A(6) ... x4
14. **A(2)**; A(7) ... x4
15. **A(2)**; A(8) ... x4
16. **A(1)**; A(9) ... x4
17. **nc**; A(10) ... x4
18. **A(3)**; A(9) ... x4
19. **A(2)**; A(10) ... x4
20. **E(2)**; E(11) ... x4
21. **E(1)**; E(2); A(1); E(6); A(1); E(2) ... x4
22. **nc**; C(2); E(2); D(5); E(2); C(2) ... x4
23. **C(3)**; C(2); A(1); D(6); A(1); C(2) ... x4
24. **C(2)**; C(2); E(2); D(5); E(2); C(2) ... x4
25. **C(2)**; C(3); A(1); D(6); A(1); C(3) ... x4
26. **C(1)**; C(3); E(2); D(5); E(2); C(3) ... x4

Lid Sides

1. **nc**; C(4); A(1); D(6); A(1); C(4) ... x4
2. **C(1)**; C(3); E(2); D(5); E(2); C(3) ... x4
3. **nc**; C(4); A(1); D(6); A(1); C(4) ... x4
4. **C(1)**; C(3); E(2); D(5); E(2); C(3) ... x4

BEGIN HEM

5. **nc**; C(4); A(1); D(6); A(1); C(4) ... x4
6. **C(1)**; C(3); E(2); D(5); E(2); C(3) ... x4

◆ Shinjin

Finished Size: 1¾" wide x 2½" tall (4.5 cm x 6.4 cm) without finial or feet

A = Cream; Delica #621; 1,008 beads (6 grams)

B = Burgundy; Delica #103; 1,428 beads (8 grams)

C = Brown; Delica #011; 2,848 beads (15 grams)

D = Size 8 beads (any color); 16 beads

Hem/Inner Wall = Any color; 284 beads (2 grams)

A   B   C   D

Construction Techniques

For the Base: pages 224–225

For the Sides: pages 228; 232–233

For the Flat Lid: pages 237–239

This box has a tiered structure.

Begin each new tier (except the bottom one) in the same way you begin a hem row, but make decreases to complete the tier. The roofs are extensions of the top row of each tier.

Base of Box

1. **C(1)** ... x4
2. **nc**; C(1) ... x4
3. **C(3)** ... x4
4. **C(2)**; B(1) ... x4
5. **B(2)**; B(2) ... x4
6. **B(1)**; C(1); B(1); C(1) ... x4

7. **nc**; C(4) ... x4

8. **C(3)**; A(1); C(1); A(1) ... x4

9. **A(2)**; A(4) ... x4

10. **A(2)**; C(1); A(1); C(1); A(1); C(1) ... x4

11. **C(1)**; C(6) ... x4

12. **nc**; C(1); B(1); C(1); B(1); C(1); B(1); C(1) ... x4

13. **B(3)**; B(6) ... x4

14. **B(2)**; C(1); B(1); C(1); B(1); C(1); B(1); C(1) ... x4

15. **C(2)**; C(8) ... x4

16. **A(1)**; C(1); A(1); C(1); A(1); C(1); A(1); C(1); A(1); C(1) ... x4

17. **nc**; A(10) ... x4

18. **A(3)**; C(1); A(1); C(1); A(1); C(1); A(1); C(1); A(1); C(1) ... x4

19. **C(2)**; C(10) ... x4

20. **B(2)**; C(1); B(1); C(1); B(1); C(1); B(1); C(1); B(1); C(1); B(1); C(1) ... x4

21. **B(1)**; B(12) ... x4

22. **nc**; B(1); C(1); B(1); C(1); B(1); C(1); B(1); C(1); B(1); C(1); B(1); C(1); B(1) ... x4

23. **C(3)**; C(12) ... x4

24. **C(2)**; C(13) ... x4

25. **C(2)**; C(14) ... x4

26. **D(1)**; C(15) ... x4

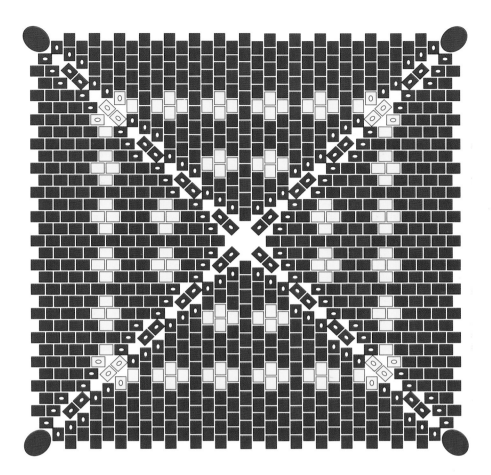

Sides of Bottom Tier

1. **nc**; C(16) ... x4
2. **B(1)**; C(1); B(1); C(1); B(1); C(1); B(1);
   C(1); B(1); C(1); B(1); C(1); B(1); C(1);
   B(1); C(1) ... x4
3. **nc**; **B(16)** ... x4
4. **B(1)**; C(1); B(1); C(1); B(1); C(1); B(1); C(1);
   B(1); C(1); B(1); C(1); B(1); C(1); B(1); C(1) ... x4
5. **nc**; **C(16)** ... x4
6. **C(1)**; A(1); C(1); A(1); C(1); A(1); C(1); A(1); C(1); A(1); C(1); A(1); C(1); A(1); C(1); A(1) ... x4
7. **nc**; A(16) ... x4
8. **C(1);** A(1); C(1); A(1); C(1); A(1); C(1); A(1); C(1); A(1); C(1); A(1); C(1); A(1); C(1); A(1) ... x4
9. **nc**; A(1); C(2); A(2); C(2); A(2); C(2); A(2); C(2); A(1) ... x4
10. **C(1)**; C(1); B(1); C(3); B(1); C(3); B(1); C(3); B(1); C(1) ... x4
11. **nc**; C(1); B(2); C(2); B(2); C(2); B(2); C(2); B(2); C(1) ... x4
12. **C(1)**; C(1); B(1); C(3); B(1); C(3); B(1); C(3); B(1); C(1) ... x4
13. **nc**; A(1); C(2); A(2); C(2); A(2); C(2); A(2); C(2); A(1) ... x4
14. **C(1)**; A(1); C(1); A(1); C(1); A(1); C(1); A(1); C(1); A(1); C(1); A(1); C(1); A(1); C(1); A(1) ... x4
15. **nc**; A(16) ... x4
16. **C(1)**; A(1); C(1); A(1); C(1); A(1); C(1); A(1); C(1); A(1); C(1); A(1); C(1); A(1); C(1); A(1) ... x4
17. **nc**; C(16) ... x4
18. **B(1)**; C(1); B(1); C(1); B(1); C(1); B(1); C(1); B(1); C(1); B(1); C(1); B(1); C(1); B(1); C(1) ... x4
19. **nc**; B(16); ... x4
20. **B(1)**; C(1); B(1); C(1); B(1); C(1); B(1); C(1); B(1); C(1); B(1); C(1); B(1); C(1); B(1); C(1) ... x4
21. **nc**; C(16) ... x4
22. **C(1)**; C(15) ... x4

Sides of Middle Tier

Bead row 1 exactly as you would bead the first hem row.

The skipped corner is considered an "**sc.**"

1. **sc**; C(15) ... x4

The next six rows use Steps 3, 4, 5, 1, 2, and 3 of a square-box decrease cycle (pages 232–233). You will then resume tubular peyote stitch.

2. **C(1)**; C(14) ... x4

3. **A(1)**; C(1); A(1); C(1); A(1); C(1); A(1); C(1); A(1); C(1); A(1); C(1); A(1); C(1) ... x4

4. **nc**; A(14) ... x4

5. **sc**; C(1); A(1); C(1); A(1); C(1); A(1); C(1); A(1); C(1); A(1); C(1); A(1); C(1) ... x4

6. **sc**; C(12) ... x4

7. **B(1)**; C(1); B(1); C(1); B(1); C(1); B(1); C(1); B(1); C(1); B(1); C(1) ... x4

8. **nc**; B(12) ... x4

9. **B(1)**; C(1); B(1); C(1); B(1); C(1); B(1); C(1); B(1); C(1); B(1); C(1) ... x4

10. **nc**; C(12) ... x4

11. **C(1)**; A(1); C(1); A(1); C(1); A(1); C(1); A(1); C(1); A(1); C(1); A(1) ... x4

12. **nc**; A(12) ... x4

13. **C(1)**; A(1); C(1); A(1); C(1); A(1); C(1); A(1); C(1); A(1); C(1); A(1) ... x4

14. **nc**; C(12) ... x4

15. **B(1)**; C(1); B(1); C(1); B(1); C(1); B(1); C(1); B(1); C(1); B(1); C(1) ... x4

16. **nc**; B(12) ... x4

17. **B(1)**; C(1); B(1); C(1); B(1); C(1); B(1); C(1); B(1); C(1); B(1); C(1) ... x4

18. **nc**; C(12) ... x4

19. **C(1)**; A(1); C(1); A(1); C(1); A(1); C(1); A(1); C(1); A(1); C(1); A(1) ... x4

20. **nc**; A(12) ... x4

21. **C(1)**; A(1); C(1); A(1); C(1); A(1); C(1); A(1); C(1); A(1); C(1); A(1) ... x4

22. **nc**; C(12) ... x4

23. **C(1)**; C(11) ... x4

Sides of Top Tier

Bead row 1 exactly as you would bead the first hem row. The skipped corner is considered an "**sc**."

1. **sc**; C(11) ... x4

The next six rows use steps 3, 4, 5, 1, 2, and 3 of a square-box decrease cycle.

You will then resume tubular peyote stitch.

2. **C(1)**; C(10) ... x4

3. **A(1)**; C(1); A(1); C(1); A(1); C(1); A(1); C(1) ... x4

4. **nc**; A(10) ... x4

5. **sc**; C(1); A(1); C(1); A(1); C(1); A(1); C(1); A(1); C(1) ... x4

6. **sc**; C(8) ... x4

7. **B(1)**; C(1); B(1); C(1); B(1); C(1); B(1); C(1) ... x4

8. **nc**; B(8) ... x4

9. **B(1)**; C(1); B(1); C(1); B(1); C(1); B(1); C(1) ... x4

10. **nc**; C(8) ... x4

11. **C(1)**; A(1); C(1); A(1); C(1); A(1); C(1); A(1) ... x4

12. **nc**; A(8) ... x4

13. **C(1)**; A(1); C(1); A(1); C(1); A(1); C(1); A(1) ... x4

14. **nc**; C(8) ... x4

15. **B(1)**; C(1); B(1); C(1); B(1); C(1); B(1); C(1) ... x4

16. **nc**; B(8) ... x4

17. **B(1)**; C(1); B(1); C(1); B(1); C(1); B(1); C(1) ... x4

18. **nc**; C(8) ... x4

19. **C(1)**; A(1); C(1); A(1); C(1); A(1); C(1); A(1) ... x4

20. **nc**; A(8) ... x4

21. **C(1)**; A(1); C(1); A(1); C(1); A(1); C(1); A(1) ... x4

BEGIN HEM

22. **nc**; C(8) ... x4

23. **C(1)**; C(7) ... x4

You will now add first the middle and then the bottom roof. Begin a new thread, and weave through the appropriate tier until your needle exits the last (top) row of the tier. (This row is indicated by the grey beads in the diagram.) You will then add one row without increasing (the corner will be a down bead) and then perform one square-box increase cycle.

Middle Roof

1. **nc**; B(12) ... x4
2. **B(3)**; B(11) ... x4
3. **B(2)**; B(12) ... x4
4. **C(2)**; B(13) ... x4
5. **D(1)**; C(14) ... x4

Middle Roof

Bottom Roof

1. **nc**; B(16) ... x4
2. **B(3)**; B(15) ... x4
3. **B(2)**; B(16) ... x4
4. **C(2)**; B(17) ... x4
5. **D(1)**; C(18) ... x4

Bottom Roof

Flat Lid

1. **C(1)** ... x4
2. **nc**; C(1) ... x4
3. **C(3)** ... x4
4. **C(2)**; B(1) ... x4
5. **B(2)**; B(2) ... x4
6. **B(1)**; C(1); B(1); C(1) ... x4
7. **nc**; C(4) ... x4

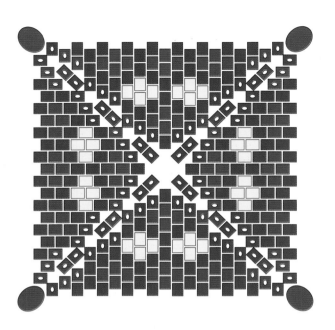

8. **C(3)**; A(1); C(1); A(1) ... x4

9. **A(2)**; A(4) ... x4

10. **A(2)**; C(1); A(1); C(1); A(1); C(1) ... x4

11. **C(1)**; C(6) ... x4

12. **nc**; C(1); B(1); C(1); B(1); C(1); B(1); C(1) ... x4

13. **B(3)**; B(6) ... x4

14. **B(2)**; C(1); B(1); C(1); B(1); C(1); B(1); C(1) ... x4

15. **C(2)**; C(8) ... x4

16. **D(1)**; C(9) ... x4

Blank Graph Worksheets
for Your Original Designs

Triangle Base and Lid

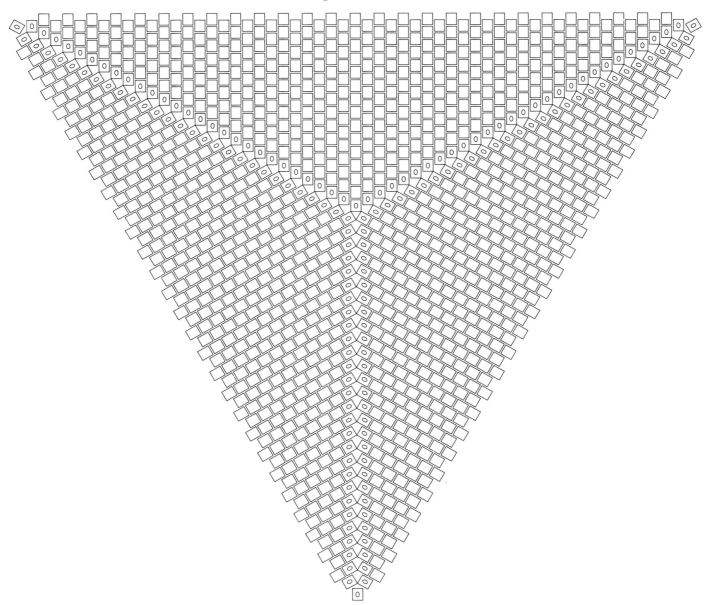

Hexagon Base and Lid

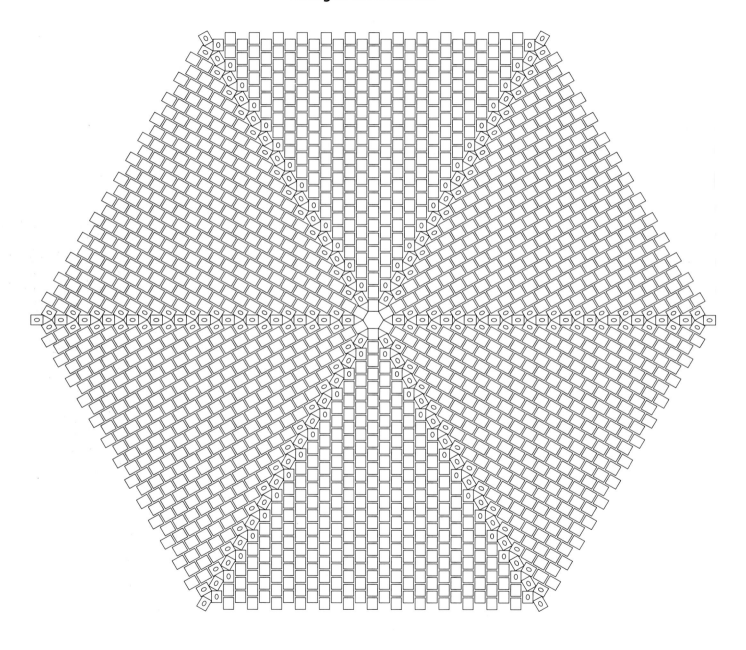

Pentagon Base and Lid

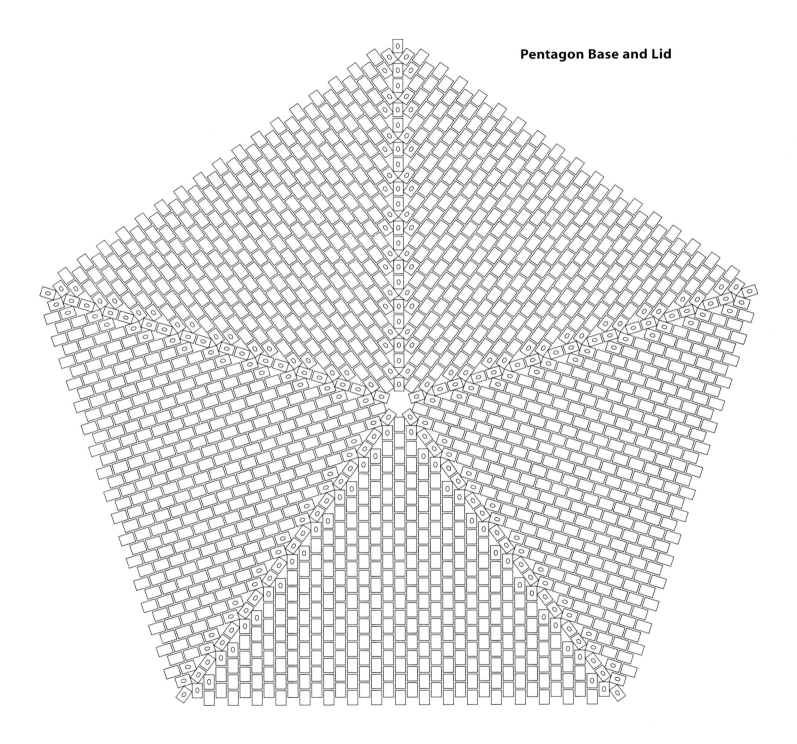

Square Base and Lid

Oblong Hexagon Base and Lid

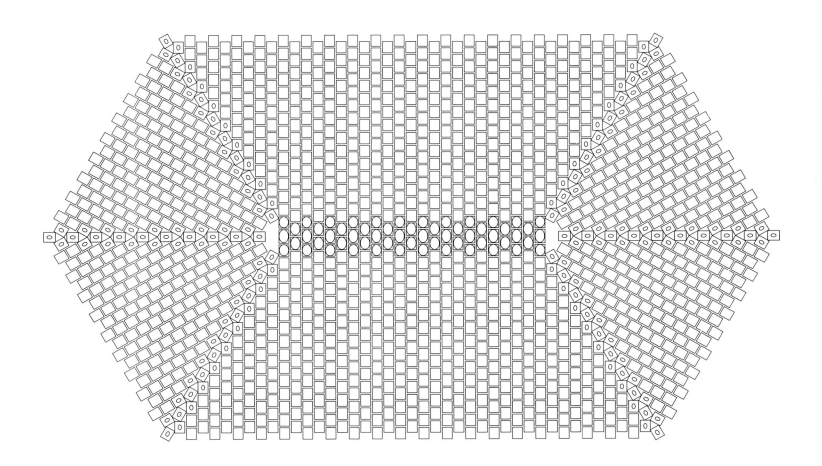

Oblong Square Base and Lid

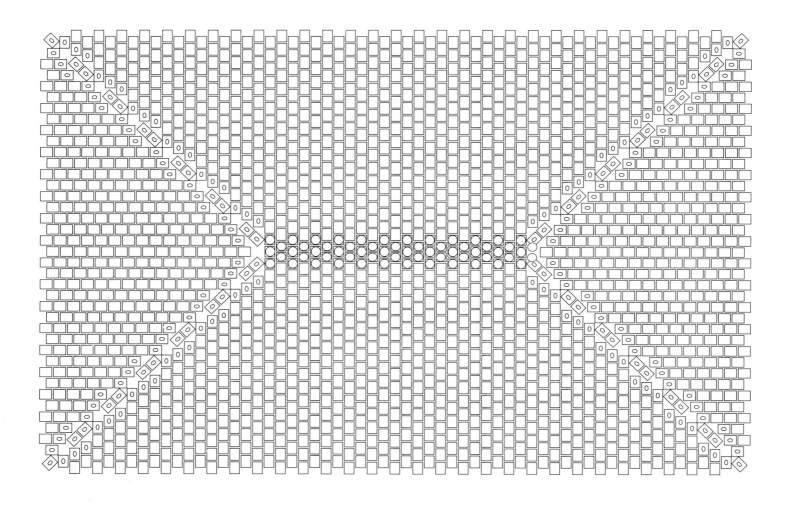

Worksheet for All Box Sides

Blank Graph Worksheets for Your Original Designs

Notes about the DVD

The video portion of the DVD will play in the DVD-ROM drive on your computer and also on your set-top player. The opening menu displays the six submenus. Beside the text on each submenu, you will see the words "left" and "right." I have provided separate visual instructions for right-handed and left-handed knitters, so choose whichever is most comfortable for you. All the menu buttons within those sections will lead to information with the same hand orientation.

The DVD contains additional information that can be viewed on your computer (but not on your television). Insert the disk into your DVD-ROM drive. Locate the DVD on your desktop (for Macintosh-based systems) or in My Computer (for Windows-based systems). Click on the DVD icon so you can view the four folders on the DVD (if you're working with Windows, right-click and choose Explore.) The folder VIDEO_TS contains video files only, so there is no need to open it.

The other folders contain:

• **Ten patterns in PDF format**

These patterns are identical to the graphed patterns in the book. In many cases, the patterns are considerably larger than those in the book. You may view them on your computer or print them out so you can mark notes as necessary as you work.

• **Ten word maps in PDF format**

These are the word maps for the patterns included in the book.

• **Blank graph worksheets**

These blank graph worksheets—one for large beads, one for smaller ones, and a blank graph for each of the projects in this book—are available in JPEG and PDF formats so that you can open them in any graphics program to design your own patterns. You can also download these blank graphic worksheets from my website, www.darkharebeadwork.com.

INDEX

Notes: Page numbers in italics indicate figures.

Antiquity Purse, 90–96, *91, 95*

bags. *See* bead knitted bags
bases, 215–216
    building, 218–227
    hexagon boxes, 220–222, *220–221*
    oblong boxes, 226–227, *226–227*
    pentagon boxes, 222–223, *222–223*
    reading patterns for, 243–244
    square boxes, 224–225, *224–225*
    triangle boxes, 219–220, *219–220*
bead boxes, 214–315. *See also specific shapes*
    bases of, 215–216, *217,* 218–227, 243–244
    Deco Pagoda, 265–269, *265–269*
    decrease cycles for, 228–233, *228, 230, 231,*
        232
    dragon, 288–292, *288–289, 291*
    Egypt, 251–254, *251–254*
    feet of, 241, *241*
    finials, 240, *240*
    Flower, 283–287, *283–287*
    getting started, 214–217
    glossary of terms, 217
    hems of, 217, 234–235, *234–235*
    hexagon boxes, 220–222, *220–221,* 230, *230,*
        261–278
    inner columns, 233, *233*
    Kaleidoscope, 248–250, *248–250*
    lids of, 217, *217,* 237–240, *237–240,* 242–244
    materials for, 215
    New School, 270–278, *270–271, 275, 277*
    oblong boxes, 226–227, *226–227*
    patterns for, 242–246, *242–245,* 247–260
    pentagon boxes, 222–223, *222–223,* 230–231,
        231, 279–292
    Red Knot, 255–260, *255–256, 259*
    replacing broken beads, 236, *236*
    Shinjin, 302–308, *302–308*
    sides of, 216–217, 228–236, 242–243, 315
    square boxes, 224–225, *224–225,* 232–233,
        232, 293–308
    Star, 280–282, *280–282*
    straight and recessed tops, 228–233
    Tempest, 294–296, *294–296*
    Tomcat, 297–301, *297–299, 301*
    tools for, 215
    tops of, 243
    triangle boxes, 219–220, *219–220,* 228–229,
        228, 247–260
    Tuffet, *262–264*
    word maps for, 245–246, *245*
bead knitted bags, 8–109, *8–110, 32–33. See also*
    purses
    Antiquity Purse, 90–96, *91, 95*
    assembly of, 102–105, *102*
    Blue Garden Drawstring Purse, 60–67, *61, 63*

China Sea Bag, 84–89, *85, 87*
decreases within a row, 109
Dragon Bag, 54–59, *55, 57, 59*
edge decreases, 39–40, *39,* 108, *108*
edge increases, 38–39, *38,* 108, *108*
edge shaping, 40, *40*
finishing techniques, 97–101
increases within a row, 109, *109*
lining for, 11, 103, *103–105, 103,* 104, *104,*
    105, *105*
Luna Purse, 78–83, *79, 81, 83*
materials for, 10–11
Olive's Star Box, 48–53, *49, 51*
shaping, 38–40, *38, 39, 40*
Tumble Bag, 74–77, *75–77*
bead knitting, 8–11
bead knitting needles, 10
beaded neckpieces, *133*
    assembly of, 126–129, *126–129*
    Chartreuse, 152–157, *152–157*
    choosing beads and colors, 119, *119*
    clasp attachment, 136, *137*
    counterweight attachment, 136, *137*
    decorative elements, 130–133, *131, 133*
    Drab, 158–165, *158–165*
    Eagle Feather, 196–203, *196–203*
    elements of, 114–117. *See also specific elements*
    Ember, 174–179, *174–179*
    ending and beginning threads, 128, *128*
    finding attachment, 134–135, *134–135*
    finding sizes, 138
    finishing techniques, 134–137, *134–135*
    fringe for, 132, 133, *133*
    getting started, 110–119
    Gradient, 188–195, *188–195*
    helpful tips, 138–139, *138–139*
    making a template, 118–119, *118*
    materials for, 113
    Meadow, *166–173*
    measuring for, 118
    New Mexico, 144–151, *144–151*
    projects, 138–212
    Spike, 180–187, *180–187*
    supplies, 113
    surface embellishment for, 132, 133, *133*
    Trellis, 204–211, *204–211*
    Urchin, 141–143, *141–143*
beading needles, 11
beads, 11, *11*
    choosing, 119, *119*
    replacing broken, 236, *236*
binding off, 22–23, 70–71
blocking, 26
Blue Garden Drawstring Purse, 60–67, *61, 63*
boxes. *See* bead boxes
bracelets, 30–31, *30–31*
broken beads, replacing, 236

casting on, 12–13, *13*
chains, 11

Chartreuse, 131, *131,* 152–157, *152–157*
China Sea Bag, 84–89, *85, 87*
circular peyote stitches, 218
circumference, measuring for, 118
clasps, 11, 136, *137*
closures, 117, *117*
collars. *See* beaded neckpieces
colors, choosing, 119, *119*
combination method, 17
continental bead knitting, 21, *21*
cords, 11
cotton, 11
cotton thread, 11
counterweights, 117, 136, *137*
crochet cotton, 11
crochet hooks, 11

cutting thread, 24

Deco Pagoda, 265–269, *265–269*
decorative elements (for beaded neckpieces),
    130–133, *131, 133. See also specific elements*
double knitting, 68–96
    binding off, 70–71
    double knit increases, 71–72, *71–72*
    rows with beads, 69–70, *69*
    rows without beads, 68–69, *68*
    separating the sides, 70, *70*
    working with multiple needles, 72–73, *73*
Drab, 158–165, *158–165*
Dragon, 288–292, *288–289, 291*
Dragon Bag, 54–59, *55, 57, 59*
dropped stitches, picking up, 23–24, *23*
Dusk Necklace, 44–47, *45, 47*

Eagle Feather, 196–203, *196–203*
Egypt, 251–254, *251–254*
Ember, 133, *133,* 174–179, *174–179*
eyelets
    crocheted, 98–100, *99*
    knitted, 97–98, *97–98*

feet, 241, *241*
findings, 11, 134–135, *134–135*
finials, 240, *240*
finishing techniques
    bead knitted bags, 97–101
    beaded neckpieces, 134–137, *134–135*
flat lids (for bead boxes), 237–239, *237–238*
Flower, 283–287, *283–287*
fringe
    for bags, 100, *100,* 101, *101*
    basic, 101, *101*
    for beaded neckpieces, 116, *116,* 132, 133, *133*
    branched, 101, *101*
    crocheted, 100, *100*
    looped, 101, *101*
    netted, 101, *101*

Gradient, 131, *131,* 188–195, *188–195*

hems, 217, 234–235, *234–235*
hexagon boxes, 220–222, *220–221*, 310
    Deco Pagoda, 265–269, *265–269*
    decrease cycles for, 230, *230*
    New School, 270–278, *270–271, 275, 277*
    oblong hexagon boxes, 227, *227*
    patterns for, 261–278
    Tuffet, *262–264*
hooks, 11, 136
how to use this book/DVD, 9–10

joining thread, 24, *24*
jump rings, 11

Kaleidoscope, 248–250, *248–250*
knit rows, 38, *38*, 39–40, *40*
knit stitches, 14–15, *14, 17*, 18–19, *19*
knitting, 8–11
    double knitting, 68–96
    knitting tutorial, 12–17
    shaping the, 38–67

ladders, 114, *114*
    ending, 123–124, *123*
    estimating the length of, 125
    extending, 124, *124*
    joining subsequent, 129, *129*
    joining the first two, 127–128, *127*
    joining with picots, 131
    making, 120–125
    one-needle method, 120–122, *120–122*
    pinning to the template, 126, *126*
    two-needle method, 122–123, *122–123*
layering, 115, *115*, 133, *133*
lids (of bead boxes), 217, 237–240, *237–240*
    flat lids, 237–238, *237–238*
    reading patterns for, 242–244
    with sides, 239–240, *239–240*
lining, 11, 103–105, *105*
    a flat bag, 103, *103*, 105
    flat bead knitting, 103
    a round bag, 104, *104*
lining fabric, 11
lobster-claw clasps, 136
Luna Purse, 78–83, *79, 81, 83*

magnetic clasps, 136
Mary Thomas's Knitting Book, 8
materials
    for bead boxes, 215
    for bead knitted bags, 10–11
    for beaded neckpieces, 113
Meadow, 131, *131, 166–173*
measuring, for beaded neckpieces, 118
mistakes, fixing, 23–26, *24, 25*

necklaces, 44–47, *45, 47*
neckpieces. *See* beaded neckpieces

needles, 10, 11, *11*, 73, *73*
netting, 114–115, *114*, 130, 131, *131*
New Mexico, 144–151, *144–151*
New School, 270–278, *270–271, 275, 277*

oblong boxes, 226–227, *226–227*
    oblong hexagon boxes, 227, *227*, 313
    oblong square boxes, 227, *227*, 314
Olive's Star Box, 48–53, *49, 51*

patterns. *See also* projects; word maps
    for bead boxes, 242–246, *242–245*
    designing, 106–109, *106*
    graphed, 28–29, *29*
    for hexagon boxes, 261–278
    pentagon boxes, 279–292
    reading, 28–29, *29*, 242–245
    square boxes, 293–308
    for triangle boxes, 247–260
    working with, 27–37, *29*
pentagon boxes, 222–223, *222–223*, 279–292, 311
    decrease cycles for, 230–231, *231*
    dragon, 288–292, *288–289, 291*
    flower, 283–287, *283–287*
    star, 280–282, *280–282*
perle cotton, 11
peyote stitches, 218, *218*, 228, *228*
picots, 116, *116*, 133
Pinwheel Purse, 32–37, *32–33, 35, 37*
purl rows, 39–40, *39–40*
purl stitches, 15–16, *16, 17*, 20–22, *20, 22*
purses. *See* bead knitted bags

Red Knot, 255–260, *255–256, 259*
row, within a shaping, 40–43
rows
    decreasing within, 42–43, *43*
    increasing within, 41–42, *41*
    removing multiple, 25–26, *25*

S hooks, 136
samples, making, 18–26, *19–25, 21, 22, 23*
seed beads, 10
shaping
    decreasing in knit rows, 39–40, *40*
    edge decreases, 39–40, *39*
    edge increases, 38–39, *38*
    edge shaping, 40, *40*
    increasing in knit rows, 38, *38*
    increasing in purl rows, 39, *39*
    within a row, 40–43
Shinjin, 302–308, *302–308*
sides (of bead boxes), 216–217, 228–236
    decrease cycles for, 228–229, *228*
    reading patterns for, 242–243
    straight and recessed tops, 228–233
    worksheets for, 315
silk threads, 11
simple bind-off, 22
sizes, finding, 138

Spike, 133, *133*, 180–187, *180–187*
square boxes, 224–225, *224–225*, 293–308, 312
    decrease cycles for, 232–233, *232*
    oblong square boxes, 227, *227*
    Shinjin, 302–308, *302–308*
    Tempest, 294–296, *294–296*
    Tomcat, 297–301, *297–299, 301*
Star, 280–282, *280–282*
steel crochet hooks, 11
stitches
    circular peyote stitches, 218
    Eastern knit stitches, 17
    knit stitches, 14–15, *14, 17*, 18–19, *19*
    peyote stitches, 218, *218*, 228, *228*
    purl stitches, 15–16, *16*, 17, 20–22, *20, 22*
    removing, 24–25, *25*
    tubular peyote stitches, 218, 228, *228*
    Western knit stitches, 17
straps, attaching, 105
supplies. *See* materials; tools
surface embellishment (for beaded neckpieces), 115, *115*, 132, 133, *133*
suspended bind-off, 23

tails, estimating the length of, 12
tapestry needles, 11
Tempest, 294–296, *294–296*
templates, making, 118–119, *118*
threads, 11
    cutting, 24
    ending and beginning, 128, *128*
    joining thread, 24, *24*
    silk threads, 11
toggles, 136
Tomcat, 297–301, *297–299, 301*
tools
    for bead boxes, 215
    for bead knitted bags, 10–11
    for beaded neckpieces, 113
tops (of bead boxes), 228–229, *228*, 243
Trellis, 133, *133*, 204–211, *204–211*
triangle boxes, 219–220, *219–220*
    decrease cycles for, 228–229, *228*
    Egypt, 251–254, *251–254*
    Kaleidoscope, 248–250, *248–250*
    patterns for, 247–260
    Red Knot, 255–260, *255–256, 259*
tubular peyote stitches, *218*, 228, *228*
Tuffet, *262–264*
Tumble Bag, 74–77, *75–77*
tutorial, 12–17
Two Easy Cuff Bracelets, 30–31, *30–31*

Urchin, 141–143, *141–143*

Western knit stitches, 17
wire needles, 11
word maps, reading, 28–29, 245–246, *245*
worksheets, blank, 309–317